Making Instructional Design Decisions

SECOND EDITION

BARBARA SEELS
University of Pittsburgh

ZITA GLASGOW

Merrill,
an imprint of Prentice Hall

Upper Saddle River, New Jersey   *Columbus, Ohio*

Library of Congress Cataloging-in-Publication Data

Seels, Barbara.
   Making instructional design decisions / Barbara Seels, Zita Glasgow. — 2nd ed.
   p.   cm.
   Rev. ed. of: Exercises in instructional design. c1990.
   Includes bibliographical references and indexes.
   ISBN 0-13-520602-2
   1. Instructional systems—Design. 2. Instructional systems—
Design—Problems, exercises, etc. 3. Curriculum planning.
   I. Glasgow, Zita. II. Seels, Barbara. Exercises in instructional
design. III. Title.
   LB1028.38.S4   1998
   371.33—dc21   97-13742
                                                  CIP

Editor: Debra A. Stollenwerk
Production Editor: Mary Harlan
Design Coordinator: Julia Zonneveld Van Hook
Text Design: Custom Editorial Productions, Inc.
Cover Designer: Brian Deep
Cover Photo: Comstock
Production Manager: Laura Messerly
Editorial/Production Supervision: Custom Editorial Productions, Inc.
Illustrations: Custom Editorial Productions, Inc.
Director of Marketing: Kevin Flanagan
Marketing Manager: Suzanne Stanton
Advertising/Marketing Coordinator: Julie Shough

This book was set in Utopia by Custom Editorial Productions, Inc., and was printed and bound by Banta Company. The cover was printed by Phoenix Color Corp.

©1998 by Prentice-Hall, Inc.
Simon & Schuster/A Viacom Company
Upper Saddle River, New Jersey 07458

Earlier edition, entitled *Exercises in Instructional Design,*® 1990 by Merrill Publishing Company.

Printed in the United States of America

10 9 8 7 6 5 4 3 2 1

ISBN: 0-13-520602-2

Prentice-Hall International (UK) Limited, *London*
Prentice-Hall of Australia Pty. Limited, *Sydney*
Prentice-Hall of Canada, Inc., *Toronto*
Prentice-Hall Hispanoamericana, S. A., *Mexico*
Prentice-Hall of India Private Limited, *New Delhi*
Prentice-Hall of Japan, Inc., *Tokyo*
Simon & Schuster Asia Pte. Ltd., *Singapore*
Editora Prentice-Hall do Brasil, Ltda., *Rio de Janeiro*

Preface

The development of qualified instructional designers is an evolutionary process that begins with formal education and continues for many years on the job. Graduates of instructional design courses enter a broad market. There are jobs for instructional designers in the training and development departments in health and industry settings, in faculty development or resource centers of educational institutions, and in instructional/training divisions in the civilian and military sectors of government.

One purpose of *Making Instructional Design Decisions* is to provide a set of exercises that requires students to apply design concepts and skills to job-related areas. However, this book is more than a series of exercises. It is a reference on theory and a self-instructional resource. The book may be used as text or supplemental material in basic courses. Because it is organized in a logical sequence with exercises, it is suitable for independent study or external degree courses. It is also suitable for short-term programs aimed at correcting or developing selective skills.

This book can be used for one course or over two courses. If it is used for one course, the instructor should select the most appropriate chapters. If it is used for two courses, students can complete chapters 1 through 6 on basic ISD in the first course. In the second course students can do chapters 7 through 12, which are about more advanced theory. In this situation, at the end of the first course a student could submit an individual design project generated through dyad exercises. During the second course, students could work on a team project in a field setting. There are also the options of having students work in teams during both courses or individually in each course.

The theoretical basis for instructional design is often abstract and confusing for the beginner. In writing this book we tried to help the future practitioner by (a) reconciling theories when they were in conflict; (b) integrating theories with practice in order to simplify design tasks; and (c) generating theory when we found gaps or inadequacies. In doing so we dealt primarily with procedural or "how to" theory. For example, in preparing the chapter on analyzing the problem we found inconsistent theory about what was included in front-end analysis. Moreover, theory about relationship among procedures was inadequate. Based on our experience and the literature, we developed theory about relationships among components of needs analysis.

ORGANIZATION

As a text for students entering the field, this book is organized in two parts: Part One, "The Seels & Glasgow ISD Model I: For Novices," and Part Two, "The Seels & Glasgow ISD Model II: For Practitioners." Part One covers the basic information that a novice designer needs to start designing. It presents the six steps in the design process known as the ADDIE model. On the assumption that the novice becomes more experienced and is able to handle a more complicated model, Part Two elaborates on the model for novices and incorporates it in an iterative model for practitioners that is more typical of approaches used by designers in the field.

FEATURES

To become competent in ISD, students or trainees will need to recall knowledge, comprehend concepts, and apply procedures. This book is constructed so that all three types of learning are practiced at the end of each chapter. The exercises in both Parts One and Two. are oriented towards three levels of practice: individual, small group, and project.

Most of the exercises provide for individual practice. We call this the first level of practice. Chapters also offer exercises for a dyad situation in which the roles of instructional designer and subject-matter expert (SME) are rotated. The purpose of the dyad exercise practice is to provide a motivational setting in which to start each step of a design project. This setting allows students to practice interviewing and teaming skills used throughout the instructional systems design process. The presence of a partner allows for peer review and playing the devil's advocate. These dyad exercises can also be done in a small group or team setting. This second level of practice produces output that allows feedback about necessary revisions.

A project exercise is also given at the end of each chapter. The third level of practice, therefore, is a project that can be based on what is done during the second level of practice or can be on a completely new topic. This level of practice is complete when a project is submitted and feedback reviewed. The second and third levels of practice will be the last exercises to appear in a chapter. Answers to exercises are given at the end of each chapter. Ideally, second- and third-level exercises will be reviewed by an instructor, too. Students should be told that they need to do the exercises to become competent in instructional design.

In addition to the exercises and answers, each chapter includes (a) an overview of the chapter; (b) questions intended to orient students to concepts presented in the chapter; (c) learning objectives; and (d) references. Students are expected to acquire the behaviors stated in the objectives, but it is left to the instructor to specify the performance standard. Thus, the instructor has the flexibility to adjust to individual differences when evaluating performance.

NEW TO THIS EDITION

The first edition of this text was titled *Exercises in Instructional Design*. However, major changes have been made to this edition. The new title of this second edition, *Making Instructional Design Decisions*, reflects these changes:

◆ There is an increased emphasis on instructional design as a decision-making process.

◆ The book has been reorganized to reflect differences between novices and practitioners. Part One introduces instructional systems design procedures. Part Two elaborates on them and adds steps to the ISD process.

◆ Two new, up-to-date ISD models are provided, a linear one for novices and an iterative one for practitioners that provide for concurrent activities, including design and development and for three stages of project management.

◆ New sections and chapters have been added, including chapters on Assessing Learning, Managing a Project Team, and Implementing Instruction, and sections on distance education technologies, instructional design paradigms, and contextual and cost analysis.

◆ Exercises have been refined, and new exercises added. Each chapter includes exercises to be done individually and exercises to be done in a subject matter expert/designer dyad or in a group.

◆ Answers to exercises are provided at the end of each chapter instead of in a separate instructor's manual.

◆ New text has been added to elaborate and update information about concepts and procedures.

◆ Format and graphics have been improved.

These changes make this edition easier for both the instructor and the student to use. In addition, the changes ensure that the book remains up to date.

USE OF THIS TEXT

Skills practice does not diminish the book's presentation of concepts. The book is organized so that Part One gives an overview of steps in instructional design, whereas Part Two elaborates on each of the steps and adds steps. Thus, Part Two considers (a) alternate ISD models and theoretical differences between paradigms; (b) concepts and procedures related to analyzing the problem; (c) theory about project teams and their management; (d) the theoretical basis for instructional analysis and instructional strategies; and (e) considerations in implementing instruction.

We believe that learning classification theory is an important theoretical basis for instructional design. In this text, we provide information on two such theories: the domains of educational objectives and Gagné and Briggs' theory of learning outcomes including their hierarchy of intellectual skills. It is our experience that beginning designers find their learning classification theory difficult to apply. Therefore, you will find this introduced late in the book in chapter 10. We urge you to spend extra time checking exercises and project tasks related to this theory. To be comfortable with the theory, students will need more practice than we are able to provide in this text.

The authors are willing to provide an audioconference for your class if you think this will be helpful. We would also like to hear from you about reactions to the text.

In writing the book we assumed that the systematic approach is the theoretical force that allows findings from psychology and communications research to be applied to the design of instruction. Although this approach may be adjusted to reflect trends in research and practice, the basic approach remains an important tool for synthesizing guidelines from learning and communication theory. The order of steps may change and steps may be added or expanded, subtracted or reconceptualized, but a systematic approach to design remains vital.

ACKNOWLEDGMENTS

Many colleagues have reviewed drafts and given valuable advice. We appreciate the suggestions and comments of the following reviewers: Gayle V. Davidson, University of South Alabama; Francis Dwyer, Pennsylvania State University; Sarah Huyvaert, Eastern Michigan University; Mable Kinzie, University of Virginia; and Gregory C. Sales, Seward Learning Systems, Inc.

We are especially grateful to the students in the Program in Instructional Design and Technology at the University of Pittsburgh who helped formatively evaluate the text and exercises. Their comments highlighted many areas of confusion and many errors in time for us to make changes.

As experienced authors, we consider ourselves blessed to have worked with Amy Lemmon-Bowen, our copy editor, and Jim Reidel of Custom Editorial Productions, our project editor. Both these individuals were committed to thoroughness and correctness. It would have been a book of different quality without them.

We would also like to acknowledge these people at Prentice Hall who made major contributions to the first and second editions: Debra Stollenwerk, our editor, who initiated the project and gave us the benefit of her wealth of experience; Mary Harlan, our production editor, who always took our requests seriously; Ben Ko, the production editor on the first edition, who provided a strong base for us to build on; and Jeff Johnston, publisher for Prentice Hall, for his continued support.

Barbara Seels
Zita Glasgow

Contents

This book is dedicated to
Fiona and Jody Seels
and Frances Kochan Mussano

Introduction

Instructional design is the process of solving instructional problems by systematic analysis of the conditions for learning. To do this one makes decisions related to each step in the Instructional Systems Design (ISD) process. Some of these decisions are common to all projects, and some vary from project to project. The designer can be sure that a series of questions related to each step will have to be answered. The linearity of this process may vary, but the need to answer questions in order to make decisions will not.

The competencies required for an instructional designer are a set of highly integrated behaviors involving extracting, analyzing, organizing, and synthesizing information. Students of instructional design draw upon theory and knowledge from psychology, education, communications, and technology to develop their skills. This is because instructional design is based on (a) learning and instructional theory, and (b) theory related to communications and technology. These two sources of theory are synthesized through systems theory as this visual representation shows:

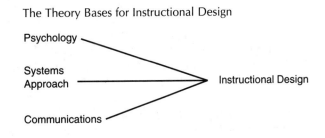

The Theory Bases for Instructional Design

In Part I you will study the basic steps required for ISD. These are presented as the ADDIE model. This ADDIE model is expanded through the Seels & Glasgow ISD Model I: For Novices, which uses questions to be answered at each step in the process. In Part II we expand this decision making model into the Seels & Glasgow ISD Model II: For Practitioners, which is both less linear and more detailed. This model incorporates the Seels & Glasgow ISD Model I: For Novices and continues the use of questions as a basis for making decisions. Thus, both models are decision-making models.

In Part II we elaborate on the use of models and paradigms, teaming and project management, procedures for needs analysis, instructional analysis, instructional strategies, and considerations in implementing instruction, such as summative evaluation and dissemination. In Part II we also offer a three-phase model of project management.

Another change will be the nature of group practice exercises. In Part I your ISD project could to be done individually with help from a dyad partner. In Part II your ISD project can be a group project developed by a team. The reason for this is to create a more realistic context for practice. Most ISD projects are the result of teamwork for a variety of reasons that are explained in Chapter 9. You need to do the exercises—not just read the text—if you expect to become competent in instructional design.

Next, each of the chapters will be described briefly and the relationship of the chapters will be represented visually.

Chapter 1, "Using an ISD Process," introduces you to the five phases of ISD. Each phase is driven by a set of questions, the answers to which provide the basis for decision making and lead to the next phase and a new set of questions. This chapter also covers the benefits of ISD, the types of jobs instructional designers occupy, and the values and competencies required of instructional designers.

Chapter 2, "Analyzing Tasks," covers how to extract information about understanding and performance from a variety of sources, as well as how to employ flowcharting and other visual techniques as tools for analyzing learning outcomes. This chapter presents a two-stage analysis: task analysis, to define what the expert performer does, and instructional analysis, to determine what the target audience already knows and what they must learn in order to achieve the desired outcomes. The skill of task analysis is developed in this chapter. The skill of instructional analysis is developed later, in Chapter 10.

Chapter 3, "Writing Objectives," and Chapter 4, "Assessing Learning," address how to describe knowledge and skills in terms of observable evidence. Both chapters are concerned with using objectives to guide design and evaluation. Chapter 3 explains how to write behavioral objectives. Chapter 4 explains the assessment process and how it relates to objectives.

Chapter 5, "Selecting and Developing Delivery Systems," relates to both the design and development phases of a systems approach. On the design side, the chapter covers delivery system options and a selection model. On the development side, the chapter presents guidelines for maintaining the integrity of the design during production of the instructional materials. You will need to learn more about instructional technologies than can be presented in this chapter; however, this chapter will help you get started.

Chapter 6, "Evaluating ISD Decisions," is about collecting evidence to validate the decisions made in each phase of the ISD process: analyzing, designing, developing, implementing, and evaluating. In this chapter, formative evaluation is presented as feedback that is used for improvement of products at all phases. Emphasis is given to the use of try-out data for revising and refining instructional materials and programs, and for prototype development that allows the designer to evaluate decisions about delivery systems. This is the last chapter in Part I.

Chapter 7, "Using Models and Paradigms," introduces some of the best known instructional design models. Different models are applicable to different situations; therefore, designers must usually adapt an existing model or developing one to suit their needs. This chapter presents the Seels & Glasgow ISD Model II: For Practitioners, which incorporates and elaborates on the Seels & Glasgow ISD Model I: For Novices presented in Part I. This chapter also presents three learning paradigms—behaviorism, cognitive science, and constructivism—and their relevance to the ISD process. By reviewing the theoretical positions offered by these paradigms and the questions they raise, the implications of learning paradigms for ISD are explored.

Chapter 8, "Analyzing the Problem," presents procedures for (a) assessing needs, prioritizing goals, and writing problem statements; (b) identifying performance problems, determining whether instruction is the best solution, and determining instructional requirements; and (c) describing the context before, during, and after instruction and the implications of this context. Thus, this chapter explains needs assessment and performance and contextual analysis.

Chapter 9, "Managing a Project Team," presents the skills necessary to achieve instructional design goals through teams. This chapter covers important considerations in ISD project management. In order to develop an effective project plan a person must have knowledge of the elements to be planned. This chapter discusses how to prepare oneself to be an ISD project manager.

Chapter 10, "Determining Prerequisites," explains how to analyze and diagram prerequisite learning, including how to draw hierarchies and entry lines. This chapter introduces Gagné's theory of types of learning. To become proficient in classifying learning according to Gagné's taxonomy, you will need more practice than can be presented in this chapter.

Chapter 11, "Planning Instructional Strategies," emphasizes basing instructional decisions on empirical evidence and covers principles of learning derived from theory and research. You are given the opportunity to devise strategies for learning that adhere to these principles.

Chapter 12, "Implementing Instruction," covers ensuring diffusion of the innovation, planning for implementation, evaluating summatively, and disseminating information about the project. It describes activities essential for acceptance—that is, activities that ensure the organization utilizes the finished product. Under planning for implementation, instructor training and logistical arrangements are discussed. The chapter concludes by explaining ways to do summative evaluation and how to write a design report.

The conceptual relationship among these chapters is shown in the concept map on the following page.

Barbara Seels
Zita Glasgow

The Relationship of Concepts in this Text

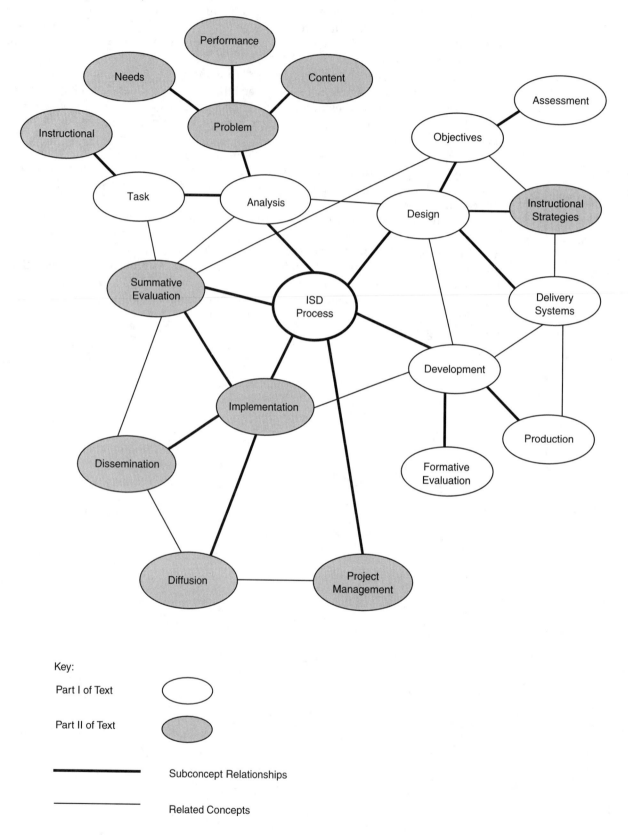

Key:

Part I of Text

Part II of Text

Subconcept Relationships

Related Concepts

Part One

The Seels & Glasgow ISD Model I: For Novices

Chapter

Chapter

1

Using an ISD Process

OVERVIEW

Instructional systems design (ISD) is based on the premise that learning should not occur in a haphazard manner, but should be developed in accordance with orderly processes and have outcomes that can be measured. Basically, ISD requires defining what is to be learned, planning an intervention that will allow learning to occur, measuring learning to determine if objectives were met, and refining the intervention until objectives are met.

ISD procedures and their application have evolved through practice as well as through research and expansion of theory. Many models of the ISD process have been developed. The Instructional Development Institutes (IDI) model for public school personnel was developed under the auspices of the U.S. Office of Education, and a number of scholars in the field (Gagné, Briggs, & Wager,1992; Kemp, Morrison, & Ross, 1994; Dick & Carey,1996) have developed models.

Although there are many ISD models, a generic model can be extracted from their common features (Gibbons, 1981; Hannum & Hansen, 1989). No matter what the configuration, all of these models include the processes of analysis, design, development, implementation, and evaluation, which can be defined as follows:

- ◆ **Analysis**—the process of defining what is to be learned.
- ◆ **Design**—the process of specifying how learning will occur.
- ◆ **Development**—the process of authoring and producing the materials.
- ◆ **Implementation**—the process of installing the instruction in the real world.
- ◆ **Evaluation**—the process of determining the impact of instruction

Several disciplines contributed to the development of the field, including psychology, communications, and general systems theory. As the field grew, roles for researchers and practitioners evolved. A generally accepted premise is that ISD should have a research base.

ISD has been formally adopted by large organizations such as the military, industries, and universities. It is used in a variety of settings, from the banking industry to schools and hospitals. ISD can be used to develop a sophisticated curriculum for a large school system or on a micro level to improve a one-hour presentation. Its benefits are that it is a systematic process that helps the instructional designer make decisions about the nature and scope of instruction.

ORIENTING QUESTIONS

What is ISD?
What disciplines have contributed to the field of ISD?
How is instruction produced by ISD different from the instruction in most classrooms?
What are the benefits of an ISD approach?
What do instructional designers do?

OBJECTIVES

1. Given the phases of the ISD process, identify the products produced during each phase.
2. Given an instructional design activity, match the ISD phase with the activity.
3. Given innovations and methods associated with ISD, name the decade when they were first introduced.
4. Given a description of an ISD project, state how it employs the principles of ISD presented in this chapter.
5. Given a description of a colleague's experience in planning an approach to instruction, compare it to the five phases of the ISD approach.
6. Given descriptions of job activities, match an ISD activity with each description.
7. Given statements describing the interests of ISD researchers and practitioners, identify whether the statements are true or false.
8. Given a matching question, identify which ISD products are produced primarily by researchers and which primarily by practitioners.
9. Given job descriptions, identify which jobs are performed primarily by researchers and which primarily by practitioners.

THE GENERIC INSTRUCTIONAL DESIGN MODEL

The generic model is so simplified it is unlikely to be used without modification or elaboration. As shown in Figure 1.1, each stage is driven by a set of questions, the answers to which are the basis for the next stage and a new set of questions. As the instructional designer discovers the answers to the "driving questions," decisions are made about the type and scope of instruction needed for the particular circumstances at hand.

An instructional situation can range in scope from a module, lesson, or experience to an entire curriculum, environment, or course. Four important characteristics of ISD are as follows:

1. Content selection based on data from the field.
2. Instructional strategies based on research and theory.
3. Assessment based on standards of performance.
4. Technology used to optimize effectiveness, efficiency, and cost (Campbell, 1980).

The following discussion elaborates on the processes of analysis, design, development, implementation, and evaluation.

Analysis

There is a great deal of uncertainty at the start of an ISD effort. The client agency may be uncertain about its needs and have unrealistic expectations of what can and cannot be done given the allocated resources. The subject matter may be new to the designer, who is faced with trying to make sense of the many ambiguities and contradictions associated

Figure 1.1 Generic ISD
Model Elaborated with
Decision Questions

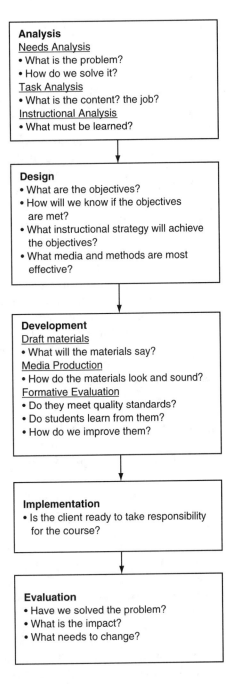

Analysis
<u>Needs Analysis</u>
• What is the problem?
• How do we solve it?
<u>Task Analysis</u>
• What is the content? the job?
<u>Instructional Analysis</u>
• What must be learned?

Design
• What are the objectives?
• How will we know if the objectives
  are met?
• What instructional strategy will achieve
  the objectives?
• What media and methods are most
  effective?

Development
<u>Draft materials</u>
• What will the materials say?
<u>Media Production</u>
• How do the materials look and sound?
<u>Formative Evaluation</u>
• Do they meet quality standards?
• Do students learn from them?
• How do we improve them?

Implementation
• Is the client ready to take responsibility
  for the course?

Evaluation
• Have we solved the problem?
• What is the impact?
• What needs to change?

with this new information. The designer's job is to make sense of these inconsistencies, to work with others such as *subject matter experts (SMEs)*, to develop a coherent solution to the problem, and to gain the client's acceptance of the proposed solution. These responsibilities are accomplished by collecting data about the performance requirements of the job or content, about the context in which the job is performed or the content used, and about the people who perform the job or use the content. The data is then analyzed to answer the questions of the analysis phase, sometimes referred to as front-end analysis because it occurs first in the ISD process.

In this text, we distinguish three types of "front-end" analyses: *needs analysis, task analysis,* and *instructional analysis.* The different types of analyses are distinguished more by the questions they answer than by the techniques they use. For example, the analyst may interview job holders when performing needs analysis as well as when performing task analysis. Although interviews are used to collect information in both instances, the purposes are quite different. Each type of analysis requires a different mental set of the instructional designer.

Needs Analysis.   Needs analysis is a method of determining whether the instruction the client called for is really needed and, if so, determining how much instruction is needed. It asks, "What is the problem?" and "How do we solve it?" A needs analysis involves getting the answers to specific questions that will circumscribe the precise nature of the problem.

Many times instruction is seen as a solution to a performance problem when it is not. Mager and Pipe (1970) distinguish between competence ("can do") and performance ("does do"). They advise the instructional designer to ask, "Could the potential students perform the task if their lives depended on it?" If the answer to the question is yes, then the poor performance cannot be attributed to a lack of competence. The analyst should look for non-instructional solutions such as introducing incentives or removing "obstacles" that keep people from performing adequately.

If there is an instructional problem, the designer wants to define the discrepancy between what the target audience already knows and what members need to know to achieve acceptable performance levels. The designer must get a general overview of the performance requirements for the job or content and the context in which performance takes place, identify learner characteristics, including educational levels, attitudes, and value systems that might affect learning, and describe the instructional environment in which the new instruction will take place.

A general solution to the problem is proposed as a goal. To this end, the designer collects information to determine whether there are adequate resources available for developing and delivering the needed instruction. Although much remains to be established about the new instruction, general estimates are made about the level of effort, time frames, and cost of developing the needed instruction. At this point, the designer and the client determine what is feasible and practical given the available resources and the size of the performance discrepancy.

Task Analysis.   Once the parameters of the problem and its solution have been defined, the designer begins defining the job or topic to be learned using the techniques of task analysis. Task analysis asks, "What is the job?" or "What is the content?"

During needs analysis, content or duties to be learned are defined at both a global and a general level. In task analysis, tasks or content are defined more specifically. The designer may review relevant documents, observe proficient performers doing the tasks to be learned, and consult with experts in the field.

When the content or job is well defined, the analyst can usually rely upon accepted practices and procedures in order to document the tasks and the conditions and circumstances under which they are performed. When experts disagree or the content or job is poorly defined, the analyst's job is to work with the experts and help them define the behavior or content. Often, expert performers are unable to describe what they do; it is second nature to them. The success of the analysis will depend on the designer's skills in focusing the SMEs on the instructional goal and extracting the relevant information about what tasks or content must be learned in pursuit of that goal.

The analysis is performed until the instructional designer arrives at an appropriate level of detail for the target audience given the knowledge or performance discrepancy. Figure 1.2 shows an analysis of a task associated with fighting small fires in underground mines. No standardized procedures existed when the project began. The designer worked with a team of three SMEs to define the sources of small fires in underground mines and to develop the specific procedures for fighting them.

Instructional Analysis.   When the task analysis is complete, a database exists that describes the job or content in detail. Next, the designer uses techniques of instructional analysis to determine what must be learned.

Figure 1.2   Flowchart for the Procedures Miners Should Follow

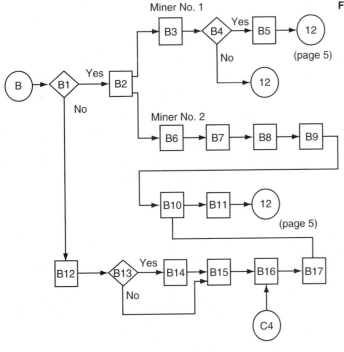

Fires Involving Electrical Equipment With Trailing Cables

B1.   If at least two miners are present at the fire site, go to Step B2. If not, go to Step B12.

B2.   Miner No. 1 (probably equipment operator) performs Steps B3 through B5. Miner No. 2 (probably equipment helper) performs Steps B6 through B11.

B3.   Shut off equipment power switch.

B4.   If the equipment has automatic fire suppression gear, go to Step B5. If not, go to Step 12 of General Procedure.

B5.   Activate automatic fire suppression gear. Go to Step 12 of General Procedure.

B6.   Shut off all section power at power distribution boxes.

B7.   Report fire to Section Foreman.

B8.   Alert other nearby miners to fire.

B9.   Call for mechanic.

B10.   Return to fire site with dry chemical extinguisher.

B11.   Go to Step 12 of General Procedure.

B12.   Shut off equipment power switch.

B13.   If the equipment has automatic fire suppression gear, go to Step B14. If not, go to Step B15.

B14.   Activate automatic fire suppression gear.

B15.   Shut off all section power at power distribution boxes.

B16.   Tell other miners to report fire to Section Foreman.

B17.   Call for mechanic. Go to Step B10.

From *Development of a Training Program for Fighting Small Fires in the Mining Industry: Task Analysis Report* (Contract No. J0395060), 1981, by W. Laird, S. Bhatt, T. Bajpayee, Z. Glasgow, and D. Scott, Bruceton, PA: U.S. Department of Interior, Bureau of Mines.

The designer analyzes each task or content area to determine what the student must know in order to perform this task or learn this content. In this way, the prerequisite competencies are identified. Then, the designer compares the prerequisite competencies needed to perform the task or learn the content with the competencies the learner already has. The gap between the two determines how much instruction is needed to learn the new material. If there is great variability among the members of the target audience, some students will need more and different instruction than others to reach the same goal. A knowledge of learning theory and research is necessary to define the competencies and their prerequisite relationships.

Design

Information from the analysis phase forms the foundation for the design phase. During analysis, the designer made decisions about *what* will be taught. Now, decisions are made about *how* it is taught. The design phase is driven by a search for the answers to the following questions:

◆ What are the objectives?

◆ How will we know if they are met?

◆ What teaching strategies will achieve the objectives?

◆ What delivery systems are most cost-effective?

The purpose of the instruction is to improve performance on the job or improve competency in some subject area. With these aims in mind, the instructional designer must devise a strategy based on research about how people learn given the type of learning involved. The strategy should be designed to help the learner bridge the gap between the performance required by the learning and the performance required on the job or in the real world outside the classroom. This is accomplished by replicating in the instructional setting situations that reflect relevant job situations and real-world contexts. Information gained from the earlier needs and task analyses is the springboard for devising authentic learning experiences.

The designer must be familiar with the research on which instructional methods, media, and strategies are most effective given the types of learning involved and the characteristics of the target audience. Practical concerns about cost-effectiveness, resource availability, and the staffing needs for course development come into play.

Development

In the development phase, the materials are authored, reviewed, produced, and validated. The activities carried out during development will depend on the instructional media to be produced. The driving question during production is, "How will the materials look and sound?" The physical features of the material are produced during this phase, and it is the designer's job to ensure that the principles of learning are incorporated into the materials as specified during the design phase. Depending on the media requirements, the instructional designer may work closely with writers, film or video producers, directors, actors, editors, artists, photographers, and computer programmers.

Material development also involves a process of formative evaluation whereby the materials are tried out. Formative evaluation answers the questions, "Do the materials teach?" and "How do we improve them?" Evaluative information is gathered in two ways. First, SMEs and ISD colleagues review and critique the materials in draft form. An SME reviews the materials to determine whether the materials are accurate, while instructional design colleagues review the materials to determine whether the materials are developed in accordance with ISD standards. Secondly, the materials are tried out on students typical of the target population before they are finalized. The tryouts are aimed at finding out whether students learn from the materials. It may take several levels of tryout to achieve the desired level of learning. In this way, materials are revised until objectives are met.

Implementation

The ultimate success of a course depends on whether it is implemented as intended. To ensure this, the designer must develop guidance for administrators and teachers in order to prepare them to carry out their prescribed responsibilities.

During the early stages of implementation, there are often a number of problems as people learn to use the new materials. If the materials are highly complex or the course uses unfamiliar methods and media, it takes some time for people to learn to accept them and use them effectively. Users may need a great deal of support until they are familiar with the new way of doing things. As people gain a better understanding of how the new version of a course works, the need for support drops off. The driving question for the implementation phase is, "Is the client ready to take responsibility for the course?"

Evaluation

The evaluation phase is driven by a search for the answers to following the questions:

◆ Have we solved the problem?

◆ What is the impact?

◆ What needs to change?

The evaluation in this phase is called *summative evaluation,* and differs from *formative evaluation* carried out during the development phase. Formative evaluation is used to identify deficiencies in the materials while they are being "formed" in order to correct deficiencies. Summative evaluation is intended to help the client agency assess the impact of the new materials in a broader sense. Summative evaluation is often carried out by an independent evaluator, not the instructional designer who is closely connected to the finished product and, therefore, may be less objective. Ideally, it takes place after the implementation phase, when the novelty of the program has worn off and bugs are worked out.

Once the course has been implemented, summative evaluation helps the client determine how well the problem was solved and the value of the solution to the organization. Depending on the size and nature of the organization, summative evaluation of instructional systems can be quite complex. Questions asked to assess organizational impact are: What does it cost? How long does instruction take? How are job performance and/or graduation rates affected? What is the impact of learning the new material on the organization? To assess instructional effectiveness, measures are taken periodically to determine if standards are slipping, learning objectives are still being met, and materials are being used correctly, as well as whether the course is still timely, or the content is obsolete.

 ISD OUTPUTS

The ISD process is as important as the product, because confidence in the product is based on the process. To be confident of the product, the phases of the generic ISD model must be followed. For each phase a series of tasks must be performed and specific output generated, as illustrated in Table 1.1.

Whatever job you assume, you may be responsible for any of a variety of products. The products of ISD can vary in scope and sophistication. Scope encompasses variation in

Table 1.1   Tasks and Outputs of the Instructional Design Process

Phase and Definition	Sample Tasks	Sample Outputs
Analysis—the process of defining what is to be learned	Needs analysis Task analysis Instructional analysis	Problem statement Behavioral task statements Learner entry level
Design—the process of specifying how it is to be learned	Write objectives Develop tests Plan instruction	Measurable objectives Criterion-referenced tests Design specifications
Development—the process of authoring and producing the materials	Work with media production staff Develop instructional materials Tryout materials	Storyboard Script Exercises Revisions based on student performance
Implementation—the process of installing the project in the real world context	Train teachers and administrators Plan resource allocation Develop maintenance system	Teacher and administrator guides Systems for tracking student progress Procedures for monitoring resource consumption
Evaluation—the process of determining the impact of the instruction	Survey graduates Review administration, maintenance, and costs	Recommendations for change Project report

Table 1.2   Dimensions of ISD Products

Project Scope	*Technological Sophistication*		
	Low	**Moderate**	**High**
Large: Curriculum Efforts	Correspondence Course	Telecourse	Computer-based Self-instructional Course

Medium:
  Programs
  Units
  Workshops
	Programmed
	Instruction Unit
		Mediated
		Workshop
			Videodisc
			Simulation

Small:
  Modules
  Lessons
  Presentation
	Workbook
	Exercises
		Videotape
		Presentations
			Computer Game

size or content, while sophistication encompasses variations in curriculum or media. At the smallest level of scope are lesson plans and modules. The next level includes courses, programs, workshops, and units. Courses, curriculum, and environments would be examples of large-scope products. At the highest level of sophistication are interactive learning delivery systems, such as interactive video, while the lowest level of sophistication is paper and pencil, with audiovisual materials in the middle. As Table 1.2 shows, products can fall on any coordinates of the scope and sophistication dimensions. An example of a product is given in the project profiles in Table 1.3.

DERIVATION OF THE GENERIC MODEL

ISD is a decision-driven process based upon theories that have been substantiated by empirical research. The integrated set of steps that make up ISD evolved from general systems theory. The generic model evolved over time. Shock (1995) notes that, rather than a linear progression of well-documented innovations, the history of instructional development is the story of a gradual confluence of ideas, which took place over several decades. Table 1.4 shows the evolution of the ISD process by decade.

Support for ISD comes from (a) surveys of procedures used in the field, (b) internal review, and (c) developmental research (Burt & Geis, 1986; Geis, Burt, & Weston, 1984; Kennedy, Esque, & Novak, 1983; Weston, Burt, & Geis, 1984; Wileman & Gambill, 1983). Surveys of procedures entail reviewing the literature in the field in order to determine the consensus and issues relating to a phase. Internal review consists of an examination of how the phases were followed or adapted and an examination of the product. Developmental research involves implementing a product and testing its effectiveness (Richey, 1966).

What is the status of knowledge about each phase? The phases of analysis, development, and implementation derive their theoretical base largely from reports from the field and theoretical papers. These phases are also supported by logic. You cannot design a solution until you have correctly identified the problem. You must develop materials in order to implement, and implement in order to evaluate.

The phases of design and evaluation developed from quasi-experimental and field studies. Communication theories on how information is transferred from one person to another have had a major impact. One area of research from the communications field is directed at matching the learner characteristics with media capabilities. Knowledge about the design phase is supported by research from the field of psychology, including learning

Table 1.3   Project Profile for College Course

Applied Phonics Course
Directors: Barbara A. Petry & Mayhouse Edwards
1984

Purpose: The course was individualized in order to meet the needs of a diverse population of students (graduate, undergraduate, international, linguistics majors, communicative disorders majors). The course requires a high level of skill development, and traditional instruction was not resulting in this level for all students.

Description: Elaboration theory was selected as a theoretical base, so the course begins with an overview of sound and speech, then proceeds to specific classes of sounds and skill development. Laboratory sessions were designed to closely correspond with class sessions. Parameters affecting the difficulty of transcription tasks were identified and manipulated through easy-to-difficult sequences. Students were allowed to work at their own speed until mastery was achieved.

Development process: A team from the University Center for Instructional Development used an instructional development model. The components developed included a student manual, a workbook and accompanying audio tapes, laboratory exercises, and test answers for all except the final test in the workbook.

Results: Students' scores remained the same although content and skill requirements were increased. Students reported more positive attitudes towards the revised course. Although the project's scope expanded beyond the original intent, the investment was returned in improvement of instruction.

Note: This course was developed for the Syracuse University Communicative Disorder Program. Adapted from "Systematic Development of an Applied Phonetics Course," by B. Petry and M. L. Edwards, 1984, *Journal of Instructional Development, 7*(4), pp. 6–10.

and instructional theory. Some researchers have thoroughly explored questions such as "What are the most effective conditions for practice?" in order to generate guidelines (Jurgemeyer, 1982; Salisbury, Richards, & Klein, 1985). Starting in the early 1970s, the cognitive sciences began studying how knowledge is structured in memory, and guidelines evolved to answer the question: "How can we present new information to aid learning?" (West, Farmer, & Wolff, 1991). Guidelines from other research questions (such as "What treatments are best for what learning styles?") have only recently evolved (Jonassen & Grabowski, 1993).

The design phase component is relatively well researched because the field of psychology is older than other contributing fields. Findings from research on learning have been translated into prescriptions for ISD. For this to happen, several stages of research must occur. Many studies must be conducted and synthesized before principles for design can be accepted.

Many studies support the use of specific evaluation strategies and techniques. Knowledge about evaluation is produced by experimental studies and field studies (Burt & Geis, 1986; Geis, Burt, & Weston, 1984; Weston et al., 1984). Formative evaluation, which is intended to improve the learning materials during the development phase, is a recognized and respected part of ISD. Formative evaluation practices are well established (Tessmer, 1993). Guidelines for summative evaluative are set forth by a number of writers (Morris, 1978; Popham, 1988). In addition, many areas related to evaluation, such as criterion-referenced testing, have been studied extensively.

Exercises A, B, C, and D at the end of this chapter provide practice on understanding the ISD process.

Table 1.4   Evolution of the ISD Process

Decade	Innovation	Comments
1920s	Objectives & Individualized Instruction	Personnel at the San Francisco State Normal School developed self-instructional materials that allowed learners to progress at their own pace with a minimum of teacher direction.
		The Winnetka Plan made use of self-paced, self-instructional, and self-corrective workbooks. It incorporated diagnostic placement tests and self-administered tests.
		The Dalton Plan, implemented in Dalton, Ohio, and New York City, centered on "contract learning." After agreeing on contracts, students were free to complete instructional units at their own pace.
1930s	Behavioral Objectives	In the Eight-Year Study launched from Ohio State University, Ralph W. Tyler, a member of the Bureau of Educational Research, refined the procedure for writing instructional objectives in terms of student behavior (i.e., behavioral objectives)
	Formative Evaluation	Objectives and their assessments were used to revise and refine the new curricula until they produced the "appropriate level of achievement." (The term "formative evaluation" would not be coined for another 35 years.)
1940s	Instructional Media	Faced with the need to train military personnel during World War II, thousands of training films and other mediated learning materials were developed by the Division of Visual Aids for War Training within the U. S. Office of Education.
	Research and Development (R and D)	Many of the people hired by the military to work on wartime training were well established researchers. Consequently, military training became a well funded research and development effort directed toward education, and predisposed the military toward innovative instructional system concepts.
	Instructional Design Teams	During the process of creating military films, the basic instructional design team evolved consisting of a professional instructional designer, an SME, and a producer with expertise in filmmaking.
1950s	Programmed Instruction	B. F. Skinner's research into operant conditioning and animal learning was the foundation for the programmed instruction movement. Programmed instruction is characterized by behavioral objectives, small steps of instruction, self-pacing, active learner response, and immediate feedback. Programmed instruction shifted the focus to the outcome behavior of the learner and away from the process or the behavior of the teacher.
	Task Analysis	Work that began during WWII on observing and analyzing human behavior continued, and task analysis procedures were developed for military applications. In the 1950s, the term *task analysis* was used by the Air Force to refer to procedures for anticipating job requirements of new equipment under development.

Table 1.4 *Continued*

Decade	Innovation	Comments
1960s	**Instructional System Design (ISD)**	The ideas expressed in previous decades coalesced to form an identifiable field. ◆ The military was rapidly infusing ISD into their standard training procedures. ◆ ISD was encouraged by the passage of the Elementary and Secondary Education Act (ESEA), which established 20 federally funded R and D labs. ◆ Many instructional technology R and D efforts were carried out in the private and public sectors. ◆ The AV field moved from a preoccupation with curriculum products to a focus on message design.
1970s	**Models**	There was a proliferation of models as scholars and practitioners sought to define and describe more thoroughly the processes they advocated.
	Needs Assessment	Needs assessment was an important addition to ISD models.
1980s	**Microcomputers**	The instructional applications of computers dominated much of the design literature and facilitated research in cognitive psychology. Tremendous growth in the use of computer-based instruction took place in business, industry, and the military.
1990s	**Cost Effectiveness**	More and more businesses and government agencies see high-tech delivery systems as a way to maintain high training standards while reducing costs. Included are the following: **Electronic Performance Support Systems (EPSS).** EPSS delivers to personnel working in highly computerized work environments on-line references, automated decision support, and "just in time" training that the user can access on demand to meet task-related information requirements. **Distance Learning Technologies.** New communication technology has the capability to deliver instruction wherever students are in whatever groups they choose to form. For example, web-based training can deliver computer-based instruction on-line as well as interactions with the instructor via live chat. Secure e-mail allows submission of written tests.

Adapted from "A Brief History of Instructional Development" by S. A Shock, in *Instructional Technology: Past, Present, and Future,* 2nd ed. (pp. 11–19), by G. A. Anglin (Ed.), 1995, Englewood, CO: Libraries Unlimited, Inc.

THE BENEFITS OF ISD

Although ISD has been adopted by many corporations, the military, and many government agencies, the impact of ISD in public schools has been low. Some of the reasons for this low impact are that (a) the responsibility and authority over instruction are vested in the teacher's direct contact with students, rather than in the development of systematically designed materials; (b) the rigidity of the daily schedules are defined in terms of hours spent in a classroom with a teacher, rather than the learning outcomes achieved; and (c) the amount of discretionary funding available to support systematically designed technology-based instruction is low (Heinich, 1991, 1995). For ISD to become more prominent in school settings three changes would have to take place: (a) a reduction of amount of time spent by teachers and students in traditional classes, (b) more individualization within the curriculum, and (c) implementation of low-cost delivery systems (Melmed, 1986).

Heinich (1991, 1995) believes our educational institutions, with their certification requirements, accreditation standards, state financial aid policies, state department of public instruction policies and standards, and contracts negotiated between teacher groups and boards of education, mitigate against the acceptance of instructional technology. He cites incidents where educational personnel actively worked against the acceptance of instructional programs despite the demonstrated success of these programs. Indeed, the history of instructional design indicates that ISD evolved largely outside of the educational system.

The benefits that accrue from instruction produced by ISD are presented next.

A Systematic Decision-Making Process

The principal benefit of ISD is that it is a systematic process that helps the instructional designer make decisions about the nature and scope of instruction. The ISD process brings objectivity and orderliness to the process of planning instruction so that the quality of instruction is assured. ISD is a problem-solving approach where cause and effect relationships can be identified, studied, and managed. Although it has not reached a level of scientific exactness, its application reduces reliance on intuition or trial-and-error planning.

If decision points are properly documented, there exists an audit trail whereby decisions made during the process can be evaluated and examined reliably. In a well executed ISD project, data collected during the analysis phase establishes a database that documents the nature of the problem, the performance requirements, the characteristics of the learners, and the types of learning and prerequisites involved. Because ISD focuses on learning outcomes, instructional objectives show everyone (administrators, teachers, parents, and students) the goals of instruction. Performance standards provide a way to determine whether or not those goals have been met. Furthermore, users can have confidence in the effectiveness of the instruction, because it is tried out and revised until objectives are met before it is implemented.

Standardized Instruction

In traditional classrooms, there is considerable variability in the quality of instruction. Learning varies as a function of many factors, including the ability of the instructor, the classroom climate, the student-teacher ratio, the adequacy of resources, and the heterogeneity of the student body. Conversely, in ISD the instructional materials and the procedures prescribed for their use bear the burden of instruction. Thus, ISD can greatly reduce the variability of learning outcomes because it is able to deliver instruction the same way every time. Where individual differences exist among the student population, instruction developed within the ISD framework can be tailored to meet individual needs by providing alternate paths through the course of study and by building in remedial instruction for those who need it.

Replicability and the Economy of Scale

The technological developments and inventions of the industrial revolution allowed cheaper production of goods for greater numbers of people. In contrast, artisans produced luxury items that few could afford. The items produced by artisans are expensive because they are one-of-a-kind products and are labor intensive to produce. Heinich (1991, 1995) sees our educational system as composed largely of artisans because face-to-face instruction in traditional classrooms is labor intensive. Although an instructor may teach the same content and use the same instructional methods each time a course is presented, each presentation of the course is a new event that takes the same level of effort on the part of the instructor.

Furthermore, the inherent nature of face-to-face instruction limits the number of people who can reasonably be taught. Using a student-teacher ratio of 20:1, it would take five offerings of a course to teach 100 students. On the other hand, a course taught via computer-assisted instruction can be cost effectively delivered again and again to countless students. The labor costs for the instructor and the overhead costs for the classroom facilities are eliminated. In fact, the longer the life of the course, the lower the per-student cost as more and more students enroll. By using technology to replicate the course, the cost of the instruction on a per-student basis drops dramatically.

ISD has the capacity to amortize the cost of development over large enough populations to realize the benefits of large-scale distribution. Due to advancements in computers and telecommunication technologies, we have the capability to deliver instruction to students wherever they are and in whatever groups they choose to form.

For this reason, many large entities such as the U.S. Office of Personnel Management are moving away from traditional classroom training to the production of distance-learning methodologies (U.S. Office of Personnel Management, 1996). For example, the Federal Election Commission plans to develop training for election officials using video and audio tapes because VCRs and cassette players are so accessible (Glasgow, 1993). The tapes can be used in settings such as the office, home, or in the case of audio tapes, car. These initiatives contrast sharply with the delivery systems of most educational institutions—namely, face-to-face interactions between teacher and students in a classroom setting.

ISD technologies have the potential for producing changes in the institutions that deliver education in much the same way that the printing press expanded the distribution of knowledge, thereby changing the social fabric of western Europe. In today's economy, the cost of maintaining instructor-based courses and funding resident institutions often puts a strain on already tight budgets. Self-paced mediated courses are often more cost effective because students take less time to complete them and they can be administered by nonprofessionals since the materials carry the burden of instruction (Glasgow, 1985; Glasgow & Cox, 1993).

For many of the above reasons, Gagné and Medsker (1996) recommend the ISD process when

◆ large numbers of learners must be trained;

◆ a long lifetime is expected for the program;

◆ standardized training requirements must be maintained;

◆ high mastery levels are required;

◆ economic value is placed on the learner's time; or

◆ training is valued in the organizational culture.

EXAMPLE OF THE APPLICATION OF ISD TO DEVELOPMENT OF A COURSE

The following case study of an actual ISD project to develop a course on "Commercial Loan Documentation" shows how one designer handled the job. The client is an association that provides training support to banks nationwide.

Needs Analysis

What is the problem? During this phase, the instructional designer wants to learn as much as possible about (a) loan documentation and the conditions under which bank employees perform that task, (b) the background and competencies of employees when they start doing loan documentation, and (c) the environment in which they might be trained. By gaining an understanding of the problem, the designer has enough information to formulate a solution to the problem.

In brief, the designer learns several facts about the problem. Loan documents present a "paper trail" on the agreements and understandings that protect the bank in case the borrower defaults on the loan. Lending arrangements can be quite complicated, and the documentation requirements differ with different types of business entities and the terms of the loan.

Generally, people given the responsibility for loan documentation have had at least three years experience working in other areas of the bank. They understand the basic concepts of banking, but cannot perform documentation tasks adequately as measured by a test. Thus, they need to know the technical points of loan documentation.

The amount of information to be learned is voluminous. Employees responsible for commercial loan documentation have to know

◆ how to determine the identity of the borrower and a person's authority to act on borrower's side;

◆ dos and don'ts for completing forms;

◆ how to prepare the promissory note and subsequent amendments;

◆ how to document third party involvement;

◆ what to say in letters that obligate the bank to make a loan and letters that do not;

◆ how to document the various types of collateral used to secure a loan;

◆ how to document unsecured loans; and

◆ how to document the understandings on both sides.

The association provides courses on loan documentation in a workshop format. Instructors are employees from member organizations with expertise in their own areas of specialty and trained in teaching skills. Workshops typically last three to five days, depending on the complexity of subject to be taught. Although all instructors work from a standard lesson plan provided by the association, the quality of instruction varies greatly, depending on the expertise and delivery skills of the instructor.

The course is followed by a period of on-the-job training, during which the employees work under the guidance of an experienced person within their banks. It takes considerable time before an employee is proficient in loan documentation.

What is the solution? The amount of information to be learned is too much to be committed to memory within the time spans typically allotted for instruction. Therefore, the designer recommends against attempting to teach all the information. Instead, she recommends a desk reference on loan documentation.

Instruction would focus on how to use the desk reference given the various types of lending arrangements. Case studies typical of the range of lending agreements encountered on the job would be developed. The instructor's role would change from that of lecturer to a facilitator who helps students apply the information in the desk reference to realistic loan situations in the case studies.

This approach has the following advantages:

1. It reduces or eliminates the amount of time currently spent learning loan documentation on the job. Employees could consult the desk reference for answers when they were uncertain about how to proceed. The expectation is that after training, new employees would need help from in-house experts for only a small number of the most complex situations. Thus, training would be more efficient.

2. The course is materials-based rather than instructor-based. The presentation of information would be dependent on the materials, that is, the Reference Guide and the case studies that are tried out and revised during formative evaluation. Thus, the same course could be delivered to large numbers of bank employees nationwide with less variation than presentations made by instructors. The approach shifts the burden of instruction from the instructor to the materials.

3. The course uses job-relevant case studies intended to aid the transfer of learning. Students' experiences in the classroom will closely replicate the real-world loan documentation conditions and thus help them transfer what is learned in the workshop back to the job.

Task Analysis

What is the job? The instruction designer's aim is to develop a usable reference guide and associated instruction directed at only the skills and knowledge actually needed to perform loan documentation. To define the job, the designer studies various texts on loan documentation and works with a lawyer from a member bank's legal department who is an expert on the subject. First, she reviews the texts to get an overview of the types of loans and documentation. Then, a series of interviews are conducted. Gradually, by consulting the texts and interviewing the lawyer, the designer documents (a) the conditions that trigger the need for loan documentation, (b) the behaviors associated with loan documentation, and (c) the standards for an acceptable set of loan documents.

Instructional Analysis

What must be learned? At this point, the designer analyzes the tasks to determine the types of learning involved and to ascertain their prerequisite relationship and verify the sequence for learning. She also collects more information on the target audience. The designer interviews bank employees and their supervisors in the commercial loan department to define more specifically what the prospective students already know about the tasks to be learned. This information is used to make decisions about the structure and amount of information to be contained in the guide, what must be learned, and in what order.

Design

Using the results of the analysis phase, the designer develops specifications for the workshop. Decisions made during the instructional analysis about types of learning feed into the decisions about which instructional strategies are appropriate for the learning tasks. She relies on her understanding of learning theory and pays special attention to research on job performance aids.

Two levels of objectives are then developed: Those that specify the performance expected at the end of the course, and those that specify the learning steps that lead up to the end-of-course objective.

How will we know if the objectives are met? Test questions are developed for each of the topic areas to measure learning of the learning steps. However, the best measure of the employees' understanding of loan documentation is actually to prepare the documents for typical cases. Thus, case studies of typical loan situations are developed to assess end-of-course performance. In addition, exercises appropriate for this type of learning are developed to assess component steps.

What teaching strategies will achieve the objectives? What delivery systems are most cost effective? The delivery system, an instructor-led workshop whereby employees learn to use a desk reference for decisions about loan documentation, was selected during the needs analysis. Therefore, the answers to these questions are constrained by that decision. The designer specifies the following materials: an instructor's guide on how to conduct the course, the desk reference, a participant's manual that contains instructional materials for each lesson, practice exercises, case studies, and blank forms for the exercises and case studies. The organization and structure of the desk reference is specified as well.

Computer-assisted instruction would be natural for this course. The desk reference materials could be accessed via computer, and the instruction could be presented in that way as well. Computer-assisted instruction enhances the replicability and reliability of the training. However, the designer did not make that recommendation for the following reasons:

1. The development of computer-assisted instruction is labor intensive, and the budget is too small for such an effort.
2. Hardware and software compatibility problems have to be resolved. No standardization of computer systems exists among the various banking institutions.
3. The association's staff has little experience with computer-assisted instruction. There would be implementation problems as they learn new ways of doing things.

Instead, she recommended a modified version of the workshop format that was familiar to the client and its instructional staff. However, the designer moves the client away from teacher-based instruction towards instruction that embodies the benefits of ISD: systematic development, standardization, and replication and the economy of scale. The reference guide and participant's manual could later provide the basis for computerizing instruction, if feasible.

Development

How do the materials look and sound? The designer develops the materials starting with the reference guide. During development, materials are reviewed by the lawyer to ensure accuracy, and by the bank's training staff to be sure they are consistent with the design specifications.

Does the course teach? The course is tried out in draft form on 20 bank employees representative of the target audience. Tryout results are analyzed and changes in the materials are made where employees had difficulty. Then materials go into final production where decisions are made about graphics and packaging.

Implementation

Is the client ready to take responsibility for the course? Bank personnel worked closely with the instructional designer during all phases. The designer obtained the client's cooperation at each point along the way. There are no surprises about what is taught and how it is taught. The client provided the pilot facilities and participants and concurred with the recommendation for revisions. The basic approach was one familiar to the client; thus, there were virtually no implementation problems.

Evaluation

Have we solved the problem? The evaluation is conducted by the association's staff. Each time the course is offered, the association reviews performance on the final exercise and on a questionnaire assessing participants' perceptions regarding the relevancy of the course to their job situations. In addition, supervisors back on the job are surveyed about participants' productivity and accuracy after training. This feedback system ensures that instructional standards do not slip and that the impact of the instruction on the commercial loan department's processing of loan documents is assessed annually. The legal department reviews the content and form of the documents to keep the course current.

Exercises E and F at the end of this chapter provide practice in comparing course development efforts to how well they realize the benefits of the ISD process.

 # ISD COMPETENCIES

Because the ISD process is prescriptive, it may seem that anyone can produce quality instruction if the process is strictly followed. Thus, practitioners may follow ISD in a lock-step manner, especially in settings where the organizational leadership does not understand that ISD is both a process and a domain of knowledge. This approach fails to recognize that ISD is based on a set of values, specialized knowledge, and intellectual skills and methodologies. Professionals responsible for applying ISD must bring the discipline to the process.

ISD is an intellectual process requiring higher-level thinking skills (Nelson, Macliaro, & Sherman, 1988). To perform this activity you will need entering skills and aptitudes plus training and education. Wallington (1981) lists the generic skills necessary to perform ISD as interpersonal skills, communication skills, and problem-solving skills, as well as skills in extracting and assimilating chunks of information and working them into a logical framework, applying principles of behavioral sciences, and systematically searching for related information.

Personal Aptitudes

In addition to study of the field there are certain aptitudes relevant to instructional design. An instructional designer needs to be able to think both in the abstract and the concrete. A great deal of design work involves checking for logical consistency of ideas. At the same time a designer is looking at the general and abstract, however, he or she must also attend to details. Thoroughness is required for quality products.

A designer must enjoy working with visual presentation modes and writing, because a good deal of design work entails visualizing, writing, or editing. If you don't enjoy writing or working with visuals, instructional design may not be for you.

Because much design work is done in teams, designers need to be task-oriented and yet still be able to work productively with others. Designers must be open to ideas and able to accept constructive criticism. Their tolerance for ambiguity should be high because design can be described as giving structure to a mass of ambiguity.

Gagné describes the personal characteristics of instructional technologists as falling into three categories: attitudes or values, specialized knowledge, and intellectual skills or methodologies. According to Gagné (1985), a designer needs to value empirical evidence as a basis for action, and needs to be able to analyze learning outcomes and conditions, use measurement techniques, and construct tests. In addition, a designer needs statistical and communication skills (Gagné, 1987).

When Mountain Bell Corporation wanted to develop employees without training in ISD into designers, they considered writing, oral, and analytical skills. They found these skills were basic to the functions an instructional designer had to perform (Maxwell & Seyfer, 1984).

You will also need the interpersonal and process skills used by consultants. Whether you are contracted temporarily to solve a specific problem or are assigned to give instructional advice as part of your regular duties, as an instructional designer you will often be in a consulting role. You will be asked to help a client temporarily with judicious sharing of your knowledge. You will need to be able to determine what the instructional problem is, whom it affects, and how it can be dealt with. You will need to be able to convince people to work with you voluntarily. You do not want to make the organization dependent on you; rather, you want to share your skills. The combination of enthusiasm and restraint that characterizes the effective consultant also characterizes the effective instructional designer.

Roles

An instructional designer's role can change depending on whether the subject to be presented is technical or non-technical, and depending on the composition of the design team. If an area is highly technical, the designer needs to instruct the content expert in design. If the subject is not overly technical, the designer can function more independently with the assistance of content expertise. Designers can work as external consultants who are responsible for all tasks, as in-house employees who are assisted by subject-matter experts, or as in-house employees who assist subject-matter experts. The following instances illustrate the variety of roles a designer can have, depending on the relation to content expertise.

1. A content expert adds instructional systems design and technology competencies and fulfills the role of designer without needing the assistance of content expertise.
2. An instructional designer is asked to work in a content area that may be familiar, but the designer still feels the need to work with a content expert.
3. A designer may be asked to manage development or research in an unfamiliar content area, and therefore needs to select and work with several content experts.

It is also important to distinguish between researcher and practitioner roles because the requirements for success in each differ. An ISD researcher is interested in studying variables and developing theories related to the delivery of instruction. An ISD practitioner is interested in applying research and theory in the development of instructional methods and materials. One role leads to operating as a generalist (practitioner) and the other to operating as a specialist (researcher). Table 1.5 contrasts the interests of both roles for each phase of the ISD process.

Depending on how the job is described, a practicing designer can perform each ISD step from analysis through evaluation. If the designer's job is defined narrowly, then he or she may perform fewer steps, leaving the production, implementation, and evaluation steps to others.

Research in the field is broad enough to incorporate experimental research as well as product development research. Some areas, such as behavior modification, have been explored all along the basic-to-applied-research continuum. Other areas, such as affective learning, need more research, basic as well as applied.

Table 1.5   A Comparison of Interests and Goals of Researchers and Practitioners

Generic ISD Model	*Researcher Role*	*Practitioner Role*
Phase 1: Analysis	Study methods for problem identification	Application of methods for problem identification
	Study effect of learner characteristics	Prescriptions for learner characteristics
	Study of content area	Using research on content area
Phase 2: Design	Study message design variables	Use of prescriptions for design of instruction
	Develop instructional strategies	
Phase 3: Development	Study team processes	Working with producers to develop scripts
Phase 4: Implementation	Ethnographic studies of variables in environments	Design and management of environment and variables in instruction
	Identification of variables affecting implementation	
Phase 5: Evaluation	Studies of issues related to evaluation	Application of evaluation research and theory

The discipline of instructional systems design is nearly 40 years old (Seels, 1989). It is the researcher's role to promote the growth of ISD theory. Because this is an applied field, the researcher's role may seem isolated and less important, but without theoretical progress the field will stagnate. As a designer, you can progress further along your career path if you are aware of the research associated with each step. This book deals with ISD theory relevant to product development research. Other research methodologies are not discussed. Richey (1996) offers an overview of developmental research methodology.

Table 1.6 compares the role profiles for two different instructional designers—the first a researcher and the second a practitioner. In short, researchers develop theories and study issues associated with phases of the ISD process and its practitioners.

Exercises G, H, and I at the end of this chapter provide practice on the roles of practitioners and researchers.

Table 1.6   Role Profiles: ISD Researcher and ISD Practitioner

	ISD Researcher	*ISD Practitioner*
Definition	An instructional design researcher's role is to build knowledge about steps for development of systematic instruction. The role requires identifying questions that need study, planning a project that will yield information, conducting such projects, and reporting project results.	An instructional design practitioner has the role of applying knowledge from many fields to the steps in a systematic process for the development of instruction. The role requires defining what is to be learned, planning an intervention that will allow learning to occur, measuring learning to determine whether objectives were met, and refining the intervention until objectives are met.
Critical Outputs	Instructional theories Information on variables Methodologies Research proposals	Problem statement Needs assessment Performance requirements Learning requirements Learning objectives Instructional strategies Tests Evaluation strategies Project proposals
Critical Competencies	Questioning assumptions, reviewing literature, stating hypotheses, selecting methodology, designing research, analyzing data, writing proposals and reports, and investigating environments.	Gathering, analyzing, learning, synthesizing, evaluating, restructuring, and translating information, writing, creating environments, messages, and systems.
Comments	The ISD researcher needs to be interested in parts of the ISD process rather than the whole ISD process. The researcher must have strong competencies in quantitative and qualitative research and an interest in publication and specialization.	The ISD practitioner needs a tolerance for ambiguity, an ability to move back and forth continually from the abstract to the concrete, and a high task orientation with effective interpersonal skills.

EXERCISES

Complete and correct the exercises, using the chapter as a reference. Then check your answers in the back of the chapter. Discuss with your instructor items that are confusing.

A. An Exercise to Identify the Products of Each Phase of the ISD Process

Circle the correct answer. There may be more than one correct answer.

1. Which of the following outputs are produced in Phase 1, Analysis?
   a. Objectives
   b. Assumptions about learners
   c. Characteristics of the process
   d. Student measurement procedures
   e. Assumptions about needs
2. Which of the following outputs are produced in Phase 2, Design?
   a. Objectives
   b. Instructional strategy
   c. Student comments
   d. Criterion-referenced tests
   e. Project report
3. Which of the following outputs are produced in Phase 3, Development?
   a. Task requirements
   b. Storyboards
   c. Characteristics of learners
   d. Slide-tape presentations
   e. Prototype
4. Which of the following outputs are produced in Phase 4, Implementation?
   a. Maintenance plan
   b. Principles of learning
   c. Sequence of objectives
   d. Description of constraints
   e. Problem statement
5. Which of the following outputs are produced in Phase 5, Evaluation?
   a. Instructional strategy
   b. Project report
   c. Interpretation of test results
   d. Revised prototype
   e. Media prescription

B. An Exercise to Measure Your Knowledge and Understanding of ISD

Complete the statements below, using one of the following phases:
   Phase 1: Analysis
   Phase 2: Design
   Phase 3: Development
   Phase 4: Implementation
   Phase 5: Evaluation

1. Instructional materials are tried out on a sample of the target audience. This activity takes place during _____ .
2. Job incumbents are surveyed to determine what tasks they perform and under what conditions they perform these tasks. This activity takes place during _____ .
3. Instructional requirements are translated into measurable objectives. This activity takes place during _____ .

4. Tasks and content to be included in the instruction are identified. This activity takes place during _____ .

5. A plan of instruction is developed. Methods and media are selected. This activity takes place in _____ .

6. Course administration procedures are printed and distributed. This activity takes place during _____ .

7. A student workbook is developed. This activity takes place during _____ .

8. User groups are surveyed to determine whether the job performance of course graduates is satisfactory. This activity takes place during _____ .

9. More practice exercises are added on the basis of tryout data. This activity takes place during _____ .

C. An Exercise in Matching the ISD Phase with the Activity Performed at That Phase

Match the phases in the first column with the activities in the second column.

Phases in ISD Model	Activities
Phase 1: Analysis	____ a. Interpret and report test results
Phase 2: Design	____ b. Work with producers
Phase 3: Development	____ c. Conduct a needs assessment
Phase 4: Implementation	____ d. Train teachers
Phase 5: Evaluation	____ e. Write objectives
	____ f. Sequence instruction
	____ g. Write a problem statement

D. An Exercise Designed to Test Your Knowledge of the History of ISD.

Using Table 1.4 as a guide, indicate the decade in which the following events or methods took place.

1. Programmed instruction movement
2. Behavioral objectives
3. Distance learning technologies
4. ISD models
5. Cognitive psychology facilitated by computer
6. Self-instructional materials
7. Computer-based instruction
8. Task analysis
9. Elementary and Secondary Education Act (ESEA)
10. Mediated training

E. An Exercise in Comparing ISD with Other Approaches to Instruction

Critique the example of the application of ISD in this chapter as to how well it delivers the benefits of ISD. For each benefit, check whether the principle applies and tell why.

1. Systematic Decision Making ____ Yes ____ No ____ Not applicable
Explain your answer:

2. Standardization ____ Yes ____ No ____ Not applicable
Explain your answer:

3. Replicability and the Economy of Scale ____ Yes ____ No ____ Not applicable
Explain your answer:

F. A Group Exercise in Comparing Approaches to Instruction

Choose a partner. Interview each other about a time when you had to teach. What did you do as an instructor? How did you decide what to teach? What steps did you follow? How did you conduct the lesson? How did you know if the student(s) had learned from the lesson? The group should then discuss how other approaches to instruction compare with the five phases in the ISD approach. Record the consensus of the group for each phase.

1. Analysis _____

_____

2. Design _____

_____

3. Development _____

_____

4. Implementation _____

_____

5. Evaluation _____

_____

G. An Exercise in Recognizing the Interests of Researchers and Practitioners.

Decide whether each statement is true or false.

_____ 1. The ISD practitioner is more interested in experimental research on learning principles than in the application of such principles.

_____ 2. The ISD researcher is more interested in studying a step in the process than in developing an instructional system.

_____ 3. Both the ISD researcher and the ISD practitioner are interested in prescriptive theories of instruction.

H. An Exercise to Measure Your Understanding of the Types of Products Produced by Researchers and Practitioners.

Identify which of the following are *produced* primarily by:
R: ISD researchers
P: ISD practitioners

_____ 1. Experimental study
_____ 2. Ethnographic study
_____ 3. Unit
_____ 4. Module
_____ 5. Curriculum
_____ 6. Small group discussion task
_____ 7. Message design principles
_____ 8. ISD models or constructs

I. An Exercise to Measure Your Understanding of What ISD Researchers and Practitioners Do.

Match the ISD role with the job description.

a. Researcher
b. Practitioner

_____ 1. Manage the design and development of instructional materials for performance improvements within financial institutions. Perform the following duties: conduct content research, analyze needs, write instructional materials, communicate with division directly about project planning, complete reports, and conduct project evaluations.

_____ 2.   Manage research activities for establishing educational planning systems and methodologies.

_____ 3.   Analyze training materials; provide direction to course developers; conduct project review meetings; and apply knowledge of task analysis, design specification, media selection, and data processing.

_____ 4.   Work on project to identify principles of message design, literature search, writing of proposals, and publication. Apply skills in experimental design, literature search, writing of proposals, and publication.

◇ REFERENCES

Burt, C. W., & Geis, G. L. (1986, April). *Guidelines for developmental testing: Proposed and practiced.* Paper presented at the 70th annual meeting of the American Educational Research Association, San Francisco, CA. (ERIC Document Reproduction Service No. 270 500)

Campbell, C. P. (1980, December). *An instructional systems development process.* Paper presented at the annual convention of the American Vocational Association, New Orleans, LA. (ERIC Document Reproduction Service No. 194 805)

Dick, W., & Carey, L. (1996) *The systematic design of instruction* (4th ed.). New York: Harper/Collins College Publishers.

Gagné, R. M. (1985). What should a performance improvements professional know and do? *Performance & Instruction, 24*(7),6–7.

Gagné, R. M. (1987). Characteristics of instructional technologists. *Performance & Instruction, 26*(3), 26–28.

Gagné, R. M., Briggs, L. J., & Wager, W. W. (1992). *Principles of instructional design* (4th ed.). Fort Worth, TX: Harcourt, Brace, Jovanovich.

Gagné, R., & Medsker, K. L. (1996). *The conditions of learning: Training applications.* Fort Worth, TX: Harcourt Brace College Publishers.

Geis, G. L., Burt, C. W., & Weston, C. (1984, April). *Instructional Development: Developmental testing.* Paper presented at the 68th annual meeting of the American Educational Research Association, New Orleans, LA. (ERIC Document Reproduction Service No. 243 793)

Gibbons, A. S. (1981). The contribution of science to instructional development. *National Society for Performance & Instruction Journal, 20*(Sept.), 23–25.

Glasgow, Z. (1985). *Videodisk instruction for senior training managers.* Contract No. F41689-83-C-0048. Randolph, AFB, TX: USAF Occupational Measurement Center (ATC).

Glasgow, Z. (1993). *Final Report: Needs analysis of the training and education of election officials.* (Contract No. FE2AC034). Washington, DC: Federal Election Commission's National Clearinghouse on Election Administration.

Glasgow, Z., & Cox, D. (1993). *Evaluation of selected courses for conversion to individualized instruction and distance delivery.* (Contract No. EME-92-C-0349). Emmitsburg, MD: Federal Emergency Management Administration, Emergency Management Institute (EMI).

Hannum, W. H., & Hansen, C. (1989). *Instructional systems development in large organizations.* Englewood Cliffs, NJ: Educational Technology Publication.

Heinich, R. (1991). Restructuring, technology, and instructional productivity. In G. J. Anglin (Ed.), *Instructional technology: Past, present, and future* (pp. 236–243). Englewood, CO: Libraries Unlimited, Inc.

Heinich, R. (1995). The proper study of instructional technology. In G. J. Anglin (Ed.), *Instructional technology: Past, present, and future* (pp. 61–83). Englewood, CO: Libraries Unlimited, Inc.

Jonassen, D. H., and Grabowski, B. L. (1993). *Handbook of individual differences, learning, and instruction.* Hillsdale, NJ: Laurence Erllbaum Assoc.

Jurgemeyer, F. H. (1982). Programmed instruction: Lessons it can teach us. *Educational Technology, 22*(5), 20–23.

Kemp, J. E., Morrison, G. R., and Ross, S. M. (1994). *Designing effective instruction.* New York: MacMillan College Publishing.

Kennedy, P., Esque, T., & Novak, J. (1983). A functional analysis of task analysis procedures for instructional systems design. *Journal of Instructional Development, 6*(4),10–16.

Laird, W., Bhatt, S., Bajpayee, T., Glasgow, Z., & Scott, D. (1981). *Development of a training program for fighting small fires in the mining industry: Task analysis report.* (Contract No. J0395060). Bruceton, PA: U.S. Department of Interior, Bureau of Mines.

Mager, R. F., and Pipe, P. (1970). *Analyzing performance problems.* Belmont, CA: Fearson.

Maxwell, K., & Seyfer, C. (1984). Selection by design. *Performance and Instructional Journal, 23,* 8–10.

Melmed, A. S. (1986). The technology of American education: Problem and opportunity. *Technological Horizons in Education, 14*(2), 77–81.

Morris, L. L. (1978). *Program evaluation kit.* Beverly Hills, CA: Sage Publications.

Nelson, W. A., Macliaro, S., & Sherman, T. M. (1988). The intellectual content of instructional design. *Journal of Instructional Development, 2*(1), 29–35.

Petry, B., & Edwards, M. L. (1984). Systematic development of an applied phonetics course. *Journal of Instructional Development, 7*(4), 6–10.

Popham, W. J. (1988) *Educational evaluation* (2nd. ed.). Englewood Cliffs, NJ: Prentice Hall.

Richey, R. C. (1996) Developmental research. In D. H. Jonassen (Ed.), *Handbook of research in educational communications and technology* (pp. 1213–1246). New York: Macmillan.

Salisbury, D. F., Richards, B. F., & Klein, J. D. (1985). Designing practice: A review of prescriptions and recommendations from instructional design theories. *Journal of Instructional Development, 8*(4), 9–19.

Seels, B. (1989). The instructional design movement in educational technology. *Educational Technology, 29*(5), 11–15.

Shock, S. A. (1995) A brief history of instructional development. In Anglin, G. J. (Ed.), *Instructional technology: Past, present, and future* (2nd ed.) (pp. 11–19). Englewood, CO: Libraries Unlimited, Inc.

Tessmer, M. (1993). *Planning and conducting formative evaluations.* Philadelphia: Kogan Page.

U.S. Office of Personnel Management. (1996). *Research and development in instructional systems development, performance management, workforce productivity, compensation, and employee relations* (Solicitation OPM RFP 96-01595VHB). Washington, D.C.: Author.

Wallington, C. J. (1981). Generic skills of an instructional developer. *Journal of Instructional Development, 4*(3), 28–33.

West, C. K., Farmer, J. A., & Wolff, P. M. (1991). *Instructional design: Implications from cognitive science.* Englewood Cliffs, NJ: Prentice Hall.

Weston, C., Burt, C. W., & Geis, G. L. (1984, April). *Instructional development: Revision practice.* Paper presented at the 68th annual meeting of the American Educational Research Association, New Orleans, LA. (ERIC Document Reproduction Service No. 243 794).

Wileman, R. E., & Gambill, T. G. (1983). The neglected phase of instructional design. *Educational Technology, 23*(11), 25–32.

◆ ANSWERS

A. An Exercise to Identify the Products of Each Phase of the ISD Process

1. b, c, and e
2. a, b, and d
3. b and d
4. a
5. b and c

B. An Exercise to Measure Your Knowledge and Understanding of ISD

1. Phase 3: Development
2. Phase 1: Analysis
3. Phase 2: Design
4. Phase 1: Analysis
5. Phase 2: Design
6. Phase 4: Implementation
7. Phase 3: Development
8. Phase 5: Evaluation
9. Phase 3 Development

C. An Exercise in Matching the ISD Phase with the Activity Performed at That Phase

a. Phase 5: Evaluation
b. Phase 3: Development
c. Phase 1: Analysis
d. Phase 4: Implementation
e. Phase 2: Design
f. Phase 1: Analysis
g. Phase 1: Analysis

D. An Exercise Designed to Test Your Knowledge of the History of ISD

1. 1950s Programmed instruction movement
2. 1930s Behavioral objectives
3. 1990s Distance learning technologies
4. 1970s ISD models
5. 1980s Cognitive psychology facilitated by computer
6. 1920s Self-instructional materials
7. 1980s Computer-based instruction
8. 1950s Task analysis
9. 1960s Elementary and Secondary Education Act (ESEA)
10. 1940s Mediated training

E. An Exercise in Comparing ISD with Other Approaches to Instruction

1. Yes. The ISD process was followed.
2. Yes. The reference guide specifies all the requirements

for loan documentation and cannot be altered. The materials and case studies are fully developed, and if the instructor's manual is carefully followed, different instructors would produce consistently high learning outcomes. A monitoring and feedback system is in place to ensure that standards are maintained, although this is no guarantee that the instructor will deliver the course as designed.

3. Yes. The course is materials based. They can be printed in large numbers and distributed nationwide to banks needing training on loan documentation. The same course would be delivered to all members of the banking association.

The course has a set format that depends on face-to-face interactions between the instructor and students; therefore, costs are incurred for travel to the training site. However, because the use of reference guide reduces the need to learn voluminous amounts of information and case studies help students make the transfer from the workshop to the job, the course is more cost-effective than previous courses on loan documentation.

F. A Group Exercise in Comparing Approaches to Instruction

Your answer should contrast ISD and other approaches by elaborating on the decision points in the five steps of the generic ISD model in Figure 1.1. The differences might include:

1. Decisions on what to teach are based on several types of analyses in ISD, rather than on personal or institutional preferences.

2. Although traditional instruction often incorporates objectives, instructional strategies, and tests, teachers seldom look at the logical consistency from one to the other. An instructional designer must examine the logical consistency between the products of each step in the ISD process.

A wide range of method and media options are considered in ISD and a systematic approach is used for selection of methods or media. In contrast, traditionally, few methods of media are considered and selection is arbitrary.

3. A common method of instruction is lecture followed by a question-and-answer period. In ISD, the emphasis is on learning by doing and more attention is paid establishing practice conditions consistent with research and theory.

In ISD, instructional materials are tried and revised until objectives are met. In traditional instruction, textbooks and other instructional materials are rarely subjected to a formative evaluation.

4. No significant differences.

5. No significant differences.

G. An Exercise in Recognizing the Interests of Researchers and Practitioners.

1. False
2. True
3. True

H. An Exercise to Measure Your Understanding of the Types of Products Produced by Researchers and Practitioners.

1. R
2. R
3. P
4. P
5. P
6. P
7. R
8. R

I. An Exercise to Measure Your Understanding of What ISD Researchers and Practitioners Do.

1. b
2. a
3. b
4. b

Chapter

2

Analyzing Tasks

OVERVIEW

Needs analysis precedes task analysis, and task analysis precedes instructional analysis. But the instructional designer will find that he or she moves back and forth among the different types of analysis, because analysis is an iterative process. It consists of collecting information for a specific purpose, analyzing the data, and making decisions based on that data. The data collection and analysis process moves from the general to the specific. It begins with the needs analysis step that involves getting the answer to specific questions that will circumscribe the precise nature of the problem. Once it is clear that some sort of instruction is the solution to the problem, it moves to the task analysis step to answer increasingly specific questions about what is the job or content. Finally, the instructional analysis step answers questions about the students' competencies with respect to the job or content and what must be learned.

Figure 2.1 shows how the three types of analyses relate to each other. Although conceptually distinct, they do not have clearly defined beginning and end points. Task analysis begins when the needs analysis is completed. Data collected during the needs analysis, however, will be relevant to subsequent task analysis; therefore, needs and task analyses overlap. Early on, the evidence from the needs analysis may indicate that instruction is needed to overcome a particular performance problem. But the data are usually still too general and diffuse for task analysis. Ordinarily the data tell you only what the next set of questions should be to answer questions about how tasks are performed. As the answers to initial task analysis questions are uncovered, new questions arise and additional information is collected. This process continues until, in the judgment of the designer, sufficient data exist as a basis for beginning the instructional analysis process. Task and instructional analysis also overlap in that task analysis provides some of the answers to the questions posed during instructional analysis.

The analysis process is akin to discovery learning. Information is gathered and examined. On the basis of this information, new hypotheses are formed and tested. As an understanding of the instructional problem evolves and relationships among tasks and content become clear, answers slowly emerge regarding what is to be learned to bridge the gap between the student entry level and the learning outcome to be accomplished.

The focus of this chapter is task anslysis. Needs and instructional analyses are covered in Part II of this text. The task analysis step introduces many of the competencies you

Figure 2.1   Expansion of the Analysis Phase of the ISD Process (Seels & Glasgow ISD Model I: For Novices)

Analysis

What is the problem?
How do we solve it?

What is the job or content?
What must be learned?

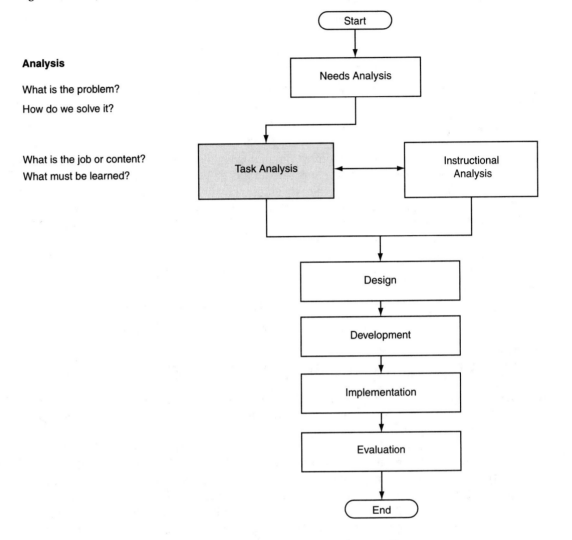

will need to perform effectively. These include the ability to collect and document evidence about jobs and content that are the goal of instruction.

The object of task analysis is to identify the subtasks, information flow, inputs, and decisions required to perform a task as objectively and explicitly as possible. The designer uses a number of methods and techniques to collect task data and reveal the relationships among task elements.

Developing a clear description of the topic or job to be learned helps the designer understand the subject or job. In turn, during subsequent steps of the ISD process, this understanding helps him to establish clear-cut instructional objectives, select the most suitable instructional techniques, and evaluate instructional effectiveness of the completed course. A task analysis is also a way to verify with others the designer's understanding of the job or topic.

When instructional designers are expert in the field to be taught, they draw on their own knowledge to define the answer to the question: "What is the job or content?" Usually, however, instructional designers are faced with the job of analyzing tasks in an unfamiliar field. Under these circumstances, designers must gather information from expert sources and translate it into a behavioral form. To do this, the designer must select from a repertoire of data collection methods those appropriate to the situation. The ability to work with unfamiliar subject matter is an essential prerequisite for virtually all designers.

ORIENTING QUESTIONS

What is the aim of task analysis?
What data is collected for a task analysis?
What methods are used to collect task analysis data?
How do we document a task analysis?
What does the instructional designer do when faced with an unfamiliar content area?

OBJECTIVES

1. Given brief job descriptions, write three-part statements that describe the inputs to the worker, the action he must take, and the outputs he will produce.
2. Given an event from everyday life, inventory the major duties and elaborate them by identifying tasks, subtasks, information flow, and the knowledge base required to perform the duties.
3. Given a task analysis situation, select the most appropriate method for collecting task data.
4. Given a task analysis situation, select the most appropriate format for recording task data.
5. Given flowcharting conventions used incorrectly, correct the errors to display the information properly.
6. Given an SME for a job or content area, interview the SME to elicit the information needed to flowchart the procedure.

WHAT TASK ANALYSIS IS AND IS NOT

Task analysis answers the question: "What is the job or content?" Its purpose is to determine the operational components of a job, skill, or subject matter in order to describe what expert performers do and how they think.

Task analysis may be the most confusing aspect of ISD to those entering the field. One reason for the confusion is that it is performed in many different ways depending on the type of tasks being analyzed, the designer's training and experience, and the resources allocated to the process by management. Another reason for the confusion is the imprecise use of terminology. Many writers blur the distinction among needs, task, and instructional analysis by using the term "task analysis" to describe all three. Most likely this is because analysis is an iterative process. The designer moves back and forth among the different types of analysis so that the distinctions blend together in practice although they are conceptually distinct.

Jonassen, Hannum, and Tessmer (1989) contend that most of the confusion is the result of uncertainty about what the process of task analysis involves. Table 2.1 shows the distinction between task analysis functions and instructional analysis functions as they

Table 2.1   Task Analysis Functions Versus Instructional Analysis Functions

Task Analysis: **What is the job or content?**	**Instructional Analysis:** **What must be learned?**
Task inventory lists the general duties or topics that make up the job or content.	Selecting tasks eliminates the tasks that are NOT the object of instruction from further study.
Describing tasks elaborates the duties or topics to identify the tasks, subtasks, information flow, and knowledge base required to perform a job or use the content.	Analyzing task and content levels determines the types of learning to be acquired. Sequencing tasks or content determines the order in which learning will occur

are defined in this text. Task analysis defines the job or content, while instructional analysis answers the question, "What must be learned?" Not everything about a job or field of knowledge must be learned. Employees may already know how to do some tasks and will not need instruction on them. Likewise, in an academic field, students may bring to the course a background of knowledge of basic facts or concepts that the new instruction will build on.

WRITING TASK STATEMENTS

Task analysis moves from the general to the specific. First, the general topics or duties of a topic or job are inventoried, then the tasks are defined. Next, tasks are described. Describing tasks is the process of elaborating the tasks to identify the subtasks, information flow, inputs, and decisions required to perform a task as objectively and explicitly as possible. The analysis continues until the designer arrives at a level of detail appropriate to define the task relative to the target audience. Difficult tasks will require more levels of analysis than easier tasks.

When information is related to a specific job or task, it isn't difficult to write statements of observable actions. In school settings, however, knowledge is not always directly related to an observable task. The goal of instruction is to instill knowledge and/or teach mental operations. When the behavior is covert, your job is to specify behavior that provides evidence that the knowledge or mental skills have been learned (e.g., "Interprets sentences with clauses at the beginning or end by paraphrasing them").

In some settings, the instruction you develop will concern behavior associated with attitudes and values. For example, you may wish to teach radiology technicians to maintain a professional relationship with their patients. It will be your job to define these behaviors, which you can do in observable terms by getting good information during the task analysis about what technicians do when they demonstrate a professional relationship with patients. Most likely, the analysis will reveal several ways technicians exhibit this relationship and you will write several corresponding statements to make the behavior explicit so that it can be taught.

Types of Information Contained in Task Statements

The object of the task analysis is to document in behavioral terms what the competent performer does in response to the various conditions of performance. Documentation includes describing as objectively as possible all inputs to the performer, actions taken by the performer, and outputs produced by the action. Figure 2.2 shows a simplified diagram of a task statement broken down into three components: inputs, actions, and outputs. Constructing inputs, actions, and outputs charts is an effective tool that the designer can use to make the task to be analyzed explicit. It is an especially effective tool when analyzing tasks in an unfamiliar area.

Inputs can be classified into four types: (a) cues that prompt performance, (b) resources used during performance, (c) organizational inputs affecting performance, and (d) environmental conditions affecting performance. A cue is any stimulus or event that starts the performance of a task (e.g., a supervisor's or teacher's directions, completion of other tasks, other verbal, visual, or auditory signal). Resources are performance aids or references, such as dictionaries, calculators, computers, meters, look-up charts, or tables, used to guide performance. Resources also include the equipment or tools used to perform a task. Organizational inputs are the policies and practices, standard operating

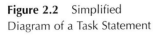
Figure 2.2 Simplified Diagram of a Task Statement

procedures, chains of command, and management directives put in place by an organization that directly affect task performance. Organizational inputs may facilitate or impose constraints on performance. Environmental conditions are physical and psychological factors. Physical factors include weather, lighting, time of day, temperature, noise levels, etc., when these conditions are relevant to performance of the task. Psychological conditions that may affect performance include fatigue, stress, and anxiety.

Actions are what the performer does. They include the overt actions that we can plainly see or hear and the covert actions that take place internally. Action statements describe how the job or function is done and in what sequence subtasks are performed.

Outputs are produced as a result of an action. Outputs may take many forms and include products as diverse as a written report, a painted surface, a speech, a typed letter, a completed project, or a correctly spelled word. Two characteristics of outputs are the following:

1. Indications or cues to the performer that mark the end of the tasks.   (How do you know when you are done?) In some instances, task completion is self-evident. But for many tasks, what constitutes a satisfactory outcome must be learned. For example, a cook must learn when a sauce is at the right consistency, a woodworker must know when a wood finish is correct, and an instructional designer must be able to determine when one step is adequate before moving on to the next step in the design process.

2. Standards of acceptability.   (How well must the task be performed?) The answer to this question will influence the standards of the instructional objectives. Sometimes standards of acceptance may be easy to set (e.g., a typist's words-per-minute rate), but sometimes they are difficult to define (e.g., aesthetic criteria for a work of art). Often you will find that standards for a job or tasks do not exist and that poor performance may have resulted from the performers' not knowing what was expected of them. If this is the case, instruction may not be the best solution to the performance deficiency. The establishment of a clear standard may solve the performance problem. If after you have investigated the problem instruction remains the solution, you will have to arrive at a standard acceptable to the people involved.

An output is usually the input for the next step in a task, as shown in the example in Figure 2. 3.

Tasks in the task inventory will almost always be too broadly written to adequately describe performance. You will have to break the task down into subtasks and subtask

Figure 2.3   Diagram of a Repair Task

An instructional designer observes the following on a job study for maintenance tasks. When a blue light flashes, the repair person replaces the XYZ component. When a red light flashes, the repair person turns off the equipment, calls the supervisor to report the problem, and requests a senior repair person to handle the job.

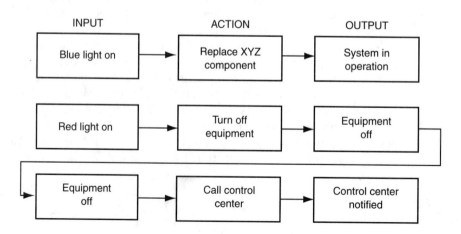

components. The breakdown should continue until the task is adequately described at a level appropriate for the target audience.

Task analysis also involves identifying the underlying knowledge base associated with each subtask. There are two types of knowledge bases: (a) knowledge that is associated with a specific task, and (b) general job or content knowledge that applies to a number of tasks. Task knowledge is concerned with facts about the task such as why and when to do it (e.g., "the sound made by a malfunctioning component is associated with the specific repair task"); nomenclature (e.g., "uses correct names of tools"); categories (e.g., "mammals are classified as either herbivores or carnivores"); and rules that guide performance of the task (e.g., "if/then"). Job or content knowledge is concerned with the "jargon" of the job or field and with general rules and principles.

EXAMPLE OF A TASK ANALYSIS

Table 2.2 presents the results of part of a task analysis for a photography course for amateurs. Table 2.3 presents the inputs, actions, and outputs for the sub-subtask "select lens." Due to space limitations, the complete analysis for each subtask component is not shown.

Table 2.2   Analysis for the Task, "Take a picture with a manual 35mm single-lens-reflex camera"

Subtasks and Sub-subtasks	*Task Knowledge*
Subtask 1. Prepare camera	
a. Select film with appropriate speed	Rule: For bright lighting conditions, use low-speed film; for low lighting conditions use high-speed film.
b. Select lens	Terms: Focal length, depth of field
	Fact: Subject magnification is dependent upon focal length. A short focal length shrinks the image, a long focal length enlarges the image.
	Classes of lens: Wide-angle lens (20mm to 35mm), Standard lens (50mm), telephoto lens (70mm or higher).
	Rules: The shorter the focal length, the wider the angle view; the longer the focal length, the narrower the angle view.
	The shorter the focal length, the greater the depth of field.
c. Check battery	
d. Detach and attach lens	
e. Load film	
f. Connect flash	Rules: Use for indoor shots. Use flash for outdoor shots with low lights. Use flash when you want to capture detail of subject in front of another light source (e.g., person in front of outdoor light from a window)

Table 2.2 *Continued*

Subtasks and Sub-subtasks	Task Knowledge
g. Mount on tripod	Term: Camera shake
	Rules: Use when a subject is very dark and shutter speed is slower than 1/30. Use for B (Bulb) shutter speed setting.
Subtask 2. Set exposure adjustments	
a. Set shutter speed	Fact: The higher the number, the faster the shutter speed.
	Rule: Increase the shutter speed as the speed of the moving subject increases.
b. Set lens opening	Terms: f-stop, aperture
	Facts: The lower the number, the wider the lens opening. Depth of field becomes progressively greater as the lens opening becomes smaller.
Subtask 3. Shoot picture	
a. Compose picture through viewfinder	
b. Focus lens	Fact: The distance at which the lens is focused affects depth of field. It increases as you get further away from the subject.
c. Shoot picture	
d. Advance film for next picture	
Subtask 4. Rewind and unload film	
a. Recognize indicators that all shots are used	Fact: All shots are used when film does not advance or exposure indicator displays number corresponding to film capacity.
b. Rewind and remove film	

General knowledge for task:

Names and locations of camera parts.

Dynamic relationship among film speed, shutter speed, lens opening, and focus adjustment.

Figure 2.4 displays the general conditions and actions for subtask 1b, "Select lens." Table 2.3 sets forth the specific inputs, actions, and outputs to be taught in the course. The table clearly defines the range of possible photo objectives and the proper lens for each objective in order to produce a photo with an acceptable angle.

Exercises A and B at the end of this chapter provide practice on writing task statements.

Figure 2.4 Analysis of Subtask 1b, "Select lens"

Table 2.3   Task Analysis for Subtask 1b, "Select lens"

Input: *Photo Objective*	→	Action: *Select lens*	→	Output: *Objective achieved*
Architecture or a panoramic scene	→	Select 24mm	→	Photo with correct angle for photo objective
Large groups, interiors, or scenery	→	Select 28mm	→	Photo with correct angle for photo objective
Natural viewing—perspective of the human eye in close quarters	→	Select 35mm	→	Photo with correct angle for photo objective
Natural viewing—perspective of the human eye	→	Select 50mm	→	Photo with correct angle for photo objective
Portrait in available light	→	Select 85mm	→	Photo with correct angle for photo objective
Distant subject, such as a cathedral, little background desired	→	Select 120mm	→	Photo with correct angle for photo objective
Portion of distant subject, such as the roof of cathedral	→	Select 135mm or 150mm, depending on level of detail.	→	Photo with correct angle for photo objective
Detail of a distant subject, such as a gargoyle on a cathedral	→	Select 200mm or higher, depending on desired level of detail.	→	Photo with correct angle for photo objective

SOURCES OF INFORMATION FOR TASK DATA

Is there one best way to do a task analysis? Some researchers think not. Kennedy, Esque, and Novak (1983) conducted an exhaustive review of all articles dealing with theory or application of task analysis published between 1979 and 1982. The researchers found that most, if not all, task analysis procedures were generated primarily for idiosyncratic application. They concluded that it is not possible to recommend one best method of task analysis for all problems.

On the other hand, Jonassen et al. (1989) make a set of recommendations about which procedures might be appropriate for different purposes. The process involves a sequence of decisions about the nature and scope of the job or subject being analyzed and the task analysis function being performed.

Rarely do procedures used in one set of circumstances apply exactly to another. The designer must consider the nature of the task to determine which analytic procedures are most appropriate.

The ability to work with unfamiliar subject matter is one of the competencies that distinguish experienced designers from novices. Bratton (1981) asked ISD practitioners at six institutions of higher education, "How do experienced developers work in unfamiliar fields?" Most answered that, when embarking on a new project in an unknown area, they read texts and/or discussed the content area with an SME.

In collecting information about a field, major sources are either some form of permanent documentation (verbal or visual) or SMEs. SMEs may be current or previous job holders, managers, or academicians.

Document Review

When you are faced with the challenge of designing instruction in an area about which you have little personal knowledge, it is a good idea to begin the task analysis by collecting all available written material about the job or function. This will give you a chance to become familiar with the terms and basic structure of the field before you encounter an SME.

Sources of written information include technical manuals, books, information sheets, professional journals, policy manuals, manufacturer's instructions, operating procedures, and job or performance aids. Existing instructional materials are another good source if the lesson plans and student materials are accurate. Finally, when the materials are too technical or too complex, go to the library and try to find the simplest possible presentation of the subject. When assigned to a project on mine safety, for example, one designer found that reading high school library books on mining practices was a good way to learn the basics about mining.

To come to grips with new topics, read actively. Outline, take notes, paraphrase key concepts, identify areas where you must seek further clarification, and write out specific questions to ask an SME. Constructing flowcharts, charts, and tables may help you discover the basics of the new job or topic.

Interviews

The background you gain from written materials will help you work better with SMEs. Some of the information found in the documentation will be contradictory, some will be out of date, some will be redundant, and some will involve alternative ways of achieving the same objective. Accordingly, take nothing for granted. One of the goals of the SME interview is to clarify ambiguities. The designer who is afraid to ask a "dumb" question will probably generate deficient task data. Do your homework beforehand. Interviews are most productive when the designer is conversant with the basics and with the language of the new field.

The ISD practitioners surveyed by Bratton (1981) suggested that a critical factor in learning about a new field from an expert is interviewing strategy. The practitioners reported interviewing the client with specific goals in mind; they used inductive reasoning (from the particular to the general) and deductive reasoning (to infer a conclusion from reasoning) strategies in asking questions. As a means of clarifying their own understanding of the content, they offered analogies and presented tentative conclusions to the SME during the discussion.

If there are different points of view on a topic or different ways of performing a job, task analysis data should be collected from expert performers who represent the full range of approaches to acceptable performance. When a number of experts must be consulted and time is a constraint, or when differences regarding how tasks should be performed must be resolved, consider group interviews. The advantage of a group interview is that the members of the group stimulate each other to recall information that otherwise might have been overlooked, which often elicits better information. Also, the pros and cons of each viewpoint are more likely to surface when they can be challenged by those holding differing opinions.

When travel time or money is a constraint, however, interviews can be conducted by telephone. Faxes and modems facilitate the exchange of visual information and documentation. However, telephone interviews are best reserved for contacting the SMEs for clarification and elaboration once a working relationship has been established. Face-to-face interviews probably elicit better information because it is easier to achieve rapport, there is usually more time to explore questions, and reference material can be consulted jointly. It is important that the designer have a good working relationship with the SME, and this is best established by face-to-face contact.

Bratton notes that the experienced interviewers he surveyed were not specifically trained during their professional development for conducting interviews in unfamiliar areas. He suggests that designers adopt the interview strategies of scientists who study human cultures. His reasoning is that ethnographers and designers have much in common, as they both must rely on personal interviews as the primary means of gaining understanding. Bratton (1981) described three major types of questions for eliciting ethnographic information. The questions move from the general to the specific. The outcome of the first level of questioning is an inventory of the duties or major topics and the tasks and functions associated with each. Levels 2 and 3 are aimed at describing the tasks and content at greater levels of specificity.

Level 1: Questions are global; they are designed to encourage the respondent to talk. ("Tell me what it is you do when you tune a guitar.")

Level 2: Questions are more specific; they are used to gather detailed information about a particular topic. ("We've been talking about diagnosing a defective circuit. What are the symptoms of this type of problem?") Structural questions also can be used to confirm the interviewer's understanding of the content. ("Let's see if I understand that point. If the test is acceptable at this point, you assume that the trouble does not exist in this section of the circuit.")

Level 3: The contrast question is still more specific. It is directed at discovering the meaning of discrete facts and concepts and the relationship among them. ("Some of the clinical signs of diabetes are also symptoms of other diseases. How do you clinically differentiate diabetes?")

Other writers recommend the general-to-specific strategy. For example, Gropper's (1971) strategy for interviewing starts with the "big picture" and systematically narrows questioning to the appropriate level of specificity. The interview begins with an orienting question designed to get at the major areas of information ("When you plan an instructional design project, what are the major factors you consider?"); then more detailed questions are posed until the desired level of specificity is reached ("How do you go about selecting an SME?").

You can help focus the interview's general-to-specific movement by combining questioning with visuals. Use a chalkboard or flip chart during the interview, or diagram, flowchart, or outline the information. Relationships and sequences can be shown for each subset of the procedure or function under study. These are good techniques for verifying your understanding of the content. They are especially useful for group interviews because the visualizations help members verify each other's perceptions and, when differences surface, arrive at a consensus. Also, if these illustrations are kept available for later reference, the interviewees will have the opportunity to review what was said and to revise, correct, or elaborate on information.

Observation

The analyst watches an expert performer and writes down what the performer does. Observations may be made in person or videotaped for later viewing. In either case, the analyst looks for connections between what is done and what is produced and is especially alert to sequencing. The analyst's job is to develop a behavioral description which consists of the inputs for the observed behavior, actions, and outputs. Observation methods of task analysis are especially useful in motor skill areas that include tasks such as machine repair, equipment assembly, and maintenance tasks.

Usually, however, after watching the job cycle until every move is known, the analyst must ask questions such as, "How did you decide that the finish was adequately polished?" or "What factors do you consider when you when you perform quality control?" Thus, few tasks can be described accurately through observation alone. Most tasks involving mental operations must be captured by questioning the expert performer.

Figure 2.5 summarizes the general steps for carrying out an analysis for procedural tasks that lend themselves to collecting data by observation. Note that the analysis procedure continues until the flowchart can serve as a set of instructions to do the task. According to Yelon (1971), a task analysis is complete when "a student can proceed through the task . . . though not as quickly or as accurately as a trained person" (pp. 8–17). When practical,

Figure 2.5   Collecting Data by Observation

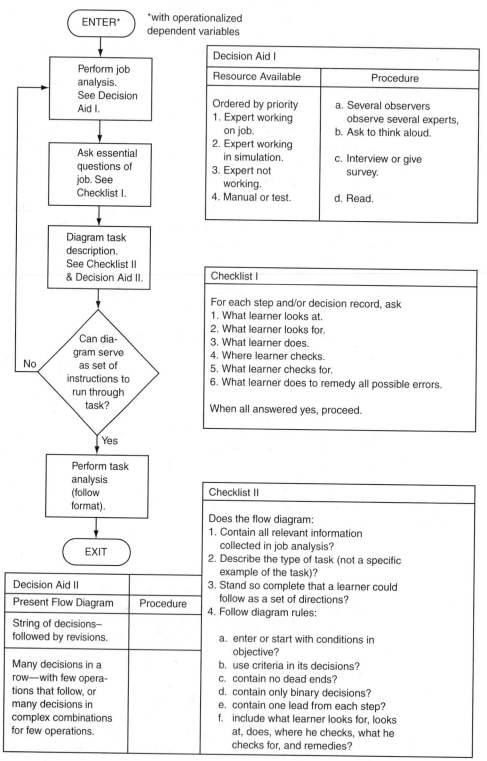

Analyzing Operationalized Dependent Variables

ENTER*   *with operationalized dependent variables

Perform job analysis. See Decision Aid I.

Ask essential questions of job. See Checklist I.

Diagram task description. See Checklist II & Decision Aid II.

Can diagram serve as set of instructions to run through task?   No   Yes

Perform task analysis (follow format).

EXIT

Decision Aid I

Resource Available	Procedure
Ordered by priority 1. Expert working on job. 2. Expert working in simulation. 3. Expert not working. 4. Manual or test.	a. Several observers observe several experts, b. Ask to think aloud. c. Interview or give survey. d. Read.

Checklist I

For each step and/or decision record, ask
1. What learner looks at.
2. What learner looks for.
3. What learner does.
4. Where learner checks.
5. What learner checks for.
6. What learner does to remedy all possible errors.

When all answered yes, proceed.

Checklist II

Does the flow diagram:
1. Contain all relevant information collected in job analysis?
2. Describe the type of task (not a specific example of the task)?
3. Stand so complete that a learner could follow as a set of directions?
4. Follow diagram rules:

   a. enter or start with conditions in objective?
   b. use criteria in its decisions?
   c. contain no dead ends?
   d. contain only binary decisions?
   e. contain one lead from each step?
   f. include what learner looks for, looks at, does, where he checks, what he checks for, and remedies?

Decision Aid II

Present Flow Diagram	Procedure
String of decisions— followed by revisions.	
Many decisions in a row—with few operations that follow, or many decisions in complex combinations for few operations.	

From "Appendix 8: Task Analysis in Instructional Design and Technology" (p. 8-2) by S. L. Yelon. In Thomas E. Harries, Ed., *The Application of General Systems Theory to Instructional Development*, 1971.

flowcharts that meet Yelon's standard should be developed. If the task can be performed simply by following the flowchart, the need for instruction will have been reduced or eliminated. If the student is not sufficiently proficient at the task, all that may be needed is practice using the flowchart as a performance aid to bring him to the required level. If the student's performance using the flowchart is satisfactory, no instruction will be needed. It is not always possible or desirable to use the results of the task analysis for formal instruction purposes. The designer should be alert for opportunities to reduce the time and effort of downstream development activities.

Questionnaires

Ideally, the analyst should observe or interview performers face to face. But performers may be located far and wide. In organizations such as the military, there may be thousands of people performing similar jobs all over the world. Even under the best of circumstances, travel budgets may preclude in-person data collection, and even telephone interviews may sometimes be impractical. The problem then becomes one of devising a collection plan that will produce the best results within the resources available.

When jobholders are at many locations and performing under a variety of circumstances, consider using questionnaires—but understand their limitations. There are two major problems in obtaining accurate and valid responses through the use of questionnaires.

1. Are the respondents willing to respond? Many people think questionnaires are a bother. Often, respondents are unwilling to devote the time and thought required to provide the kind of detailed task data necessary for analysis. Even when a response is mandatory, answers are likely to be perfunctory and, consequently, of limited value.
2. Will the respondents respond reliably? It is highly unlikely that most respondents will have the skills to describe tasks in the behavioral terms needed for instructional design. If respondents are untrained and responses are unstructured, reducing the data to make sense of it will be an overwhelming task.

Questionnaires are not useful for obtaining descriptions of how tasks are done because of problems in recording and interpreting results. However, they can be effectively used to inventory tasks. Organizations such as the military find them a good method for surveying large numbers of widely dispersed people about tasks performed at various facilities. Questionnaires should be used only when data collection is restricted to obtaining information about fairly straightforward, generally known tasks. The questionnaire's purpose should be to confirm which tasks are performed, where they are performed, and by whom, not to describe how the tasks are performed. Response requirements should be as simple and easy as possible—ideally, a check mark or a yes or no answer.

FORMATS FOR RECORDING DATA

The format used for recording data will depend on the type of data under study.

Procedural Tasks

Flowcharts are appropriate for procedural tasks. Overt (e.g., "changing a tire") and covert (e.g., "calculating the future value of a savings account") procedural tasks lend themselves to flowcharting. A flowchart is simply a description of the sequence of physical and mental actions and decisions involved in a procedure's performance. Analysts have employed this technique for jobs such as medical diagnosis, computer repair, and insurance claims processing.

Any procedure can be flowcharted. A number of different performances have been analyzed using flowcharts. Figures 2.6, 2.7, 2.8, and 2.9 illustrate flowcharts for various tasks.

Figure 2.6   Flowchart for Determining Black Lung Claims

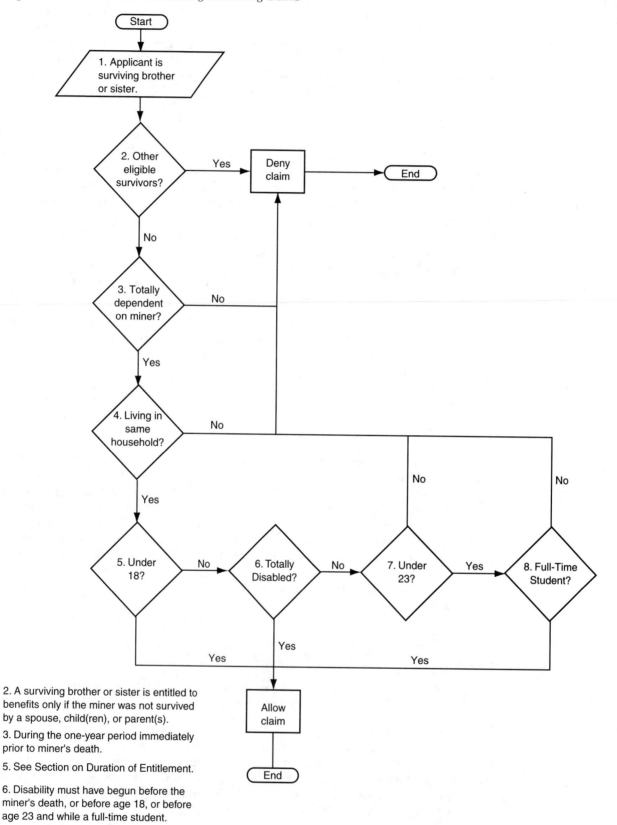

2. A surviving brother or sister is entitled to benefits only if the miner was not survived by a spouse, child(ren), or parent(s).

3. During the one-year period immediately prior to miner's death.

5. See Section on Duration of Entitlement.

6. Disability must have begun before the miner's death, or before age 18, or before age 23 and while a full-time student.

From *Course for Black Lung Claims Examiners,* by V. Johnson, G. Schneider, & Z. Glasgow, 1979, p. 106.

Figure 2.7   Steps in the
Planning Process

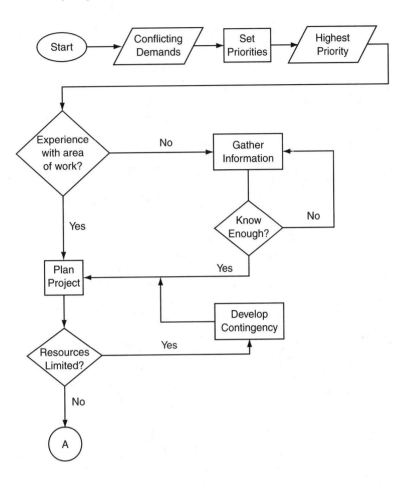

There are at least three good reasons for using flowcharts:

1. They help to focus on the specific practices that make experts out of novices. Graphic devices facilitate communication between the designer and the SME. They help to zero in on the subtasks critical to correct performance and provide a means of checking understanding.
2. They lead to easier ways to perform tasks or expose dead-end steps. Procedures used by expert performers may be out of date or inefficient. SMEs continue using old ways out of habit. Visual displays help them see the task in a new light and consider alternative ways to achieve the same end. Gaps and deficiencies are readily identified. Used correctly, visual tools often lead to a more rigorous analysis.

Figure 2.8   Flowchart for Performing a Process Analysis

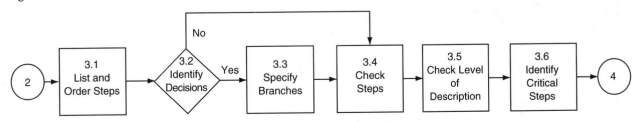

From *Task Analysis Procedure (ETAP): User's Manual* by C. H. Reigeluth, D. Merrill, R. K. Brandon, R. Begland, and R. Tarr, Fort Monroe, VA: U.S. Army Training Development Institute, 1980.

Figure 2.9   Flowchart for the Instructional Objective, "Given a list of mixed decimal fractions, the pupil is able to order them from smallest to largest."

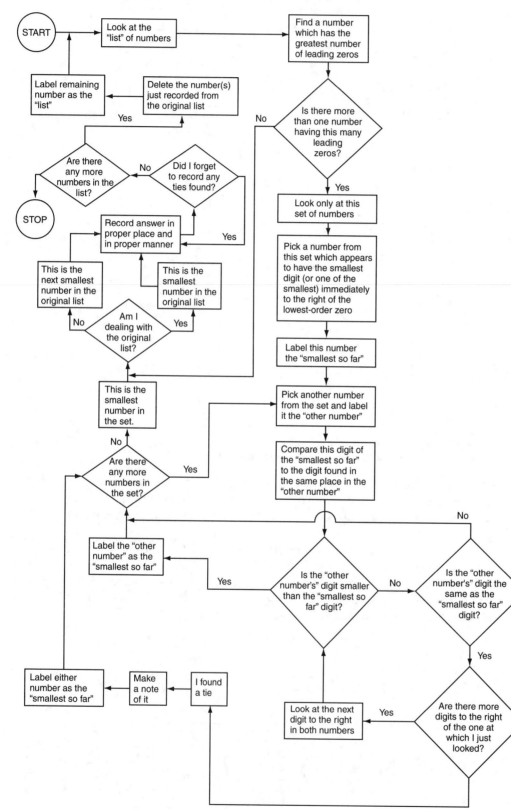

From "Charting as a Technique in Instructional Design" by A. J. Nitko, 1976, in D. T. Gow (Ed.), *Design and Development of Curricular Materials, Vol. 2.*, Pittsburgh, PA: University of Pittsburgh, p. 218.

3. The display may provide all the guidance necessary to perform a task. Many equipment-related tasks can be performed using only the information in a flowchart. Also, having reference sources at hand reduces dependence on memory. One instructional design project (Johnson, Schneider, & Glasgow, 1979) resulted in a set of flowcharts to describe complex rules for determining an insurance claimant's eligibility for benefits. Previous instruction on this task had consisted of having students learn the rules, but now, instead of trying to commit the complicated regulations to memory, students were simply taught to use the flowcharts. Instruction was thereby substantially reduced.

Flowcharting Conventions

Flowcharting has a language of its own. Following are the generally accepted conventions for flowcharting.

Start/End. This symbol is used as the beginning symbol pointing to the first task and as a symbol indicating that no more tasks are to be performed. A flowchart has only one starting point; therefore, there is only one "start" symbol. However, there can be more than one "end" point.

Input/Output. A parallelogram represents either an input task or an output task. An example of an input task is keying the account number of a savings account in a bank. An example of an output task is printing a report or displaying the results of a computation. An output at the end of a chain creates the input for the next step.

Process. A process is a simple procedure, an operation, or instruction on what to do. Processes do not include tasks requiring a decision. A process is represented by a rectangle. Calculating simple interest, typing a report, and taking a test are examples of processes.

Decision. Decision symbols are used when two alternative sequences are possible depending upon the outcome of the decision. Usually decisions are posed as questions requiring a yes or no answer. However, any two-way alternative may be posed.

Connector. A connector is represented by a circle and may serve one of two functions:

1. It is a junction point gathering flowchart segments leading to a common task. The junction point is given a label such as a capital letter. No two connectors can have the same label.
2. It connects flowchart segments from one page to another. This situation arises when space limitations make it necessary to continue a flowchart on a different page. In this case, the same label must be used.

Lines with Arrowheads. An arrowhead at the end of a line is used to indicate the direction of flow from one symbol to another. All the elements in a flowchart are connected in one way or another by lines with arrowheads. The sequence in which the symbols are ordered indicates the sequence in which steps must occur. The following flowchart indicates the sequential order for steps A, B, and C.

$$A \rightarrow B \rightarrow C$$

The following flowchart indicates that steps A, B, and C may be taken in any order, but all must be completed before proceeding to step D.

Annotation.   Descriptive notes may be required to explain a task in a flowchart. Annotations are usually numbered and placed on the lower portion of the sheet. A corresponding number or notation is placed in the symbol for reference to the annotation, as shown in Figure 2.6.

Often this annotation is shown as

This symbol indicates that an explanation of this box will be given elsewhere on the page by the letter A. It could also indicate an associated flowchart or cluster diagram on a separate page.

Procedures for Constructing a Flowchart

The procedure is fairly straightforward. The SME explains what he or she is doing or thinking while performing the task. A process/decision flowchart is developed and revised until it is correct. The starting step for constructing a flowchart is a list of the tasks involved in the procedure to be flowcharted. There are three general steps.

1. If there are more than ten tasks, collapse them into five to seven major tasks. List and order the major tasks in optimal procedural order. Draw a simple flowchart to show the flow of the major tasks. Show any branching as a consequence of a decision point. If there are alternative ways to do the tasks, show them as branches.
2. Using the general flowchart as a starting point, draw an expanded flowchart that shows the flow of the subtasks for each major task. Continue expanding and elaborating the steps until you have arrived at an appropriate level of detail. All tasks should be at approximately the same level of description.
3. Confer with a subject matter expert to determine the flowchart's accuracy. This step will be integral with Steps 1 and 2 if the construction is done with an expert.
   a. Ensure that all decision points are present and that all steps are sequenced in the optimal order.
   b. Make sure all tasks are stated at the appropriate level of detail. The flowchart should not be so general as to be meaningless to anyone except an expert, nor should it be so detailed as to describe what is obvious even to the uninitiated.

Facts and Cognitive Tasks

Tabular or matrix formats are effective for structuring knowledge because they allow the distinctions and commonalities of a topic to be made explicit. Table 2.4 shows how a columnar format is used to distinguish singular and plural noun-verb associations. It makes explicit the basis of exclusion or inclusion of nouns in a class, and lists examples of each. Table 2.5 shows an example of the format applied to rule learning, where the rules applied to various situations are defined.

Outlines are often the simplest and best format of all for learning facts, as shown in Table 2.6.

Attitudes

The designer attempting to perform a task analysis of attitudes must specify the overt behavior that will be accepted as evidence that an attitude is learned. The student will undertake some action, make a statement, or make a choice consistent with the attitude. The overt behavior will be in the form of a psychomotor skill, an intellectual skill, or verbal information. The task analysis technique appropriate for these overt behaviors is used to describe the attitude.

Exercises E, F, and G at the end of this chapter provide practice on collecting and recording task data.

Table 2.4   Columnar Format Used to Distinguish Attributes for the Concepts "Noun" and "Verb"

Personal Pronouns	*Use Present Tense of Verb "To Be"*	*Correct Subject-Verb Pair*
He	Say "Is"	Singular Pair
She		
It		
We	Say "Are"	Plural Pair and Singular "You" Exception
You		
They		
I	Say "Am"	First Person Singular Pair

Table 2.5   Format Applied to Rule Using

Rules about the Use of Criterion Visuals in Instruction

Situation	*Rule*
1. A job diagram indicates that the job-holder must discriminate between or generalize across CRITERION OUTPUTS that are VISUAL.	Provide opportunity in training for learner to practice discriminating between or generalizing across the CRITERION VISUAL INPUTS.
2. A job diagram indicates that the job-holder must discriminate between or generalize across CRITERION INPUTS that are VISUAL.	Provide opportunity in training for learner to practice discriminating between or generalizing across the CRITERION VISUAL OUTPUTS.
3. A job diagram indicates that the job-holder must associate an input and CRITERION ACTIONS that are VISUAL.	Provide opportunity in training for learner to practice associating inputs with CRITERION VISUAL ACTIONS.

From *Criteria for the Selection and Use of Visuals in Instruction: A Handbook*, (p. II. 13), by G. L. Gropper and Z. Glasgow, 1971, Englewood Cliffs, NJ: Educational Technology Publications.

EXERCISES

A. An Exercise to Define Inputs, Actions, and Outputs

Your assignment is to read job description narratives and record inputs, actions, and outputs. Figure 2.3, a diagram of a repair task, is an example of what your answer should look like.

1. An instructional designer interviews a soldier about the correct procedures for camouflaging and concealing a vehicle under field conditions. The designer is told that there are several steps in the procedure and that they are the same regardless of weather conditions or time.
    a. Place the vehicle under natural vegetation.
    b. Cover all reflecting surfaces of the vehicle with natural or artificial materials.
    c. Ensure that the color and texture blend with the surrounding areas.
    d. Drape the net to conceal the vehicle.
    e. Brush and cover the vehicle's tracks.

Table 2.6   Outline Format for Recording Recall of Facts, "Recall pathological lesions that may be associated with diabetes"

I. Pathological Lesions

A. Retinopathy

1. Cataract
2. Microaneurysms
3. Glycogen in vacuolated iris epithelium
4. Hemorrhages and exudates
5. Proliferate retinopathy

B. Neuropathy

1. Patchy demyelinization of the peripheral nerves
2. Hydropic vacuolization of the sympathetic and parasympathetic ganglion cells

C. Nephropathy (in order of progressive onset)

1. Basement membrane thickening
2. Hyalinization of afferent and efferent arterioles
3. Fibrosis and hyalinization of renal glomeruli
4. Vacuolization of Henle's Loop

D. Angiopathy

1. Micro
   a. Thickening of peripheral basement membrane
   b. Mesangial areas (diabetes of long duration)
2. Macro
   a. Atherosclerosis
   b. Monckeberg's sclerosis
   c. Arteriosclerosis

E. Xanthopathy

1. Xanthochromia
2. Xanthelasma pelpebrarum
3. Papular xanthoma
4. Necrobiosis diabeticorum
5. Diabetic dermopathy
6. Bullosis diabeticorum
7. Mal perforans
8. Bacterial/fungal infections

2. An emergency medical technician describes the following procedure for performing mouth-to-mouth resuscitation on a victim who is apparently unconscious and not breathing:
   a. Start resuscitation immediately.
   b. Continue as long as there is a pulse
   c. Stop resuscitation if the victim breathes on his or her own or if relieved by medically trained personnel.

B. A Group Exercise to Perform a Task Analysis

This is a group exercise to analyze the tasks associated with planning a Super Bowl party for about 20 people. By analyzing familiar tasks, you will be able to focus on the task analysis process and not have to struggle with unfamiliar content.

There are five parts to the exercise.

1. Develop a task inventory.   Working together, develop an inventory of three or four major duties to be carried out to get ready for the party. The inventory should be complete, and stated at a global level.

2. Describe a task and associated knowledge.   Select a duty from the inventory developed in the previous step, break it down into three to five tasks and subtasks, if appropriate. Identify the specific knowledge base associated with the tasks or subtasks and the general knowledge for the entire duty, if any.

3. Define the components of a subtask or sub-subtask.   Select a task or subtask from the previous step that is a procedure and diagram the inputs, actions, and outputs.

4. Critique the results.   Select a member of the group to present your group's analysis to the other groups in the class. After each presentation, the analyses will be critiqued against Yelon's (1971) standards for a task analysis. Namely, a task analysis is complete when "a student can proceed through the task . . . though not as quickly or as accurately as a trained person" (pp. 8–17). In making your critiques, state the rationale for the evaluation, including whether the following are true:

◆ All duties, tasks, and subtasks are specified at the appropriate level of detail.

◆ Statements are written as observable actions.

◆ All inputs, actions, and outputs are identified.

5. Improve your task analysis given the results of part 4.

C. An Exercise to Identify the Most Appropriate Task Analysis Data Collection Methods

Select the best method of data collection for each situation.

1. A department store receives complaints about its appliance department sales staff. No one is sure of the exact cause of the complaints. What data would you collect and emphasize? In each situation, you might also collect other types of data.
   a. Interviews with customers who made complaints about the sales staff.
   b. Interviews with the sales staff.
   c. Observations of the sales staff with customers.
   d. Questionnaires surveying customer satisfaction with the sales staff.
2. You are assigned to develop a basic course for aircraft maintenance jobs. The course is intended to teach tasks common to all aircraft maintenance, regardless of the type of aircraft the jobholder works on. After learning the tasks that are common to all types of aircraft, students will be assigned to receive training on the specific aircraft they will be working on. A group of SMEs developed an inventory of common tasks. Verify the accuracy of the inventory.
   a. Interview with employees in all jobs.
   b. Study of maintenance manuals.
   c. Observation of employees in all jobs.
   d. Questionnaires surveying all employees, asking them to check off the tasks they do in their jobs.
3. You are assigned to develop instruction for drug and alcohol abuse counselors.
   a. Interview clients about counselor currently performing the job.
   b. Interviews with counselors.
   c. Textbooks and references on the subject.
   d. a and b.

4. You are assigned to develop instruction for workers who assemble water sampling kits. Because of the high demand for the kits, the company is expanding its current 10-person assembly staff to 100 people in the next month.
   a. Survey users about the kits.
   b. Interview the 10 employees.
   c. Observe the 10 employees assembling the kits.
   d. Study manuals describing water sampling procedure.

D. An Exercise to Select the Most Appropriate Format for Data Recording

Identify which of the following formats are most appropriate to record task data for the following situations.

a. an outline
b. a flowchart
c. a table or matrix contrasting attributes
d. a list

_____ 1. Learning to troubleshoot a photocopy machine. The procedures involve many more chains.
_____ 2. Learning to visually classify flying aircraft as "friend" or "foe."
_____ 3. Learning the radio voice codes for the letters of the alphabet.
_____ 4. Learning to identify symbols on a weather map.
_____ 5. Learning which instruments are associated with a wide variety of surgical procedures.
_____ 6. Learning how to do an intake interview at a clinic.

E. An Exercise to Recognize Correctly Constructed Flowcharts

Consider the flowchart in Figure 2.10. There are four errors in the use of flowcharting conventions. Correct the errors.

F. A Group Exercise to Collect Information in an Unfamiliar Area

This is an exercise for two people. Each person will take a turn at playing an SME describing and demonstrating a procedural task and an instructional designer gathering information to define the task behaviorally.

The SME should select a procedural task unfamiliar to the instructional designer. The task should be simple enough to describe in a single interview—for example, operating a VCR or playing a game of cards. Equipment or objects used during performance should be available for demonstration.

The instructional designer should conduct the interview using whatever strategy and support materials are judged necessary. Afterward, the interviewer will prepare a task analysis report. The report will be evaluated by the SME using the following criteria:

1. All steps are correct.
2. The steps are arranged in logical and optimal order.
3. Flowchart conventions are used correctly.

Figure 2.10

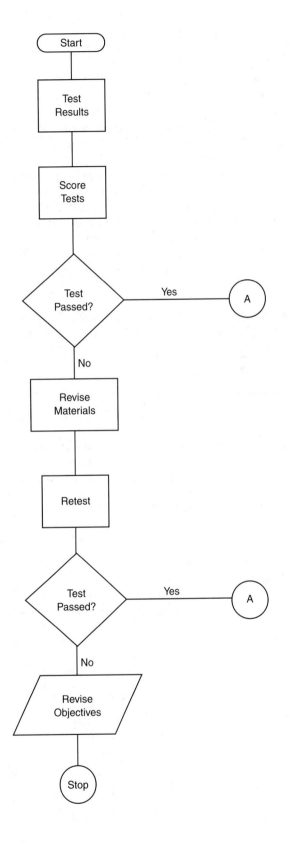

REFERENCES

Bratton, B. (1981). Training the instructional development specialist to work in unfamiliar content areas. *Journal of Instructional Development, 4*(3), 21–23.

Gropper, G. L. (1971). *A technology for developing instructional materials: Handbook A: Plan study of criterion behavior*. Pittsburgh, PA: American Institutes for Research.

Gropper, G. L., & Glasgow, Z. (1971). *Criteria for the selection and use of visuals in instruction: A handbook*. Englewood Cliffs, NJ: Educational Technology Publications.

Johnson, V., Schneider, G., & Glasgow, Z. (1979). *Course for black lung claims examiners* (Contract No. J-9-E-7-0188). Washington, DC: U.S. Department of Labor, Office of Workers' Compensation Programs, Employment Standards Administration. Butler, PA: Applied Science Associates.

Jonassen, D. H., Hannum, W. H., & Tessmer, M. (1989). *Handbook of task analysis procedures*. New York: Praeger.

Kennedy, P., Esque, T., & Novak, J. A. (1983). Functional task analysis procedures for instructional design. *Journal of Instructional Development, 6*(4), 10–16.

Nitko, A. J. (1976). Charting as a technique in instructional design. In D. T. Gow (Ed.), *Design and development of curricular materials: Vol. 2* (pp. 216–221). Pittsburgh, PA: University of Pittsburgh.

Reigeluth, C. H., Merrill, D., Brandon, R. K., Begland, R., & Tarr, R. (1980). *Task analysis procedure (ETAP): User's manual*. Fort Monroe, VA: U.S. Army Training Development Institute.

Yelon, S. L. (1971). Appendix 8: Task analysis in instructional design and technology. In T. E. Harries (Ed.), *The application of general systems theory to instructional development* (pp. 8-1–8-24). University Consortium for Instructional Development & Technology (UCIDT) Instructional Development Institutes. Syracuse, NY: Syracuse University.

ANSWERS

A. An Exercise to Define Inputs, Actions, and Outputs
Figures 2.11 and 2.12 show how one designer did the exercise. Your chart may not look exactly like this. You should check to make sure the output of the previous step becomes the input of the next step.

B. A Group Exercise to Perform a Task Analysis
Your answer should meet the criteria in the exercise. If it does not, the critiques should provide specific feedback on why it does not.

Figure 2.11   Answer to Exercise A.1

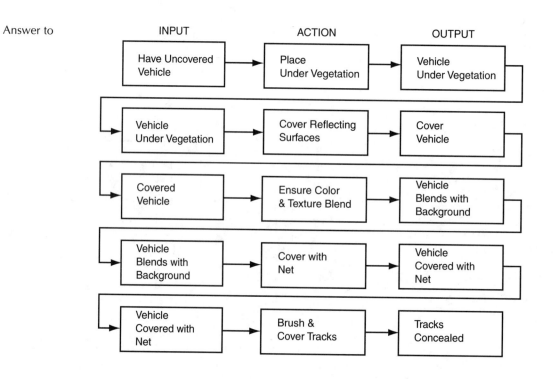

Figure 2.12 Answer to
Exercise A.2

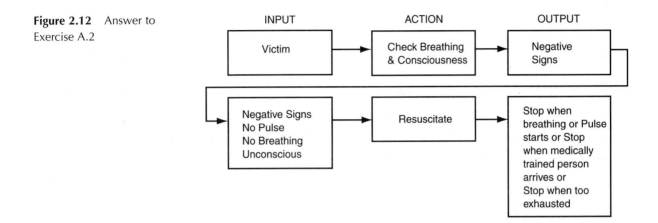

1. Develop a task inventory. You might have had the following duties:
Invite guests
Plan menu and decorations
Prepare food
Set up party site

2. Describe a task and associated knowledge. Here are the tasks one designer listed for the duty "Invite guests." Subtasks for this task were too trivial to include in the analysis. Your answer should have tasks and subtasks, if appropriate, for each duty listed in your answer to part 1.

Tasks	Task knowledge
Determine list of guests Prepare invitations	
Address envelopes	Correct spelling for guests' names. Addresses or how to obtain them
Mail two weeks in advance of Super Bowl	
General knowledge: Not applicable	

3. Define the components of a subtask or sub-subtask. Figure 2.13 is how one designer constructed an input, action, output chart for the task "Prepare chili."

4. Critique the results. The results should meet the criteria in the exercise.

C. An Exercise to Identify the Most Appropriate Task Analysis Data Collection Methods

1. a. The best way to find out the exact cause of the complaints is to ask the customers who made them. Interviews with sales staff are not likely to provide objective reports. Observations of the sales staff entail waiting until an incident occurs, which could take a very long time. Also, the presence of an observer could change the behavior of the sales staff. Questionnaires are best when the required

reponses can be checked off or short, straightforward answers given. Since you don't know the nature of the complaints, it would be impossible to construct options to be checked off that isolate the reasons for the complaints.

2. d. You need only a yes or no answer for each task on the inventory. A questionnaire is the best way to achieve the goal. Other methods are too impractical.

3. e. Counselors who are performing the job can describe what they do. References and textbooks are a good source for what counselors should do.

4. c. Observation is one of the best ways to analyze a procedural task.

D. An Exercise to Select the Most Appropriate Format for Data Recording

1. b
2. c
3. d
4. d
5. a
6. b

E. An Exercise to Recognize Correctly Constructed Flowcharts

The flowchart contains these four errors:

1. "Stop" should be shown with an oval.
2. Two connectors are labeled "A." They should be labeled differently.
3. "Test Results" should be in a parallelogram because it's an input to the next step, not a process.
4. "Revise Objectives" should be in a rectangle, not a parallelogram. It's a process.

F. A Group Exercise to Collect Information in an Unfamiliar Area

The students should critique each other using the criteria given in the exercise:

1. All steps are correct.
2. The steps are arranged in logical and optimal order.
3. Flowchart conventions are used correctly.

Figure 2.13   Answer to Exercise B.3

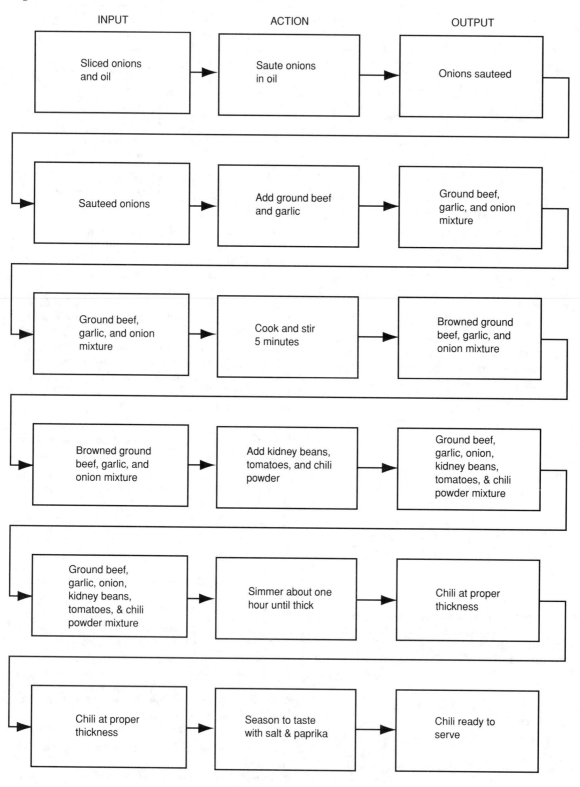

Chapter

3

Writing Objectives

OVERVIEW

Learning is a relatively permanent change in attitude, behavior, or cognitive schema due to experience. The goal of the instructional designer is to plan the experiences that will change current behavior or cognition to some new, as yet unlearned behavior or mental processing. The designer begins by identifying the nature of the learning. Human capabilities can be divided into three domains: cognitive, psychomotor, and affective. The *cognitive domain* deals with mental tasks, such as remembering facts and the intellectual skills involved in thinking; the *psychomotor domain* deals with physical actions, such as manipulative skills and gross motor skills; and the *affective domain* deals with feelings and emotions, such as attitudes, interests, and values.

Consider the job of the coach of a Little League baseball team. To prepare the team to play baseball, the coach must have the team develop capabilities in all three domains. Hitting the ball, running, and catching are the psychomotor skills the players will need to develop. Knowing the rules of the game and making judgments about when to attempt to steal a base are two of the cognitive skills of baseball. The coach will also have to motivate the players to put forth the effort necessary for winning.

Not all learning is the product of instruction. In fact, most learning occurs without the benefit of any deliberate instruction. We learn how to behave socially from our parents, then later from other sources such as television and our peers. Emotional learning, which includes our attitudes, values, and beliefs, comes from the same sources. Experience from everyday life is constantly shaping and molding our behavior in unpredictable ways. These changes are also defined as learning.

Instructional design begins with a defined learning goal that represents a domain of learning (or more than one domain). It concludes with a plan to reach that goal. This plan specifies the instructional events and materials that will provide the conditions for learning. "Instruction" is planned by instructional designers, teachers, students, or other mediators. While instruction is intended to provide the conditions for learning, it never provides learning. "Learning" is done by students; it is an internal phenomenon. Instruction, however, is an external phenomenon. Thus, what a designer can do is limited to the choice and arrangement of external conditions that will help the internal process of learning to occur. Out of theory and research, a substantial body of knowledge has evolved about how to establish conditions that will enhance the likelihood that learning will occur.

An underlying premise of ISD is that the behavior to be learned must be made explicit in order to design instruction that will achieve objectives, and to know when these objectives have been achieved. Figure 3.1 expands the decision-making model presented in chapter 1 by elaborating on questions that must be answered during the step of writing objectives.

The purpose of an instructional objective is to make clear what evidence of learning is required or how learning will be measured. This chapter explains verbal conventions for describing learning outcomes in observable and measurable terms. Whenever possible, tasks are consolidated before objectives are written. Then, a format is chosen, and tasks are written to match the task analysis. At some point during the process of writing objectives, the designer must distinguish between enabling objectives (EOs) and terminal performance objectives (TPOs). Finally, the objectives written are critically reviewed by the group, using criteria for judging the adequacy of objectives written for a design product or learning process.

Figure 3.1   Expansion of the Design Phase of the ISD Process (Seels & Glasgow ISD Model I: For Novices)

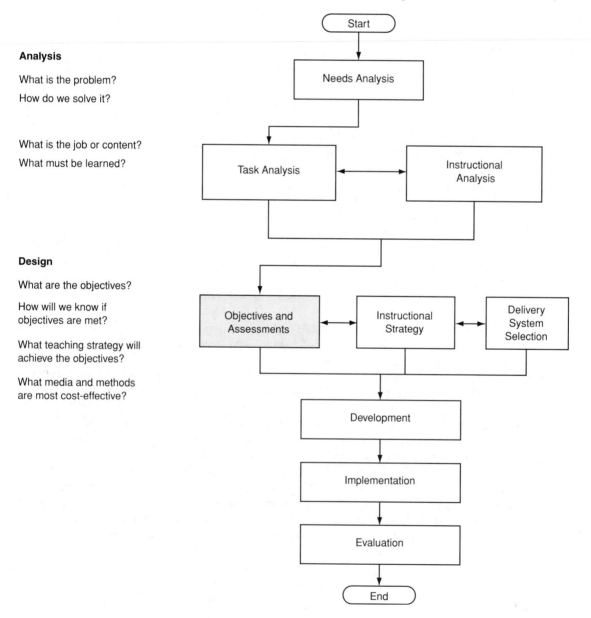

ORIENTING QUESTIONS

What is learning?
What are the different domains of learning?
How does a designer make task statements more specific?
How does the designer move from task and instructional analysis to behavioral objectives?
How does the designer relate enabling objectives to terminal objectives?
What format is used for writing behavioral objectives?
What are the criteria for effective use of objectives?

OBJECTIVES

1. Given learning outcomes, you will be able to classify them according to the three learning domains.
2. Given statements of learning outcomes, you will be able to identify those that are observable and measurable.
3. Given unacceptable statements of learning outcomes, you will be able to rewrite them to make them acceptable.
4. Given job titles and associated requirements, you will be able to write statements that describe observable and measurable behavior.
5. Given behavioral objectives, you will be able to label the component elements of each objective.
6. Given a task or topic, you will be able to write a behavioral objective using the Mager or ABCD format.
7. Given a list of related tasks, you will be able to classify them as TPOs or EOs.
8. Given an essay question, you will be able to describe common problems associated with instructional objectives.

INSTRUCTIONAL OBJECTIVES

We all have been students. Think back to those courses in which you misunderstood what the instructor wanted. The instructor lectured on one thing and tested on another. Or remember the course you registered for based on the course description. Partway through it, you realized that it was headed in a direction different from where you had intended to go. The course description had not clearly described the course's goal or purpose.

These and similar problems you encountered as a student are the very ones that as instructional designers you should strive to avoid. In order to design instruction, you need to define learning outcomes precisely. Kemp, Morrison, and Ross (1994) state that objectives perform three important functions: (a) they guide the instructional design process; (b) they provide a framework for evaluation; and (c) they guide the learner.

In education and training, the term "objective" connotes something external, extrinsic, and explicit. When you write objectives for instruction you are putting your internal ideas or goals into external form so that you can share them with others. You are going to visualize the purposes of instruction by writing them so precisely that all who use them perceive the same meaning. By writing goals specifically, you will later be able to determine whether the learner reached them.

To develop an instructional design plan, start by turning your task statements into objectives. To do this, identify the domain of learning that you need to address and the format that you will use for writing objectives. You start by identifying domains of learning because (a) there are many resources to guide a designer in developing objectives for different domains, and (b) adjustments may need to be made depending on the domain. For example, psychomotor and affective objectives are often paired with cognitive objectives, and the condition statement may need to be personalized in an affective objective. After you write objectives, the instructional systems process requires that instruction be developed, media selected, implementation planned, and evaluation data collected.

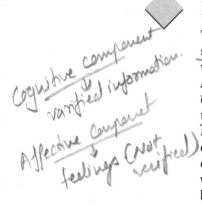

[margin handwriting: Cognitive component ↓ verified information. Affective Component ↓ feelings (Not verified) ... taxonomies.]

IDENTIFYING DOMAINS

While we can distinguish three domains of learning theoretically, in practice the relationship among them is not clear. How much difference is there between what we know and what we feel about a subject? What is the cognitive component of a psychomotor task? Actually, all learning involves the three domains to varying degrees. Attitudes consist of a cognitive component and an affective one. The *cognitive component* of an attitude refers to the perceptions and information one has about the attitude object. The *affective component* refers to one's feelings of liking or disliking the attitude object. Similarly, many psychomotor outcomes have a large cognitive component. When performance is highly proficient, the domains become so integrated that they are no longer distinguishable. Thus, when we classify a learning outcome as being in one of the three domains, we do so on the basis of its primary focus and intent.

Educators have developed classification schemes for defining the types of learning within each domain. These schemes, called taxonomies, are organized from the simplest to the most complex type of learning. This hierarchical organization means that the lower level skills must be learned before one can acquire the higher level skills. Look at the simple version of a hierarchy in Figure 3.2. Before a student can perform at the top level, he or she must acquire all the lower types of learning in the sequence shown in the taxonomy.

While taxonomies share certain general characteristics, it is difficult to make comparisons between any two of them. No two learning theorists break learning down into the same number of categories or the same types of learning.

Despite these difficulties, taxonomies (a) assist the designer in determining the type of learning which is to be the object of instruction, (b) are useful for sequencing learning when the learning outcomes are known, and (c) reduce the work associated with planning the conditions of learning by grouping learning outcomes into similar types of capabilities.

Cognitive Domain

A number of educators have developed taxonomies for the cognitive domain (Bloom, Englehart, Furst, and Krathwohl, 1956; Gagné, 1977; Gerlach & Ely, 1980; Merrill, 1983). Jonassen and Hannum (1995) compare taxonomies of learning in a chart. The simplest level is usually some type of associative learning, such as naming, and the highest levels are complex intellectual tasks, such as might be performed by a debater in preparing to argue a position or an instructional designer attempting to solve a learning problem. Bloom's taxonomy for the cognitive domain is one of the best known and is summarized in Table 3.1.

The cognitive taxonomy was published in 1956, and its purpose was to develop a classification system to describe behavior and therefore enable educators to communicate about test items, educational goals, and testing procedures. The behaviors are divided into six categories with corresponding subcategories. The categories are

Figure 3.2   Model of a
Simple Learning Hierarchy

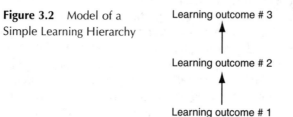

Table 3.1 Taxonomy of the Cognitive Domain   *Bloom's Taxonomy*

Type of Learning	Definitions and Examples of Behavior
6. Evaluation ↑	Making judgments about the value of ideas, works, solutions, methods, materials, etc. Judgments may be either quantitative or qualitative.
	Examples: To argue, to decide, to compare, to consider, to contrast.
5. Synthesis ↑	Putting together elements and parts to form a new whole.
	Examples: To write, to produce, to plan, to design, to derive, to combine.
4. Analysis ↑	Breaking down material or ideas into their constituent parts and detecting the relationship of the parts and the way they are arranged.
	Examples: To distinguish, to detect, to employ, to restructure, to classify.
3. Application ↑	Knowing an abstraction well enough to apply it without being prompted or without having been shown how to use it.
	Examples: To generalize, to develop, to employ, to transfer.
2. Comprehension ↑	Understanding the literal message contained in a communication.
	Examples: To transform, to paraphrase, to interpret, to reorder, to infer, to conclude.
1. Knowledge	Remembering an idea, material, or phenomenon in a form very close to that in which it was originally encountered.
	Examples: To recall, to recognize, to acquire, to identify.

Adapted from *Taxonomy of Educational Objectives: Handbook I: Cognitive Domain* (pp. 201–207), by B. S. Bloom (Ed.), M. D. Englehart, E. J. Furst, and D. R. Krathwohl, 1956, New York: David McKay Co.

arranged hierarchically from simple to complex, the simplest being recollection of specific bits of information, and the most complex being judgments about the value of some object, idea, or process.

Martin and Briggs (1986) summarize the studies to validate the psychological assumptions and hierarchical relationship of the taxonomy. Results of studies are mixed and inconclusive. There is fairly strong support for the hierarchical structure of the lower levels of the taxonomy, but less for the upper three levels. Criticisms of the taxonomy reported by Martin and Briggs are that (a) the categories are not mutually exclusive; (b) there are problems of consistently classifying behavior due to the vagueness of the descriptors; (c) although useful for formulating learning outcomes, structuring learning sequences, and assessment procedures, it is of little value for curriculum development; and (d) the taxonomy is weighted toward knowledge rather than the higher mental processes (p. 71). Postlewaite (1994) goes even further in criticizing the taxonomy. He claims that (a) distinctions between any two levels may be blurred; (b) it is more a set of categories than a hierarchy; and (c) the lockstep sequence based on complexity or difficulty which underlies the taxonomy is naive. Nevertheless, he believes that the cognitive taxonomy spurred educators to emphasize higher order objectives rather than the learning facts, as was done in the 1960s and 1970s. Therefore, it allowed both curriculum and evaluation to expand their use of objectives beyond simple knowledge.

Table 3.2   Taxonomy of the Affective Domain

Type of Learning	Definitions and Examples of Behavior
5. Characterization by Value or Value Set	Acts consistently in accordance with the values he or she has internalized.
	Examples: To revise, to require, to be rated high in the value, to avoid, to resist, to manage, to resolve.
4. Organization	Relates the value to those already held and brings it into a harmonious and internally consistent philosophy.
	Examples: To discuss, to theorize, to formulate, to balance, to examine.
3. Valuing	Willing to be perceived by others as valuing certain ideas, materials, or phenomena.
	Examples: To increase measured proficiency in, to relinquish, to subsidize, to support, to debate.
2. Responding	Committed in some small measure to the ideas, materials, or phenomena involved by actively responding to them.
	Examples: To comply with, to follow, to commend, to volunteer, to spend leisure time in, to acclaim.
1. Receiving	Being aware of or sensitive to the existence of certain ideas, material, or phenomena and being willing to tolerate them.
	Examples: To differentiate, to accept, to listen (for), to respond to.

Adapted from *Taxonomy of Educational Objectives: Handbook II: Affective Domain* (pp. 176–185), by D. R. Krathwohl, B. S. Bloom, and B. B. Masia, 1964, New York: David McKay Co.

Affective Domain

The best known of the affective taxonomies was developed by Krathwohl, Bloom, and Masia (1964). It is summarized in Table 3.2. Affective capabilities are difficult to translate into behavior that reveals the learned capability. Since attitudes, interests, and values are not easily defined in behavioral terms, it is difficult to know when an attitude or interest is acquired. On top of this, it takes a long time, perhaps years, to achieve this type of learning. Martin and Briggs (1986) distinguish between long-term and short-term objectives for attitude learning. They note that an objective such as willingness to receive information on a fairly non-controversial, limited topic (e.g., soccer as a hobby or as an elective physical educational activity) may be quickly established. On the other hand, taking a studied position on a complex, highly controversial topic, such as abortion, may require a long period of information learning, debate, soul-searching, and position-taking (p. 365). Krathwohl et al. (1964) note that instructional objectives are rarely set at the highest level of the taxonomy.

The taxonomy is ordered according to the principle of *internalization*. Internalization refers to the process whereby a person's affect toward an object passes from a general awareness level to a point where the affect is internalized and consistently guides or controls the person's behavior.

Validation studies reported by Martin and Briggs (1986) indicate that the categories seem to be correctly ordered. But, as with the cognitive taxonomy, the support is stronger for the lower categories of receiving, responding, and valuing, with tenuous support for the higher categories. Criticisms of the taxonomy cited by Martin and Briggs are that it is too general and abstract, overly dependent on cognition, and limited in scope because it fails to include the affective constructs of self-development (self-concept, self-esteem) and motivation.

Psychomotor Domain

The psychomotor domain is organized on the basis of the degree of coordination required. The lowest level is simple reflexes and the highest levels are tasks requiring complex neuromuscular coordination. The best known taxonomy is Harrow's (1972). She classifies six types of capabilities and corresponding subcategories in the psychomotor domain. The classification scheme includes involuntary responses as well as learned capabilities.

The categories and examples of corresponding behaviors are presented in Table 3.3. Reflex movements in category 1 are not learned capabilities; they are functional at birth. Harrow (1972) includes them because they are prerequisites for the development

Table 3.3 Taxonomy of the Psychomotor Domain

Type of Learning	Definitions and Examples
6. Nondiscursive communication	Communication through bodily movements ranging from facial expressions through sophisticated choreographics.
	Examples: Body postures, gestures, and facial expressions efficiently executed in skilled dance movement and choreographics.
5. Skilled movements	The result of the acquisition of a degree of efficiency when performing a complex task.
	Examples: All skilled activities obvious in sports, recreation, and dance.
4. Physical activities	Endurance, strength, vigor, and agility, which produce a sound, efficiently functioning body.
	Examples: All activities that require (a) strenuous effort for long periods of time; (b) muscular exertion; (c) a quick, wide range of motion at the hip joints; and (d) quick, precise movements.
3. Perceptual	Interpretation of various stimuli that enable one to make adjustments to the environment. Visual, auditory, kinesthetic, or tactile discrimination. Suggests cognitive as well as psychomotor behavior.
	Examples: Coordinated movements such as jumping rope, punting, catching.
2. Basic fundamental movement	Inherent movement patterns that are formed by combining of reflex movements and are the basis for complex skilled movements.
	Examples: Walking, running, pushing, twisting, gripping, grasping, manipulating.
1. Reflex movements	Actions elicited without learning in response to some stimuli. Examples: Flexion, extension, stretch, postural adjustments.

Adapted from *A Taxonomy of the Psychomotor Domain* (pp. 100–150), by A. J. Harrow, 1972, New York: David McKay Co.

of higher-order movement patterns learned during the first year of life. Obviously, instruction is not developed for reflexes. While the movements included in category 2, basic fundamental movements, are learned capabilities, they unfold as the child matures, rather than being taught. Instructional designers do not usually develop instruction at this level either, unless a child is having problems in this area. Categories 3 and 4, perceptual abilities and physical abilities, are developed through maturation and learning. Structured learning programs facilitate the acquisition of these abilities. Category 5, skilled movements, builds upon the student's perceptual abilities and stage of physical development. Skilled movements, in turn, are the prerequisites for the aesthetic movements patterns in category 6, nondiscursive communication. A proficiency continuum exists in both categories 5 and 6; that is, there are degrees of excellence that a learner may attain.

Exercises A and B at the end of this chapter provide practice on domains of learning.

DERIVING OBJECTIVES

Objectives are derived from goals, which are general statements of intent. These statements of intent are too broad and vague about evidence of learning to function as objectives that guide the designer. Goals must be translated into statements of behavior that can provide evidence of learning. To derive objectives from goals, the designer uses the process of identifying behaviors associated with goals and the process of stating those behaviors in observable and measurable terms.

Goal Analysis

A good source on how to derive objectives from goals is Mager's *Goal Analysis* (1972). Mager proposed a procedure which he called "goal analysis." Good analysis is similar to task analysis. The designer often starts with general statements of intent about valuing, being creative, appreciating, and understanding. For example, a student should "value safety procedures in airplanes and hotels," "demonstrate creativity in science," "appreciate excellence in photography," and "understand establishing communication." By using the procedure, behavioral indicators of goals such as these could be derived. Mager's procedure can be simplified to a process in which goals yield behaviors and each behavior yields many sub-behaviors, which in turn yield further sub-behaviors as conditions change.

Using this procedure, a designer can break a goal into behaviors and sub-behaviors until many levels are shown. Let's take the goal "conducts oneself in a professional manner." Some of the behaviors that would indicate achieving this goal are "dresses appropriately, is respectful of colleagues and clients, keeps up-to-date about field and specialty, uses knowledge base and skills of field, meets commitments, and maintains involvement with professional associations." The list is then edited to delete "dresses appropriately," which is essential only some cases (e.g., safety). The remaining phrases are still too vague for deriving objectives. They have to be stated as more specific behaviors. For example, "is respectful of colleagues and clients" can become several behaviors: "speaking with respect," "listening to a colleague or client," and "refraining from derogatory remarks about a colleague." Figure 3.3 illustrates how this goal could be analyzed. In the figure only selected behaviors lead to sub-behaviors. If every sub-behavior had been analyzed at each level, the resulting graphic would have been cluttered and confusing. This is not to say the designer can ignore analyzing each sub-behavior. A designer's final analysis should be more complete than Figure 3.3.

Goal analysis gives us the basis for writing statements of observable and measurable behaviors such as these, observed of an employee during a meeting:

1. Avoids derogatory words when speaking with clients and colleagues.
2. Acknowledges the expertise of others when speaking.

Figure 3.3   Example of a Goal Analysis

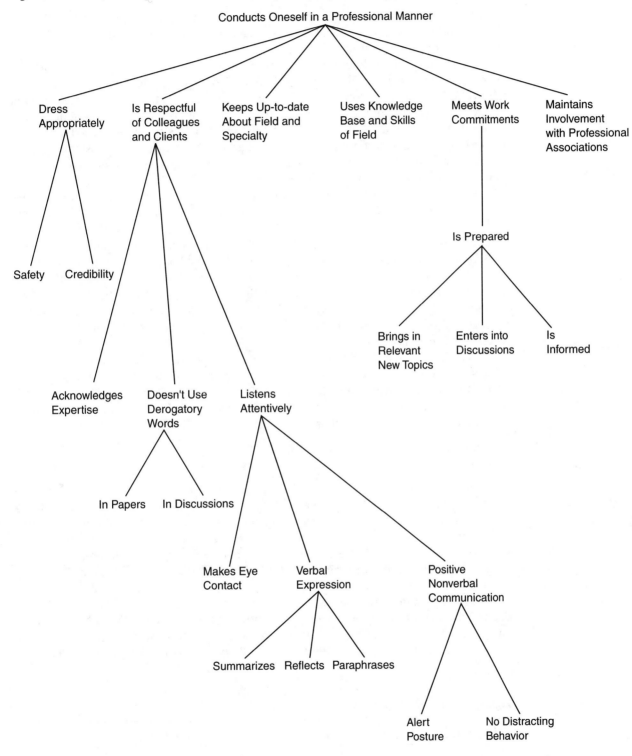

3. Makes eye contact when listening.
4. Verbally shares their professional knowledge and skills.
5. Is familiar with materials provided before the meeting.

This is only a partial list of behaviors that would indicate that the employee has reached the goal of "conducts oneself in a professional manner."

Observable and Measurable Behaviors

A key concept in instructional design, then, is that learning outcomes are described in terms of observable student activity; that is, what does the student do after instruction that indicates he or she has learned what was taught?

Why is this concept important? Simply because an instructor can't read the student's mind to see how well he or she understands; only through the student's observable activity can skill or knowledge be measured. Defining the precise behavior to be taught begins with the analysis step in the ISD process. With a clear description of the topic or performance to be learned, you will be able to establish clear-cut instructional goals that provide a basis for developing performance measures, tests, or other means of assessment; permit selection of the most suitable instructional techniques; and permit evaluation of the completed course's instructional effectiveness.

Statements that lead to these outcomes describe observable and measurable behavior. When you describe an observable action, focus on using precise verbs. Consider, for example, the two groups of statements in Table 3.4. The verbs in column A describe observable actions, and the statements communicate what a student will have to do to determine whether learning has occurred. The verbs in column B, however, are imprecise; it is not clear how learning will be evaluated. Does "Be familiar with fuses" mean the teacher will be satisfied with a definition of fuses? Will "critical thinking" be demonstrated by the answer to a multiple-choice question or by performing an experiment? Column B does not make clear what the teacher will observe in order to judge whether learning has taken place.

In addition to using precise verbs, you can further clarify behavior with active-voice, subject/verb/object sentence structure. In other words, say what the student is to do to what. The sentences in column A leave no doubt as to how performance will be evaluated.

Good sentence structure doesn't always prevent confusion; sentences must contain unambiguous words. Consider these statements:

1. Handle classified defense documents.
2. Analyze hazardous materials.

"Handle" and "analyze" are certainly observable, but because the terms are open to interpretation, they are unacceptable. Does handle mean, for example, storing documents, following regulations for circulating documents, or labeling documents according to how they are classified? The term "analyze" also has a number of meanings. Likewise, "hazardous materials" is too general because there are different types of hazardous materials and different analytic techniques associated with each. The statement is ambiguous.

How can statements be improved? The method of making them specific will depend on the nature of the performance they describe. It may be possible simply to change the verbs. If "handle" means following a set of procedures for circulating the documents, then changing "handle" to "circulate" makes the statement acceptable.

Table 3.4   Observable and Unobservable Behaviors

Column A	Column B
Write the formula for Ohm's Law	Know Ohm's Law
Solve circuit problems	Think critically
Replace fuses	Be familiar with fuses

From *Module 9: Preparing Task/content Hierarchie s: Student Resource Book* (p. 7), by D. Frezza, 1985, Randolph AFB, TX: USAF Occupational Measurement Center (ATC).

However, if a verb denotes a variety of actions, several statements must be written to describe each one. The statement on hazardous materials may have to be expanded into a series of statements in order to define the specific type of analysis required for each type of material. In sum, to effectively communicate intentions that are not open to different interpretations, statements must describe observable, measurable, specific behavior.

Behaviors That Are Not Observable

In cognitive and affective areas it is sometimes difficult to describe observable behaviors. Some of these problems are described next.

Cognitive Operations.   When information is related to a specific job or task, it isn't difficult to write statements of observable and measurable actions. In school settings, however, knowledge is not always directly related to an observable task. Frequent goals of instruction are to instill knowledge and/or teach mental operations. When the behavior is covert, your job is to specify observable, measurable actions that the student can display as evidence that the knowledge or mental skills have been acquired. Table 3.5 shows acceptable statements written for the cognitive domain.

Affective Behavior.   In some settings, the instruction you develop will concern affective behavior. For example, you may wish to teach radiology technicians to maintain a professional relationship with their patients. It will be your job to define "professional relationship." You can define these behaviors in observable and measurable terms by getting good information during the task analysis about what technicians do when they demonstrate a professional relationship with patients. Most likely, the analysis will reveal several ways they exhibit this relationship and you will write several corresponding statements to make the behavior explicit, so that it can be taught. Table 3.6 shows behavioral statements written for the affective domain.

Exercises C, D, and E at the end of this chapter provide practice on observable and measurable behaviors.

Table 3.5   Statements of Observable and Measurable Behaviors in the Cognitive Domain

Instructional Goal	*Behavior Taken as Evidence of Learning*
Recognize nutrients and their functions	Matches a list of nutrients to a list of their functions
Apply principles of planning	Constructs a plan for conducting a task analysis, given a description of the problem, a list of resources, and a due date
Classify levers according to their properties	Labels illustrations of levers as belonging to Class I, II, or III
Recognize symptoms of paranoid personality	Selects symptoms from a list of statements about behavior OR Identifies symptoms from video presentations of patients
Apply criteria for instructional design	Rates three instructional designs for adherence to criteria OR States which elements of an instructional design meet the criteria and where the design is deficient

Table 3.6   Statements of Observable and Measurable Behaviors in the Affective Domain

Instructional Goal	Behavior Taken as Evidence of Learning
Interest in reading	Asks to read a book OR Selects statements consistent with an interest in reading OR Subscribes to a magazine OR Reports activities that involve reading (e.g., joins a book club, goes to the library)
Pleasure in gardening as recreation	Purchases a book on gardening OR Collects articles on gardening OR Responds favorably to statements about pleasure of gardening
Devotion to freedom of speech	Agrees with statements consistent with value OR Argues against limiting the expression of views with which the student strongly disagrees OR Reports protests against perceived infringements (e.g., writes letters to others to support freedom of speech, enlists aid of others in support of cause)
Alertness to nutrition principles	Voluntarily selects reading material on nutrition OR Rates high statements about sound nutrition

WRITING OBJECTIVES

The first step in writing objectives is to identify the domain of learning the objective will represent. This is done so that the type of behavior to be demonstrated is clear and that words appropriate to that domain can be used in writing the objective. The next step is to derive the behaviors from the goals and state them in observable and measurable terms. If you have completed both these steps, you are ready to write behavioral objectives. This means you will use an acceptable format to state the objective so that everyone understands the behavior expected and the criteria for success in achieving the objective.

Formats for Behavioral Objectives

Formats are simply different ways of making the desired behavior explicit. There are many formats for writing objectives (Popham, 1979; Popham & Baker, 1970; Dick & Reiser, 1996). The Mager format and the ABCD (IDI) format are recommended for the instructional designer. You may even find it desirable to develop your own format by modifying one of these approaches. The formats can all be described as behavioral objectives because they make the expected behavior explicit. Mager's instructional objectives and comparable formats are called behavioral objectives or performance objectives. "A behavioral objective is a statement of certain behaviors that indicate a student has some skill, attitude, or knowledge" (Morris & Fitz-Gibbon, 1978, p. 19).

Mager Format.   Robert Mager published *Preparing Instructional Objectives* in 1962. Few books have had as wide an impact on education and training. James Popham (1979, p. 10) has said that "without question the most important advance in education during the 1960s was the widespread advocacy and increased use of behavioral objectives." Mager (1987) describes how he wrote this programmed instruction text in branching or scrambled book form. In this branching text, a multiple-choice question is asked. Depending on the student's answer, he or she is directed to another page that provides the instruction appropriate for that answer. This classic, easy-to-read book teaches you how to write behavioral objectives in a short time.

Here are Mager's requirements for a behavioral objective:

1. Identify the terminal behavior or performance by name.
2. Decide under which conditions the behavior will occur.
3. Specify the criteria of acceptable performance.

In other words, what must the learner do, under what conditions, and how well? Mager offers this correct example: "Given a list of thirty-five chemical elements (condition), the learner must be able to recall and write the valences (behavior) of at least thirty (criterion)" (Mager, 1962, p. 30). Mager describes the audience only as the student or the learner, or uses the "you will be able to" form. A convention often used by designers is "SWBAT," meaning "the student will be able to."

ABCD Format.   The ABCD format was used by the Instructional Development Institutes (IDI) described in chapter 7 (University Consortium on Instructional Development and Technology, 1968). It is a mnemonic device that helps the designer remember to include four elements: audience, behavior, condition, and degree. It is similar to Mager's format but adds a requirement for identification of the audience. Here is an example: "Given a 10-item matching question (C), a seventh grader in the Social Studies 101 section (A) will match each general with his battle (B) with no errors (D)." Note that the audience is described more specifically here than in the Mager format.

As a beginning instructional designer, use the format approach that functions best for your project. There is general agreement that conditions, behavior, and criteria are essential components of any behavioral objectives format. Historically, in instructional systems design theory, objectives have been written in behavioral formats. However, newer applications of instructional systems theory have experimented with variations on behavioral objectives and with using more than one format for writing objectives. These variations will be discussed in chapter 7, "Using Models and Paradigms."

Writing the Objective

Whatever the format, the written expression should meet the standards for good writing. The behavioral objective must be clear and specific. You will often change the order so that you start with the condition or situation and end with the criterion or degree statement. The behavior usually appears in the middle of the sentence. The format may be ABCD but it is usually written "C," "ABD," or "C, B, D." This procedure helps prevent the misplaced phrases that tend to occur as you string modifying phrases out at the end. Also avoid run-on phrases and sentences. Be as specific as possible. For example, what's wrong with this objective?

> The nurse will administer an intravenous solution from the steps of gathering the supplies to monitoring the patient when given an inventory of supplies and a patient and then will be evaluated on a checklist.

It reads more clearly as:

> When given an inventory of supplies and a patient in a bed, the nurse will administer an intravenous solution from the step of gathering supplies through monitoring the patient. She must receive 100 points on an evaluation checklist.

You need to communicate how the behavior will be measured, not how it will be taught. In your condition statement, describe the situation the student will encounter when making the response. Do not describe the instruction which leads to the response. For example, here are two objectives; which expresses the measurable behavior best?

1. Given two weeks of instruction in emergency childbirth, you will answer 90% of the questions on procedures to use during the four stages of labor to birth correctly.
2. Given a 40-item objective test containing true/false, matching, and completion questions on procedures to use during the four stages of labor and birth, you will answer at least 36 of the questions correctly.

Example 1 is wrong because the condition describes the instruction, not the test. It should read, "Given a 40-item multiple-choice test," and so on.

The degree part of an objective is often the most difficult to write. Under no circumstances write "to the teacher's satisfaction" as a criterion because this is simply not a replicable or reliable method. It does not communicate well because it has a different meaning for each reader or teacher. With affective objectives, there are times when you want to make the degree component flexible to allow for personal variation. In this case, your criterion might be "a positive change"—without specifying the amount of change. You will have to think clearly about whether it is desirable simply to allow for a change or whether you need to be more specific.

Exercises F, G, and H at the end of this chapter provide practice on formats and writing objectives.

FROM TASK ANALYSIS TO OBJECTIVES

Suppose you are at the stage of using a task analysis as a basis for writing objectives. How should you proceed? You could start by consolidating tasks to reduce the number of subtasks that must be taught and tested separately. Then you could identify goals and sub-objectives by writing final performance objectives and identifying sub-objectives.

Consolidating Tasks

Let's take an example. The needs assessment you perform reveals that city school students who must use transportation authority buses to reach school are absent because they do not understand the schedules, routes, and pay options offered by the authority. Your task analysis reveals that a competent bus rider knows how to read published literature on schedules, tours, and costs, how to obtain information about buses by telephone, and how to determine and choose the best alternative tours, schedules, and pay options. How would you consolidate the prerequisite tasks in order to plan for efficient instruction? You would look for like tasks—in this case, knowledge necessary to understand many pieces of transit authority literature. For example, instead of teaching each route and pay schedule, you might consolidate tasks and teach how to read a bus schedule and how to choose a payment option.

The Air Force manuals for instructional designers call for the consolidation procedure of deriving common elements in order to make specific objectives more efficient and to simplify sequencing of objectives (Department of the Air Force, 1978). In the Air Force example, behavioral objectives to match each task were written first; then the designer looked at other tasks involving the XYZ calculator and determined that setting up for multiplication was a common element. Table 3.7 is an example of the common elements approach used by Air Force instructional designers.

Table 3.7   Sample Objectives for the Job "Use of Electronic Calculator"

Objective (Task 8)	*(1)*	
Condition(s)	*Performance*	*Standard(s)*
Given an XYZ calculator and a list of 25 three-digit numbers with decimals,	student will enter number and multiply each by a constant.	All 25 products calculated and corded within one minute, without error (timing begins after setup of calculator is completed).

Sub-objective (Activity 8.78)	*(2)*	
Condition(s)	*Performance*	*Standard(s)*
Given lists of three-digit numbers and XYZ calculator,	student will enter numbers and press ± key after each number is entered.	Without looking at keyboard touch rate of 40 numbers in one minute with less than 5% error.

Common-Element Objective (Activity 8.1)		
Condition(s)	*Performance (3)*	*Standard(s) (4)*
Given an XYZ calculator,	student will demonstrate steps of the procedure for setting up a calculator to perform multiplication.	No more than one error of sequence.

From *Handbook For Designers of Instructional Systems: Vol. III. Objectives and Tests* (AF Pamphlet 50–58) (pp. 3–6), 1978, Department of the Air Force, Washington, DC: Author..

TPOs and EOs

All objectives are derived from goals. After you derive an objective, you can break it down into sub-objectives. Thus, objectives at each stage become goals from which a more specific level of objective is derived. A *terminal performance objective* (*TPO*) is a final performance goal stated in behavioral format; it represents the most complex behavior to be demonstrated. *Enabling objectives* (*EOs*) are sub-objectives; they are the prerequisite learning stated in behavioral format. This is a TPO:

> Given an extemporaneous topic, speak for five minutes on that topic following the principles of rhetoric summarized in a ten-point checklist. You must score an average of eight or more on the checklist of three trained observers.

Either or both of these could be an EO:

1. Given a topic for a ten-minute speech, orally outline what you would say about the topic including introduction, major points, and conclusion.
2. Given a rule of extemporaneous speech, orally provide one illustration of following that rule in a speech.

In both cases the implied criterion is mastery; the learner either performs the task completely and correctly or he doesn't.

The designer must be careful not to describe instructional activities as enabling objectives. Instruction can occur through a variety of activities, but usually methods of assessment are specific to an objective. If you ask the question, "Does this objective describe something that could be done in other ways?" and the answer is yes; then the objective may describe an activity, not an enabling objective. This principle is illustrated by comparing these objectives:

1. Given a videotaped presentation, the student will discuss the causes of the Civil War shown in the tape.
2. Given an essay question, the student will explain the causes of the Civil War. The essay must cover the points raised in the videotape "Roots of the Conflict" and meet the criteria given in the Peters Middle School Writing Manual.

Sometimes there is also more than one way to determine the achievement of an enabling objective. When this happens the question "Could this be done in other ways?" confuses more than illuminates. In this case, the designer can ask, "Is this something that needs to be assessed, or is it part of the instruction that enables to student to master the objective?"

When the relationship of a TPO and EOs is diagrammed, the TPO is shown at the top of a hierarchy and the EOs form levels beneath. An example of such a relationship is shown in Figure 3.4.

Figure 3.4   Example of TPO/EO Relationship

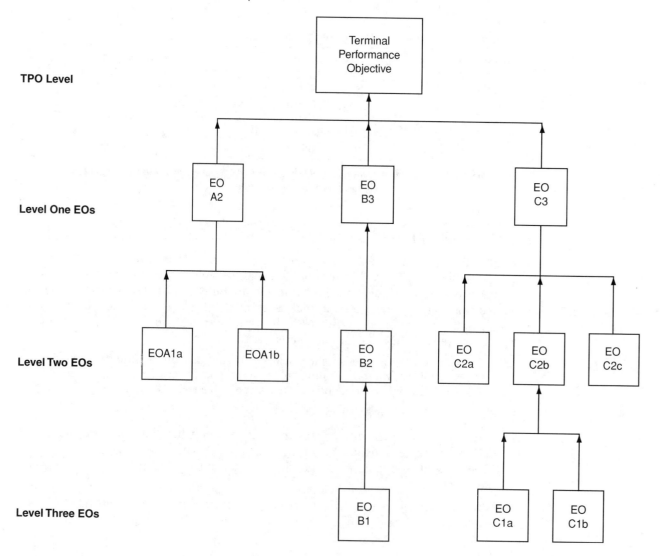

Both TPOs and EOs should be written in behavioral objectives format. If EOs are not written as measurable observable behaviors, the designer may be unable to determine whether all the objectives were achieved through instruction and whether all of the objectives were necessary for instruction. If the TPO is not achieved, measuring EOs makes it clearer where instruction fell short.

Levels of Objectives

Objectives are described by their function. Thus, there are levels of objectives. The most general are program objectives, which describe competency goals for a curriculum area or a program, such as a writing program. Course objectives, on the other hand, describe more specifically. They describe planned outcomes of courses in terms of major objectives. Unit objectives are even more specific and describe sub-objectives that must be achieved in order for course objectives to be achieved. Next, there are lesson objectives which are sub-objectives for parts of units. All these objectives should relate to the goals identified for instruction (Yelon, 1991). As you move from task analysis to objectives, you may find some tasks represent one level of objectives, and some tasks another level. Keep tasks at different levels of objectives separate. In other words, associate tasks with the level of objective they represent. Here is an example of a design plan calling for different levels of objectives:

Curriculum Objective. Be able to write cohesive, grammatically correct paragraphs.
Course Objective. Be able to write paragraphs which have a topic, beginning, middle, and end.
Unit Objective. Be able to use words of transition in paragraphs.
Lesson Objective. Be able to edit paragraphs so that they make sense. There are TPOs and EOs within each level and for across all levels. In the latter case, lesson and unit objectives become EOs, and course objectives become TPOs.

Exercise I at the end of this chapter provides practice on identifying TPOs and EOs.

Criteria for Objectives

Thiagarajan (1973) identified several criteria for determining whether objectives as a group are written correctly:

- Objectives should be related in several ways.
- The objectives should be complete in that each subtask necessary to the final goal should be listed.
- Only objectives that are necessary to achieving the final goal should be listed.
- Objectives that are stated differently but that are basically redundant should be eliminated.
- Trivial objectives such as those that identify pre-entry skills, especially very basic ones, should not be included.
- The language used should be clear, fluent, and unambiguous.
- The major components of a behavioral objective should be included: condition, behavior, and criterion (even if it is a personalized criterion).

The criteria suggested include relevance, completeness, clarity of language, necessity, and avoidance of unnecessary triviality, fragmentation, or redundancy.

The use of behavioral or performance objectives can result in problems such as proliferation and fragmentation of objectives, overemphasis on lower-level tasks, and inattention to affective goals. The instructional systems design approach can prevent these problems by (a) examination of the design based on these criteria, (b) examination of the design based on logical consistency and clarity, (c) emphasis on interrelationship of objectives with other parts of instruction, and (d) use of formative evaluation to determine effectiveness of instruction.

Current concerns about the use of behavioral objectives focus on the limitations on construction of knowledge imposed by predetermining goals for students and on the resulting emphasis on teaching or delivery, as opposed to learning in the sense of student exploration. Some educators take the position that these problems cannot be resolved when an ISD approach is used; others believe alternate versions of the ISD paradigm which will solve these problems are evolving.

Exercise J at the end of this chapter provides practice in describing problems associated with instructional objectives. Exercise K provides practice in critically reviewing objectives.

EXERCISES

A. An Exercise to Classify Behaviors According to Domain

Classify each statement by writing the correct letter as follows:
A: Affective Domain
C: Cognitive Domain
P: Psychomotor Domain

1. Chooses the best of two solutions to a geometry problem.
2. Displays good manners toward elders.
3. Lists the names and contributions of five key curriculum developers.
4. Knits a baby blanket.
5. Votes for a political candidate.
6. Plans daily menus in accordance with nutritional principles.
7. Reports to work on time, 100% of the time.
8. Defeats three inexperienced players at ping-pong.
9. Recites the Gettysburg Address from memory.
10. Voluntarily attends lectures on higher mathematics.
11. Evaluates conclusions drawn from a body of data.

B. Another Exercise to Classify Learning Outcomes According to Domains

Classify each of the learning outcomes as cognitive, affective, or psychomotor using C, A, or P according to the domain of learning each represents. Then, identify the level of learning required according to the domain. Use Figures 3.1, 3.2, and 3.3 to guide you in identifying the level within the domain.

1. Wrap an ankle, given an elastic bandage and a plastic model of an adult's foot.
2. List the U.S. Air Force enlisted and officer ranks from memory.
3. List five causes of the Civil War as cited in *The Civil War and Reconstruction* by D. S. Randall.
4. Given a list of chemical elements, recall and write the valences of at least 30.
5. Solve electrical circuit problems, using Ohm's Law.
6. Interpret written instructions to determine sequence of two or more actions.
7. Encode data for radio and teletype transmission.
8. Using a year's data from atmospheric data-gathering systems, compute the annual mean wind velocity.
9. Find West 33rd Street on a map of Manhattan.
10. Label the components of a carburetor.
11. Participate in a public discussion on the transportation of hazardous materials.
12. Change an automobile tire in 10 minutes.
13. Attend the theater regularly.
14. Volunteer to answer a crisis hotline telephone.

15. Contribute to a political party.
16. Type 60 words a minute.
17. Visually track a moving object.
18. Troubleshoot defective equipment to detect cause of breakdown.
19. Follow investment guidelines to obtain highest possible income.
20. Diagnose disease from clinical symptoms

C. An Exercise to Identify Correctly Stated Learning Outcomes

Check the statements of learning outcomes that can be readily observed and measured.

1. Possess interpersonal communication skills.
2. Complete maintenance data collection forms.
3. Develop manual dexterity.
4. Read a barometer and record the atmospheric pressure.
5. Translate a news report in a Russian newspaper.
6. Solve formulas containing statistical symbols.
7. Know when to notify a superior of a problem.
8. Perform safety procedures while repairing a malfunction in a stereo receiver.

D. An Exercise to Revise Poorly Written Learning Outcomes

Rewrite each of the statements from the previous exercise that did not meet the "observable and measurable" criteria. To be correct, your statements must be phrased in verb-object sequence and must describe an observable learning outcome. The statements may be written for any job or content area.

E. An Exercise in Writing Observable and Measurable Learning Outcomes

For each of the following jobs, write a statement that describes a readily observable and measurable learning outcome.

1. Firefighter: Ability to operate types of hand-held fire extinguishers.
2. Statistician: Ability to use visual conventions to display annual incomes.
3. Communication Specialist: Ability to use Morse code by receiving and sending messages.
4. Art Historian: Ability to distinguish different painting styles.
5. Pianist: Ability to read music.
6. Comptroller: Ability to plan budget requirements. End product is a dollar amount.
7. Geologist: Dependability on the job.
8. Climatologist: Knowledge of specific facts about weather in northeastern U.S. cities.
9. Soldier: Knowledge of military convention for telling time.
10. Electronics Technician: Ability to apply Ohm's law.
11. Woodworker: Attitude consistent with good workmanship.

F. An Exercise on Component Parts of Behavioral Objectives

Bracket, then label above the brackets, the component parts of each objective. For objectives written in Mager format use condition, behavior, and criteria as components. For objectives written in ABCD format use audience, behavior, condition, and degree as components.

1. (Mager)   Given a battery, light bulb, socket, and pieces of wire, demonstrate the making of an electronic circuit by connecting wires to battery and socket and testing the lighting of the bulb.

2. (Mager)   Given a list of 35 chemical elements, the learner must be able to recall and write the valences of at least 30.
3. (ABCD)   Given all the basic shapes—cone, cylinder, cube, and sphere—each second-semester geometry student will identify orally each shape.
4. (Mager)   Given a meter scale, the learner is to be able to identify the value indicated by the position of the pointer as accurately as the construction of the meter will allow.
5. (ABCD)   Using tape recorded readings of the tryout sessions for the school play, students in the drama class will select the proper voice for each character as indicated in the drama text.

G. Another Exercise on Identifying Component Parts of Behavioral Objectives

Bracket and label the component parts of each objective using Mager's approach.

1. Given an essay question and no references, the student will explain four causes of the Civil War as covered in chapter 8.
2. Given a properly functioning camcorder unit and time before on-location shooting, the student will set the controls so that the picture and sound will have adequate technical quality as determined by the supervisor.
3. Given the names and pictures of four prescription drugs, the second-year medical student will identify orally which one is appropriate for the treatment of high blood pressure in patients with no other health problems.
4. Given a videotaped role playing situation, the sales trainee will identify by writing on the response sheets provided which steps in the proposal selling procedure were not properly demonstrated.
5. When he or she is observed unobtrusively in informal conversations with other students, the student will choose to speak about the teaching and grading in Sociology 101, Section C, positively.

H. An Exercise in Writing Behavioral Objectives in Diverse Areas

Write an objective in Mager or ABCD format on the topic specified.

1. Use the dummy Resuscitation Annie (with sensors) to demonstrate proficiency in CPR.
2. Use nutritional principles in planning a well-balanced daily menu.
3. Write a short article suitable for publication in a business newsletter.
4. Demonstrate counting 1 to 10 on an abacus.
5. Identify the paintings of Van Gogh.

I. An Exercise in Identifying TPOs and EOs

There are four objectives for competency area. Label each objective as the terminal performance objective (TPO) or as an enabling objective (EOs). Give each of the enabling objectives a number to indicate which behavior is prerequisite. The first level of prerequisite should be given number EO1. The level closest to the TPO should be given EO4, with the levels in-between given EO2 and EO3 in order.

1. Interviewing Techniques
    a. Given a list of questions, the student will write next to each question the type of PROBE it represents. Accuracy should be at least 75%.
    b. Given a resume and a job description, the student will conduct a simulated employment interview segment in which he or she successfully demonstrates application of the PROBE interviewing technique by asking appropriate questions to identify an event, role, or outcome.

c. Given a list of PROBE terms and a list of definitions, the student will match the terms to the definition. The terms will be primary/secondary, open/closed, leading/neutral, redirective, mirror, and nudging.

d. Given a definition of the PROBE interview technique, the student will label that definition as true or false.

2. Valuing Extracurricular Activities

a. Given information on events, the student will voluntarily attend three events sponsored by extracurricular organizations.

b. Given an orientation session on extracurricular activities, the student will listen attentively as evidenced on a checklist of nonverbal behaviors completed by an observer.

c. Given time and transportation after school, the student will join an extracurricular activity and participate in preparation for one of that organization's events.

d. Given the opportunity to elect an extracurricular activity-related course rather than another academic course, the student will elect the extracurricular-related course.

3. Performing Dance Sequences

a. Given a dance partner and a simple routine, the dance student will perform the routine and make adjustments in movements as necessary to maintain balance and extension.

b. Given a musical sequence, the dance student will develop and perform an interpretive dance that includes skilled movement and utilizes the whole body.

c. Given a series of exercises, the dance student will perform them by stretching, bending, and twisting so that the body is extended in all movements.

d. Given a solo ballet sequence requiring strenuous effort and highly skilled movement, the dance student will perform the complete sequence without stopping.

J. An Exercise in Describing Problems with Objectives

Write a short essay on errors that can arise when objectives are written. Your essay should address several of the problems summarized by Thiagarajan (1973). Each of the problems discussed should be illustrated with a new example.

K. A Group Exercise in Critically Reviewing Objectives

This exercise is designed to be a role play between a designer and an SME. However, at different points in the process, each could assume the role of writer of objectives. Often, objectives are written by the designer and SME together. Using the task analysis you developed during chapter 2, write behavioral objectives using the Mager or ABCD approach. Have your partner review the objectives using the criteria provided by Thiagarajan, i.e., relevance, completeness, necessity, redundancy, triviality, specificity, and language. Organize these objectives by relationships between TPOs and EOs and submit them for review.

You must include behavioral objectives based on your task analysis in your final project. Refinement and reorganization of these objectives can be done by you from feedback and reference to this chapter on objectives.

◈ REFERENCES

Bloom, B. S. (Ed.), Englehart, M. D., Furst, E. J., & Krathwohl, D. R. (1956). *Taxonomy of educational objectives: Handbook I: Cognitive domain.* New York: David McKay Co.

Department of the Air Force. (1978). *Handbook for designers of instructional systems: Volume III. Objectives and tests* (AF Pamphlet 50-58). Washington, DC: Author.

Dick, W., & Reiser, R. A. (1996). *Planning effective instruction* (2nd ed.). Boston: Allyn & Bacon.

Frezza, D. (1985). *Module 9. Preparing task/content hierarchies: Student resource book* (Contract No. F41689-83-C-0048). Randolph AFB, TX: USAF Occupational Measurement Center (ATC).

Gagné, R. M. (1977). *The conditions of learning.* New York: Holt, Rinehart & Winston.

Gerlach, V. S., & Ely, D. P. (1980). *Teaching and media: A systematic approach.* Englewood Cliffs, NJ: Prentice-Hall.

Harrow, A. J. (1972). *A taxonomy of the psychomotor domain.* New York: David McKay Co.

Jonassen, D. H. & Hannum, W. H. (1995). Analysis of task analysis procedures. In G. H. Anglin (Ed.), *Instructional technology: Past, present and future* (pp. 197–209). Englewood, CO: Libraries Unlimited, Inc.

Kemp, J. E., Morrison, G. R., & Ross, S. M. (1994). *Designing Effective Instruction.* New York: Merrill.

Krathwohl, D. R., Bloom, B. S., & Masia, B. B. (1964). *Taxonomy of educational objectives. Handbook II: Affective domain.* New York: David McKay.

Mager, R. F. (1962). *Preparing instructional objectives.* Palo Alto, CA: Fearon.

Mager, R. F. (1972). *Goal analysis.* Belmont, CA: Fearon Publishers.

Mager, R. F. (1987). Why I wrote . . . . [25th Anniversary Issue]. *The Best of Performance and Instruction,* 37.

Martin, B. L., & Briggs, L. J. (1986). *The affective and cognitive domains: Integration for instruction and research.* Englewood Cliffs, NJ: Educational Technology Publications.

Merrill, M. D. (1983). Component display theory. In C. M. Reigeluth (Ed.), *Instructional design theories and models: An overview of their current status* (pp. 279–334). Hillsdale, NJ: Lawrence Erlbaum.

Morris, L. L., & Fitz-Gibbon, C. T. (1978). *How to deal with goals and objectives.* Beverly Hills, CA: Sage Publications.

Popham, J. (1979). Instructional objectives 1960–1970. *National Society for Performance and Instruction Journal,* 18(10), 10–12.

Popham, J. & Baker, E. L. (1970). *Establishing instructional goals.* Englewood Cliffs, NJ: Prentice Hall.

Postlewaite, T. N. (1994). Validity vs. utility: Personal experiences with the taxonomy. In L. W. Anderson & L. A. Sosniak (Eds.), *Bloom's Taxonomy: A Forty-year Retrospective (Ninety-third Yearbook of the National Society for the Study of Education, Part II).* Chicago: University of Chicago Press.

Thiagarajan, S. (1973). Good objectives and bad: A checklist for behavioral objectives. *Educational Technology,* 13(8), 23–28.

University Consortium for Instructional Development and Technology. (1968). *Objective marketplace game.* Syracuse, NY: Instructional Development Institutes, Syracuse University, IDDE.

Yelon, S. L. (1991). Writing and using instructional objectives. In L. J. Briggs, K. L. Gustafson, & M. H. Tillman, (Eds.), *Instructional design: Principles and applications.* Englewood Cliffs, NJ: Educational Technology Publications.

◆ ANSWERS

A. An Exercise to Classify Behaviors According to Domain

1. C
2. A
3. C
4. P
5. A
6. C
7. A
8. P
9. C
10. A
11. C

B. Another Exercise to Classify Learning Outcomes According to Domains

1. P (5-Skilled Movement)
2. C (1-Knowledge)
3. C (1-Knowledge)
4. C (1-Knowledge)
5. C (3-Application)
6. C (2-Comprehension)
7. C (2-Comprehension)
8. C (3-Application)
9. C (3-Application)
10. C (1-Knowledge)
11. A (3-Valuing)
12. P (5-Skilled Movement)
13. A (2-Responding)
14. A (2-Responding)
15. A (3-Valuing)
16. P (5-Skilled Movement)
17. P (3-Perceptual)
18. C (4-Analysis)
19. C (4-Analysis)
20. C (4-Analysis)

This exercise demonstrates the difficulties practitioners have with the taxonomies. The categories are not mutually exclusive, and there are problems with consistently classifying behavior due to the vagueness of the descriptors. The answers given here reflect the authors' best effort at this tax. Other experts may disagree.

C. An Exercise to Identify Correctly Stated Learning Outcomes
(Statements marked with an "X" are correct.)

1.
2. X
3.
4. X
5. X
6. X
7.
8. X

D. An Exercise to Revise Poorly Written Learning Outcomes
Here are some examples of how to rewrite the statements in the preceding exercise. The correct answers will depend on the tasks the students choose.

1. maintain eye contact during an interview
3. type 60 words per minute
7. notify a superior of a problem by writing a memo

E. An Exercise in Writing Observable and Measurable Learning Outcomes

1. Operates a hand-held fire extinguisher by performing each of the steps in the correct sequence.
2. Uses test data to make a bar chart comparing results for three groups.
3. Transmits this message, "Come to deck A."
4. Distinguishes between impressionist and post-impressionist paintings in a museum.
5. Plays a new piece from sheet music.
6. Prepares cost estimates for 500 copies of a brochure from concept through production.
7. Completes reports on time.
8. States average annual snowfall for Syracuse, New York.
9. Translates military time into civilian time.
10. Solves a problem in resistance.
11. Selects the proper grade of sandpaper for a finishing task.

F. An Exercise on Component Parts of Behavioral Objectives

1. (Mager). Given a battery, light bulb, socket, and pieces of wire (condition), demonstrate the making of an electronic circuit by connecting wires to battery and socket (behavior) and testing the lighting of the bulb (criteria).
2. (Mager). Given a list of 35 chemical elements (condition), the learner must be able to recall and write the valences (behavior) of at least thirty (criteria).
3. (ABCD). Given all the basic shapes—cone, cylinder, cube, and sphere (C)—each second-semester geometry student (A) will orally identify (B) each shape (D).
4. (Mager). Given a meter scale (condition), the learner is to be able to identify the value indicated by the position of the pointer (behavior) as accurately as the construction of the meter will allow (criteria).
5. (ABCD). Using tape recorded readings of the tryout sessions for the school play (C), students in the drama class (A) will select the proper voice for each character (B) as indicated in the drama text (D).

G. Another Exercise on Identifying Component Parts of Behavioral Objectives

1. Given an essay test and no references (condition), the student will explain four causes of the Civil War (behavior) as covered in chapter 8 (criteria).
2. Given a properly functioning camcorder unit and time before on-location shooting (condition), the student will set the controls so that the picture and sound have adequate technical quality as determined by the supervisor.
3. Given the names and pictures of four prescription drugs (condition), the second-year medical student will identify orally (behavior) which one is appropriate for the treatment of high blood pressure in patients with no other health problems (criteria).
4. Given a videotaped role playing situation (condition), the sales trainee will identify by writing on the response sheets provided (behavior) which steps in the proposal selling procedure were not properly demonstrated (criteria).
5. When he or she is observed unobtrusively in informal conversations with other students (condition), the student will choose to speak about the teaching and grading in Sociology 101, Section C (behavior), positively (criteria).

H. An Exercise in Writing Behavioral Objectives in Diverse Areas

1. Given Resuscitation Annie, the workshop participant will demonstrate the CPR stroke for two minutes using proper positioning and pressure of hands.
2. Given one day's meals to plan, the tenth-grade home economics student will prepare a menu that satisfies the requirements for balanced nutrition according to the food pyramid.
3. Given a topic and a 5" column space, the beginning journalism student will write a short article suitable for publication. This means the article will have the correct number of words, grammar, and syntax and will be coherent.
4. Given an abacus, the first-grade student will count from 1 to 10 correctly using the abacus.
5. Given a series of slides on post-impressionist paintings, the tenth-grade art history student will identify all those painted by Van Gogh.

I. An Exercise in Identifying TPOs and EOs

1. Cognitive Domain
   a. EO3
   b. TPO
   c. EO2
   d. EO1

2. Affective Domain
   a. EO2
   b. EO1
   c. EO3
   d. TPO
3. Psychomotor Domain
   a. EO2
   b. TPO
   c. EO1
   d. EO3

J. An Exercise in Describing Problems with Objectives

Your essay should illustrate with an example each of the criteria for reviewing objectives as a group. You can illustrate proper or improper use but be sure to explain which use the example represents. Here is one approach:

Two seventh-grade language arts teachers have been hired for two weeks during the summer to develop the curriculum guide for their subject and level. They produce a lengthy document that includes many objectives at the knowledge stage, such as "know the bow wow theory of language development," "recognize the meaning of correction symbols," "compare and contrast different theories of language development," and "understand editing symbols when used on papers."

After reviewing these objectives, the designer finds that the relationship of knowing theories of language development and using editing symbols is not clear. Furthermore, objectives related to each topic are not identified by level (e.g., unit, lesson). In addition, some of the objectives seem unimportant for seventh graders whose curriculum goal is writing skills. However, the redundancy of the objectives is seen as necessary because both knowledge and understanding goals are important.

There are tasks identified in the required state syllabus for the year which are not addressed by the objectives. Therefore, the match between the state syllabus and the objectives needs to be examined more closely.

K. A Group Exercise in Critically Reviewing Objectives

The first attempt to do this should be evaluated and corrected by your partner in the role of designer. In addition, you can have your instructor review and critique your initial draft. Your later drafts will be reviewed by peers in class. The use of objectives in your final design plan will be reviewed by your instructor according to the criteria for domain objectives, format, TPOs and EOs, and examination of the whole set forth in this chapter.

Chapter

4

Assessing Learning

OVERVIEW

Figure 3.1 in the previous chapter showed an expansion of the objectives and assessment step. Decisions about assessment are usually made in response to the following questions:

- ◆ How will we know if objectives are met?
- ◆ How can assessment be made valid and reliable?
- ◆ Are tasks, objectives, and criterion items logically consistent?
- ◆ Are assessment items constructed in accordance with established principles?

In chapter 3 you studied how to derive observable and measurable objectives from goals and how to write these enabling objectives in behavioral format. Writing behavioral objectives requires predetermination of means of assessment. The means of assessment chosen must be consistent with the tasks identified. Because tasks vary greatly, a designer needs to be comfortable with the area of assessment. The step of formative evaluation, which is explained in chapter 6, also requires knowledge of assessment principles and techniques.

In order to be competent in assessment, an instructional designer must understand basic measurement concepts including criterion- and norm-referenced measurement and validity and reliability. Assessment procedures must be consistent with both principles of measurement and ISD. This means that a designer needs to know how to develop assessment instruments and write test items.

In addition, a designer needs to be familiar with different types of assessment, because a designer must check to be sure the method of measurement is consistent with the objective's stated intent. For example, you cannot measure problem solving skills with a true/false test, and you cannot judge ability to play the tuba from a paper and pencil exercise. There should be logical consistency between tasks, behavioral objectives, and assessment measures. To determine consistency between the products of steps in ISD, use a task/objectives/criterion chart.

ORIENTING QUESTIONS

What can be assessed?

How are assessment, testing, measurement, and grading related?

What concepts must be understood by the instructional designer in order to fairly assess and measure learning?

What are the functions of criterion-referenced testing?

How can you increase the validity of an achievement test?

How can you increase the reliability of an achievement test?

What types of assessment are commonly used?

How can the designer check for consistency between tasks and objectives and objectives and criterion-referenced items?

What is a table of specifications?

How are the different types of criterion-referenced items selected and written?

What is an error matrix?

OBJECTIVES

1. Given a description of a measurement procedure, you will be able to identify what is being assessed.
2. Given statements describing tests, you will be able to identify those that apply to criterion-referenced tests.
3. Given a description of an item and a method for scoring it, you will be able to identify the item and the method likely to be more reliable.
4. Given statements of learning outcomes and associated test items, you will be able to identify the items that reflect the outcomes.
5. Given a task, you will be able to identify appropriate ways to assess learning.
6. Given a task, you will be able to write an objective and a criterion item consistent with that task.
7. Given an objective, you will be able to write a task and a criterion item consistent with that task.
8. Given a criterion item, you will be able to write a task and an objective consistent with that item.
9. Given information about learning requirements, you will be able to construct a table of specifications.
10. Given objectives, you will be able to write an item appropriate for the objective and consistent with item writing rules.
11. Given rules for writing test items, you will be able to develop a mnemonic, visual, or sentence that helps you remember the rules for each type of item.
12. Given test results, you will be able to construct and interpret an error matrix.
13. Given objectives, you will be able to develop an assessment plan and instruments for a unit.

ASSESSMENT IN ISD

Each of us assesses many times during a day. We assess our likelihood of finishing a task, the competency of a colleague, and our own productivity. When we assess, we estimate or judge the value of a person, activity, or situation. When we approach assessment from this point of view, it becomes easier to understand that assessing learning is not equivalent to grading. While one function of assessment can be to provide a basis for grading, that is not its primary function. Methods of assessment can serve multiple functions. The most obvious of these functions are measuring, diagnosing, or instructing. Assessment that serves a pedagogical function enhances learning by creating awareness, cuing attention, or providing practice. In ISD, assessment serves all these primary functions: measuring, diagnosing, and instructing. The information gained may then be used for secondary functions, one of which is evaluating ISD; another might be grading.

Research documents that tests are learning events. Ideally, learners clearly understand when a test is being used for diagnosis or instruction, when it is being used for grading, and when it is being used for more than one of these purposes. The reason for this is that learners can be inhibited from making errors when they think they are being graded. Since making errors can be an important part of learning, they will be deprived of this opportunity (Druckman & Bjork, 1994). Portfolios, for example, differ depending on the purposes for which they are intended. "A portfolio system that promotes self-assessment and self-confidence in students as readers and writers, for example, will look very different from a portfolio that provides a valid and reliable basis for a statewide evaluation of student performance in literacy " (Wolf & Siu-Runyan, 1996, p. 30).

Approaches to assessment differ depending on what is being assessed. Cognitive learning is often assessed with paper and pencil tests. Performance, or demonstrations of the ability to apply learning, are assessed through observation or examination of products often through checklists. Attitudes can be determined through inventories or self-reporting instruments. However, sometimes attitudes are determined through observation that yields indicators of valuing. Psychomotor objectives can be assessed through all three approaches. Paper and pencil tests can be used to determine knowledge of the cognitive component of a psychomotor skill. Attitude inventories can determine feelings towards regular performance of the skill. Performance measures can be used to collect data on ability to execute the skill.

Exercise A at the end of this chapter provides practice on identifying what is being assessed.

BASIC PRINCIPLES OF MEASUREMENT

In order to develop assessment plans that include testing instruments, you need to understand the concepts of criterion-referenced testing, reliability, and validity. Instruction is designed to bring about learning, and tests or other means of assessment are used to determine whether learning occurred. Tests that measure what a person has learned to do are called *achievement tests*. There are two types of achievement tests: criterion-referenced tests (CRTs) and norm-referenced tests (NRTs). The same concepts can refer to methods of assessment in general, not just tests.

CRTs

Criterion-referenced assessment uses the term "criterion" to refer to the relationship between the objective and method of assessment and to the level of performance required for mastery. To determine whether a test item is criterion-referenced, determine whether the performance required is congruent with the behavioral objective and whether the level of proficiency required is specified. CRTs are sometimes called content-referenced or objective-referenced tests. A test is criterion-referenced when its score can be translated into a statement about what a person has learned relative to a standard; a CRT score provides information about a person's mastery of a behavior relative to the objective and reflects that person's mastery of one specific skill. A person who passes a state's automobile driving test can be said to have the competencies set as a standard for driving in that state. Success on a CRT means being able to perform specific competencies. Usually, a cut-off score is established, and everyone reaching or exceeding the score passes the test. There is no limit to the number of test takers who can pass a CRT.

NRTs

On an NRT the score tells where the person stands relative to other persons who have taken the test. The Scholastic Aptitude Test (SAT) is an NRT; its score tells where a person stands relative to other potential college entrants.

Success on an NRT is defined as being ahead of most of the other test takers. NRTs are designed to "reliably" select the best performers. NRTs seldom provide specific information about mastery of a specific skill, because they are designed to measure a person's relative standing in a group with respect to some broadly defined capabilities.

Purposes of CRTs

CRT scores let everyone (students, parents, administrators, and teachers) know exactly how well students stand relative to a standard. CRTs can be constructed to measure separate prerequisites. This prerequisite analysis serves as a blueprint to enable the designer to plan testing systematically.

When instruction begins, tests are administered to determine which competencies students have already mastered. The test results help the teacher decide where to place the student based on how much instruction is needed to achieve the desired competency level. As instruction on each level is completed, end-of-lesson tests (post-tests) reveal whether mastery has occurred and whether the student can move on to the next lesson.

CRTs are also used to evaluate the instruction itself. If an acceptable number of students are achieving mastery, then the instruction is obviously working. If there are too many failures, test results can be analyzed to determine where the instruction failed and to plan the necessary revisions. Gagné (1988) compares the concept of mastery learning with ISD and finds that they have a great deal in common in that they both advocate improving instruction until criteria can be met.

Sometimes the "criterion" in criterion-referenced measurement is misinterpreted to mean a required cut-off score. Actually, "criterion" has a broader meaning. It refers to the behaviors used to measure achievement of an objective. In some cases, this may mean a criterion-referenced test with a cut-off score required to achieve criterion. In other cases, it may mean demonstration of a behavior or cognition where no test scoring is required.

Another common misconception is that criterion-referenced testing means a master (as compared with novice) level must be demonstrated. There is a difference between a master level and mastery of specific behaviors or cognitions. The latter may be achieved without achieving all the behaviors or cognitions required to qualify for a master level. In some cases requirements are adjusted depending upon performance of the group with respect to the criterion. For example, it may become clear that for most to achieve criterion, more time would have to be devoted to the instruction. Instead of providing more time, the criterion may be adjusted. The consequence will be that the lower criterion will be mastered, but the students may not reach mastery level.

When criterion measures have to be related to grading, it is possible to have levels of meeting the criterion, with the higher levels indicating expert or master achievement and the lower levels indicating minimum level of performance. Again, the essential requirement is that students be assessed in relation to standards based on criterion-referenced measurement or assessment, not in relation to the achievement of other students.

Nevertheless, there are often problems with implementation of "pure" criterion-referenced measurement that cause adjustments to be made. Sometimes those adjustments reflect attention to the variability of the group as described by norm-referenced measurement techniques, such as frequency distributions (Cross, 1995). Although "pure" criterion-referenced measurement has been implemented in the military, in schools and higher education adjustments are made because schedules preclude mastery learning for all. In addition, while the military controls who is trained, there will be more variability in groups in schools and institutions of higher education. The pressures of group heterogeneity, schedules, and grading often lead to some modifications in criterion-referenced measurement.

Nevertheless, in the final analysis assessment is criterion-referenced if judgments are made in relation to performance standards, rather than in relation to normative data, such as distribution on the bell curve. Criterion must be clearly specified for CRT to work.

Reliability

Reliability means that a test yields a dependable measure, that if the test is repeated the same results will be obtained. Reliable tests have consistency and temporal dependability.

Consistency.   A student may correctly answer a question by guessing, or answer a question incorrectly because it was phrased misleadingly. A single item is not sufficient evidence to conclude that a student has or has not mastered an objective. To draw a conclusion confidently from a test, it is necessary to determine whether the student's performance is consistent on other items aimed at the same objective.

A student who answers several test questions correctly is more likely to have mastered the objective than a student who can answer only one or two questions. To increase the internal consistency of an NRT, developers simply increase the number of items on the test. This is not always a practical solution for CRT developers who must strive to assess each separate competency a test covers. If this rule were rigidly followed, tests might last longer than the course. The following are factors that affect the number of items developed:

1. Consequences of misclassification: What is the cost of judging a master a non-master, and vice versa? The greater the cost, the greater the need for multiple items.
2. Specificity of the competency: The more specific the competency, the smaller the number of test items needed to assess competency. This is especially true in performance tests of simple motor skills, for example, playing the C scale. Once is usually enough.
3. Resources available for testing: When it is impossible to allot long periods of time to testing or when the costs of extensive testing are prohibitive, a strategy will have to be devised for selecting competencies for testing to make maximum use of time or money (Shrock, Mansukhani, Coscarelli, & Palmer, 1986).

Temporal Dependency.   Each time the test is administered, it should produce similar results. The student's demonstration of mastery should be the same on Tuesday as it is on Friday. Temporal dependency is usually determined by administering the tests on two occasions to the same group of students. A high degree of correspondence between scores suggests good reliability. Statistics employed for traditional norm-referenced reliability are not appropriate here. The comparison can be done by a simple percentage.

Test-retest reliability is enhanced by constructing unambiguous items and by making scoring as objective as possible. The most objective tests are those that can be scored by machine or by anyone with a scoring key. By contrast, subjective items must depend upon the judgment of experts who may have varying opinions about correctness. Subjective tests get varying results from the same students on different days. Table 4.1 illustrates types of written tests and their degree of objectivity.

Validity

Validity means that a test measures what it is supposed to measure. There can be no validity without reliability. The performance on a CRT must be exactly the same as the performance specified by the objective. Consider this example: If the test item says that an automotive repair student must remove a brake drum, then to be valid, the test must be designed to provide an automobile and the equipment to actually remove the drum. A multiple-choice test requiring students to recognize the correct procedure for removing the drum is not a valid test of the objective, nor would the test be valid if it required the student to recite from memory the procedures for removal. Neither test provides evidence of

Table 4.1 Types of Written Tests and Degrees of Objectivity

Objective	Less Objective	Subjective
Multiple choice	Production items (case studies or problems) when answers are specific and not open to interpretation	Essay in which a student is required to discuss a topic
Completion when answers are short, requiring a specific phrase		Completion answers when answers can be phrased in various ways
True-false when indisputably factual or not factual		True-false when dependent on context

From *Handbook for Designers of Instructional Systems: Volume III* (pp. 4–16), by Department of the Air Force (AF Manual 50-58), 1978, Washington, DC: Author.

the student's ability to use the actual equipment. Responses to such a test may be interpreted as a memorized verbal chain. Only when the test and the objective are congruent is the test valid.

Achieving validity is not always straightforward. Frequently, it is not possible to test the actual performance of a task, because it is difficult to obtain the resources to develop and administer the test. For example, consider the problem of obtaining equipment for the test on automotive repair. Practical considerations may necessitate a scaled-down version of the actual performance. Therefore, the objective must be written to take these constraints into consideration while still obtaining a valid measure. In cases such as these, it is a good idea to obtain the judgment of others about whether the objective and the test truly reflect the purposes of the lesson.

The best approach to establishing a test's validity is to empirically demonstrate that a test correctly distinguishes between masters and non-masters. One acceptable method is to administer the test to approximately thirty persons rated as masters and thirty rated as non-masters. If the test is valid, most of the masters should be able to answer each item on the test and most of the non-masters should not. Items that do not distinguish between masters and non-masters should be dropped from the test or revised.

Exercises B, C, and D at the end of this chapter provide practice in applying principles of measurement.

WHEN ASSESSMENT IS USED

Assessment techniques can be used for pre-assessments, embedded items, and post-assessments. Sometimes the same or similar items are used in each. The difference is one is given before instruction, one during, and one after.

Pre-assessments

Pre-assessments can serve multiple functions. They can diagnose which entry skills need remedial attention. They can provide a baseline that allows comparison with post-test scores, thus providing gain scores. Pre-assessments, such as pre-tests, can affect learning by cuing, providing practice, or creating awareness. In the ISD example in chapter 1 on "Commercial Loan Documentation," a written pre-test on basic concepts was given in order to establish the level of those entering. Even after that level was determined, the pre-test was continued because it had a self-awareness effect. Participants tended to enter believing they knew more than they did. The pre-test created self-awareness that was motivational.

Care must be taken in the presentation of pre-assessments, because poor performance on them can demoralize employees and affect instruction. Pre-assessments, then, can measure entry level or mastery of the objectives that will be taught. They can provide the basis for recommending inadmissibility, remedial instruction, or bypassing parts of the instruction.

Embedded Items

Embedded items are used throughout the instruction to determine whether enabling objectives have been achieved. It should be remembered that achievement on embedded criterion items does not necessarily mean that the learning will be retained or transferred. These embedded items can also serve a motivational function by creating self-awareness through feedback. They can ensure that learners do not progress to another objective until they have achieved a prerequisite objective.

Post-assessments

If achievement of enabling objectives hasn't been reliably determined earlier, then post-assessments, such as post-tests, should cover both enabling and terminal objectives. If this is not done, learners may be successful on the terminal objectives, but the designer will not know if all the enabling objectives were necessary. Perhaps the learners would have been successful with less instruction. On the other hand, students might be unsuccessful because they had not achieved some enabling objectives, and the designer would not know which enabling objectives had been achieved.

Assessment techniques are not limited to one part of the assessment process. Portfolios can be used for both pre- and post-assessment, as can objective tests. Observations are appropriate before, during, and after instruction.

MATCHING ASSESSMENT TO OBJECTIVES

What information is collected as evidence of learning achievement will depend on the nature of the competency being measured.

Cognitive Tests

For learning requiring acquisition of knowledge, the appropriateness of paper and pencil tests is self-evident. Verbal chains may be measured by recitation. Knowledge of facts and other types of information may be assessed by test questions that require the student to make mastery explicit. Intellectual skills are assessed by having a student solve problems, apply rules, or classify objects.

Unobservable cognitive tasks are usually made visible by some form of a written test. There are six types of tests that apply to cognitive tasks: multiple-choice, true-false, fill-in, matching, short answer, and essay. Each of these tests will be discussed in detail later in the section on constructing tests.

Performance Tests

In contrast to tests that measure cognitive abilities, performance tests measure a student's ability to do something. For example, a student's ability to perform a motor task is evaluated by observing and judging his behavior. In the test, the student is directed to perform a task and his performance is evaluated against some predetermined standard. If the output is a process, performance is evaluated as it occurs. Tasks evaluated this way include actions performed by athletes, performing artists, and equipment operators.

Figure 4.1. Visualization of the Five Types of Performance Assessment.

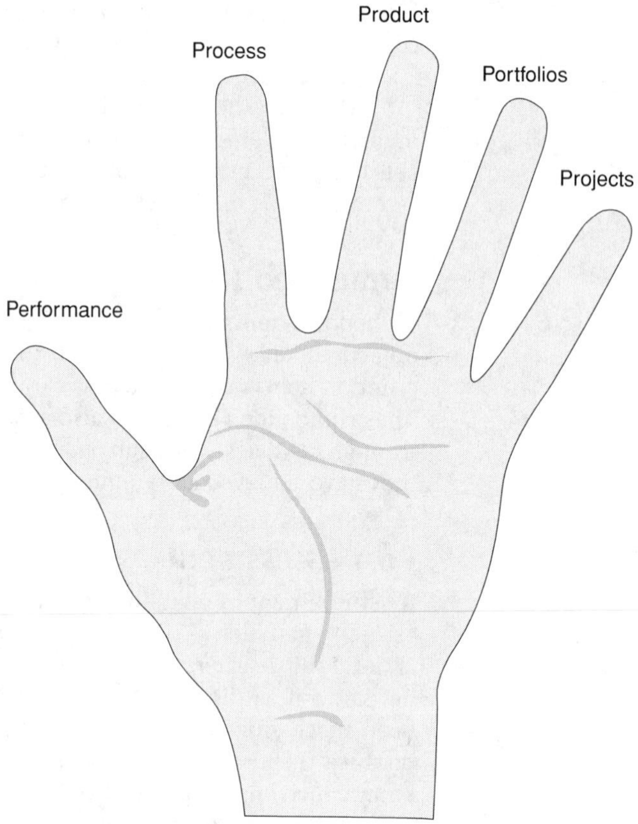

Because performance tests directly measure capability, they are inherently more valid than written tests. But because performance tests usually require judgment by the examiner, they tend to be less reliable than most cognitive tests. There are several types of performance assessment, and they are easily remembered because they all start with the letter "p" (see Figure 4.1). They include process and products, and two forms of product—portfolios and projects. If you visualize a splayed hand with a "p" at the tip of each digit standing for "product," "process," "portfolios," and "projects," and on the thumb for "performance," you will find it easy to remember these forms of tests.

Before each form is discussed, the concept of authentic assessment will be introduced because it is generating great interest currently in areas such as science and mathematics.

Authentic Assessment.   The concept of authenticity in assessment means that employee performance is examined directly on "real" tasks. The opposite of authentic assessment is a paper and pencil test from which learning must be inferred. Wiggins compares authentic assessment with more traditional means of assessment:

◆ Authentic assessment achieves validity and reliability by emphasizing and standardizing the appropriate *criteria* for scoring such (varied) products; traditional testing standardizes objective items and, hence, the (one) right answer for each.

◆ "Test validity" should depend in part upon whether the test simulates real-world tests of ability. Validity on most multiple-choice tests is determined merely by matching items to the curriculum content (or through sophisticated correlations with other test results).

◆ Authentic tasks involve "ill-structured" challenges and roles that help students rehearse for the complex ambiguities of the "game" of adult and professional life. Traditional tests are more like drills, assessing static and too-often arbitrarily discrete or simplistic elements of those activities. (Wiggins, 1990, p. 1)

The major problem with this type of assessment is that it is very labor intensive and therefore costly. Wiggins places the cost at $2 per employee, as compared with one cent per employee for a multiple choice test. He argues, however, that the increased gains more than offset the increased costs. Process, product, portfolio, and project assessments can be ways to assess authentically.

Process.   Objectives can be process objectives. This means that students are expected to learn ways of doing things, such as problem solving and discussing. Problem-based learning, which will be discussed in chapter 7, uses process objectives. In other words, students are expected to learn procedures for problem solving. Johnson (1996a) discusses Socratic seminars in which students are judged on the extent to which they develop the ability to articulate issues and participate with others in conversation about these issues. To assess such outcomes, criteria are established and applied, sometimes through rubrics and sometimes through observation checklists.

A rubric is a table, list, or scale used for scoring performance on assigned tasks. It can be designed to allow comparison between levels of achievement or aspects of a task. Figure 4.2 is an example of rubrics used for participation in a seminar. Another form of process assessment is using checklists to determine whether the employee can execute a procedure or demonstrate applying a rule.

Figure 4.2 Example of a Rubric for a Process Objective

> ### Boom to Bust Exhibition #1: Piner High School Literature Seminar and Essay Rubric
>
> SEMINAR (credit/no credit)
>
> **Oral Participation**
>
> 1. Addresses the question using evidence from the book. Cites examples, passages, characters from the book to support answers. Comments show that student has read and understood the book and is making connections between the book and the ideas generated by the seminar.
>
> 2. Makes relevant comments during the seminar which show response to previous speakers' ideas. Helps to enlarge understanding of the text and ideas generated in the seminar.
>
> 3. Takes the initiative in participating; does not have to be prompted.
>
> 4. May ask questions to clarify and deepen the discussion of ideas.
>
> ---
>
> **Other Participation**
>
> 1. Is on time for the seminar.
>
> 2. Shows attentiveness through body language: sitting up straight, looking at the speaker, giving the speaker the floor.
>
> 3. Does not belittle or criticize others' comments.

Adapted from *Performance Assessment Handbook: Volume One: Portfolios & Socratic Seminars* (p. 110), by B. Johnson, 1996, Princeton, NJ: Eye on Education. Reprinted with permission.

Products.   The outcome of a procedure is a product which is evaluated against a standard. Products may take many forms. A sample of the student's handwriting may be compared to an ideal sample of correct penmanship, or an apprentice cabinetmaker's work may be evaluated against certain workmanship standards. A learner may demonstrate the ability to do double entry bookkeeping by recording debits and credits from paper records such as check stubs and invoices. The product can be in the form of written language, such as a report; or it can be in graphic form, such as a chart; or it can be in edible form, such as a cake; or it can be a dramatic performance or a speech. Criteria are established to facilitate feedback on the product. Figure 4.3 is an example of criteria used to assess a writing sample.

Products can take many other forms, such as athletic performance. Whatever the form, assessment of performance can require more time and resources than administering written tests when there are many learners to assess. One teacher can administer a written test to 30 students with no help. To give a performance test to 30 students, the teacher may need help to fit all the assessments in the time available or to teach other students while one is observed.

Portfolios.   One of the alternate assessment practices increasingly used is portfolios. They have the advantage of providing a basis for both process and product review. Portfolios are a product because they contain examples of work that can be examined. An example of an objective for a portfolio might be:

> Given 3 months and a research topic and resources, the student will be able to write a formal paper that demonstrates mastery of the topic, including original interpretations and thoughts. The paper will meet standards summarized in a rubric, and the portfolio will include evidence of growth and collaborative reflection on the experience and will meet standards set forth in a checklist.

The portfolio concept has been used before by models, artists, and even instructional designers. Paulson and Paulson (1991) define a portfolio as follows:

> A purposeful, integrated collection of student work showing student effort, progress, or achievement in one or more areas. The collection is guided by performance standards and includes evidence of students' self-reflection and participation in setting the focus, selecting contents, and judging merit. (p. 295)

The key phrase in this definition is "guided by performance standards." How does one set standards for portfolios, which are works in process and involve both process and product approaches to performance assessment?

One way is to set standards for parts as they evolve and to use these standards in addition to review of the portfolio as a whole and evidence of involvement and reflectivity. Many problems arise from this approach: (a) personal standards must be integrated with criterion-referenced standards, (b) assignments must be relevant to the individual student, (c) time for evidence of growth and achievement must be provided on an individual basis, and (d) time for collaborative reflection is required (Seely, 1994). These problems require flexibility and emotional investment beyond the usual, but can yield rich assessment data and instruction, but as with any assessment practice, portfolios can also distract from instruction and yield superficial data. The latter sometimes happens when portfolios become a collection of products rather than a reflection on growth.

Portfolio generation is a process, not just a simple procedure. It requires many procedures, from decisions about what will be included, to when it will be reviewed periodically, and how reflection and feedback will occur. The questions that are generated for each stage and procedure are very important. Often rubrics are used. Rubrics present criteria in a graphic form that allows an evaluator to give feedback that stimulates reflection. Teachers and students should define standards and rubrics collaboratively.

The teachers have to develop many forms, rubrics, lists of questions or considerations to be used during their process. They have to continually reflect on how well the process is working. Because the portfolio assessment process is subjective, there can be problems with reliability. Students can question the fairness of feedback unless the relationship of student and teacher criterion-referenced standards is negotiated and communicated clearly.

Figure 4.3 Example of Criteria Used to Assess a Writing Product

---

Narrative JBHS Writing Rubric

Directions: Read the piece of writing holistically and give a single holistic score on a six point scale ("6" is exemplary and "1" is very poor). In determining that single score judge the quality of the piece of writing as a whole, giving greater weight to longer and more substantive pieces and rewarding variety and creativity.

6. A piece of writing that is **exemplary** in overall quality. It is characteristically substantial in content and mature in style. It demonstrates an ability to use language creatively and effectively. Voice is strong and there is a sophisticated sense of audience, task, and choice of form. The writer demonstrates insight, synthesizing complex ideas and generating original ideas. The organization is clear and artful. The content, sentence structure, and word choice are rich and sophisticated. The use of mechanics furthers the meaning.

5. A piece of writing that is **commendable** in overall quality. It suggests the excellence that a "6" demonstrates, but is less developed, less creative, or takes fewer risks. The writing is clear, interesting, appropriate, and generally rich and sophisticated. It demonstrates an effective use of voice, details, and language. There are few errors in mechanics, usage, or sentence structure.

4. A piece of writing that is **effective, but flawed** in overall quality. The writing has minor flaws, but is effective. There is a sense of audience and task and appropriate use of form, but some of the writing may seem formulaic. There is some insight, but tends to demonstrate minimal risk taking and original thinking. It is acceptable, generally correct, and the errors do not interfere with the meaning.

3. A piece of writing that **approaches effective** in overall quality. The writing has flaws that interfere with meaning. The pieces may be too brief or underdeveloped. The writing shows awareness of task, audience, and writing conventions but is often awkward or simplistic. There are attempts at analysis but little insight or originality.

2. A piece of writing that is **poor** in overall quality. The writing is incomplete or has major flaws. The piece may be either too short and undeveloped or abstract and vague. The writing demonstrates a poor sense of audience and task and no variety. Details are either repetitive or missing. It has many errors that interfere with meaning and little sense of conventions.

1. A piece of writing assessed as **errors block meaning.** There are many weaknesses and few, if any, strengths. The piece of writing shows very little time and thought. The writing is very limited, inappropriate, meaningless and/or demonstrates no sense of conventions.

From *Performance Assessment Handbook Volume 2: Performances and Exhibitions* (p.138), by B. Johnson, 1996, Princeton, NJ: Eye on Education. Reprinted with permission

Assessment decisions must also be made about what products to include in a portfolio. Anything that documents the process of learning is appropriate. Grace (n.d.) recommends that decisions about what to include be based on the purpose of the portfolio. For example, if the purpose is for the child and teacher to reflect on personal growth, drafts should be included. If, on the other hand, the purpose of the portfolio is assessment for placement, then it might not be appropriate to include drafts. In any event the material in a portfolio should be organized. Work samples could be arranged chronologically or by assignment.

Projects.   Another form for product assessment is projects. According to Katz (1994),

> A project is an in-depth investigation of a topic worth learning more about . . . The key feature of a project is that it is a research effort deliberately focused on finding answers to questions about a topic . . . The goal of a project is to learn more about the topic rather than to seek the right answers to questions posed by the teacher. (p. 1)

When an objective is assessed through a project, a rubric or checklist can be used (Priestly, 1982). Figure 4.4 is an example of a rubric for assessing a project. Johnson (1996a, 1996b) offers group and individual project rubrics.

Attitudinal Objectives

Ways to assess attitudes include interviews, surveys and polls, questionnaires, and rating scales. You can also use logs, journals, diaries, and self-reporting instruments. Sociometric procedures, observation reports, and examination of records are also valid techniques for measuring attitudes. Other methods include oral tests, essay test items, problem solving items, behavioral checklists, tally charts, and sentence completion sheets (Ackerson, 1992). A tally chart is a count or tally of the number of times a behavior is observed. Sentence completion sheets call for filling in the blanks at the end of sentences with phrases or words that express feelings.

Another common technique is to use an attitude inventory. If affective objectives are the major point of a design project, you will probably want to use several of these methods. Attitude inventories are usually constructed with scales that indicate feeings towards others, ideas, or objects. There are several types of scales: Likert, semantic differential, and Thurstone (Gay, 1985). Items can be constructed using each. An item using the Likert scale asks an individual to indicate extent of agreement on a continuum. A Likert scale item might look like this:

> It is important to study the information on fire safety procedures immediately upon checking into a hotel.

Strongly agree   Agree   Undecided   Disagree   Strongly disagree

Another type of scale is the semantic differential. An item that uses this scale requires the respondent to give a quantitative rating to a bipolar adjective. A mark on a continuum indicates an attitude. An item which uses a semantic differential scale will look like this:

> Student representatives should serve on all Board of Education committees.

Necessary __ __ __ __ __ __ __ Unnecessary

Desirable __ __ __ __ __ __ __ Undesirable

Good __ __ __ __ __ __ __ Bad

To use a Thurstone scale you need to construct a series of statements that represent different points of view. The respondent selects the ones with which they agree (or

Figure 4.4 Example of a Rubric for Assessing a Project

Sciences Core
The Physics of Sports and Recreation

Rubric for Science Fair Projects

Fulton Valley Prep

Mastery:	**Distinguished:**

Mastery:

1. Display Board clearly reflects the product development process.

2. Display Board includes summaries of all experiments and the results, with appropriate illustrations, measurements, calculations, and graphs.

3. Display Board includes a model or drawing of the final product.

4. Display Board includes writeup with appropriate conclusions based on data.

5. Display Board includes thorough explanation of the relevance of the principles of Newtonian physics to the performance of the product.

6. Notebook is a thorough record of the process of the development of the final product, including lab writeups, answers to assigned questions, vocabulary exercises, and reflective writings about concepts, experiments, and results.

7. Product exhibits care in thought, planning, and construction. Attention to detail is evident.

Distinguished:

Overall: Display Board is striking, attractive, well-organized, thorough and shows careful attention to detail.

1. See *Mastery.*

2. See *Mastery.* Also, neatly written, thorough, in-depth summaries of experiments, including quantitative data, measurements, calculations, and graphs.

3. See *Mastery.* Also model or drawing is to scale, neat, clearly labeled, and detailed.

4. See *Mastery.* Also, conclusions show thoughtful and significant insight into the experimental results and data.

5. See *Mastery.* Also shows clear connections between the performance of the product and the Newtonian principles involved.

6. See *Mastery.* Notebook entries are thoughtful and in-depth and reflect clear insight into the connections between the experiments, readings, and concepts.

7. See *Mastery.* Product also shows originality and creativity.

From *The Performance Assessment Handbook Volume 2: Performances and Exhibitions* (p. 43), by B. Johnson, 1996, Princeton, NJ: Eye on Education. Reprinted with permission.

disagree). Point values are assigned for each statement through a systematic process. Self-reporting instruments, such as those for self-concept and communication style, are other ways of gathering information on attitudes. Rating scales and self-report items are only as accurate as the individuals responding are truthful, rather than merely politically correct.

When you assess attitudes, it is desirable to place the learner in a voluntary situation in order to collect data. Otherwise, the learner may indicate a preference just to please the examiner rather than being honest. This means that you measure preference for reading indirectly by counting books signed out from the library, not by collecting a book report done to fulfill an assignment. Affective objectives are measured by criterion items that are often voluntary and indirect. They can have a flexible, personalized level for success.

The following objective is an example of attitude assessment through a journal or diary kept on a voluntary basis:

> Given a budget and the opportunity to participate in a research study, the teenage volunteer will show preference for a balanced diet in reports on a five-day eating period in restaurants. The balanced diet will be judged on a five-day rather than a meal-by-meal basis.

Appropriateness of Items

How do you go about writing valid criterion items? You write a criterion item consistent with the objective. The taxonomies of objectives include sample test items that can be used as models (Bloom, Englehart, Furst, Hill, & Krathwohl, 1956; Krathwohl, Bloom, & Masia, 1964; Harrow, 1972).

An assessment procedure may be more appropriate for some learning outcomes than others. This is not to say that multiple-choice items cannot be used for knowledge and attitude assessment. However, it is difficult to measure application of a psychomotor skill with multiple choice items. Items can be constructed to be suitable for different learning outcomes. Still, there are domains for which an item is most suitable, as shown in Table 4.2.

There are several bases on which the logical consistency between assessment and other aspects of design can be determined. One is matching the objectives to the criterion (Mager, 1973); another is matching the type of assessment to the type of learning; and a third method is matching the data collection method to the purpose of assessment. To use an extreme example, one does not use observation with a written test on cognitive learning. However, some data collection methods appropriate for performance assessment can also be used for assessment of attitude change. Still, there are methods more suitable for one than the other. Self-report methods, the oral or written responses of individuals, are an effective way of assessing attitude change. Observation, on the other hand, is a method equally useful for performance or attitude change assessment. However, checklists used by observers are generally more useful for performance assessment, and rating scales used by observers are generally more useful for assessment of attitude change. In either performance or attitudinal change situations, it is necessary for observers to use forms to record data.

Task/Objective/Criterion Charts

Each objective must be examined for a correct match between the means of evaluation and the type of learning or behavior. Criterion-referenced measures define achievement on the basis of a pre-established standard stated in an objective. Students either reach this standard or they don't. Criterion items are those on which the student must demonstrate mastery by performance.

Table 4.3 shows a good way to check the validity of your objectives by matching the task on your instructional analysis with its objective and criterion item. If the chart indicates discrepancies across columns, then rewrite the objective.

Exercises E and F provide practice in determining appropriateness of assessment procedures.

Table 4.2 Type of Item Most Appropriate for a Learning Domain

KEY
Very Appropriate For
C Cognitive
P Psychomotor
A Affective

Type of Item	Domain Most Associated with	Comments
Objective		
True False	C	Efficient for items with only two logical responses
Completion	C	Natural for brief responses
Multiple-Choice	C	Use when answer is long—reduces effect of guessing, so can have fewer items
Matching	C	Efficient but not for higher level learning tasks
Essay		
Essay	C	Score systematically
Extended Report	C	Clarify required components
Activity		
Lab Reports	C	Type of learning used for depends on content and structure
Exercises	C, P	Separate use for testing from use for instruction
Projects	C, P, A	Good for multi-domain learning
Observation		
Checklists	P, A	Excellent for procedural knowledge and practice
Rating Scales	P, A	Self or observational, degrees of subjectivity
Anecdotes	A	Subjective
Interviews	A	Revealing, can have degree of objectivity
Application		
Problem Solving	C, A	For higher level of learning
Product	C, P, A	Especially for interactive domain learning

Table 4.3 Task/Objective/Criterion Chart

Task	Objective	Criterion
Identify data. Identify editing. Identify saving. Identify printing. Identify on-screen help.	Given an oral example of a procedure, the student will identify the procedure by naming it correctly as data entry, editing, saving, printing, or on-screen help.	When you select a sentence, then copy, cut, and paste, you are using a(n) _____ procedure.
Determine distance and travel.	Given two locations on a map and a rate of travel, the student will determine the distance and time of travel.	Determine the distance from Syracuse, New York, to Washington, D.C., and the time of travel at an average of 50 mph.
Identify/trace routes on the map using the correct legend.	Given a bus schedule, circle 3 route stops on the schedule map.	Select a bus route and circle 3 stops on the schedule map for that route.
Pay correct bus fare.	Given a predetermined location, select the appropriate payment.	What is the designated fare in the downtown area?
Recognize the order of events in the first stage of labor.	Given events in the first stage of labor, the student will list the order of events as they occur in labor.	Put numbers in front of these events to indicate the order in which they occur in labor. Make the first event #1.
Distinguish rhythm through syllabification.	Given 5 poems, the student will write at the end of each line the number of syllables in that line.	At th end of each line in the poem "The Road Not Taken," write the number of syllables in that line.

CONSTRUCTING AND ANALYZING TESTS

This section will cover techniques and guidelines for constructing assessment procedures and items and interpreting the results. This subject is covered extensively in measurement theory. Only those techniques most relevant for novice designers will be addressed.

Table of Specifications

The purpose of a table of specifications is to increase the likelihood that all objectives will be measured and that only objectives will be measured. It's a blueprint for a test. The same technique can be used to specify all the assessment procedures to be used. To make a table of specifications, list the content categories you wish to assess on the vertical axis and the behavioral outcomes to be assessed on the horizontal axis. Thus, if you are going to assess

Table 4.4 Table of Specifications for a Test on Punctuation

Behavioral Outcomes

Content	Know Marks	Comprehend Rules	Apply Rules	Punctuate Original Paragraph	TOTAL
Comma	1	5	3	1	10
Period	1	4	2	1	8
Semicolon	1	6	4	1	12
Quotation	1	4	2	1	8
TOTAL	4	19	11	4	38

learning of punctuation, you may list on the vertical access: commas, periods, semicolons, quotation marks. On the horizontal axis you might list know marks, comprehend rules, apply rule, and punctuate original paragraph. Then in each cell formed by the matrix, indicate how many items will be used for that objective, e.g., knowing comma mark. Table 4.4 is the resulting table of specifications for this example. Table 4.4 suggests that learning marks and period and quotation mark rules is easier than applying rules when writing and learning comma and semicolon rules. In this example the numbers in the cells refer to how many items will be included.

Another way to use a table of specifications is to put the numbers of the items on the test that measure the objective in the appropriate cell. Thus, if items 1–4 and 10 will measure comprehending comma rules, then in the first cell made by the intersection of comprehending rules and comma write 1–4, 10.

Rules for Item Construction

Developers must also consider guidelines for writing items. We offer here some general and specific rules for writing items; they are derived from several sources and are summarized in Table 4.5 (Remmers, Gage, & Rummerl, 1965; Payne, 1968; Nitko, 1983; Gay, 1985). The types of items covered range from true/false items to essay items and problem-solving items.

Table 4.5 Rules for Writing Test Items

General Rules

Be careful not to provide cues to the correct answer.	Do not call for trivial, obvious, ambiguous, or meaningless answers.
Avoid dependent items where one item cues the answer in another item.	Each item should have only one correct answer.
Avoid negatives.	Use illustrations appropriately and accurately and make them clear.
Avoid unnecessary difficulty, such as use of obscure vocabulary.	Follow the rules of grammar and syntax.
Avoid direct quotations.	Avoid items that give away the answer.
	Avoid complex sentence structure.

Table 4.5 *Continued*

Multiple Choice Items

Make the stem a direct question.	Make options and the stem grammatically parallel and consistent.
Ask one definite question.	Present the term in the stem and definitions as options when testing knowledge of terminology.
Avoid making correct alternatives obviously different.	Avoid requiring personal opinion unless on attitude survey.
Avoid making correct alternatives systematically different.	Avoid redundancy in alternatives by stating once in the stem.
Present alternatives in logical order.	Avoid a collection of true/false alternatives.
Make response alternatives mutually exclusive and of similar length.	Use "all of the above" option when there are several correct answers, not a best answer.
Make response alternatives plausible but not equally plausible.	Put as much of the problem as possible into the stem.
Use "none of the above" seldom and with caution.	

Matching Items

Use response categories that are related but mutually exclusive.	Use longer phrases in the response list, shorter in the stimuli list.
Keep the number of stimuli small and have the number of responses exceed stimuli by 2 or 3.	Identify stimuli with numbers and responses with letters.
Present response in logical order (e.g., alphabetically, chronologically).	Keep everything relating to an item on a single page.
Explain the basis for matching; give clear directions.	Make stimuli and response columns similar in level of difficulty.
Avoid "perfect" matching by including one or more implausible responses.	Avoid using complete sentences in stimuli column; use phrases or words instead.

True/False, Constant Alternative Items

Be sure the item is definitely true or false.	Use quantitative language when possible.
Avoid determiners such as "always" or "often."	Place crucial elements at the end of the sentence.
Use approximately the same number of words in each statement.	Instead of true/false, you can use yes/no, right/wrong, correct/incorrect, same/opposite.
Avoid quotations or stereotypes.	Phrase items unambiguously.
Don't present items in a pattern.	

Short Answer, Completion, or Supply Items

Word items specifically and clearly.	Provide the terms and require the definition rather than vice versa.
Put the blank towards the end of the sentence.	
Use only one blank.	Specify the terms in which the response is to be given; e.g., word, phrase, sentence, inches, feet.
Avoid quoted or stereotyped statements.	Use direct questions rather than incomplete declarative sentences.
Require short, definite, explicit answers.	

Table 4.5 *Continued*

Essay Items

Focus the type of response you wish the student to make.	Word question so experts can agree on correct response.
Clarify limits and purposes of questions.	Use more than one essay question.
Avoid optional questions.	Set up a systematic scoring procedure.

Application or Problem Solving Items

Use new or novel test materials	Test ability to use materials.
Use introductory materials followed by item dependent on that material.	Use pictures or diagrams for testing.
Call for identifying or producing examples.	Use reading material for testing.
Call for identifying components or relationships.	Allow for creativity.

Using Item/Error Matrices

One way to record data from test assessments is to use an item or error matrix. Basically, they are the same, except that, when the matrix is used for embedded items, it is sometimes called an "item matrix," and when it is used for a post-test it is called an "error matrix." The terms are basically synonymous and can be used interchangeably. To use such matrices, list the students by name or number down the vertical axis. List the item across the horizontal axis. This creates a cell for each student for each item. You can then note in that cell if the student missed the item by using an x or check. This allows you to identify items that gave most students problems by seeing where the x clusters. It also can reveal which students missed enabling objective criterion items, which students had difficulty throughout, and which students had no problems. The results may indicate when material was too difficult or too easy for students. Table 4.6 is an example of an error matrix.

The matrix in Table 4.6 could be interpreted as indicating that item 4 was too difficult. In addition, one can see that Mary and Bruce are having difficulty, but Jeff is not. Item 3 may either be too easy or the instruction may be very effective. Since Mary missed everything else, it is likely it is very easy, but we can't conclude that without further examination of the material and students.

Exercises G, H, I, and J provide practice in constructing and analyzing tests. Exercise K provides practice in combining all of the elements of this chapter into an assessment plan and instruments.

Table 4.6 An Error Matrix

	Items							
Student	*1*	*2*	*3*	*4*	*5*	*6*	*7*	**TOTAL**
Mary	x	x		x	x	x	x	6
Jeff				x				1
Carole				x		x		2
Bruce	x	x		x		x	x	5
TOTAL	2	2	0	4	1	3	2	14

EXERCISES

A. An Exercise to Identify What Is Being Assessed

For each item identify what is being assessed:

    C: cognitive learning

    P: performance

    A: attitudes

1. A checklist is used while watching an electrician install a dishwasher.
2. An objective test is given to measure knowledge and understanding of concepts in instructional design.
3. An essay test is used to determine whether students understand chemical reactions.
4. An inventory that asks participants to evaluate their satisfaction with the workshop is used after instruction.
5. A time test is used to measure ability to write behavioral objectives.
6. A questionnaire is used to measure opinions before and after instruction.

B. An Exercise to Distinguish CRTs and NRTs

Read the following statements and check the ones that apply to CRTs.

1. At the end of instruction, test scores showed that 80% of the students reached mastery level.
2. Mary's math score showed that she was in the 80th percentile for students in the 10th grade.
3. Betty's test score showed that she needs tutoring in how to multiply fractions.
4. After studying test results of a group of 15 people who had completed a course on using a computer program, an instructional designer concluded the instruction would have to be revised because 10 people did not achieve mastery on two of the objectives.
5. Harry's test score showed that he was below average in abstract reasoning.
6. The teacher gave John an A because he had the highest test score in the class.

C. An Exercise in Recognizing Ways to Achieve Greater Reliability in a Test

For each learning outcome below, two types of scoring are described. Check the type of scoring which is likely to be more objective.

1. Learning outcome: Student must identify a major theme in *The Scarlet Letter.* The scorer checks to see whether
   a. The correct answer in a multiple choice item is endorsed.
   b. Ideas involved in the major theme are present in an essay.
2. Learning outcome: Student must correctly punctuate a paragraph. The scorer
   a. Rates the student on a scale of 1 to 5 for each type of punctuation. The score is the total of the rankings.
   b. Works from a correctly punctuated paragraph and compares the student's paragraph with it. The score is the number of correspondences.
3. Learning outcome: Student must compare and contrast "criterion-referenced testing" and "norm-referenced testing." The scorer
   a. Assigns points to the student's essay, depending on the student's estimate of adequacy of coverage.
   b. Has a list of characteristics the essay must cover for each type of test and adds up the number cited.
4. Learning outcome: Student mechanic must set spark plug gap to correct width. The scorer
   a. Passes instrument through gap and checks for snugness of fit.
   b. Visually inspects gap and accepts or rejects.

5. Learning outcome: Student must comply with lunchroom rules of conduct. The scorer
   a. Checks to see whether the student has received detentions for lunchroom conduct
   b. Observes the student in the lunchroom and rates the adequacy of the student's behavior against a list of the rules of conduct.
6. Learning outcome: Students must subtract four-digit numbers. The scorer
   a. Checks to see whether the student can correctly subtract his or her birth year from the current year.
   b. Checks whether the student can solve ten subtraction problems involving four-digit numbers.

D. An Exercise in Recognizing Test Items Likely to Lend Greater Validity to a Test

For each statement of a learning outcome, two test items have been developed. Check the one that better reflects the behavior in the objective.

1. Objective: Given specific travel needs, the student travel agent will prepare a travel itinerary which includes the traveler's name, date, destination, and credit card number; names of airlines, flight numbers, departures, and arrivals arranged chronologically; and the amount charged to the traveler's account.
   a. Test A presents hypothetical travel information. The student must write a travel itinerary that conforms to the criteria in the objective.
   b. Test B asks "What items should be included in a travel itinerary?"
2. Given a politician's speech, the student will identify the known facts contained in the speech and separate facts from inferences.
   a. Test A presents an entire speech and directs the student to "Underline one statement of fact. Double-underline one inference contained in the speech."
   b. Test B presents an entire speech and directs the student to "Underline all of the known facts. Double-underline the inferential portions of the speech."
3. Given a drawing of a Hopi residential structure, the student will identify the description that best characterizes the structure.
   a. Test A shows a picture and directs the student to "Study this picture and read the four sentences below it. Put a check mark in front of the one sentence that is appropriate for the structure."
   b. Test B shows a picture and directs the student to "Study this picture and read the sentence below it. Indicate by a true or false answer whether the sentence is appropriate for the structure."
4. Given a specific geographical location and a specific month, the student will name the season.
   a. Test A asks "What season would it be in Bogota during June?"
   b. Test B directs the student to "Fill in the following chart by identifying the season for each city."

City	Month	Season
Montevideo	June	
Miami	January	
Montreal	January	
Seattle	September	
Bogota	September	

5. Given an instance in which humans have altered their environment, the student will name the positive and negative effects of the alteration on the ecosystem.
   a. Test A states, "A dam is a human-made alteration of the environment. Give a negative and a positive effect on the ecosystem."
   b. Test B states, "The following are man-made alterations to the environment: dam, oil drilling, freeway, solid-waste disposal system, gravel pit, park. Provide one positive and one negative effect resulting from each."

6. Given a moving van, the student will load the van with household items so that they will not shift during movement.
    a. Test A requires the student to load a scale model of a truck with scaled-down furniture.
    b. Test B requires the student to describe the placement of the furniture in the truck.

E. An Exercise in Identifying Appropriate Ways to Assess Learning

For each of these tasks, suggest appropriate ways to assess.

1. Use the process writing approach to write an essay.
2. Choose to align yourself with the animal rights movement.
3. Sew a "scrunchy" to hold a ponytail.

F. An Exercise in Using a Task/Objective/Criterion Chart

Where a column is blank, complete it so that the row across is logically consistent.

Task	Objective	Criterion
	Given a blank 5.25" floppy disk and a flow chart, the student will generate an initialized disk within 15 minutes.	
Load DOS	Given DOS software and a microcomputer, the student will follow the recommended procedure to load DOS.	
Estimate distance to locations		What is the distance in milesbetween Indianapolis and New Orleans?
	Given a predetermined location,determine charges for travel within and between zones.	How much fare would be paid for a ride from Zone 1 to Zone 2?
Describe the events in the second stage of labor		There are at least four events in the second stage of labor. Write a paragraph about each event.
Use phonetics to distinguish rhyme		After each line in "The Raven" write the phonetic ending.

G. An Exercise in Constructing a Table of Specifications

In the additive color system red, blue, and yellow are primary colors. These primary colors are combined to make the secondary colors. Blue and yellow make green. Red and blue make violet. Red and yellow make orange. On a chart in the shape of a circle, known as a color wheel, each primary color has an opposing complementary color just as 12 opposes 6 on a clock. Green opposes red. Orange opposes blue. Violet opposes yellow. These opposing colors are known as complementary colors. Construct a table of specifications for a test on recognition and knowledge of primary and secondary colors.

H. An Exercise in Applying Test Construction Rules

Each of the behavioral objectives listed implies a type of test item. Use the guidelines in Table 4.5 to develop criterion items for these objectives.

1. Given an essay question, explain the causes of diabetic shock and the predicted effects of several modes of treatment.
2. Given the name of five inventors, match each with the name and date of the invention.
3. Given seven statements about the mechanical properties of a V-8 gasoline engine, identify all seven correctly as true or false.
4. Given a multiple-choice question about characteristics of effective introductions to lessons, identify the characteristic that does not apply to introductions.
5. Given a completion question, give the definition of each of the parts of speech, e.g., verbs.

I. An Exercise to Help You Remember Item Construction Rules

Develop a mnemonic, visual, or sentence that helps you remember some of the rules for each type of item: multiple choice, matching, true/false, completion, essay, or problem solving.

J. An Exercise in Constructing and Interpreting an Error Matrix

You have 6 students and a test with 10 items. Construct an error matrix. Fill in the following data:

Student 1 missed items 2, 4, and 6.

Student 2 missed no items.

Student 3 missed item 4.

Student 4 missed items 4, 6, 8, and 10.

Student 5 missed all the items.

Student 6 missed item 4.

Write out your interpretation of this matrix.

K. A Group Exercise to Practice Developing Assessment Items

Your partner should assume the role of instructional designer, and you should function as the SME. As a designer help your partner develop criterion items that match the objectives he or she developed in exercise K at the end of chapter 3. Then, reverse roles and have your partner help you develop assessment items. If you already have the items, have your partner review and critique them. When you have developed the items, try putting them in a task/objective/criterion chart to check for consistency.

L. An Exercise to Develop an Assessment Plan

Use the behavioral objectives you developed at the end of the previous chapter as a basis for an assessment plan. The plan should specify methods and instruments to be used for collecting data on success in achieving objectives. When the plan is complete, develop assessment items that are appropriate for the objectives. Then, describe how you would defend the reliability and validity of the assessment items. Complete the task/objective/criterion chart as a check on logical consistency and appropriateness. These elements should all be part of your individual project.

◆ REFERENCES

Ackerson, C. (1992). Affective objectives: A discussion of some controversies. *Instructional Developments, 3*(1), 7–11.

Bloom, B. S., Englehart, M. D., Furst, E. J., Hill, W. H., & Krathwohl, D. R. (1956). *Taxonomy of educational objectives: Handbook II: The cognitive domain.* New York: David McKay.

Cross, L. H. (1995). *ERIC/AE Digest: Grading students* (Report No. EDO-TM-95-5). Washington, DC: ERIC Clearinghouse on Assessment and Evaluation, The Catholic University of America.

Department of the Air Force. (1978). *Handbook for designers of instructional systems: Volume III.* Washington, DC: Author .

Druckman, D. & Bjork, R. A. (Eds.). (1994). *Learning, remembering, believing: Enhancing human performance.* Washington, DC: National Academy Press.

Gagné, R. M. (1988). Mastery learning and instructional design. *Performance Improvement Quarterly, 1*(1), 7–18.

Gagné, R. M., Briggs, L. J., & Wager, W. (1992). *Principles of Instructional Design* (4th Ed.). New York: Holt, Rinehart and Winston.

Gay, L. R. (1985). *Educational evaluation & measurement.* Columbus, OH: Merrill Publishing.

Grace, C. (n.d.). *ERIC Digest: The portfolio and its use: Developmentally appropriate assessment of young children* (Report No. EDO-PS-62-11). Urbana-Champaign, IL: ERIC Clearinghouse on Elementary and Early Childhood Education.

Harrow, A. J. (1972). *A taxonomy of the psychomotor domain.* New York: David McKay.

Johnson, B. (1996a). *The performance assessment handbook volume one: Portfolios & Seminars.* Princeton, NJ: Eye on Education.

Johnson, B. (1996b). *The performance assessment handbook volume two: Performances & exhibitions.* Princeton, NJ: Eye on Education.

Katz, L. G. (1994). *ERIC Digest: The project approach* (Report EDO-PS-94-6). Urbana-Champaign, IL: ERIC Clearinghouse on Elementary and Early Childhood Education.

Krathwohl, D. R., Bloom, B. S., & Masia, B. B. (1964). *Taxonomy of educational objectives: Handbook II: Affective domain.* New York: McKay.

Mager, R. F. (1973). *Measuring instructional intent, or got a match?* Belmont, CA: Fearon.

Nitko, A. J. (1983). *Educational tests and measurement: An introduction.* New York: Harcourt Brace Jovanovich.

Paulson, F. L. & Paulson, F. L. (1991). Portfolios: Stories of knowing. In P. Dreyer (Ed.), *Workshop 3: The politics of process* (pp. 294–303). Claremont, CA: Claremont Reading Conference.

Payne, D. A. (1968). *The specification and measurement of learning outcomes.* Waltham, MA: Blaisdell.

Priestly, M. (1982). *Performance assessment in education and training: Alternative techniques.* Englewood Cliffs, NJ: Educational Technology Publications.

Remmers, H. H., Gage, N. L., & Rummerl, J. F. (1965). *A practical introduction to measurement and evaluation.* New York: Harper and Row.

Seely, Amy E. (1994). *Portfolio assessment.* Westminster, CA: Teacher Created Materials.

Shrock, S., Mansukhani, R. H., Coscarelli, W., & Palmer, S. (1986). An overview of criterion-referenced test development. *Performance and Instruction Journal, 25*(6), 3–9.

Wiggins, G. (1990). *The case for authentic assessment* (Report No. EDO-TM-90-10). Washington, DC: ERIC Clearinghouse on Tests, Measurement and Evaluation, American Institutes of Research.

Wolf, K. & Siu-Runyan. (1996). Portfolio purposes and possibilities. *Journal of Adolescent & Adult Literacy, 40*(1), 30–37.

◆ ANSWERS

A. An Exercise to Identify What Is Being Assessed

1. Performance
2. Cognitive Learning
3. Cognitive Learning
4. Attitude
5. Performance
6. Attitude

B. An Exercise to Distinguish CRTs and NRTs

The statements that apply to CRTs are 1, 3, and 4. These are CRTs because they measure in relationship to a criterion not to other students.

C. An Exercise in Recognizing Ways to Achieve Greater Reliability in a Test

1. a
2. b

3. b

4. a

5. a (Think about why b is more valid, while a is more reliable.)

6. b

D. An Exercise in Recognizing Test Items Likely to Lend Greater Validity to a Test

1. Test A
2. Test B
3. Test A
4. Test B (There can be no validity without reliability.)
5. Test A (This item is a good example of a common error. It is often the case that an objective is written to test one level, but when the CRT is written it's harder and goes beyond the level called for by the objective.)
6. Test A

E. An Exercise in Identifying Appropriate Ways to Assess Learning

1. Since this task requires learning to apply the process writing approach, it can be assessed by examination of both process and product. One way to do this would be to use portfolio assessment employing teacher generated forms and rubrics. Another would be to use performance assessment through examination of product. For example, there might be a checklist, a list of criteria, or a rubric that provides a basis for assessment. Portfolio and product assessment of performance can both be used.

2. This is an affective task. It requires a positive attitude towards animal rights and a willingness to become personally involved even at the minimal level of listening attentively or responding. There are several ways achievement of this task can be assessed. An obvious one is to use an attitude inventory in which the student is aware that there is no personal advantage in either the positive or negative position. In other words, the student feels no pressure to be for or against animal rights. The same condition should apply if other methods of assessment are used. For example, the student could be given an essay topic which requires taking a position. A debate could be set up and a student given a choice of sides. Two meal options could be offered, one of which is vegetarian. A discussion or debriefing after an activity could be observed and the number of times a student takes a pro animal rights stance counted.

3. A "scrunchy" is a band of elastic covered by fabric which is used to hold a ponytail, or a bunch of hair at the base of the neck. The item asks for assessing performance of a procedure. One way of doing this is to examine the product against a checklist of criteria or a rating scale for a well-made "scrunchy." Another way would be to observe using a checklist for steps completed. Some steps will have to be done in order; however, some latitude may be allowed for substeps. The checklist should make this clear.

F. An Exercise in Using a Task/Objective/Criterion Chart
Examples of ways to fill in the blanks are shown in Table 4.7.

Table 4.7

Task	Objective	Criterion
Generate initialized disk	Given a blank 5.25" floppy disk and a flow chart, the student will generate an initialized disk within 15 minutes.	Initialize this disk.
Load DOS	Given DOS software and a microcomputer, the student will follow the recommended procedure to load DOS.	Load DOS.
Estimate distance to locations	Given two locations on a map, determine the distance between the locations.	What is the distance in miles between Indianapolis and New Orleans?
Determine travel charges	Given a predetermined location, determine charges for travel within and between zones.	How much fare would be paid for a ride from Zone 1 to Zone 2?
Describe the events in the second stage of labor	Given 10 minutes, write an essay describing the second stage of labor, including all four events in that stage.	There are at least four events in the second stage of labor. Write a paragraph about each event.

Table 4.7 *Continued*

Task	Objective	Criterion
Use phonetics to distinguish rhyme each line.	Given "The Raven," write the phonetic ending after	After each line in "The Raven" write the phonetic ending.

G. An Exercise in Constructing a Table of Specifications

There are many ways to do this. The important part is to place the content on one axis (vertical) and the behaviors or cognitions on the other (horizontal). Table 4.8 shows one example of how to do the exercise.

H. An Exercise in Applying Test Construction Rules

There is more than one way to write each item.

1. You have three hours to answer three questions about the treatment of diabetes. The first question (A) is required. You may select the other two questions from a choice of four.
   A. In an essay, explain the causes of diabetic shock and the predicted effects of several modes of treatment.
2. Match the inventor with the invention.

Inventor	Invention and Date
1. Alexander Graham Bell	a. cotton gin (1793)
2. Thomas Edison	b. first patented reaping machine (1834)
3. Elias Howe	c. first patented sewing machine (1846)
4. Cyrus McCormick	d. first patented electric speaking telephone (1876)
5. Eli Whitney	e. phonograph (1877)
	f. motion-picture camera (1895)
	g. television iconoscope (1923)

3. Identify each of the following statements about the mechanical properties of a V-8 engine as true or false.
   a. Power output comes from the crank shaft.
   b. Eight pistons slide in eight cylinders.
   c. Valves regulate the flow of gases to each cylinder.
   d. Eight cylinders form the engine block.
   e. A carburetor prepares fuel by mixing gasoline and air.
   f. Each cylinder is serviced by at least two valves.
   g. A flywheel is used to smooth out engine pulsations.
4. Which of the following is not a characteristic of effective introductions to lessons?
   a. Structure the information logically.
   b. Describe the objective of the lesson.
   c. Describe how the lesson will be evaluated.
   d. Describe the benefits of instruction.
   e. Relate the new learning to previous learning.
5. What is the definition of "adjective"?

I. An Exercise to Help You Remember Item Construction Rules

There is no one way to help yourself remember. Develop a method that works for you. Do not try to include all the rules. Choose the rules that you think are most important or that will cue you to remember other rules. Here is an example for each type of item.

Multiple-Choice: Stuff the stem and order the alternatives! Think Mmm-Crisp Celery!

Table 4.8

	Behavioral Outcomes				
Content	Recognize Primary	Recognize Secondary	Know How Secondary Is Made	Know Placement on Color Wheel	Total
Red	3	0	0	2	5
Blue	3	0	0	2	5
Yellow	3	0	0	2	5
Green	0	3	2	2	7
Orange	0	3	2	2	7
Violet	0	3	2	2	7
TOTAL	9	9	6	12	36

Matching: 1, 2, 3, A, B, C MARCH! First Column Phrases! Second Column Longer!
True/False: Always definite but never always or often!
Short Answer, Completion, or Supply Items: In a question, provide the long, require the short.
Essay: Be a camera! Help focus on response purposes, types, limits, scoring.
Problem Solving: Use an image of reading a novel with an illustration on the facing page.

J. An Exercise in Constructing and Interpreting an Error Matrix

The error matrix shown in Table 4.9 suggests that student 5 is having a great deal of difficulty with the instruction. This is more likely to be due to lack of pre-entry requirements than to problems with the overall instruction, since none of the other students missed all the items. On the other hand, the instruction may not be challenging enough for student 2. There is no way to be sure of this without further examination of the design and gathering more information from the student. The instruction for item 4 may need improvement because everyone except student 2 missed this item. This is also likely for item 6. Students 1 and 4 need to be questioned and observed as they appear to be having difficulty

which may be due to the effectiveness or appropriateness of the instructional approach.

K. A Group Exercise to Practice Developing Assessment Items

Your assessment items can be expanded to make an assessment instrument, or they can be embedded items. They can also take the form of rubrics, checklists, or criteria for evaluating performance.

L. An Exercise to Develop an Assessment Plan

Your plan should address the following:

1. What is being assessed.
2. The functions assessment will serve.
3. How reliability and validity will be ensured.
4. Appropriate ways of assessing.
5. Appropriate ways of collecting data.
6. A task/objective/criterion chart.
7. Rationale for use of pre- or post-assessment.
8. Rationale for use of embedded items or tests.
9. Table of specifications for any tests.
10. Sample items for any test of learning.
11. Sample items for any performance or attitude assessment.

Table 4.9

					Items						
Students	**1**	**2**	**3**	**4**	**5**	**6**	**7**	**8**	**9**	**10**	**Total**
1		x		x		x					3
2											0
3				x							1
4				x		x		x		x	4
5	x	x	x	x	x	x	x	x	x	x	10
6				x							1
Total	1	2	1	5	1	3	1	2	1	2	19

5

Selecting and Developing Delivery Systems

OVERVIEW

We are not going to deal with the step of instructional strategies in Part One of this book. Rather, we will present information on strategies for instruction in chapter 11. As we explained in the Preface, this textbook presents the essential steps for an ISD approach first. After these essential steps are learned, we elaborate by presenting additional steps. Thus, we take the position that the design step of the ISD process can be completed at a novice level by basing decisions about instruction on the learning situation and channels, and by taking learner characteristics into account. This step in the ISD Model for Novices is illustrated in Figure 5.1.

Delivery systems are ways to carry information from a source to a receiver or vice versa for the puposes of instruction. The term can be used to describe older technologies, such as traditional media, or newer technologies, such as distance education technologies, or a combination of both.

Learner characteristics, objectives, resources, and constraints must be identified before delivery systems are selected. Selection and justification should be based on an ISD model developed for delivery system selection. Instructional designers may select from print technologies, audiovisual technologies, computer technologies, and integrated technologies. The instructional designer determines delivery system options, then identifies whether commercial materials can be adopted or adapted, and initiates the development phase.

With computer-based and emerging technologies, the designer's role varies greatly. For example, the designer might (a) stop after the analysis and design steps, (b) continue and develop prototype segments, or (c) become part of the development team and be involved in scripting and storyboarding. The client or the designer may select the delivery system, often in consultation with the developer. The designer may also be the developer, or he or she may work with a development team chosen by a project manager. Generally, however, the designer selects the delivery systems and then works with a development team. Because it is the designer's responsibility to monitor development to ensure that materials and instructional strategies reflect design decisions, you need to be familiar with the production process.

Figure 5.1 Expansion of Delivery Systems Selection and Development (Seels & Glasgow ISD Model 1: For Novices)

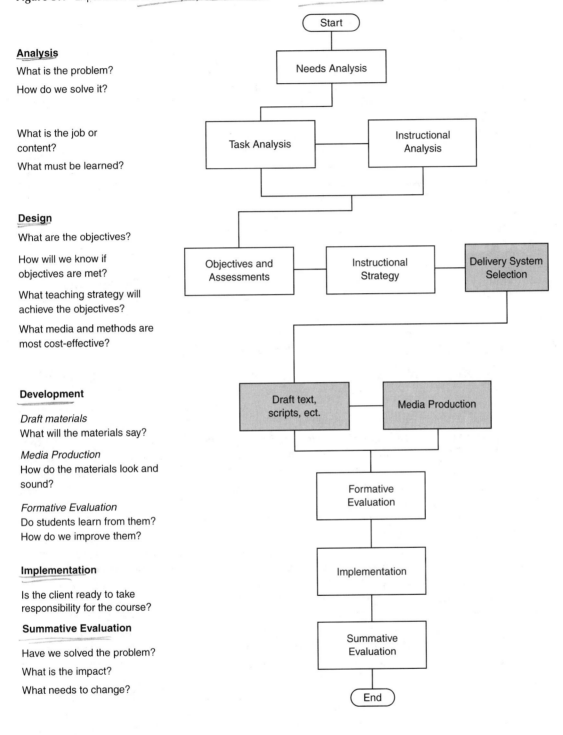

Analysis

What is the problem?

How do we solve it?

What is the job or content?

What must be learned?

Design

What are the objectives?

How will we know if objectives are met?

What teaching strategy will achieve the objectives?

What media and methods are most cost-effective?

Development

Draft materials
What will the materials say?

Media Production
How do the materials look and sound?

Formative Evaluation
Do students learn from them?
How do we improve them?

Implementation

Is the client ready to take responsibility for the course?

Summative Evaluation

Have we solved the problem?

What is the impact?

What needs to change?

ORIENTING QUESTIONS

What is a delivery system?
What is the designer's role in selecting and developing delivery systems?
What technology options are available for delivery systems?
How should you select delivery systems?
How can the designer monitor the development phase to ensure the integrity of the design and the quality of the materials?

OBJECTIVES

1. Given categories of technologies, you will be able to identify delivery systems associated with each.
2. Given learner characteristics, you will be able to develop a learner profile.
3. Given a learner profile, you will be able to recommend grouping and channel options.
4. Given objectives, you will be able to identify channel requirements.
5. Given grouping situations, you will be able to identify the delivery systems most compatible with each.
6. Given an instructional problem including learner, task, grouping, and resource information, you will be able to use a model to select delivery systems and then write a justification to support your selection.
7. Given a role-playing situation, you will be able to explain the designer's role in delivery system selection and development to a client.
8. Given a topic, you will be able to prepare a treatment and part of a script.
9. Given a topic, you will be able to prepare a storyboard for an audiovisual technology.
10. Given a table, you will be able to list ways the designer can ensure the integrity of the design by being involved in the development phase.
11. Given a design project in process, you will be able to select appropriate media and delivery systems and write a rationale for the decisions you have made.

DELIVERY SYSTEM OPTIONS

In the past the word "media" was adequate to describe delivery systems. Media are ways to carry information from a source to a receiver through a channel. With the advent of computerized systems and distance education, however, the word "media" was supplemented with phrases such as "technologies for instruction" and "delivery technology." Media were still used as vehicles for materials, but emerging technologies, such as the World Wide Web and interactive video, presented materials through support systems and had new capacities for interactivity. The combination of media and support systems came to be called delivery systems. Moreover, today when media for instruction are described the term "technology" is often used instead.

A system consists of components that are integrated to work as a whole. Delivery systems are integrated components that facilitate communication by carrying information through channels. Delivery systems are defined as "ways to carry information from a source to a receiver, or vice versa, for the purposes of instruction." The term can be used to describe older technologies, such as traditional media, or newer technologies, such as distance education technologies, or a combination of both.

Delivery system options are grouped by technology areas in order to facilitate discussion and study of these options. The technology areas discussed in this chapter are the subcategories of the Development Domain proposed by Seels and Richey (1994): print, audiovisual, computer, and integrated technologies. These technology categories are given in historical order. Print technologies developed before audiovisual technologies, which developed before computer technologies, which in turn gave rise to integrated technologies. Of course, there were periods of overlap as one technology evolved into another form; for example, motion picture production procedures were used at the beginning of television production. Moreover, the old technologies did not disappear as new technologies evolved. They continued to be used and were often incorporated in new technologies. Thus, motion pictures change form and are incorporated in interactive multimedia. Remember that each technology area includes production, storage, and delivery formats. Sometimes these are the same, but sometimes they differ in significant ways. For example, a dynamic visual presentation may be produced through motion picture film, stored on videotape, and delivered via broadcast television. On the other hand, the presentation might be produced, stored, and delivered via videotape.

Years of practical experience and research are reported in books and articles about choosing and using these technologies. There is far too much information to be covered in this chapter. Instead, we will introduce you to the nature of these technologies and the best references to use to learn the advantages and disadvantages of technologies.

Print Technologies

Print technologies are ways to deliver materials, primarily through mechanical or photographic printing processes. Any medium or material produced through text, graphic, or photographic representation and reproduction falls in this area. These technologies generate materials in hard copy form. Text displayed by a computer is an example of computer-based technology. However, when that text is printed in hard copy to be used in instruction, it is an example of delivery in a print technology form. The options in this category are verbal text materials, visual materials, and materials that combine both forms. Print technologies are usually static with one-way communication, but they have the advantage of allowing the user to reorganize, restructure, and control the pace of learning.

The advantages of print technologies are as follows:

◆ Advances in printing technology make reproducing large quantities of printed material easy and inexpensive.

◆ Desktop publishing makes high-quality presentations easy to create.

◆ Printed information is easily duplicated on office copiers.

◆ Printed information is easily transmitted via telephone lines by fax.

◆ The capacity for information is unlimited; it can range from one page to many volumes.

◆ Print materials do not require equipment for use and are eminently portable.

Audiovisual Technologies

Audiovisual technologies are ways to produce or deliver materials by using mechanical or electronic machines to present auditory and visual messages. Audiovisual machines make possible the projection of motion pictures, the playback of sounds, and the display of large visuals. Thus, audiovisual instruction is characterized by the use of hardware in the teaching/learning process. It does not depend exclusively on students' ability to comprehend words. Sounds and pictures also contribute to learning. Most audiovisual instruction uses a sophisticated combination of audio and visual cues and information. Options within this technology include films, videotapes, audiotapes, slides, transparencies, or any medium based on film or magnetic tape. When television production is combined with computer production, the medium moves to the integrated technologies category. Audiovisual technologies are often teacher centered and involve a lower degree of learner interactivity.

The advantages of audiovisual technologies are as follows:

◆ They are usually easy to use and comprehend because they tend to be linear in nature.

◆ They can present dynamic (having motion) or static visuals or make static visuals dynamic.

◆ The designer can pre-determine the manner in which they are presented and used.

◆ They allow the designer to incorporate principles from both behaviorism and cognitive psychology.

Computer-based Technologies

Computer-based technologies are ways to produce and deliver materials using microprocessor-based resources. They are distinguished from other technologies because information is stored electronically in the form of digital data, rather than as print or visuals in analog form. Computer-based technologies use screen displays to present information to students. The most well known application is computer-based instruction that can deliver tutorials, drill and practice, games and simulations, and databases as learning tools. Computer-based instruction can be used in random, nonsequential ways as well as in linear ways. Content is usually presented abstractly in words, symbols, and graphic displays. Computer-based instruction can provide for a great deal of learner interactivity.

Computer-based technologies have these advantages:

♦ They can be used in random or nonsequential, as well as in linear ways.

♦ They can be used the way the learner desires, as well as in ways the designer/developer has planned.

♦ They are a way to present abstract ideas with words, symbols, and graphics.

♦ It is easy to incorporate principles of cognitive science.

♦ Learning can be student-centered and incorporate high learner interactivity.

Integrated Technologies

Integrated technologies are ways to produce and deliver materials that encompass several forms of media under the control of a computer. There is also a trend to include delivery systems that integrate more than one type of technology, including computers, even though the overall control might not be computerized. Integrated technologies encompass two main types of delivery systems: telecommunications systems used for conferencing, and multimedia systems based on digitized information.

Teleconferencing technologies use computers to enable reception and interactivity across distances when information is transmitted in one of several ways, including telephone lines, microwaves, or cable transmission. Even when transmission is in analog form, computers facilitate necessary connections. These technologies are used for distance learning. As with multimedia technologies, they allow incorporation of other technologies, such as audiovisual technologies. The instructor and students are separated in space, but not in time. When setting the schedule for use of teleconferencing technology, the number of time zones to be covered must be considered. If the goal is to deliver the course to all participants in all time zones during normal business hours, a series of afternoon sessions may have to be scheduled. These technologies connect near and far sites, such as the originating classroom and the remote classroom.

There are many forms of multimedia technologies for instruction, including CD-ROM, videodisc technologies, digital audio technologies, and virtual reality. Integrated technologies involve digital information and systems that integrate powerful hardware and software. They have the advantage of learner control features, which can allow for interactivity and the advantage of combining realistic visuals with text and sound. These technologies can be used in a linear way but usually allow random access. Still, their greatest capability is the integration of words and imagery from many sources with the control for these sources provided through computer software.

Integrated technologies have these advantages:

♦ They can be used in random or nonsequential, as well as linear, ways.

♦ They can be used the way the learner desires, not only in ways the developer planned.

♦ They have the capability to present ideas realistically in a context that the learner can experience.

♦ The learner can determine what is relevant and attend only to that.

♦ Principles of cognitive science and constructivism can be incorporated.

♦ Knowledge can be constructed as the lesson is used, rather than being predetermined.

♦ Materials can incorporate a high degree of interactivity.

♦ Materials can integrate words and imagery from many sources either synchronously or asynchronously.

Sources on Selection

Good references on the advantages and disadvantages of the various technologies are Hackbarth (1996) and Heinich, Molenda, Russell, and Smaldino (1996). There are many books on the production of audiovisual materials, including books by Simonson and Volker (1984) and Kemp and Smellie (1994). References on computer-assisted instruction for the beginning designer include *The Computer-based Training Handbook* by Lee and Mamone (1995) and *Computer-based Instruction: Materials and Development* by Alessi and Trollip (1985). Smith and Boyce (1984) have written about "Instructional Design Considerations in the Development of Computer-assisted Instruction." References for the novice on the characteristics of integrated technologies include *New Technologies for Education* (1997) and *Multimedia Technologies for Training* by Barron and Orwig (1995). *Designing Electronic Performance Support Tools* by Stevens and Stevens (1995) is a good tool for understanding the capabilities of electronic performance support systems. Case studies of distance learning applications are found in *T.H.E. Journal: Technological Horizons in Education.*[1]

DISTANCE LEARNING TECHNOLOGIES

When instruction is delivered at one site and transmitted to another site, distance learning technologies are used. Distance learning utilizes technologies in each of the categories just presented: print, audiovisual, computer-based, and integrated. Table 5.1 presents some of the technologies used for distance education.

In the next section we review and elaborate of each of the technologies presented in Table 5.1.

Print Technologies

Print technologies employ mechanical or photographic printing processes. A medium or material produced through text, graphic, or photographic representation and reproduction falls into this category.

Instructional Printed Materials.   In instructional settings, print materials are used to present written discourse on abstract knowledge and verbal information, as well as instructions on concrete performances, such as assembly and procedural tasks. Print media range from student workbooks used in traditional instructor-led training to self-instructional programmed texts. In programmed test form, print can provide a fair amount of interactivity.

Job Performance Aids (JPAs).   A job aid is a tool that assists workers in performing parts of their job by minimizing the need for recall. In print form, JPAs present procedures and illustrations in formats tailored to the user and to the job requirements. JPAs support and, in some cases, control performance, often dramatically changing the way the job is done. The two most common types are:

◆ *Step-by-step instructions for procedural tasks.* There are two forms: linear and branched. In linear, one step follows another until the task is complete. Most component assembly, or component removal and installation, procedures are linear. In branched procedures, what the next step should be depends on the outcome of the previous step. Troubleshooting tasks are branched because the outcome of one test or reading determines the next appropriate step.

---

[1] *T.H.E. Journal: Technological Horizons in Education* is published monthly by the T.H.E. Journal L.L.C., 150 El Camino Real, Suite 112, Tustin, CA 92680-3670.

Table 5.1 Types of Technologies and Selection Criteria for Distance Delivery

TYPES	PRINT	AUDIOVISUAL	COMPUTER-BASED	TELECONFERENCING	MULTIMEDIA
Definition	Way to deliver text and static visual materials, primarily through mechanical or photographic printing processes.	Way to produce or deliver materials by using mechanical or electronic machines to present auditory and visual material.	Way to produce or deliver materials using microprocessor-based resources	Ways to deliver instruction when the instructor and students are separated in space, but not in time	Way to produce or deliver materials that encompass several forms of media under the control of a computer so that words and images from many sources are integrated
Attributes	• Text is linear • Provides one-way reception • Visuals are static • Learner-centered • Information can be easily reorganized or restructured	• Linear in nature • Visuals are dynamic • Sequence usually predetermined • Presents physical representations of real people and events as well as abstract ideas • Instructor centered • Low degree of interactivity • Presented in real time or on delayed basis	• Used in random, nonsequential, or linear ways • Sequence may be determined by learner or instructional designer • Information presented with words, graphics, photos, and simple animation • Learner centered • Capable of high interactivity	• By definition a live event where the instructor delivers the message using visual aids • Instructor centered • Techniques must be developed to facilitate interactivity	• Used in random, nonsequential, or linear ways • Sequence may be determined by learner or predetermined by instructional designer • Presents physical representations of real people and events as well as abstract ideas • Learner centered • Capable of high interactivity
Examples	• Programmed instruction texts and other instructional documents • Job performance aids (JPAs)	• Videotapes • Audiotapes	• Computer based instruction (CBI) • Electric performance support systems (EPSS) • Web-based training	• Audio teleconferencing • Audiographic teleconferencing • Video teletraining options are: one-way video and two-way audio; two-way video and two-way audio, one-way video and one-way audio • Desktop teleconferencing	• Interactive Videodisc (IVD) • Compact Disc (CD) • Digital Versatile Disc (DVD) • Other technologies

Table 5.1 *Continued*

TYPES	PRINT	AUDIOVISUAL	COMPUTER-BASED	TELECONFERENCING	MULTIMEDIA
Criteria for Distance Delivery	**Text material** • Presentation requirements do not include need for moving visuals or dramatizations • No need for branching (students are relatively homogeneous) • Portability is important **JPAs** Students have competencies to perform task, but: • Seldom-used information tends to be forgotten • Information is too voluminous or procedures are too complex to commit to memory • Consequence of error is detrimental	**Audiotapes** • Presentation requirements for verbal information such as lectures or discussions • Students have low reading ability • No need for branching **Videotapes** • Presentation of moving or still visuals or dramatizations are essential for learning • No need for branching	**CBT & Web-based** • Presentation requirements do NOT include need for physical representations of real people and events • Students are diverse; instruction needs to accommodate individual differences **Web-based** Same as above and • Material is NOT proprietary • Content is fluid. There is need for frequent updates • On-line interactions are essential to learning **EPSS** • Students need tutorials or "just in time" training to perform work processes • Students need on-line help programs or databases to support work processes	**Audio and audiographics** Objectives require voice communication and exchange of graphic displays **Video teletraining that is one-way video and one-way audio** No interaction with students needed **Video teletraining that is one-way video and two-way audio** Instructor does not need to observe students, but students need to see a demonstration and/or visual information **Video teletraining that is two-way video and two-way audio** Same as above, but instructor must observe student performance **Computer conferencing** • Involves interactive data exchange • Participation limited to groups of three or four	**IVD, CD, DVD** • Presentation of physical representations of real people and events are essential for learning • Students are diverse; instruction needs to accommodate individual differences

◆ *Reference manuals.* References may range from simple look-up charts to extensive documentation formatted so that expert performers can quickly obtain the information needed to perform specific, complex tasks. A dictionary is an everyday example of a reference-type JPA.

Audiovisual Technologies

Audiovisual technologies are ways to produce or deliver materials by using mechanical or electronic machines to present auditory and visual messages.

Video-based instruction.   Video-based instruction makes possible the presentation of realistic images and dramatizations, in motion and color, along with sound. It can store and transmit other media forms (slides, transparencies, films, etc.). In instructional settings it can support learners' attention with visual effects such as compressed time (i.e., time lapse), expanded time (i.e., slow motion), enlarged close ups, and telephoto views. In addition, it is teacher centered and involves a low degree of interactivity. Instructional videos used for self-instructional purposes should be accompanied by a guide that focuses the viewer's attention on key elements and summarizes the presentation.

Audio-tutorial instruction.   Audiocassette recordings are an easy-to-use medium for presenting verbal information, such as lectures and discussions. They are most appropriate for self-instructional learning and for individuals with low reading ability. Audio-tutorial instruction can be accompanied by printed material containing specific illustrations referred to in the discussion, or can be listened to when examining or handling an item that is the object of instruction.

Computer-based Technologies

Computer-based technologies are ways to produce and deliver materials using microprocessor-based resources.

Computer-based Training (CBT) or Instruction (CBI).   Computer-based training or instruction can deliver tutorials, drill and practice, and games and simulations. The advantages of CBT and CBI are that they can do the following:

◆ Present a great deal of information, manipulate this information rapidly, and never make a mistake in this manipulation of data.

◆ Deliver dynamic graphics, and the character of the graphics can change through input from the learner.

◆ Ask for student response and respond to the student's response in a relatively individualized manner.

◆ Be adapted to the learner, adjusting the content based on the learner's needs.

◆ Maintain a high level of control over what the learner is allowed to attend to, or it can put the control in the hands of the learner.

◆ Retain and analyze progress records and use this information to adapt future instructional sequences.

Web-based Training.   Web-based training has the same characteristics as CBT; however, there are several factors to consider in the development of Web-based documents. Different browsers support different page markup capabilities, so a page design for a high-end browser may not be readable by a participant using a less capable browser. In addition to the features of CBT, Web-based training does the following:

- Provides instantaneous feedback mechanism to students and instructors.
- Provides instructors with the ability to revise instructional content as often as necessary.
- Uses live chats with instructors to review sessions. Time zones must be considered when scheduling chat sessions. Other software considerations come into play when interactive chats and discussion groups are used.
- Integrates a bulletin board system into a website to encourage student cooperation on specific subjects and assignments. These discussion groups can serve as a vehicle for the dissemination of new instructional materials, new assignments, and review sessions.
- Allows students, through secure e-mail, to submit work of a more qualitative nature such as an essay.
- Provides information in a more timely manner than CBT disseminated via diskette or CD-ROM. To furnish timely updates for a CBT solution, it may be necessary to use a type of on-line vehicle such as a File Transfer Protocol (FTP) site or a PC-based bulletin board system. It is much more cost effective to update the content of a website.

Electronic Performance Support Systems (EPSS).   Electronic performance support systems are a way to deliver instruction to personnel in highly computerized work environments with on-line references, automated decision support, and just-in-time training that they can access on-demand to meet task-related information requirements. EPSS is most effective when supporting routine standardized tasks that can be accurately documented and that require standardized actions. Elements that make up EPSS include:

- information in the form of databases (text, visual, audio, and knowledge bases);
- systems that support achieving a performance objective, such as expert systems that help solve problems (e.g., spreadsheet applications, help systems that give demonstrations, assessment systems that evaluate skills, and feedback systems);
- an interface that facilitates the use of applications that require a variety of software; and
- a system for tracking performance and recording data that can be helpful to students, employers, and designers.

Some advantages of EPSSs are:

- Standardizing training and performance throughout the organization. When the work force is using the same tools, references, and training materials, consistency is maximized.
- Reducing the amount of time spent on off-line training, because workers learn on the job.
- Updating information on an immediate and consistent basis.
- Reducing errors, because all workers have immediate and constant access to expert support.

Just as there are levels of interactivity in computer-based instruction, there are levels of performance support that require increasing sophistication. Although the first level does not require CBI, levels 2 through 4 do. The first level is on-the-job training in which a supervisor or colleague provides support. Level 2 consists of separate computer applications that support instruction, such as databases, help programs, and tutorials. Level 3 occurs when several of these functions are programmed within one application, such as Hypercard. Level 4 is reached when an interface is used to integrate several computer applications that serve several functions. At this level, the computer also allows sophisticated tracking that is used by an organization for monitoring performance and learning. This is the level that EPSS represent.

Teleconferencing

Teleconferencing technologies are classified as integrated technologies, because they operate to some extent through computer technologies and use digitized information for telecommunications. They also integrate several types of technologies into a system for instructional purposes.

Audio Teleconferencing.   Audio teleconferencing provides voice communication only. It closely resembles a normal telephone conference call. Transmissions are analog and require little more than a simple audio bridge that routes calls from multiple remote locations. The calls can be placed by the instructor, or all participants can call into a designated number at a scheduled start time. To facilitate interaction, the instructor will have to poll participants.

Audiographic Teleconferencing.   This is a form of audio conferencing with the addition of graphic exchanges through facsimile and computer technologies. Effectively, this is a fancy phone call wherein users can share PC managed data while maintaining voice communications. Audiographics is a mainstay of desktop teleconferencing. The majority of interaction is with the data portion of a shared screen. Audiographic applications software does not necessarily work from one vendor to another.

Video Teletraining.   Video teletraining combines full motion video with audio in a synchronous mode. Transmission technologies are satellite or terrestrial (microwave, cable, or telephone). By definition VTT is a live event. The key to success is ensuring the desired level of interactivity from the remote sites to meet the training objectives. Full interactivity may not always be feasible, and a poorly processed video signal may diminish screen resolution and become a communication barrier. Networking problems are exponential when networking multi-point to multi-point sites, especially when audio and video signals are being sent from multiple sites in addition to control data in the transport layer. There are limits on the number of locations that can be linked. Some design options that must be considered when implementing VTT are:

◆ one-way video and two-way audio;

◆ two-way video and two-way audio;

◆ one-way video and one-way audio;

◆ analog or digital transmission; and

◆ classroom or individual workstation configuration.

Computer Conferencing.   Computer conferencing involves interactive data exchange between multiple terminals, normally over standard telephone lines. In addition to routine data passing, computer conferencing systems hosted by mini or main-frame systems are able to collect document sets and maintain a full file. In less sophisticated systems, files are overwritten with the entry of a new file document. All data passed is digital, and a modem is required for external communication. E-mail and electronic bulletin boards can be used for computer conferencing. Less formal computer conferencing, such as group debriefing, is also possible using commercial software products. Computer conferencing has the advantage of allowing users to meet interactively in a synchronous conference or receive, store, and forward in an asynchronous mode (e.g., e-mail). Configurations of the workstations and screen size limit the number of people who can participate in a synchronous computer conference at a location.

Interactive Multimedia

Interactive multimedia technologies are considered integrated technologies because they are ways to produce, store, and deliver materials that encompass several forms of media under the control of a computer.

Interactive Videodisc (IVD).   Interactive videodisc combines the positive instructional benefits of video-based instruction and computer-based instruction. It uses an 8- or 12-inch laser disc that stores information optically. Frames can be accessed with barcode readers, remote controls, or computers. These video and recording and storage systems record audio-visual signals on plastic discs rather than magnetic tape.

Compact Disc (CD).   A disc on which a laser has recorded information digitally, such as audo, video, or computer data. Although it measures about 4.72 inches in diameter, a CD is usually described as a five-inch disc. Different forms of CD technology include Digital Video Interactive (DVI), Compact Disc-Interactive (CD-i), Compact Disc-Read Only Memory (CD-ROM), and Compact Disc-Audio (CD-Audio).

For example, DVI is a technology used to digitize video before storing it on a CD. It allows over an hour of full motion video to be stored on a five-inch CD. This is possible because audio and video are compressed and decompressed to create multimedia applications.

CD-i, on the other hand, is a technology for using CDs interactively. A CD-i system requires both hardware and software, i.e., a computer and television system, that utilizes a CD for storage. CD-i discs combine audio, video, graphics, and text that provide a basis for interactivity when used with a CD-i system consisting of a display monitor and computer programming.

CD-ROM is a storage medium. Like other digital multimedia technologies, CD-ROMs have built-in compatibility with the computer. A CD-ROM is a prerecorded disc that stores over 600 megabytes of data. This is equivalent to about 300,000 pages of text, 10,000 photographic images, or over an hour of video. Basically, the technology stores data, text, visuals, and graphics in digital form on a CD so that it can be retrieved by the computer. When combined with digital audio circuitry and speakers, a CD-ROM can turn a personal computer into a multimedia computer. However, sometimes CD-ROM technology is used to store text and graphics only, such as when an encyclopedia or parts manual is stored on CD-ROM. The CD-ROM becomes interactive only when it is linked with a computer hardware configuration that provides this capability.

CD-Audio is a storage medium that provides for 74 minutes of sound. The audio stored on a CD cannot be changed or revised. A CD-Audio does not allow for interactivity, although it can be used when developing interactive multimedia materials, because the audio is easy to access through time code.

Digital Versatile Disc (DVD).   This is a new generation of CD format that is being developed by a consortium of the largest computer, consumer electronics, and entertainment companies. It provides for increased storage capacity and performance, especially for video and multimedia applications. Eventually, it may replace half-inch videotape (VHS), CD-Audio, and CD-ROM because it increases storage capacity and access and transfer speeds. The process of authoring can differ for CD and DVD technologies.

Virtual Reality.   Through computer interfacing a virtual reality system presents a three-dimensional representation of an environment and responds to the user's motion within that environment. It is a form of advanced simulation that allows learners to manipulate objects using simulation control devices such as gloves and headsets. The learner feels the sensations of moving about and being in that environment. A series of still pictures of a room can be turned into a tour using virtual reality which adds motion and creates objects that are perceived in 3-D form.

Exercise A provides practice in identifying media and delivery system options.

SELECTING DELIVERY SYSTEMS

It is important to clarify the meanings of "media systems" and "delivery systems." Although these terms are often used interchangeably, they have different roots historically. The term "media" has been used for a long time to connote a means of communication, a way to carry information between a source and receiver. Another way of describing a medium would be materials used over a channel to facilitate communication. We all think of newspapers and television as mass media, and slides and photographs as media used in teaching. More recently, however, a new type of medium has evolved that uses traditional media in combination with support systems to deliver instruction. For example, the World Wide Web and interactive television (two-way video) are delivery systems because they provide instructional materials via a computerized system. Thus, the term delivery system has come into usage with the move to integrated technologies. Typically, new technologies become absorbed in the larger palette of media options and are considered just another way of communicating, in other words another media.

Procedures for selecting media and delivery systems have been presented in forms of ISD models known as media selection models. Examples of such models are Kemp, Morrison, and Ross (1994) and Reiser and Gagné (1983). Many of these models incorporate similar criteria for selection of delivery systems. The selection criteria commonly used include learner and task characteristics, grouping, and practicality or feasibility. The Seels and Glasgow Model for Selecting Media and Delivery Systems presented in this chapter incorporates these criteria. Selection criteria will be discussed next.

Selection Criteria

Learner Characteristics.   Another criterion is learner characteristics. For example, motivation or preferences can affect attention and learning. Learners who find a medium frustrating will learn less. Materials must be appropriate for the learner's level of ability. Learners need the pre-entry skills necessary for success with the media or delivery system.

You can use information on learner characteristics to profile the intended learner. Such a profile can include age, sex, educational level, achievement level, socio-economic background, learning style, experience, attitudes, role perceptions, and perceived needs. In addition to providing a basis for delivery system selection, such information may also be useful when you decide on objectives or assessment strategies and when you choose an instructional strategy or design messages. For example, some research suggests that high-ability students achieve less when provided with more instructional support such as cues, structure, and provision for frequent responding. You can take this information about the learner into account when selecting instructional strategies (McGowan & Clark, 1985). If you know that the learners have low verbal skills, you will be more careful about the verbal form of your test items. You will not use all the information, but it is difficult at this point to know which information may be useful. The best strategy is to collect any information you think may be useful. If you are sure you will not need certain kinds of information, such as sex or educational level, you need not waste time collecting it.

To construct a learner profile you need to find out about both individual learners and the range of learners in a class. Then, you fill the information in on a chart such as shown in Table 5.2.

Task Characteristics.   Task characteristics refer to unique requirements for learning related to learning goals. They can include appropriateness to types of learning and to channel requirements. Using concrete objects when physical discriminations have to be learned is an example of choosing a medium appropriate for the type of learning. "Channel" refers to the sensory mode in which the instruction is delivered. A learner has a choice of audio, visual, audiovisual, kinesthetic, or tactile channels. For most learners and most learning tasks an effective combination of audio and visual is most effective.

Table 5.2 Learner Profile Chart

Characteristic	Representative Learner	Range for Learners
Age		
Sex		
Educational Level		
Achievement Level		
Socio-economic Background		
Learning Style		
Verbal Ability		
Relevant Experience		
Attitude		
Interest		

Grouping.   The choice of media depends on whether instruction is to be by a large group, small group, or independent study method. A television tape prepared for a large group lecture can differ from one prepared for a small discussion group. A filmstrip can be suitable for independent study but generally not for a large group lecture. A decision about grouping determines whether the instruction will be in a large group, small group, or independent study situation. This decision has important implications for the use of technology. The technologies appropriate to each situation differ as does the way a technology should be used. Large group presentations demand different uses of technology than small group or independent study situations. A series of slides used for large group instruction is probably going to be presented in a lecture. The same slides used for self-instruction will probably be incorporated through a manual or computer program. Projected visuals are an important technology for large group instruction. In a small group the only technology needed might be an experienced teacher or group leader. In other words, technology might not be needed. On the other hand, maybe an audio conference is warranted, and microphones and speakers are required for a discussion group.

Practicality.   A final critical consideration is practicality. If there is no time for production or no resources to produce a medium, do not select it. The most expensive or time-consuming medium is not always the best. If the equipment necessary for production or development, for delivery, or for storage is not available and there are no funds for rental of such equipment, then the delivery system is not feasible.

A Model for Selecting Delivery Systems

The model for selecting media and delivery systems shown in Figure 5.2 assumes that one set of decisions should be based on another set of decisions.

Figure 5.2 The Seels & Glasgow Model for Selecting Delivery Systems

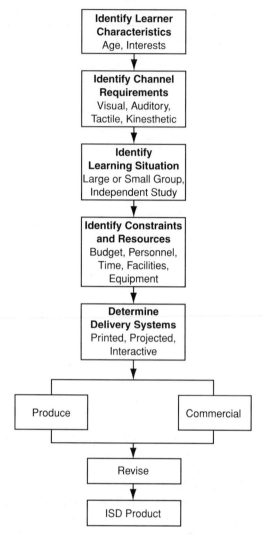

Identify Learner Characteristics.   It is good to begin by identifying relevant learner characteristics, such as age, attention span, language ability, learning style, preferences, and interests. This criterion encompasses demographic characteristics, such as age, maturity, socio-economic background, and geographic region; cognitive style characteristics, such as sequential/global, sensory/intuitive, inductive/deductive, active/reflective, and field dependent/independent; ability characteristics, such as language, attention span, intelligence, interpersonal skills; and attitude characteristics, such as preferences, interests, and motivation. Learning style refers to traits that characterize how a learner prefers to learn. A student may find one perceptual channel more comfortable than another. Generally, we speak of tactile, visual, and auditory learners.

Learner characteristics may be psychological, physical, or sociological. Each characteristic has implications for media selection. Psychological characteristics, such as ability, motivation, and learning style, should be used to determine the desired difficulty and appeal of the material. Physical characteristics, such as need for mobility, can influence the decision about which media will be most effective. Sociological characteristics, such as socio-economic background, may have a bearing on entry level skills.

Identify Channel Characteristics.   It is important to identify channel requirements early in the process of selection. The channel is the perceptual modes needed for presentation, practice, and feedback. Usually, the same modes are used for each, but sometimes they differ. For example, a student may study music theory from a book, practice it on a piano, and respond to an audiotape when being assessed. It is best to assess in the same media used for instruction. Perceptual mode requirements come from objectives and learning characteristics. The designer can select from audio, visual, audiovisual, kinesthetic, tactile, or olfactory sensory inputs. If the task is to discriminate visually, use the visual channel. If the learner prefers to learn visually, that is another reason for using the visual channel through a medium that offers pictures.

Identify the Learning Situation.   You can identify the learning situation based on whether instruction will be large or small, group or independent study. A textbook may be effective in independent study, but not in a large group presentation where group pacing is required. Each of the technology categories (print, audiovisual, computer-based, and integrated) offers options for each grouping. However, some categories have more affinity for one type of grouping. For example, print technologies are more likely to be appropriate for independent study. Computer-based technologies are also often most appropriate for independent study. Audiovisual technologies, on the other hand, are easily adapted to all three grouping situations. Audiotapes are most useful for independent study. Slides and videotapes can be used for each of the grouping situations. Integrated technologies can be projected, but are usually used in independent or small group situations. Still, it is not the technology option, but whether it can be designed for the purpose of the grouping situation, that should be the basis for selection.

Identify Constraints and Resources.   Constraints are limitations or parameters that must be taken into account in the design specifications. Resources give you the flexibility necessary to take constraints into account. This information allows you to determine options for production, storage, and delivery. Resources are determined by the expertise, equipment, and budget available.

Determine Delivery System Options.   After options appropriate for the learner characteristics, channel requirements, learning situation, and constraints and resources are identified, then the type of media or delivery systems to be used are selected. Remember that feasibility is an important criterion when you select options.

Obtain or Produce Materials and Revise.   Because media and delivery systems require materials, you must determine whether commercial materials are available and, if so, whether they need revising. If not, you must determine what materials will be produced. These materials can be produced locally or obtained commercially. Sometimes they are even produced non-locally. Often, a combination of locally produced and commercially available materials are used. To determine what is available, searches of indexes, sourcebooks, and catalogs are done.

The information gathered through steps 6 through 8 may lead you to choose another medium or delivery system or to modify your plans. Decisions about modification should involve all stakeholders including clients, designers, producers, evaluators, and users. Nevertheless, the designer continues to be responsible for the integrity of the design and to bear the major responsibility for monitoring the design through the ISD process.

If you decide to use commercial materials, be sure you follow any provisions of the copyright law that affect your use of them. This means you must obtain permission to include or adapt the materials in the final product. A good source on copyright provisions for utilization of commercial materials is Heinich et al. (1996). This book also has lists of comprehensive and specialized information sources on commercial materials. The specialized sources are divided by type of media or delivery system.

Searches for materials can now be done electronically through on-line services and CD-ROM discs. The most comprehensive sources that can be searched electronically are the NICEM (National Information Center for Educational Media) indexes. NICEM offers these indexes on both CD-ROM and in printed directories: *International Directory of Educational Audiovisuals*, which contains 300,000 entries, and A-V Online on SilverPlatter, which contains 420,000 entries. These electronic indexes cover library collections including the Library of Congress and publisher's catalogs.

Other comprehensive sources are the *Guides to Free and Inexpensive Materials* published by Educators Progress Service, *The Multimedia and Videodisc Compendium* published by Emerging Technology Consultants, and the media resource catalogs available from the National Audiovisual Center. This center is responsible for distribution of all U. S. government produced media.

It is the designer's job to determine what materials if any can be obtained to be used with a delivery system. This means that (a) you decide what materials would be appropriate, (b) you search for commercially available materials, and (c) you identify what materials could be produced and/or purchased.

Make Final Selections. The media selection process is completed when final media and delivery system decisions about an ISD product are made.

This model is useful only when you can connect decisions to media characteristics. The ability to do this comes from broad experience with using media. An instructional designer should try to obtain such experience. A lengthy discussion of this topic, however, is beyond the scope of this book.

The decisions you have made so far enable you to specify delivery systems and media at this stage. Sometimes you have to defend your decisions orally, sometimes in writing, and sometimes not at all. Regardless, to be sure of the quality of your decisions, it is best to write a delivery system justification explaining your choices of delivery system, media, and materials. This justification or rationale is based on the process you just followed. Explain the constraints and resources you identified and how they relate to possible options and materials. Then, explain why you narrowed the options to the ones you are recommending, for example, on the basis of feasibility within timelines. Relate the choices to cost and need. Traditionally, written justifications are used in ISD as a way to increase the possibility of budget approval.

In summary, this model provides a rationale for media selection; the rationale illustrates how a systematic process was followed to determine appropriate media and delivery systems. Thus, a designer can justify decisions because the connections between parameters and media or delivery systems are made logically. The systematic process the model provides ensures the logic will be complete and consistent.

AN EXAMPLE OF SELECTION OF DELIVERY SYSTEMS

Let's examine a product in use to see how the selection of delivery systems relates to other steps in ISD. The product we will examine, Standard First Aid, is typical of courses offered by the American Red Cross. It is based on a task analysis done from the Standards and Guidelines established by a national conference on cardiopulmonary resuscitation and emergency cardiac care, and on information provided by the Division of Medical Science, National Academy of Sciences, National Research Council. Medical care professionals and educators, as well as representatives of volunteers, staff, and field personnel, constituted the design and development team. The content is divided into discrete topical units presented in sections with emergency action units in one section and secondary action units in the other section.

The course went through technical review and field testing at many Red Cross chapters. The learner was defined as an adult who assumes responsibility for care of another adult until emergency medical services arrive. The learner is told that he or she will learn to stay calm because they will know what to do and to make decisions and take appropriate steps to keep a victim alive.

The course begins by explaining that pre-entry conditions (known as health precautions guidelines) include freedom from infection and informing the instructor of any infections, and knowledge of guidelines for sterile precautions and prevention of stress. The course itself consists of materials, activities, and assessment procedures. The materials used include a textbook with objectives, information, and action guides in the form of skill sheets to guide and assess practice. The skill sheets consist of photographs and text that illustrate proper positions and actions sequentially. In addition, videotaped demonstrations of skills are used, and a manikin is used for practice.

Several activities are used to integrate the use of materials. One activity takes the form of practice on a partner and a manikin. Skill checks are done by partners and by instructors. Thus, two other types of assessment are incorporated in the course: written tests and skills tests. Questions are tested after each section of the course, and instructors check skill performance using checklists. At the end of the course, the learner takes the textbook for reference and receives a certificate if successful.

This course is described because it exemplifies an ISD product that takes into account a small group instruction setting and the availability of an instructor. This course is a good example of media and delivery system selection based on constraints, such as a wide range of learner characteristics and one session training, and resources, such as instructors, manikins, and print materials as needed. Other delivery options may have been considered, but the final decisions were appropriate based on feasibility (American National Red Cross, 1993).

Exercises B, C, D, E, and F provide practice in selecting media and delivery systems.

THE DESIGNER'S ROLE

The instructional designer has many functions to fulfill during the delivery systems step. The designer can function as a decision-maker who selects technology options, as a quality control expert who sees that instructional design recommendations are implemented, or as a manager who initiates and evaluates development. In this chapter you will read about the designer's role in the realization of the design, the options available for delivery systems, how you make decisions, and how you initiate and monitor the development process.

You must consciously limit your role to the functions you can perform and finish effectively. Beware of also becoming the media producer, the photographer, or the programmer. It is challenging to try to make others understand that you will not be able to do all the production or that it may be more advisable for you to coordinate with a production team than to lead one.

Essential Responsibilities

The designer's responsibilities are to determine delivery system options, select the delivery systems, determine how the materials necessary for implementation will be obtained or produced, and as either a team member or leader monitor the development process. You cannot do all this well if you also serve as photo researcher, scriptwriter, photographer, and editor. This does not mean that you never produce or help edit. It means that you are aware of your guidance function and your skill limitations. You know, for example, that your group process skills are more developed and will be more useful than your photographic skills.

Often the designer is told at the beginning of the project what delivery systems are to be used. If this is the case, it is the designer's responsibility to examine the choice and counsel the client on the appropriateness. Often, the same design results can be achieved through one of several technologies. This is because how the technology is used is as important as the choice of technology. If, however, the learning situation seems a poor match to the delivery system chosen, perhaps for reasons of cost, then the designer should make the client aware there are cheaper or better delivery systems for the situation. Suppose the client has reasons for staying with the original delivery system decisions. It could be that use of that delivery system increases chances of receiving funding. What does the designer do in this situation? It is quite reasonable to accept that delivery system and modify parts of the design or situation so that justification is still possible. The delivery system then becomes a design constraint as well as a resource and as such must be taken into account.

Confronting Costs

Often it is necessary to help the client decide whether to make the financial commitment required for a recommended delivery system. Financial commitment involves allocating funds for development of the delivery system, allocating the start-up funds for implementing the system once it is developed, and finally allocating funds for offering the course on an on-going basis. By estimating these costs, you can present the financial requirements. The client can then decide if the investment is warranted.

Development costs start with the analysis phase of ISD and end after formative evaluation in the development phase. Start-up costs are those associated with the implementation phase of ISD. Ongoing costs are those incurred to deliver the course on a continuing basis. These costs will differ depending on the delivering system chosen and the number of students expected to take the course.

One of the best ways to present costs is to compare the cost of offering the course using different delivery systems. To help you understand how this is done, we present an example taken from a cost analysis done for the Emergency Management Institute (EMI) in Emitsburg, Maryland (Glasgow and Cox, 1993). EMI offers resident courses in a campus-like setting. Resident courses require students to be away from their jobs and homes for several days or even weeks. The demand for training at the EMI exceeded available capacity. The cost of providing training was increasing, while federal, state, and local training budgets shrank. To address these problems EMI explored a program that redeveloped resident courses into a program of distance education to improve instructional effectiveness, increase availability of the courses, improve the quality and consistency of training, and reduce overall costs to EMI and its students.

Cost Analysis.   Estimating costs for developing a new version of a course is fairly straightforward. However, it is more difficult to pinpoint startup and ongoing costs. Why do you need to include startup and ongoing costs? Because amortizing the development costs with implementation and maintenance costs presents a truer picture. Development costs associated with technology are often high, but maintenance costs are usually low compared to traditional instruction. By amortizing the costs, high development costs are offset by lower maintenance costs. To make decisions about delivery systems clients need more information than development costs. Table 5.3 defines some of the startup and ongoing cost considered in analyzing the cost effectiveness of alternative delivery systems for EMI.

Estimating startup and ongoing costs is problematic, because these costs are highly integrated, making it extremely difficult to isolate and allocate costs accurately. Facilities, equipment, and devices are often shared among departments and institutions (Levine, 1990).

One of the courses EMI considered for redevelopment was the E438 Community Rating System. This course is for National Flood Insurance Program (NFIP) State Coordinators and local and regional officials performing flood plain management services for local governments. The course consists of 10 lessons and lasts four and a half days. Approximately 165 people take the course each year.

The recommendation was to convert the course to a programmed text and offer it as a self-study course. Table 5.4 presents the cost comparisons between the classroom version of the course and the self-study version. Costs for the classroom version are based on actual costs for the current course. Costs for the self-study version are estimated on the designer's experience with similar efforts.

Redevelopment Costs.   As Table 5.4 shows, the redevelopment costs are about three times higher for the programmed self-study version.

Table 5.3 Explanation of Terms for Cost Analysis

STARTUP COSTS

Item	Definition
Instructor Training	Cost for one instructor to be trained to offer the course
Administration Training	Cost for one administrator to be trained to perform registration, tracking, and materials distribution tasks
Diffusion	Course manager's hourly rate marketing
Travel	Cost for the course manager's travel and lodging while marketing the ADF
Instructor Travel	Cost for the instructor travel and lodging during training
Capital Expenditures	Cost for one-time equipment purchases

ONGOING COSTS

Item	Definition
Instructors	Hourly rate for teaching the course
Administrator	Hourly rate for administering the course
Reduced Student Time	The amount by which costs are reduced due to early completion in self-study
Satellite Uplink	Cost associated with use of studio and transmission for videoconferencing
Lodging	Cost for student's housing and meals on campus
Student Manuals	Cost for one manual
Instructor Guide	Cost for one manual
Postage	Postage costs for mailing a course packet to a student
AV Materials	Cost for videocassettes, slides, overheads associated with the course
Diskettes	Cost for one diskette
Maintenance	Annual upkeep of AV equipment (estimated)
Travel	Cost for round trip student travel to attend training
Facility	Cost for room rentals, copy costs, postage, etc.
Telephone	Cost per minute for student/instructor conferences
AV Equipment	Cost for VCRs, TVs, slide projectors, overhead projectors associated with the course
Course Manager	Labor cost for monitoring one course offering

Startup Costs. Although the course is self-study, an instructor will be available to answer student questions. Instructor training for the programmed text is assumed to consist of a one-day orientation to the new procedures and equipment. Equipment expenditure is for installation of a voice mail and audio conferencing system to facilitate instruction and student interactions. There are costs to prepare the staff responsible

Table 5.4 Cost Comparison for E438 Community Rating System

	Redevelopment	Startup	Ongoing
Classroom	$15,675	$ 3,200	$101,160
Programmed text	$45,743	$ 63,228	$ 41,770

for handling registration, mailing self-study materials, tracking completion, and using the new system. Finally, there are costs associated with promoting the new version of the course in 50 states. Startup costs are about 20 times higher for the self-study version than for the classroom version.

Ongoing Costs.   Ongoing costs are for labor costs associated with registering, tracking, and distributing the materials, as well as instructor time for conferring with students. Savings of almost $70,000 per year are realized by the self-study version from reductions in travel and lodging costs.

Differences in Cost.   Due to savings in the ongoing costs, redevelopment and startup costs are recaptured in the second year of the alternative delivery systems. Over a seven-year period, almost $500 million are saved.

The new self-study version of the course is expected to reduce the time students spend in training and therefore away from work by about 25%. These savings accrue to state and local government entities that employ the students, not to EMI. They are not reflected in Table 5.4. However, the savings should be publicized to potential users as a benefit of the new version.

The Client's Point of View.   Based on the cost analysis, the client has the data to decide whether to make the upfront financial commitment to develop and implement the self-study course or to remain with the current program. The client may inform you that the estimated expense is not warranted. If the client won't make the necessary financial commitment, it is better to face that fact early in the project and recommend alternate delivery systems. Another result of cost analysis may be that you inform the client that more is being spent than is necessary. For example, it may be more desirable to mail out videocassettes than to use videoconferencing, especially with the cost of uplinking.

Exercise G provides practice in explaining the designer's role.

THE PRODUCTION PROCESS

The designer's input into the production process is usually a lesson plan that incorporates commercial or locally produced materials. Sometimes the project allows for materials produced with higher production values. Whatever the case, if you cannot adopt or adapt commercial materials, then you must arrange for the materials to be produced. Although it is unlikely you will produce the materials, you could be a member of the production team. Your best chance of being able to function effectively on that team is to understand the production process intimately. Every designer should have experience scripting, shooting, and editing in order to communicate with producers. To insure the integrity of the design, you need to monitor each stage of production to make sure that design guidelines are followed, that consistency is maintained from step to step, and that quality is evident.

From Treatment to Storyboard

The production process, which you initiate by contract and agreement, starts with conceptualizing by scripting and storyboarding. You may be involved creatively at this stage or you may be monitoring the work of others. In either case, it is important that you understand the process that leads to the visual (or audio) instructional material. There are many commonalities among production processes for different technologies. Production usually includes phases such as pre-production, production (including generating images), and post-production (including editing).

The process follows three steps if the end product is to be visual material. The first step is a treatment, then a script is based on the treatment, and finally a storyboard is based on the script. Each step becomes a more concrete plan for the final product.

Treatment.   Let's start with a treatment. A treatment is a one- to two-page (usually less) description of how the material will be organized, the approach to be taken, and the content. Figure 5.3 is a description of a sound slide presentation proposed for a township.

A treatment should describe the content of the visual presentation and the approach to that content. For example, a presentation can have a dramatic, humorous, factual, historical, or how-to treatment. The treatment should also specify any special aesthetic elements such as music or artwork or artwork style. You may wish to prepare for a treatment by preparing your storyline. How will your story be presented or your storylines interweave (Simonson & Volker, 1984)?

Scripting.   After a treatment is proposed and accepted, work can begin on a script. The script will make the idea even more specific by detailing the audio and visual material for each frame. At this point the visual material can be described in phrases, using abbreviations for technical terminology, rather than in sketches. LS, MS, CU, and ES, for example, stand for long shot, medium shot, close-up, and establishing shot, respectively. Figure 5.4 was written for adults who have been ordered to undergo a Magnetic Resonance Imaging (MRI) body or head scan to aid diagnosis of their medical problem. These people will range from grade school to college educated and in age from adolescent to geriatric and for the most part will possess little knowledge of MRI technology. The goal of the slide presentation will be to educate these people about what it is they will undergo in order to make them as emotionally comfortable going into the procedure as possible.

Figure 5.3 Example of a Treatment for a Slide Presentation

**Project Treatment
Recreational Parks and Our Township**

After titles and series of slides of signs at park entrances in neighboring townships, the narrator explains that the purpose of the presentation is to stimulate discussion on recreation planning in our township by presenting comparisons with similar townships.

The presentation will be organized as a series of visits to parks in neighboring townships. Facts about their recreation program, e.g., per capita expenditure, will be interspersed with the narration of their parks. The presentation will conclude with a history of our township's recreation planning and investment in parks. Graphics will be used at the end to summarize per capita investment and proportion of land. The presentation will conclude with text slides that stimulate open-ended discussion by posing questions.

Figure 5.4 Example of a Script on Having an MRI Scan

Visual (Slides)	Audio
	Flute music over
Front of MRI Center with sign as seen from driveway	Narrator: Your doctor has scheduled you for magnetic resonance imaging, or MRI. We would like you to feel as comfortable as possible during the procedure, so we have put together this program on MRI for your information.
	Flute music down
Several shots of different MRI scans: head/abd/ chest/spine "NO RADIATION" slide	MRI, also called NMR for "nuclear magnetic resonance," is used as a diagnostic tool by your physician. This technology is something like X-rays in that it produces pictures, or IMAGES, of the inside of the body. However, these images are more informative than regular X-rays. In addition, the MRI procedure exposes you to NO radiation. In fact, in extensive research with animals and in clinical trials with human beings, MRI has been shown to be a virtually harmless procedure.
Physician looking at scan	MRI will allow your doctor to see more clearly the difference between healthy and diseased tissue, and he will thus be able to develop the most appropriate treatment plan for you.
Figure 1 Figure 2	How does magnetic resonance imaging work? Your body is made up of millions of atoms. Under normal conditions, the protons in these atoms spin randomly. But when the strong magnetic fields of the MRI scanner are passed through your body, these protons line up in the field's directions.
Figure 3	Then the radio wave is transmitted to the magnetic field. This causes the protons to change direction 90° and spin together.
Figure 4	When the radio waves are turned off, the protons return to the alignment they had in the magnetic field. During this realignment, they give off a signal that is measured by a receiver antenna. This antenna is connected to a computer that compiles the information and produces an image.
	Flute music over
Close-up of MRI Center entranceway with patient coming in	Narrator: When you come to the MRI Institute for your scan, you should plan to spend 2 to 3 hours with us. First, you will be asked to complete some medical insurance information.
Tech and patient talking (MS)	Then a technician or a nurse will question you about your medical history and will answer any questions you might have.
	Flute music down
Text slide of list	You will not be able to have an MRI scan if any of the following applies to you: if you have a cardiac pacemaker in place if you have had an operation for aneurysm of the brain if you have any metal implants or shrapnel anywhere in your body if you are in the first trimester of pregnancy if you weigh over three hundred pounds
Tech giving patient tranquilizer	If you have extreme claustrophobia, please tell the technician before the start of the test. You will be administered a mild tranquilizer to help you cope with the confined quarters of the scanning tube.

Note: Script by Barbara Good, Medical Writer, Allegheny Singer Research Institute, Pittsburgh, Pennsylvania.

Interactive Media. The production planning process for interactive technologies such as those stored on CD-ROM are more complex. A typical process for this technology would be to complete a flowchart and then do screen design. Finally, text similar to a script might be written. These steps can also be done concurrently. Figure 5.6 illustrates this process. The hexagon shapes in this flowchart represent processes just as the rectangles do. A different shape was used to make it easier to distinguish layers in the navigation. The plain hexagons indicate the main menu, while the shadowed hexagons represent menu choices that lead to more extensive flowcharting shown on separate pages. The page symbol replaces the circle used for a connector and was used because it stands out from the other symbols more.

Relationship of Script/Storyboard Process to Development

The script/storyboard process is only the beginning of the development process. It is part of the pre-production stage in development. It allows the designer to discuss conceptualization with producers who bring a great deal of creativity and experience in actualization of ideas to the ISD process. After consensus is reached on conceptualization, there is still much to be done before a product is developed. The steps that follow vary from technology to technology. Moreover, they are the responsibility of the production part of the ISD team, not the designer. Therefore, they are beyond the scope of this book. Nevertheless, as stated previously, it is important for the designer to understand the production process so that communication within the ISD team is facilitated.

During the production stage the script/storyboard takes physical form as video is shot, photographs are taken, text is drafted, or programs are written. As ISD products take physical form in the pre-production, production, and post-production stages, formative evaluation is ongoing. Revisions are made continually during development and reevaluated immediately. During the post-production stage, editing and final printing occur.

It is impossible to review the production process for each media or delivery system within this chapter, especially since that process also varies project to project. One of the designer's jobs can be to develop or help develop the flowchart of the ISD process planned for the project including the development or production phase. A project manager is often responsible for the flow of the project activities and the visualization of the overall process. How to manage a project team will be discussed in chapter 9.

To give you an example, Figure 5.7 presents a flowchart of the development process used for an IVD or a digital video interactive (DVI) product. DVI products store multimedia applications on compact discs. IVD applications usually involve Level III interactivity whereby a videodisc player is controlled by a computer.

Levels of interactivity is a concept used in multimedia instruction to indicate the amount of control a learner has and the hardware and software configuration used to achieve that control.

Level I interactivity, the lowest level, is when the videodisc player is used alone without a computer attached to it. Level II interactivity can also be achieved without a computer, because a program is embedded in the videodisc itself. This program cannot be changed or updated. The user interacts through the remote control unit. With the addition of a computer for Level III interactivity, the program can branch, access databases, and store student performance data and records. This is the highest and most flexible level of interactivity (Barron & Orwig, 1995).

The product of the process shown in Figure 5.7 is intended to be used at Level III. Note that the script/storyboard phase is only a small part of the process. It is, however, the most important part of the process for the designer who participates in production.

Exercises H and I provide practice in skills in development.

Storyboarding.   The final step in the conceptualization process is often a storybo
storyboard is a script translated into still pictures. Each shows a successive fram
ment of the proposed presentation. A storyboard can take many forms—th
sketches on index cards, stick figures on a page with frames on one side and a col
narration on the other, or photographs, with comments below.

Whatever form it takes, the storyboard makes the visual part of the script m
cific so that the producer knows the camera angles and the graphics that will be i
From a storyboard a producer can prepare a shooting script in which all the sho
location and one camera set-up are grouped. These shots can then be made out
for greater efficiency. Another key role of storyboards is to communicate the conce
client and other stakeholders, many of whom may be less skilled in this type of v
tion. Figure 5.5 illustrates a storyboard for audiovisual media.

Figure 5.5 Example of a Storyboard for Audiovisual Media

Hold the hamster, Fiona. (MS)	I have to clean the cage. (MS)	It smells! (MS)
You better not do it here, Jody. (MS)	Take it to the laundry, Jody. (MS)	OK. (MS)
(MS–Taking lid off)	(CU–Dumping drawer in bag)	(CU–Dump bottom of box)
(CU–Putting chips in cage)	You can put the hamster back, Fiona. (MS)	You forgot the water, Jody. (CU)

Figure 5.6 Example of a Flowchart for Interactive Multimedia

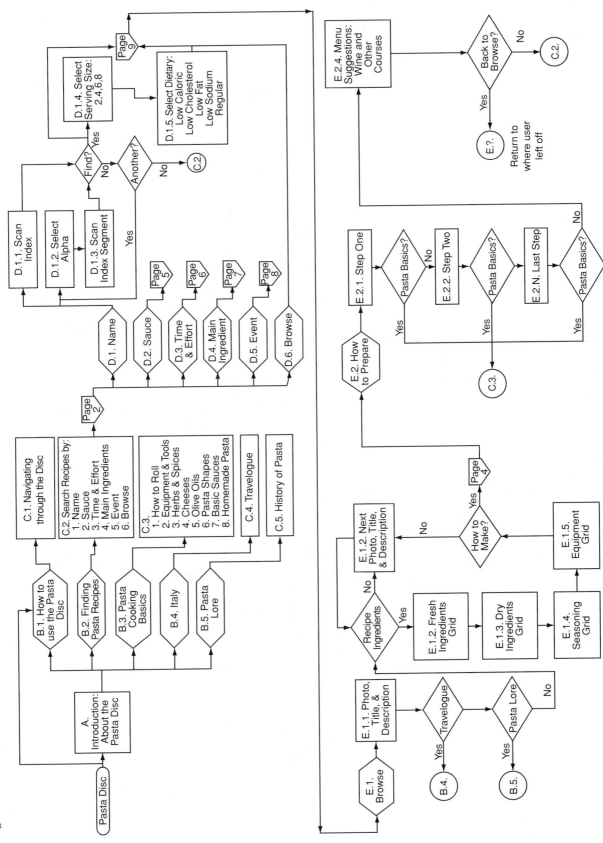

Figure 5.7 Development Phase for IVD/DVI

Development

Draft materials
What will the materials say?
How will practice exercises work?
How is feedback provided?

Media Production
How do the materials look and sound?

Formative Evaluation
Do students learn from them?
How do we improve them?

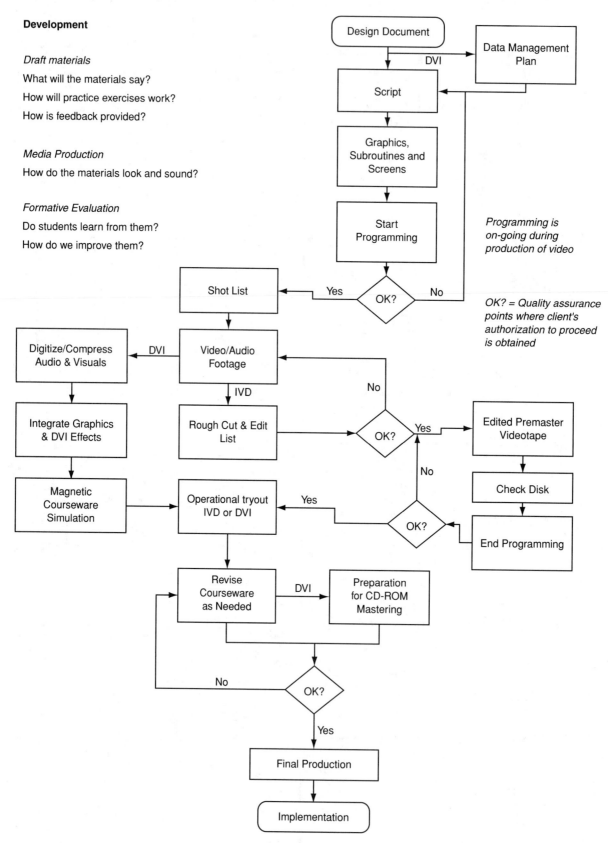

Programming is on-going during production of video

OK? = Quality assurance points where client's authorization to proceed is obtained

ENSURING THE INTEGRITY OF THE DESIGN

To take shortcuts with any of this treatment/script/storyboard process means to risk misunderstandings, greater costs, and less efficiency. Production often takes longer than design activities, and while time passes, original intent may be misinterpreted or forgotten. It is the designer's responsibility to see that specified objectives are met consistently in development. Production changes may negatively affect the project. Aesthetic changes, for example, must be consistent with instructional intent.

Suppose you have approved a storyboard for a slide-tape presentation on "What Are Non-Print Materials?" The storyboard shows a character looking at pictures on a screen. In an attempt to add interest, the artist pictures voluptuous women on the screen. The design has been compromised; the materials need to be exemplars without stereotypes, because one criterion for media selection is that the medium should not reinforce stereotypes. Another example is the use of handwriting and primitive drawings to suggest the work of an untutored adolescent. If production changes this to a printed serif font and more sophisticated drawings in order to increase legibility, the characterization necessary to the message may be lost. In this situation, the designer should negotiate ways to increase legibility without losing the "done by hand" quality of the printing and drawing.

Aesthetic changes are often improvements, but they should be made only for instructional reasons. An audiovisual producer should not be expected to know theory of instructional design in depth. His job is to see that the script is shot. The designer's job is to monitor script changes or interpretations.

There are many ways you can ensure the integrity of the design. You can (a) monitor the steps including delivery, (b) participate in decision making during the development stage, and (c) assume roles that strengthen the likelihood that quality will be maintained throughout the ISD process. More specifically, you can monitor the analysis of goals and content, the design of objectives and assessment strategies, the selection and development of media and delivery systems, and the formative evaluation process. You can participate in the development process during the pre-production, scripting, production, and post-production stages. Your roles should include monitoring the integrity of the design by communicating important aspects of design, facilitating communication with the client about progress and changes, making contributions as a team member, and making recommendations for revision based on evaluation.

Exercise J provides practice on ways to monitor development. Exercise K provides practice in applying principles for the selection of media and delivery systems.

EXERCISES

A. An Exercise on Delivery System Options
For each category of media or delivery system list three options the designer can consider in Table 5.5.

Table 5.5

Technologies			
Print	*Audiovisual*	*Computer-based*	*Integrated*

B. An Exercise to Give Practice in Developing and Using a Learner Profile

Here are the results of a needs assessment done by interviews and an examination of records. Use this information to complete the learner profile in Table 5.6 so that you will have information that allows you to analyze learner characteristics. After you have completed the learner profile, use this information to make recommendations about appropriate delivery systems.

Students in eighth-grade enrichment science classes range in age from 12 to 14, with the mean and mode being 13. There are three sections with a total of 87 students (28, 32, and 27 students per class). Forty-five are girls, and 42 are boys. Each section uses one self-contained classroom with fixed chairs and tables. There are lab tables around the walls of the classroom.

Eighty percent of the students are in other enrichment classes. The Dakota Achievement Test scores on areas related to scientific concepts and skills range from the 92th percentile to the 99th percentile for their grade level. The Metropolitan Test checks measurement, reading, logic, and graphing concepts relevant to science. On the Metropolitan Aptitude/Achievement Test, last year's eighth-grade enrichment science students all scored well above average. Last year's students were representative of this year's students.

Students must maintain a B average overall to stay in this class and have an A average in science to be recommended for the class. Most of the students come from upper-middle-class families where at least one of the parents is a professional or business executive. Many of the parents are scientists or in science-related occupations. Most of the students are well traveled. For example, last year one student visited the Thomas Edison home and museum in Florida, and another visited Edison's laboratories in Menlo Park, New Jersey. Yet another student visited the Henry Ford museum in Detroit. Most students have been to science center museums in several cities. There are also a few students who come from a lower-middle-class background and another few whose families are barely above the poverty level.

The students have had infrequent trips to a local science center and one year's experience with an independent study approach to science (Learning Activity Packages). Generally, in science they have been taught for the last three years by the traditional lecture/discussion method. In other cases, such as social studies, they frequently do independent projects. They have a range of learning style preferences and ways of approaching problem solving. About two-thirds of the students prefer hands-on activities and a variety of instructional strategies. The other third prefer to take notes from lecture/presentation and to be checked by tests. Four of the students have placed in the school science fair and one in the regional science fair.

As is usual, some of the students are very verbal and quick to respond; others are quiet and consider carefully before responding. All of the students have high verbal ability,

Table 5.6

Characteristic	Representative Learner	Range for Learners
Age		
Sex		
Educational Level		
Achievement Level		
Socio-economic Level		
Learning Style		
Verbal Ability		
Relevant Experience		

as seen in their reading, writing, and speaking. They almost all have a positive attitude toward school. However, they find enrichment science as taught by lecture/discussion and lab experiments one of their least interesting classes. When asked, they report they need science for future careers but that it's not one of their favorite subjects. They are vague when asked what they need to know in science. When pressed, many say they like to dissect and are disappointed there won't be dissecting this year.

What information on this learner profile can be used to help make delivery system decisions? List five learner characteristics that are relevant to selection of delivery systems.

1.

2.

3.

4.

5.

Are any of these characteristics related to channel or grouping recommendations? If so, which ones, and why?

Channel:

Grouping:

How does this information translate into decisions about delivery systems? What recommendations would you make based on these learner characteristics?

C. An Exercise in Identifying Channel Requirements

Below are six learning objectives. The channel requirements for instruction can be inferred from each objective. After the objective, write the implied channel requirements. The channel might be audio, visual, audiovisual, tactile, kinesthetic, or olfactory.

1. Given pictures of signs of the Zodiac, the student will identify each sign orally.
2. Given a standard transmission automobile, the student will use the clutch while operating the car.
3. Given the choice of classical or popular music, the student will listen to classical music.
4. Given an aquarium with fish, the student will orally identify five types of fish in the aquarium.
5. Given an outline of a human face, the child will locate and label parts of the face.
6. Given an egg, the student chef will separate the yolk from the white using the shell as a tool.
7. Given a piece of meat or fish and refrigeration and purchase records, the student chef will determine whether there is a likelihood of spoilage.

How does identification of the channel as in statements 1 through 7 above relate to decisions about delivery systems?

D. An Exercise in Identifying Appropriate Grouping

Here are five situations in which one of the following is more desirable: large group, small group, or independent study. Read each situation and then write which type of instruction is most appropriate—LG, SG, IS—and then give the reason why in the space provided.

1. An expert will be available as a guest speaker for one presentation and will bring transparencies and slides.

Recommended grouping:

Reason:

Relevance to delivery system decisions:

2. Students have done individual research on a topic and are now ready to share their findings and establish further directions for research.

Recommended grouping:

Reason:

Relevance to delivery system decisions:

3. Before employees can practice in a field setting, they must build a base of knowledge and skills. An excellent textbook, a workbook, and demonstration videotapes are available.

Recommended grouping:

Reason:

Relevance to delivery system decisions:

4. Some employees enter without prerequisite knowledge. But all employees must achieve the same objectives in fifteen weeks.

Recommended grouping:

Reason:

Relevance to delivery system decisions:

5. The instructor feels it is important to discuss problems and issues related to the topic.

Recommended grouping:

Reason:

Relevance to delivery system decisions:

E. A Group Exercise in Judging Appropriate and Inappropriate Uses of Delivery Systems in Grouping Situations

In a small group discuss your experiences as a student in a variety of class formats, e.g., large group lecture, small group discussion, independent study. Discuss instances in which you felt delivery systems were appropriately or inappropriately used.

F. An Exercise in Justifying Selection of Delivery Systems

Following is an instructional problem. If you prefer, develop parameters for another problem using a similar approach. Use the process presented in the Seels and Glasgow Model for Selecting Delivery Systems. Then, justify your recommendations in a written rationale.

A Spelling Problem

Goal: To improve students' spelling achievement.

Objective: To correctly differentiate among "to," "too," and "two"; "their" and "they're"; "its" and "it's."

Learner Characteristics: Ungraded classroom of fourth and fifth graders ranging in age from eight to 12 years. Some have no understanding, some partial understanding, and some full understanding of topic.

Instructional Plan: To have students practice comparing and contrasting the spellings.

Grouping Decision: Independent study.

Setting: Two large classrooms with moveable divider between them. Forty-eight students. Independent study and display areas are available. Desks are movable.

Resources: Four cassette tape players, two Macintosh computers, and duplicating facilities.

Schedule: Start study of this area in two weeks, then continue for two weeks.

G. A Group Exercise on the Designer's Role

This exercise requires a dyad for a role play. (It can also take place in a small group setting with others watching.) The topic of discussion can be the media selection and development for the design project being undertaken.

1. One person in the dyad assumes the role of client and the other the role of instructional designer. The instructional designer is to practice explaining why he or she recommends changes in the plans developed so far. In order to do this, the designer explains his role in the selection of delivery systems to the client. The client argues for the approach to media, delivery systems, and materials originally discussed with the designer. Then the roles are reversed and the scene acted out again. For example, the client may have originally discussed an interactive multimedia system to be available in all plants. Now the designer is recommending instead a videotape with support materials be mailed to all the plants. You can hypothesize a situation relevant to your individual design project.

2. One person assumes the role of leader of the development team. The other plays the instructional designer who is explaining his or her role in selection and development to this leader. In this case, leader is trying to reach an agreement with the designer on roles in development. There are points of disagreement because the designer does not want to totally relinquish control, and the producer does not want the designer making production decisions, especially ones related to treatment and aesthetics. The roles are then reversed. For example, the leader of the development team argues that they have all the information they need to proceed and the designer does not need to be involved until they have developed something to review. The designer, on the other hand, argues that he wants to be part of the development team and involved in discussions about approach, organization, and interactivity. You can hypothesize a situation relevant to your individual design project.

H. An Exercise in Writing a Treatment and Script

You have been asked to prepare a treatment and script on a topic related to nutrition. Prepare a treatment of one page or less and then develop a ten-frame script based on part of that treatment.

I. An Exercise in Developing a "How-To" Storyboard

Create part of a storyboard on how to do something. Break the process into understandable steps and use stick figures or thumbnail sketches in the frames. Make some narration and camera shot notes at the bottom of each frame. Use the form in Figure 5.8.

Figure 5.8

J. An Exercise on Ensuring the Integrity of the Design

First, list the aspects of ISD that the designer can monitor. Then, list some steps in the development process in which the designer can participate. Finally, list the roles the designer can play in the development process. Using these lists, write a short essay on how the designer's involvement in the development process can ensure the integrity of the design.

Aspects to Monitor	*Participation in Steps*	*The Designer's Roles*
1.	1.	1.
2.	2.	2.
3.	3.	3.
4.	4.	4.

K. An Application Exercise on the Delivery System Component of Your Design Plan

Use the Seels and Glasgow Model for Selecting Delivery Systems as a basis for making decisions about the project you are developing. Specify what materials must be produced or obtained. Write a rationale to support your selection.

◆ REFERENCES

Alessi, S. M., & Trollip, S. R. (1985). *Computer-based instruction: Materials and development.* Englewood Cliffs, NJ: Prentice-Hall.

American National Red Cross. (1993). *Standard first aid.* St. Louis: Mosby Lifeline Publications.

Barron, A. E., & Orwig, G. W. (1995). *Multimedia technologies for training.* Englewood, CO: Libraries Unlimited.

Barron, A. E., & Orwig, G. W. (1997). *New technologies for education: A beginner's guide* (3rd ed.). Englewood, CO: Libraries Unlimited.

Glasgow, Z. & Cox, D. O. (1993). *Evaluation of selected courses for conversion to individualized instruction and distance delivery: Final report* (Contract No. EME-92-C-0349). Emittsburg, MD: Emergency Management Institute.

Hackbarth, S. (1996). *The educational technology handbook: A comprehensive guide-process and products for learning.* Englewood Cliffs, NJ: Educational Technology Publications.

Heinich, R., Molenda, M., Russell, J. D., & Smaldino, S. E. (1996). *Instructional media and technologies for learning.* Englewood Cliffs, NJ: Merrill/Prentice Hall.

Kemp, J. E., Morrison, G. R., & Ross, S. M. (1994). *Designing effective instruction.* New York: Merrill/MacMillan.

Kemp, J. E. & Smellie, D. C. (1994). *Planning, producing, and using instructional technologies* (7th ed.). New York: HarperCollins.

Lee, W. W. & Mamone, R. A. (1995). *The computer based training handbook.* Englewood Cliffs, NJ: Educational Technology Publications.

Levine, T. K. (1990). *Going the distance: A handbook for developing degree programs using program television courses and telecommunications technology.* Washington, DC: The Anneberg/CPB Project.

McGowan, J., & Clark, R. E. (1985). Instructional software features that support learning for students with widely different ability levels. *Performance and Improvement Quarterly,14*, 17.

Reiser, R. A., & Gagné, R. M. (1983). *Selecting media for instruction.* Englewood Cliffs, NJ: Educational Technology Publications.

Seels, B., & Richey, R. C. (1994). *Instructional technology: The definition and domains of the field.* Washington, DC: Association for Educational Communications and Technology.

Simonson, M. R. & Volker, R. P. (1984). *Media planning and production.* Columbus, OH: Merrill Publishing.

Smith, P. L. and Boyce, B. A. (1984). Instructional design considerations in the development of computer-assisted instruction. *Educational Technology, 24*(7), 5–11.

Stevens, G. H. & Stevens, E. F. (1995). *Designing electronic performance support tools: Improving workplace performance with hypertext, hypermedia, and multimedia.* Englewood Cliffs, NJ: Educational Technology Publications.

◆ *ANSWERS*

A. An Exercise on Delivery System Options
Some possible answers are shown in Table 5.7.

B. An Exercise to Give Practice in Developing and Using a Learner Profile
The answer to the exercise is shown in Table 5.8.

Here is a sampling of learner characteristics relevant to delivery systems.

1. These students have high verbal skills.
2. They have experience with independent study.
3. They prefer hands-on science lessons.
4. Many have experiences relevant to science that they can share.
5. They are aged 12 to 14 and in eighth grade.

Here are some examples of channel and grouping recommendations that can be inferred from these learner characteristics:

Channel: A variety of visual channels needed to be added to the audio channels used during lecture discussion. These students are capable of reading for information and observing. In addition, tactile channels as used in hands-on activities will increase attention and memory.

Grouping: These students can do independent study in the form of projects, labs, and learning packages. As middle schoolers they probably like working in groups where boys and girls are mixed.

Here are examples of some recommendations that can be made for delivery systems based on learner characteristics:

1. These students are capable of learning through appropriate applications of technologies in any category (print, audiovisual, computer-based, or integrated) providing visuals are used.
2. Students can share science information and activities in small groups through discussion and reports.
3. Independent study activities that use verbal material with visuals and small group activities should be supplemented by laboratory or field work that involves verbal directions and tactile materials.

Further specificity in recommendations depends on the objectives.

C. An Exercise in Identifying Channel Requirements

1. audiovisual
2. tactile/kinesthetic
3. audio
4. audiovisual
5. visual
6. visual and tactile
7. visual and olfactory

This information relates to decisions about delivery systems because the designer should select a delivery system or combination of systems that can provide these channels. For example, your instruction for number 7 could not be limited to computer-based instruction unless that instruction provided for interaction with a real object or sensory cues. Luckily, most delivery systems can provide a variety of channels, depending on how they are used. It is important, though, to design for these channels. An audio CD will not be adequate for number 5 because it does not provide visual cues.

D. An Exercise in Identifying Appropriate Grouping

1. **Large Group.**
Reason: one chance
Relevance to delivery system decisions: Although all the technology categories (print, audiovisual, computer-based, and integrated) include capability for large group display, the capacity depends on the formats chosen and how they are designed. In this case, the most practical delivery system would be a lecture using audiovisual equipment, such as microphones and projectors.

2. **Small Group.**
Reason: need for dialogue with others
Relevance to delivery system decisions: You may not need a delivery system in this situation, because the student's words serve as the medium. On the other hand, the student may choose to use printed or projected visuals as ways to explain in which case print and audiovisual technologies provide delivery systems.

Table 5.7

Technologies			
Print	*Audiovisual*	*Computer-based*	*Integrated*
Textbooks	Slides	Tutorial programs	Interactive video
Photos	Video	Simulation programs	CD-ROM
Posters	Transparencies	Drill and practice programs	Virtual reality

Table 5.8

Learner Characteristics	Representative Learner	Range for Learners
Age	13	12–14
Gender	Girl	42 boys and 45 girls
Education Level	Eighth grade	Eighth grade
Achievement Level	94% Dakota Test; 89% Metropolitan Test; all classes are enrichment	Above average on Metropolitan Test; 92-99% on Dakota Test; 80% are in some enrichment classes
Socio-economic Level	Upper middle class	Lower to upper middle class
Learning Style	Hands on preferred, likes variety of strategies, methods	Wide range of styles
Verbal Ability	High	High
Relevant Experience	Trip to Thomas Edison's home in Florida	Independent study, field trips, travel common

3. **Independent Study**

Reason: resources are available

Relevance to delivery system decisions: The materials already available are in print or audiovisual form. These delivery options are adequate; therefore, why invest more money or time in preparing other delivery systems? If improvement in instruction is warranted at some point, interactive multimedia can be used to improve simulation, interactivity, and feedback by integrating the materials, enriching them, and increasing immediacy.

4. **Independent Study**

Reason: remediation, because there are individual differences

Relevance to delivery system decisions: If independent study is chosen, delivery systems can be designed so that employees can work on their own at their own pace continuing at home if necessary. Note that again it is not just the choice of delivery system but also how it is planned so that it matches the grouping choice. For example, a combination of print and audiovisual delivery system could be chosen. If it uses a package which integrates a textbook, workbook, and demonstration videotapes, it is an appropriate format for independent study. If instead, the combination is a lecture following a prepared outline with a lecture guide handout and slides, the match of delivery system and grouping is probably not appropriate.

5. **Small Group**

Reason: need for discussion

Relevance to delivery system decisions: You may not need a delivery system in this instance. The instructional strategy of small group discussion does not require visuals or individual practice.

E. A Group Exercise in Judging Appropriate and Inappropriate Uses of Delivery Systems in Grouping Situations

Often, grouping is not successful because inappropriate delivery systems were used in conjunction with the grouping format or because the delivery system was poorly designed. For example, a large group lecture with unreadable visuals and no support materials may be ineffective although the grouping format was appropriate. By no support materials we mean no way to help students follow and remember the information, such as a lecture guide, a reading, or a text. Another example might be the use of independent study where the student is given a list of readings with no questions to guide study and no materials to enrich the written material. A better solution would be an integrated set of materials that support the students in achieving specific purposes.

F. An Exercise in Justifying Selection of Delivery Systems

If you choose the spelling problem, your justification might read like this. It is also possible to use another approach to the same problem as long as it is based on the Seels and Glasgow Media Selection Model.

The process used to select delivery systems, media, and materials was the Seels and Glasgow Model for Media Selection. This model requires that decisions first be made about learner and task or channel characteristics, then about grouping plans. Resources are identified.

Constraints and resources are taken into account when determining delivery system options, and the materials needed to support these options. Practicality, feasibility, and budget are considered at this point. Then, decisions are made about how to produce or obtain the materials needed to support delivery.

In this case, the goal was an ISD process to teach discrimination between "to," "two," and "too"; "there" and "their"; and "its" and "it's." Students needed to discriminate between spellings by meaning and usage. A learner profile revealed that there was a wide range of age and abilities. An inference was made that there was also a wide range of styles and attitudes. One constraint, therefore, was that the lessons had to hold attention regardless of age, ability, attitude, and style. A second constraint was the need to provide for individual differences in pacing, practice, and channel needs. Those that already knew the spelling and meaning of these words were excused for other instructional activities as determined by tests. Successfully passing the tests became a motivational element in instruction.

The chief task characteristic is that this is factual learning, learning that must be memorized. It was determined that because it was difficult, though not impossible, to use meaning and visuals as vehicles for retention, overlearning should be a constraint. In other words, it was decided that the best way to aid retention was to provide overlearning and that whatever delivery systems were recommended had to have the capability of encouraging overlearning.

Two other constraints were identified, one related to grouping and the other to channels. Teachers have decided that independent study is the most suitable approach because of the range of individual differences and the need for intensive practice. The task requires visual discrimination, the primary channel for both instruction and responding must be visual, although audio instruction and testing could supplement the visual channel.

Although the budget is limited, the lessons are being planned for next year which gives teachers time to request and justify purchase of some commercial material. Audio cassette players and Macintosh computers are also available, as well as print duplication facilities. All are identified as options. A search for commercial materials reveals drill and practice and tutorial computer programs are available on the topic.

For the reasons just cited, a combination of computer-based instruction and audio directions for worksheets and tests is recommended. Commercial programs should be purchased. These programs should be supplemented by locally produced materials. The locally produced materials can be generated by the teachers. They should take the following forms:

◆ Separate stories for each set of words and stories using all the words with exercises requiring the students to use the words in stories (in computer-based instruction and worksheet format so students can take home as well as do in school).

◆ A Hypercard program with stacks on each set of words.
◆ Cassette tapes that cue work sheet and test items.

A search of indexes and previewing has been used to identify commercial drill and practice and tutorial programs suitable for the Macintosh computers available to teachers. A list of the recommended programs with ordering information is attached. Teachers could be employed this summer to develop the locally produced materials. The time requirements and materials required for local production are given in another attached list.

G. A Group Exercise on the Designer's Role

These are realistic problems that the designer is likely to encounter. You need to be able to articulate the roles that a designer plays in the development process and to be able to defend changes in decisions made during development which you believe do not affect the integrity of the design. Your answers to Exercise J will help you with this exercise.

H. An Exercise in Writing a Treatment and Script

The treatment should describe the content and the approach to that content. The script should have at least ten frames (a single shot or several shots plus related audio or narration). The narration is best done by relating audio and visual, by making them complementary rather than repetitive. Notes can also be made about special effects for transitions.

I. An Exercise in Developing a "How-To" Storyboard

This should be a series of thumbnail or stick figure sketches with narration and camera distance (shot) notes below. The type of shot, e.g., ES, LS, MS, or CU, clarifies the information that should be shown in the shot. The sketches should show the camera angle, e.g., high or low, directly in front. The angle tells the producer the point of view, e.g., dominant, subordinate, or objective.

J. An Exercise on Ensuring the Integrity of the Design

The answer to this exercise is shown in Table 5.9.

Your essay should explain how the designer can ensure the quality of the product by fulfilling roles, being involved during phases, and monitoring aspects of the design.

K. An Application Exercise on the Delivery System Component of Your Design Plan

The delivery system section you develop should specify recommended media, delivery systems, and materials. You should present your rationale for these decisions. This rationale can be based on the media selection model you used. Practical considerations such as cost and feasibility should enter in the decision, as should learner and task characteristics, grouping considerations, and constraints and resources.

Table 5.9

Aspects to Monitor	Participation in Steps	The Designer's Role
1. Goals & Content	1. Pre-production (conceptualization)	1. Monitor integrity of design and communicate important aspects of design
2. Objectives & Assessment	2. Scripting	2. Facilitate communication with client about progress and changes
3. Delivery Systems, Media, & Materials	3. Production (shooting)	3. Make contributions as a team member
4. Formative Evaluation: Results & Revisions	4. Post-production (editing)	4. Make recommendations for revision based on evaluation

Chapter

6   Evaluating ISD Decisions

OVERVIEW

One of the tenets of a systems approach to instructional design is that the instruction is submitted to an evaluation during its development. That is, the instruction is tried and revised until objectives are met. The term "formative evaluation" was coined by Scriven (1967) to describe the kind of evaluation performed during the developmental or "formative" stage of the instructional design process. Originally, the term applied to the tryout of materials to answer the question: "Do students learn from them?" However, nearly 30 years of experience have broadened the meaning beyond learning effectiveness to involve feedback regarding other issues, such as content accuracy, technical quality, user acceptability, and issues associated with implementing the instruction. Formative evaluation provides feedback that is used for improvement of the products at all stages of the ISD process.

Outputs of each phase of the ISD process are reviewed for accuracy and adequacy by SMEs, the client, media specialists, end users, and other instructional designers working on the project. The purpose of these internal reviews depends on what is being reviewed and who is doing the reviewing.

If complex and expensive media are being considered, a prototype may be developed to test the cost-effectiveness of the proposed delivery system and to determine the appropriateness of the new medium for the target audience. Prototypes are developed during the design phase. Lessons learned from prototyping are incorporated into a document that serves as the blue print for the development phase.

During the development phase, the instructional materials are tried on representatives of the target audience to determine how well they learn from the instruction. Elements of the instruction that are deficient are revised and tried out again. The tryout and revision cycle continues until the instructional objectives are met.

Student tryouts of instruction have been used for nearly 30 years and are included in nearly every ISD model, yet there is little research on the topic. The limited amount of research evidence, however, shows that instruction revised on the basis of formative evaluation results in better student performance than unrevised instruction (Flagg, 1990; Tessmer, 1993). Improvements were found for all types of instruction. Dick (1980) cites as barriers to research on formative evaluation outcomes the lack of funding, the complex problems associated with conducting research on one phase of the

ISD process, the difficulty in obtaining a sufficient pool of equally skilled designers available to work on the same instruction in a comparative research study, and the fact that in large organizations where systematic design is taking place, there is no time for or interest in such research.

Figure 6.1 shows how formative evaluation takes place in the ISD process.

Figure 6.1   Formative Evaluation in the ISD Process (Seels & Glasgow ISD Model I: For Novices)

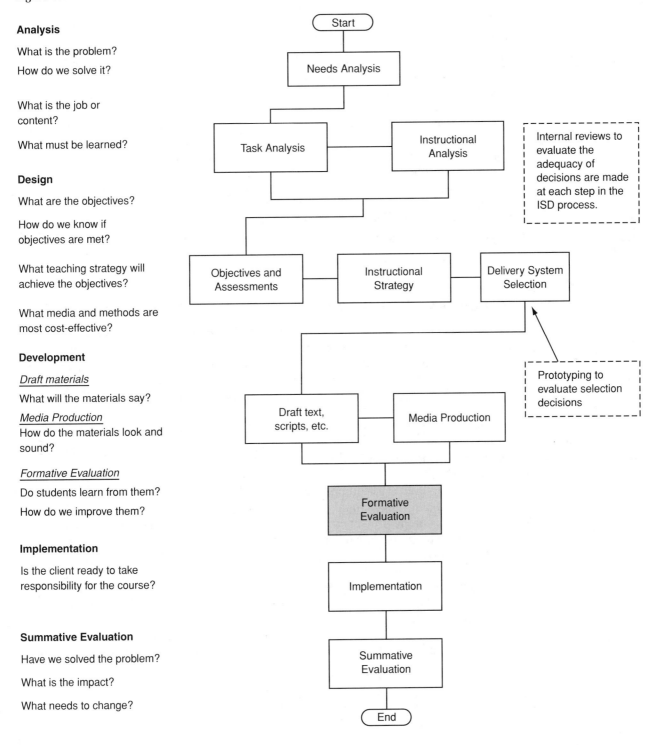

Analysis

What is the problem?

How do we solve it?

What is the job or content?

What must be learned?

Design

What are the objectives?

How do we know if objectives are met?

What teaching strategy will achieve the objectives?

What media and methods are most cost-effective?

Development

Draft materials

What will the materials say?

Media Production

How do the materials look and sound?

Formative Evaluation

Do students learn from them?

How do we improve them?

Implementation

Is the client ready to take responsibility for the course?

Summative Evaluation

Have we solved the problem?

What is the impact?

What needs to change?

ORIENTING QUESTIONS

What is "formative evaluation"?
What kind of evidence is gathered during formative evaluation?
When is "prototyping" used?
What are the steps in the formative evaluation process?
How should each step be conducted?
How can I improve instruction that doesn't work?

OBJECTIVES

1. Given descriptions of instructional design projects, state which experts should review the products developed and at what stage they should do the review.
2. Given situations appropriate for prototyping, describe what kind of prototype you would develop.
3. Given descriptions of individual tryouts, select one that demonstrates a better application of tryout guidelines.
4. Given examples of how designers collected information during small-group tryouts, identify the one who used the better method.
5. Given the results from student tryouts, identify the types of learning failures that occurred.
6. Given an instructional design project of your own choosing, develop a plan for trying out the instruction.
7. Given a plan for a student tryout, evaluate its adequacy.

INTERNAL REVIEWS

The instructional designer enlists the assistance of other instructional designers or a supervisor, SMEs, sponsors, and other knowledgeable people who review the instruction and provide comments and criticism. The internal review may be done by one person or a team. Internal reviews start with the problem definition and task analysis phases of the process and continue until the final product is turned over to the organization responsible for accepting and implementing the program.

Internal reviews can serve two functions. They provide an opportunity to spot and correct technical inadequacies and flaws early, and they serve as a mechanism for gaining acceptance of and commitment to the new materials.

Geis (1987) suggests a number of different experts who might be involved in an internal review. Table 6.1 summarizes the areas of expertise and the functions performed. Internal reviews should include potential users and sponsors who have a stake in the outcome of the project as well as people who, because they have no involvement in the specific program, provide a disinterested review. They should also be concise and constructive critics.

Depending on when the particular area of expertise is needed, expert reviews may occur at any point in the instructional design process. Sponsors and SMEs, for example, may be involved in every stage of the process, while others, such as media consultants, will be brought in during the design and development phases only.

It is often helpful to structure the review to focus the reviewer on what it is you want evaluated. Geis (1987) suggests at least three questions for reviewers of all draft materials:

1. Where does something appear to need fixing?
2. What appears to be the cause of the problem?
3. What might be done about it?

Table 6.1   Expert Reviewers and the Functions They Serve

Subject Matter Experts	Master performers who supply the content for instruction, SMEs attend to questions of accuracy and emphasis. They indicate whether the knowledge and skills to be taught are the ones used on the job and whether the examples are representative. They are most critical in the analysis and development phases.
Instructional Designers	Peers or supervisors who evaluate the prototype material for formal features (e.g., is there an introduction?) and functional features (e.g., is there adequate opportunity for practice?).
Media Specialists	Graphic artists and specialists in audiovisual presentation who can comment on the physical features of the message design (e.g., layout, color, clarity of display, and aesthetic elements).
Audience Specialists	Instructors or teachers experienced with teaching the content to the intended audience can comment on suitability of the chosen strategy for the target audience. Additionally, materials that are to be instructor-delivered can be reviewed for acceptability, practicality, ease of use, and likelihood of adoption by teachers.
Gatekeepers	Representatives of the community or organization regarding acceptability on social, ethical, legal, and moral grounds. In educational settings, they might include parents, religious leaders, ethnic leaders; in work settings, they would include decision makers and/or those responsible for insuring adherence to policy. Input would come during the analysis, design, development, and implementation phases.
Sponsors	Sponsors' reviews often serve all of the functions listed in this table. In addition, they may be directed toward matters of cost, implementation, and deadlines.
Former Students	Those who have already taken the course in another form may provide special insights about the new version, having had to learn the same content in another environment.

After "Formative Evaluation: Developmental Testing and Expert Review" by G. L. Geis, 1987, *National Society for Performance and Instruction, 26*(4), pp. 1–8. Copyright 1987 by NSPI. Adapted with permission.

Exercise A at the end of this chapter provides practice in relating to internal reviews.

PROTOTYPE DEVELOPMENT OF MULTIMEDIA INSTRUCTION

The purpose of formative evaluation is to assess the strengths and weaknesses of instruction in order to revise the materials so that objectives are met. Altering intricate computer programming and/or authoring systems, graphic or animated sequences, and motion and still video in multimedia instruction is expensive and time consuming. Where multimedia instruction is involved, waiting until a version of the product has been created to gather tryout data ensures that major modifications cannot be made. Even when formative evaluation reveals major problems, the intricate programming and/or authoring, graphic and animation creation, and motion and still video development are difficult to modify substantially due to the substantial costs involved (Northrup, 1995).

To overcome the difficulties of making expensive post-production modifications, prototyping has emerged as a way to test design approaches and user interfaces before full scale production. Prototyping is defined by Tessmer (1993) as a hybrid of formative evaluation and design activities. As Figure 6.2 illustrates, prototype development takes place during the design phase of the ISD process. Flagg (1990) refers to prototyping during the late design phase as "pre-production formative evaluation."

When the design phase is completed, the decisions made at each step are documented in a design document. The final document reflects the lessons learned from the prototype. In the development phase the materials are authored, reviewed, produced, and validated. The physical features of the material are produced during this phase. The design document guides the production team to answer the driving question of the development phase: "How will the instruction look and sound?"

Figure 6.2   Design Phase with Prototype

What are the objectives?

How will we know if objectives are met?

What teaching strategy will achieve the objectives?

What media and methods are most cost-effective?

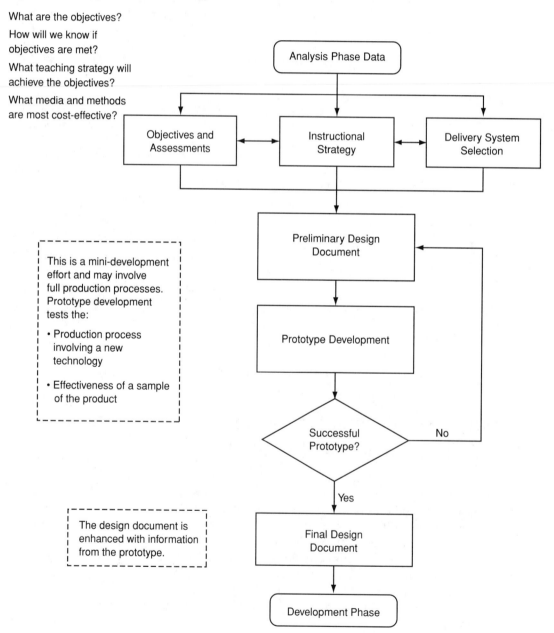

Why Develop a Prototype?

There are two reasons for developing a prototype. First, the designer may have questions about the students' ability to learn from and use the new system. Secondly, when a new technology is involved there may be questions about the design team's experience with new ways of doing things. Prototype development allows the client to assess the cost effectiveness of the new system and allows the design team the opportunity to learn new skills in an environment where the consequences are less expensive.

Compatibility with Target Audience Entry Level.   The intent of the prototype is to test approaches on the target audience. Northrup (1995) notes, "The prototype may emphasize the general flow, screen design, button placement, use of a metaphor, color, font, learner control, general interactivity, user interface, and how multiple media, including text, graphics, animation, audio, and/or video impact" (p. 28). A full blown production effort is not necessary in order to evaluate an approach. The prototype may incorporate storyboards, paper and pencil mockups, rough videos, etc. Detailed content is not needed. Northrup recommends that the prototype contain only enough descriptive information for a design team member to work one-on-one with a student to test the general approach while interacting with the prototype.

Choices of media and interactive strategies should be tested with the target audience, rather than relying on the professional experience and personal preferences of the production staff. Prototyping to answer design questions is sometimes called "rapid prototyping," because it allows quick construction of an approach in order to evaluate its effectiveness before full scale development. Flagg (1990) identifies a number of questions about user friendliness in an interactive learning environment that can be evaluated by a rapid prototype. The criteria are defined in Table 6. 2.

Cost Effectiveness.   A second reason for developing a prototype is to evaluate the cost effectiveness of the approach. Development costs, budgets, and development time are among the factors considered in media selection. If the technology to be used is untried and untested in the setting where it is to be used, or if there are concerns about its cost effectiveness, a prototype may be developed.

Prototyping is a mini-development effort for a sample of the larger program. The propose of the cost-effective analysis is to replicate the production process on a small scale. Prototype development provides the project team a chance to debug the production

Table 6.2   Criteria to Evaluate User Friendliness of Interactive Strategies

Accessibility	Was the information easily accessible? Did users understand what to do next or how to proceed through a decision-making process?
Responsiveness	Was the program responsive to the users' wishes? Did users receive timely feedback appropriate to their needs? Did users find all the tools that they wanted?
Flexibility	Could users change the parameters in the program to suit their own needs? Could users go back and change their responses after an initial decision? Could users go back and review previous content?
Memory	Could users retrieve and examine their past decisions and performance to the extent desired? Are hard copy printouts from selected portions available for later study?

Adapted from *Formative Evaluation for Educational Technologies* by B. N. Flagg, 1990, Hillsdale, NJ: Laurence Erlbaum Associates.

process when a new technology is involved. An instructional segment representative of the total production requirements is selected for prototyping. Then, to the extent possible, full scale production is carried out with an eye to answering the following questions:

◆ Are the system capabilities for graphics, interactivity, animation, etc., compatible with the objectives and instructional strategies selected? The design team's lack of familiarity with the new system may lead to misconceptions about what it can do or the level of effort required to accomplish the instructional objectives.

◆ What are the staffing requirements for each step in the production process? Does the current staff have the requisite production competencies? If not, can they learn them? Do we need to add new staff? Can we subcontract the work? etc.

◆ What are the time lines for each step in the process? How can steps be performed more efficiently?

◆ What are the costs associated with each step? If costs are too high, how can we reduce costs without reducing instructional effectiveness?

Development costs, budgets, and development time are among the factors considered in media selection. The media selection decision process takes into account resources and constraints on the project and provides flexibility by allowing trade-offs to be made. High costs may discourage development of complex multi-media courses.

However, when considering cost effectiveness, decision makers should look to the long-term life of the training to be developed. With many high-tech, self-instructional media, up-front development costs are relatively high, but implementation and maintenance of the course is low compared to traditional classroom training, where the instructor bears the burden of delivery. Furthermore, because these media deliver instruction to students in their homes or businesses, the costs of travel to a facility for instruction, if paid for by the client agency, and the overhead costs for classrooms and offices space needed for faculty and staff in traditional courses are saved. Thus, when looked at in terms of per student costs over the life of the instruction, the perception that certain media are expensive is not always supported by the facts.

Exercise B at the end of this chapter is designed to evaluate your understanding of prototype development.

◆ STUDENT TRYOUTS

The materials are tried out on naive learners to determine to what extent the instructional objectives are met. The designer responsible for developing the instruction collects information about where the instruction worked and where it did not. When instruction fails, the designer questions students to obtain as much evidence as possible about why the instruction failed; this evidence is the basis for revision.

There are three levels of student tryouts: tutorials, small-group tryouts, and operational tryouts.

Tutorial Tryouts

At the beginning of tryouts students individually go through the instruction in the presence of the designer. After a handful of students have worked through the materials, the instruction is revised and an additional group of two to five students work through the revised material. Revisions are seldom made on the basis of one student's idiosyncratic problems. Instead, the instructional designer looks for trouble spots and errors that consistently crop up. The tryout-and-revision cycle continues as long as necessary to achieve the standard specified in the objectives.

The instructional designer determines the adequacy of the instruction through feedback obtained from tests, student performance during learning, and student comments.

Student Performance During Learning and on Tests.   As students work through each exercise or task, the instructional designer notes difficulties and probes for the source of any failure. After the tryout, performance on pre- and post-tests are examined to determine any gain due to instruction. Analysis of the post-test will identify errors and help interpret learner difficulties. However, it may be too complicated and expensive to attempt to use a performance test on a pre and post basis. For example, the post-test in the loan documentation course in chapter 1 required students to actually document loans for typical lending arrangements. Because the test took about four hours to complete, it was impractical to administer on a pre-test basis. Therefore, a written test was developed for use as a pre-test during the tryout.

Student comments.   After students complete the post-test, reactions to the instructions and suggestions for improvement are obtained.

Student Sample.   Students participating in the tryouts should fall within the range of prerequisite abilities defined as the entry-level behavior of the target audience. Research using ninth graders as tryout subjects for math materials suggests that different aptitude groups in the one-to-one stage of formative evaluation provide different types of feedback (Wager, 1983). High-aptitude students can help analyze weak spots in the instruction and provide information about the strategies they use to overcome them. Low-aptitude students are able to identify more basic problems, but are unable to suggest revisions. Groups with mixed aptitudes provide a greater variety of feedback than either high- or low-aptitude groups. Wager reports that materials revised on the basis of the mixed aptitude group produced higher post-test scores and were more favorably received than materials revised solely on the basis of either high- or low-aptitude students.

Delivery System Requirements.   The medium used during the tryout will depend on what is available and economically feasible. One of the purposes of the tryout is to uncover problems before expensive production has begun. Therefore, unless the medium of choice can be inexpensively produced in a rough version, the tryout uses storyboards, scripts, drawings, or mock-ups of the instructional materials. As discussed earlier, a prototype may be developed when highly complex and expensive media systems are used. An abbreviated version of the instruction is produced for evaluation. Thiagarajan (1978) suggests that tryouts of complex multimedia instruction be done in successive stages. For example, if the finished product is to be a videotape, formative evaluation might begin with a storyboard, then use a rough cut of the video before final editing.

Tryout Practices.   Lowe, Thurston, and Brown's (1983) guidelines for conducting one-to-one tryouts are based on their experience developing vocational technology courses for students in Saudi Arabia.

◆ Conduct the tryout early in the development process to allow designers time to improve materials while still in development, thereby saving time and money.

◆ Put the student at ease by explaining that it is the instructional system and not the student that is being evaluated. Make the student feel that he or she is a part of the development team.

◆ Prepare for the tryout in advance by reviewing all material and setting up any equipment or media before the student arrives.

◆ Select a quiet place with no distractions for the tryout.

◆ Use a checklist to ensure that all necessary materials are available and procedures are correctly followed.

◆ Sit close enough to the student to see what he or she is working on, but not so close as to crowd the student.

◆ Do not help answer questions until the student has sought the answers in the materials. Question the student to locate the difficulty only when he or she is frustrated by a problem.

Exercise C at the end of this chapter provides practice identifying good tryout practices.

Revision.   Stolovitch (1982) compares 12 systems models, all of which prescribe formative evaluation. None of them, however, prescribe specific revisions to counteract learning failures. Typically the revision step in a systems approach is largely a process that draws on the designer's knowledge of the principles of learning. The designer uses posttest information as well as other subjective and objective data. If the materials have been subjected to an internal review and are the product of an experienced designer, decisions about how to revise them are usually straightforward. For a skilled and experienced designer, usually the "fix" is obvious. Practice and feedback requirements may be insufficient, or step size may be too large, and so on. That is, the materials must be broken down into smaller parts with additional guidance and practice added. But with less able designers or with complex subject matter, a number of tryouts may be necessary before learner outcomes are affected.

Glasgow (1974) developed guidelines for translating tryout data into revisions. Three types of student failures and associated revision strategies are shown in Table 6.3.

Exercise D at the end of this chapter provides practice on distinguishing types of learning failures.

Small Group Tryouts

Small-group tryouts provide an opportunity to obtain feedback about how well the course achieves the learning objectives, as well as duration of the instruction and instructor preparation requirements. The same issues applicable to tutorial tryouts are applicable to small-group tryouts.

Duration.   Each learning situation fits into a larger context with schedules. By their nature, individual tryouts will not give you good estimates on the time to complete the program. Small-group tryouts consisting of eight to 10 students are useful for estimating the duration of the instruction. For individualized instruction, the median completion time is usually calculated for each unit of instruction. In group-paced instruction, everyone moves at the same pace; therefore, the instructor's task during the tryout is to determine whether the lessons can be contained within the time limits needed to meet the learning requirements of most members of the group and the practical time constraints of the organization offering the instruction.

Instructor Preparation.   If instructional designers conduct the instruction themselves, they will learn a great deal from the instructor's point of view about problems with using the materials. Lessons learned from the tryout will have implications for the instructor's guides, lesson plans, and other materials and equipment used to prepare for and conduct the instruction. The instructional strategies may require instructors to assume new, unfamiliar roles. For example, an instructor used to delivering instruction by lecturing may have difficulty assuming the role of a facilitator in a course that makes use of group discussions and case studies. Findings about instructor competencies during the small tryout will influence the degree and scope of formal training necessary to prepare instructors to conduct the training and perform these new roles during the operational tryout, and later when the course is implemented.

Table 6.3   Types of Learning Failures and Associated Revision Strategies

Type of Failure	Examples of Failure	Revision Strategy
Failure in retention Students correctly performed during instruction, but on the test failed to remember what they learned.	• There are many steps in a procedure. On the test, the student omits a step. • On an end-of-week test, students miss items learned earlier in the week. • Students are learning a new way of doing things. Instead, they use the old procedure on the test.	• Provide more opportunities to practice the task to be learned before the test. • Provide a performance aid, a mnemonic, or visual image to help memory. For example, "RAT" will help you remember **R**etention, **A**cquisition, & **T**ransfer.
Failure in acquisition The student failed to learn the material during instruction and demonstrated that failure by errors during instruction and on the corresponding test items.	Despite repeated attempts to learn long division, students are unable to perform satisfactorily on workbook exercises and fail the test.	Compare the analysis data with the instruction to determine whether the instruction accommodates the: • learners' motivational problems and/or learning preferences; • prerequisite requirements; and • sequencing requirements for the types of learning. Review the instructional strategy to determine whether principles of learning are appropriate for the type of learning.
Failure in transfer The student correctly performed during instruction, but on a test failed to apply what he had learned to new situations.	Student correctly applies Ohm's Law on workbook exercises, but fails to apply law to new examples on the test.	• Range of examples used during instruction is too narrow. Include examples that are representative of the variety of applications (easy to difficult). • Students have misconceptions about application. Direct attention to relevant and critical properties of problems that call for the response.

Adapted from "Planning, Developing and Validating the Instruction," by Z. Glasgow, 1974, in *Handbook For Developing Instructional Systems: Vol. VI* (Contract No. F331615-72-C1363, USAF Human Resources Laboratory, Wright-Patterson AFB, Ohio). Butler, PA: Applied Science Associates.

A designer who lacks subject matter expertise required by instructor tasks may not be the right person to conduct the tryout. In such cases, the designer should work closely with whoever actually instructs during the tryouts, collecting information to detect strengths and weaknesses in the materials and procedures required of the instructor.

Exercise E at the end of this chapter helps you understand the small group tryout process.

Operational Tryout

The materials are tried out under conditions that simulate those of the actual instructional environment. The operational tryout provides an opportunity to work out administrative, equipment, facility, or any other implementation problems.

In operational tryouts, the instruction is evaluated as an integral part of the environment where it will eventually reside, and it is delivered by the instructors and administrators who ultimately will be responsible for it. In addition to providing an opportunity to work out administrative, equipment, facility, or any other implementation problems, the operational tryout ascertains students' attitudes toward the course.

Satisfaction with the training is important. Although there is not always a direct connection between high satisfaction and learning effectiveness, as a rule satisfied participants will help ensure the success of a program. Some activities essential to learning may be difficult or tedious and therefore distasteful to the students. A program that does not satisfy its students will probably not continue in business for long.

A standard approach to assess student satisfaction calls for having students use questionnaires to evaluate the environment, presenters, materials, length, and organization of the program. The survey may be done at the end of training or after some time has elapsed. These indices are disparagingly referred to as "smile" or "happiness" scales because they seldom have demonstrated reliability and validity.

Schwier (1982) points out the difficulties of developing effective scales as well as the pitfalls of using them. He cites four uses in a developmental context

1. as a placebo when student data are gathered but ignored;
2. as an ice breaker where the designer collects satisfaction data in response to client's concerns;
3. as a product appraisal where information about the difficulty, sequence, entertainment value, and instructional approach are used to provide insights to problems overlooked by designers; and
4. as an instructional appraisal where evaluations are used to identify perceived weaknesses and strengths of the instructional staff.

A number of important issues affect student evaluation outcomes. They include the reliability and validity of the instruments and intervening variables that influence students' acceptance of the course. Variables include class size, whether the instruction is compulsory or not, personality of the presenter, and the students' actual or anticipated grade. Although Schwier (1982) points out the difficulties of developing effective scales as well as the pitfalls of using them, Schwier concludes that student evaluations judiciously used and carefully constructed can contribute to assessing an instructional package.

Debriefing is another way to assess student satisfaction. A debriefing is a discussion—sometimes with an individual but usually with a group—about the activities just experienced. A debriefing session provides an opportunity to talk about emotions, such as frustration. The debriefing approach is always used with simulation/gaming activities (Heinich, Molenda, Russell, & Smaldino, 1996). A discussion or debriefing leader asks questions about emotions and about what happened, what was learned, and the relevancy of what was learned. ("How did you feel about playing the game?" "To what extent was the game realistic?" What part does chance play in the game? How realistic is this part? "What factors affect success in the game?") Notes are taken on participant's responses.

Another approach to improving instruction on the basis of student comments is the evaluation interview, which is a form of debriefing. The U.S. Department of Labor's Employment Standard Administration (ESA) has pioneered a mechanism for gathering formative evaluation data through group interviews. The mechanism allows the instructor to improve an ongoing course and collect data for future revisions. This approach employs evaluation meetings and works best for workshops and training sessions that last longer than two days. Although no formal evaluation of the approach is known, it has been used by ESA trainers for more than 10 years and by other organizations in modified forms (Stevenson, 1980; Pearlstein, 1988).

Meetings generally last 30 minutes and are attended by the instructor and representatives selected by the course participants. Evaluation meetings are held daily to determine how the course is going and to air issues that, if allowed to go unvented, might interfere with the course. Topics may include pace, problems with materials, problems with exercises or group activities, and problems with the instructors. If students are reluctant to reveal their real concerns, the instructor will have to probe—and be willing to accept and respond to negative comments.

Meetings are most effective if feedback will make a difference immediately. A meeting held at the end of the day should result in a change the next day. The instructor must be willing to follow through in the next session on any commitments, or students will feel that comments they make at the meetings are not taken seriously. On the other hand, changes that violate learning principles and harm the effectiveness of the course should not be made. A suggestion that cannot be acted upon can be handled by explaining that the basic course design is founded on principles of learning that are not subject to change. In other words, although learning is a cooperative venture, don't be coerced into altering the nature of the course.

Example of an Operational Tryout.   The example presented here shows the difficulties associated with conducting formative evaluations.

The Educational Technology Laboratory at the Medical University of South Carolina (MUSC) developed a CD-ROM program to interest middle school students in environmental careers (Mauldin, 1996). The design team wanted to evaluate ease of use, the computer program performance, and the content. Because MUSC did not have access to the target audience, tutorial and small group tryouts were not possible. However, several school systems were persuaded to volunteer as evaluation sites for operational tryouts.

Three rounds of tryouts were conducted over a one-year period. In the first round, two versions of the program with different interfaces were developed and tried out in two schools. Revisions were made based on the results of observations of students using the program and interviews with school personnel. The second round of tryouts involved two other schools. Evaluation instruments included: pre- and post-tests, observations, interviews, and questionnaires regarding students' likes and dislikes. Further revisions were made and a third round of tryouts was conducted to evaluate the latest changes in another two schools. The same evaluation procedures and instruments were used. A final set of changes were made before the CD-ROM was mastered, duplicated, and delivered to the client.

In order to obtain the cooperation of the schools, MUSC provided the schools with complete computer systems, gave the teachers written documentation on the program (including suggestions for incorporating it into the classroom instruction), and furnished teachers and administrators with letters of appreciation, sending copies to supervisors and personnel files. MUSC also publicized the schools' involvement in newspaper articles, and gave the schools credit in the finished programs for participation in the evaluation.

Exercise F at the end of this chapter provides practice developing and evaluating formative evaluation plans.

EXERCISES

A. An Exercise Designed to Identify Who Should Conduct an Internal Review and When

The following are descriptions of instructional design projects. For each project name an expert who should review the materials and the step in the instructional systems design process where the review should take place.

   Steps: Analysis, design, development, evaluation, and implementation.

1. Develop a slide-tape to explain to parents and employees the school board's plans for asbestos removal from the high school.
2. Revise an instructor-delivered course on the documentation requirements for commercial loans. Students are new employees in the commercial loan departments of banks.
3. Develop a videotape for elementary school children on safe street-crossing behavior. The videotape will employ a nationally known host of a children's television show.
4. Develop a two-hour course for emergency medical technicians on how to deal with the emotional trauma of parents whose infant dies as a result of sudden infant death syndrome (SIDS). The sponsor is the U. S. Department of Health and Human Services. The training is mandated under a law enacted as a result of the efforts of parents who have experienced SIDS.

B. An Exercise Designed to Help You Plan Prototypes

Prototypes are appropriate for the following situations. Describe what kind of prototype you would develop to answer the questions posed by the problems.

1. **Problem:**   A telecommunications course on statistical concepts is being developed for college freshmen. The designer plans to use bar graphs, line charts, scatter diagrams, and pie charts to display data.
   Question: How much explanation will the students need in order to understand the graphics?
2. **Problem:**   A computerized reading course with audio is being developed for kindergarten children. The instructional strategy uses a phonic approach.
   Question: Will children understand directions for using the mouse to point, click, and drag?
3. **Problem:**   A national chemical manufacturer is considering using DVI for its safety training for employees in processing plants throughout the country. (Figure 5.7 in chapter 5 shows the activities involved in developing DVI.) The Vice President for Human Resources wants to use the corporate training staff and its video production facilities. The staff has never developed interactive instruction.
   Question: How much will it cost us to convert our present courses to DVI using corporate staff and facilities?

C. An Exercise Designed to Help You Recognize Appropriate and Inappropriate Tryout Practices

The following are descriptions of an instructional designer's behavior during a small-group tryout. Indicate whether the designer's behavior is correct or incorrect. If incorrect, state what the designer should have done.

1. Self-instructional slide-tape art appreciation course. Target audience is ninth graders. The instructional designer set up the equipment before a ninth grader arrived for the tryout. The designer had already determined that the tryout subject's aptitude was average. When the tryout began, the designer gave the directions on what to do and left the student alone to work.

2. Self-instructional science materials for seventh grade.
   Instructional designer asks a seventh-grade teacher to provide subjects for the tryout. The teacher, wanting to make a good impression, sends the three best pupils.
3. Course to teach bank employees which forms are required to document commercial loans.
   A bank employee agrees to try out the material. The instructional designer explains to the employee that assistance is needed to find out how well the materials work. The designer points out that on the basis of the employee's comments, the materials will be revised, and that thereby the employee will contribute to the effectiveness of the training eventually to be offered to other bank workers. The designer leads the bank employee through the materials, noting difficulties and discussing possible improvements. They work as a team throughout the tryout.
4. Management training presented on videodisc.
   The scriptwriter and instructional designer try out the materials in storyboard form on typical management trainees.
5. Correspondence course for soldiers in the reserves who are being trained to do maintenance and repair radios.
   Instructional designer sends out draft materials to several reserve units after selecting subjects based on their aptitude test scores. A person assigned to each unit will administer the materials and mail them back to the designer.

D. An Exercise Designed to Help You Distinguish Among Acquisition, Retention, and Transfer Failures

Indicate whether the learning problems described below are failures in retention, acquisition, or transfer.

1. On an exercise, a student fails to select the correct form to use for a loan guarantee. She makes the same mistake on a test.
2. On an exercise, a student selects the correct form to use for a loan guarantee, but misses the item on a test.
3. On an exercise, a student selects the correct form to use when the guarantor is a spouse. On the test, when asked to select a form to use when the guarantor is a corporation, the student selects the wrong form.
4. A student is learning to use a computerized program to calculate statistics. The student is learning to select the correct statistical procedure to use given a particular request for analysis. On an exercise, the student uses the correct procedure for entering the test score on a spelling test to obtain descriptive statistics. On a test, the student is given weather data for several cities and is asked what procedure to follow to obtain descriptive statistics. The student doesn't know the answer.
5. A student photographer is learning to develop black and white film. There are many steps in the procedure that must be performed exactly right. The instructor works with the student until he or she can do all of the steps correctly. The instructor schedules a test for the following week. On the test, the student mixes the chemicals incorrectly.

E. An Exercise Designed to Help You Understand the Small-Group Tryout Process

Following are descriptions of how instructional designers approach the same problem in a small-group tryout. Select the one who is likely to obtain information from the tryout. Explain your choice.

1. Tryout of self-instructional text materials.
   Designer A.   The designer collected time data at the start and end of each day. At the end of the tryout, the designer calculated the range and median completion time for the course.

Designer B.   The designer collected time data for each module for each student, then calculated the range and median completion time for each module.

2. Tryout of instructor-led materials of a three-day workshop requiring the instructor to lead discussion groups on highly technical matters. The instructor for the small group tryout is the SME who has been working with the designer all along.
Designer A.   The designer constructs a checklist of issues he wants feedback on. At lunch and at the close of the business day, the designer and the SME/instructor review the events of the day against the checklist.
Designer B.   The designer constructs a checklist of issues that require feedback and asks the SME/instructor to complete it for each course segment. Because of the working relationship established during the course's development, the SME and the designer schedule a debriefing at the end of the course.

F. A Group Exercise to Help You Plan the Steps in Formative Evaluation and Help You Evaluate Plans for Formative Evaluation

From your own experience, select an instructional design problem or materials used in a learning environment. Briefly describe them and prepare a plan for a formative evaluation. Your plan must include tutorial, small-group, and operational tryouts. For each tryout, specify the subjects, tryout environment, tryout procedures, data collected, and the prototype to be developed, if one is warranted.

Exchange evaluation plans from this exercise with another student and evaluate each other's plans. First construct a checklist against which you will evaluate the plan, then discuss each other's evaluations.

REFERENCES

Dick, W. (1980). Formative evaluation in instructional development. *Journal of Instructional Development, 3*(3), 3–6.

Flagg, B. N. (1990). *Formative Evaluation for Educational Technologies.* Hillsdale, NJ: Laurence Erlbaum Associates.

Geis, G. L. (1987). Formative evaluation: Developmental testing and expert review. *National Society for Performance and Instruction Journal, 26*(4), 1–8.

Glasgow, Z. (1974). Planning, developing and validating the instruction. In *Handbook for developing instructional systems: Vol. VI* (Contract No. F331615-72-C1363, USAF Human Resources Laboratory, Wright-Patterson AFB, Ohio). Butler, PA: Applied Science Associates.

Heinich, R., Molenda, M., Russell, J. D. & Smaldino, S. E. (1996). *Instructional media and the new technologies for learning.* Englewood Cliffs, NJ: Prentice Hall.

Lowe, A. J., Thurston, W. I., & Brown, S. B. (1983). Clinical approach to formative evaluation. *National Society for Performance and Instruction Journal, 22*(5), 8–10.

Mauldin, M. (1996, March/April). The formative evaluation of computer-based multimedia programs. *Educational Technology,* pp. 36–40.

Northrup, P. T. (1995, November/December). Concurrent formative evaluation: guidelines and implications for multimedia designers. *Educational Technology,* pp. 24–31.

Pearlstein, G. (1988). Gathering formative evaluation data daily. *National Society for Performance and Instruction Journal, 27,* 49–50.

Schwier, R. A. (1982). Design and use of student evaluation instruments in instructional development. *Journal of Instructional Development, 5*(4), 28–34.

Scriven, M. (1967). *The methodology of evaluation* (AERA Monograph series on curriculum evaluation, No. 1). Chicago, IL: Rand McNally.

Stevenson, G. (1980, May). Evaluating training daily. *Training and Development Journal,* pp. 120–22.

Stolovitch, H. D. (1982). Applications of the intermediate technology of learner verification and revision (LVR) for adapting international instructional resources to meet local needs. *National Society for Performance and Instruction Journal 21,* 16–22.

Tessmer, M. (1993). *Planning and conducting formative evaluations.* Philadelphia, PA: Kogan Page.

Thiagarajan, S. (1978). Instructional product verification and revision: Twenty questions and 200 speculations. *Educational Communication and Technology Journal, 26,* 133–141.

Wager, J. C. (1983). One-to-one and small group formative evaluation: An examination of two basic formative evaluation procedures. *National Society for Performance and Instruction Journal, 22*(5), 5–7.

◆ ANSWERS

A. An Exercise Designed to Identify Who Should Conduct an Internal Review and When

1. Representative of school board (analysis phase)
   Representative of parents and employees (design phase)
2. SME on documentation from bank (analysis phase)
   Former instructor (design phase)
3. SME on traffic safety (analysis phase)
   Child development expert (analysis and design phases)
4. Emergency medical technician or technical SME (analysis and design phases)
   Sponsor (all phases)
   Parents (analysis and design phases)

B. An Exercise Designed to Help You Plan Prototypes

1. There is no one correct answer. This is how one designer approached the problem. Using one-on-one evaluation, the designer showed freshmen sample graphics in paper format. He asked each student to explain what the graphics mean to him or her. He taped the responses for later analysis. From the responses, he drew tentative conclusions about what freshmen understood about graphics.

Next, he projected colored slides, and played an audio tape of the narration to a small group of students. The script covered the basic information the design teams thought Freshmen needed based on information gained from the one-on-one evaluation. He administered a quiz on interpreting the graphics. Then he conducted a debriefing to get more detailed reactions from the group. (The designer could also have done a rough version of a video and tested it the same ways as the slides.)

2. There is no one correct answer. This is how one designer approached the problem. The designer did not develop a rapid prototype. Rather, she used Macintosh Basics, a program with cartoons, designed to teach use of the mouse. She conducted a series of one-on-one sessions with kindergarten children. During the sessions she worked with them on mouse skills. Another member of the design team observed her and took notes on the children's performance.

3. There is no one correct answer. This is how one training director approached the problem. After getting the OK to spend money on a prototype, the Training Director spent considerable effort selecting a segment of a course representative of the existing safety training.

He then proceeded to produce a DVI carefully tracking costs associated with the prototype. He generalized the findings to the remaining courses to derive an estimate of the final costs for redevelopment to DVI for all courses.

C. An Exercise Designed to Help You Recognize Appropriate and Inappropriate Tryout Practices

1. Incorrect. She should have stayed with the subject during tryout to collect information on why mistakes were made.
2. Incorrect. She should have obtained students who represent the full range of abilities in seventh grade.
3. Correct.
4. Correct.
5. Incorrect. The materials should be tried out by the designer. With this approach, one cannot be sure that the examiner is adhering to accepted tryout practices.

D. An Exercise Designed to Help You Distinguish among Acquisition, Retention, and Transfer Failures

1. Acquisition
2. Retention
3. Transfer
4. Transfer
5. Retention

E. An Exercise Designed to Help You Understand the Small-Group Tryout Process

1. **Designer B.** More accurate time was collected.
2. **Designer A.** When feedback is immediate, corrective action can be taken promptly.

F. A Group Exercise to Help You Plan the Steps in Formative Evaluation and Help You Evaluate Plans for Formative Evaluation

The two parts of this exercise build on each other. Plans must include tutorial, small-group, and operational tryouts. For each tryout, specify the subjects, tryout environment, tryout procedures, data collected, and the prototype to be developed, if one is warranted.

Part Two

The Seels & Glasgow ISD Model II: For Practitioners

Chapter

Using Models and Paradigms

OVERVIEW

ISD models serve as analogs for the process used to complete any design project. These visual or verbal representations of the ISD process are used to guide design in many settings (e.g., business or schools) and for many purposes (e.g., education in developing countries or training pilots). Each model emphasizes different aspects of the process. Comparable ISD models are the Instructional Development Institute (IDI) Model (1973), the Air Force Model (1975), the Gagné, Briggs, and Wager Model (1992), the Smith and Ragan Model (1993), the Kemp, Morrison, and Ross Model (1994), the R2D2 Model (1995), the Reiser and Dick Model (1996), the Dick and Carey model (1996), and the Seels & Glasgow Model (1997) used in this textbook.

The IDI Model has three phases: define, develop, and evaluate. The Air Force Model is iterative in nature; the steps are repeated and revisions are made as new information is revealed at a later step. The Gagné, Briggs, and Wager Model uses Gagné's theories about types and conditions of learning as a basis for analysis and design decisions. Smith and Ragan's model is divided into three stages: analysis, strategy, and evaluation. Kemp, Morrison, and Ross's model is very flexible. The order of steps can be modified to suit the situation. The R2D2 Model is described as a recursive, reflective design and development model consistent with the constructivist paradigms discussed at the end of this chapter. Reiser and Dick's model is appropriate for novices. Dick and Carey's model emphasizes the instructional analysis step.

Like the other models, the Seels & Glasgow ISD Model II: For Practitioners is a variation of its predecessors. It separates project management into three phases and presents diffusion as an ongoing process. The model is iterative because the products of the steps can be revised as the process proceeds. Thus, the design is continually being refined and polished by returning to a step and making adjustments. For example, you can complete a task analysis before writing objectives; however, you can also expand the task analysis and rewrite the objectives as new insights are revealed. When an instructional design process is used to solve problems, decisions must be made about which model to use and what adjustments, if any, need to be made in the model chosen. A design team may choose to develop their own model instead.

When a management plan is developed, an ISD model must be chosen to guide the process. An existing model can be adopted or adapted, or a model may be created just for the project. In either event, this step needs to be done early on so that it can provide structure for a project team.

The decision to use an ISD model may depend to some extent on the adoption of learning paradigms such as behaviorism, cognitive science, and constructivism. This is because paradigms have different positions on the use of objectives and strategies for instruction and evaluation. These positions make some ISD models more appropriate than others. In the case of constructivism, there is debate about whether ISD models can be used at all.

ORIENTING QUESTIONS

What is an ISD model?
What purposes can these models serve?
What are the similarities and differences among major ID models?
What are the components of Seels & Glasgow ISD Model II: For Practitioners?
What are learning paradigms, and how do they relate to instructional design?

OBJECTIVES

1. Given authors' ISD models, you will be able to match a schematic or descriptive phrase with each author.
2. Given an essay question, you will be able to explain the steps and flow of the Seels & Glasgow ISD Model II: For Practitioners.
3. Given a chart, you will be able to compare and contrast ISD models using date, configuration, and unique characteristics and infer reasons for the variations.
4. Given true/false statements, you will be able to distinguish between behavioral, cognitive science, and constructivist learning psychologies.
5. Given a chart, you will be able to visualize how design elements for the same instructional problem would change based on different paradigms for learning.

FUNCTIONS OF MODELS

Models can take many forms: verbal, visual, or three-dimensional. Whatever form they take, their purpose is to present a view of reality. They are used to give form and substance to conceptual relationships or procedures. Although models represent a reality, they can never be a complete representation, because you must abstract in order to translate reality into theoretical terms. Models can show variables and their interrelationship or they can represent steps in a problem-solving process.

Instructional design models give visual form to the procedures used in the ISD process. Often this is done with an accompanying description in verbal form. An ISD model is modified as it is implemented in different settings and situations.

Imagine you've finished your studies and accepted a position as instructional designer. You are assigned your first project, which is a relatively ambiguous task, such as improving the instruction in a course or changing the behaviors of employees who do performance appraisals. How do you control your anxiety? You break the task into parts. The first part is to decide on procedures you will follow in solving this problem.

The instructional systems design model is a representation of the process you or your team agrees to follow when doing instructional design. ISD models serve several purposes:

1. They visualize a systematic process, thus allowing those involved to reach consensus on that process.
2. They provide a tool for managing the process and project.

3. They allow you to test theories by integrating them within a practical model that can be applied.
4. They set tasks for the designer that can be used as criteria for good design.

Instructional design models are based on assumptions about tasks and the order of tasks. Always question these assumptions. Like all models, the ISD model is not reality; rather, it is a way to simplify and make reality visible. There are more aspects to each step than known in the model. Each step breaks down to many substeps.

Usually ISD models are adaptations of the generic model. This is because a model must be modified to fit specific situations or localities. What is new in the model is not the process, but rather the interpretation of the process.

ISD models differ in many ways. Some are accompanied by annotations or descriptions of how to implement a step. Others include only brief descriptions of a step. Most require doing each step in a prescribed order; a few allow more flexibility. Some are linear and others are iterative. The order of steps and what steps are included differs from model to model.

COMPONENTS OF MODELS

Models are constructed by showing the relationship among the steps and how the steps occur chronologically. A step is a task or phase that must be completed in order to develop an instructional design solution.

The generic model represented in chapter 1 consists of five steps: analysis, design, development, implementation, and evaluation. These steps are simply listed or shown in a line of five rectangular blocks connected by arrows. This model defines the process as five steps in fixed order performed one at a time. Other models may vary the steps, show more steps, or suggest more flexibility.

Andrews and Goodson (1980) compared 30 ISD models on the basis of 18 dimensions, including problem identification, alternative solutions to instruction, identification of constraints, and cost of instructional programs. They cautioned that many of the models represent a series of mechanical or linear steps rather than the complex analytical and cybernetic process required in order to apply the systems approach effectively.

Richey (1986) examined Andrews and Goodson's "Comparative Analysis of Models of Instructional Design." Their list of common elements was reduced to the six core elements shown in Table 7.1.

The question of whether ISD models are or should be linear is an interesting one. The word "linear" means arranged in a line or taking the form of a line. In programmed instruction, linear style means each learner follows the same path or line. Using this meaning, some of the models to be discussed, such as the IDI Model, are linear; others, such as the Air Force Model and the Kemp, Morrison, and Ross Model, are not.

The issue is whether an ISD model when applied should require a fixed sequence of steps, or whether there should be some flexibility. The flexibility in the Air Force and Kemp, Morrison, and Ross Models serves different purposes. Kemp, Morrison, and Ross's model uses flexibility to adapt to situations; the Air Force Model uses it to adapt to information resulting from a previous step. The Air Force Model still requires a prescribed sequence of steps. The consensus of ISD models is that there is a fixed order of steps to be followed, and that the process is iterative.

Several ISD models provide for flexibility in the order of steps by being iterative or by leaving options. Some of the ISD models that provide for simultaneous and interacting steps as well as linear ones are the Air Force; Kemp, Morrison, and Ross; Dick and Carey; and Seels and Glasgow models.

In his review of ISD models, Gustafson (1991) compares models on several dimensions. The first dimension is purpose. He describes some models as oriented towards

Table 7.1   A Definition of the Six Core Elements

Core Elements	*Andrews/Goodson Tasks*
Determine learner needs	Assessment of needs, problems identification, occupational analysis, competence or training requirements
	Characterization of learner population
Determine goals and objectives	Formulation of broad goals and detailed sub-goals stated in observable terms
	Analysis of goals and subgoals for types of skills/learning required
	Sequencing of goals and subgoals to facilitate learning
Construct assessment procedures	Development of pre-test and post-test matching goals and subgoals
Design/select delivery approaches	Formulation of instructional strategy to match subject-matter and learner requirements
	Selection of media to implement strategies
	Development of courseware based on strategies
	Consideration of alternative solutions to instruction
Try out instructional system	Empirical tryout of courseware with learner population, diagnosis of learning and courseware failures, and revision of courseware based on diagnosis
Install and maintain system	Formulation of system and environmental descriptions and identification of constraints
	Development of materials and procedures for installing, maintaining, and periodically repairing the instructional program
	Costing instructional program

From *Theoretical and Conceptual Bases of Instructional Design* by R. Richey, 1986, New York: Nicols Publishing. Copyright 1986 by Rita Richey. Reprinted with permission.

classroom instruction, others towards product development, and others towards course development. Depending on their orientation, the models require different resources. For example, classroom instruction development is done individually with few resources, little needs analysis, and tryout and revision. The results are not disseminated. Product and course orientations, on the other hand, generally require team development using extensive resources, with some needs analysis and extensive tryout and revision. The results are widely disseminated.

VISUAL DIFFERENCES

One of the reasons for using visual models is that you can see at a glance the nature of the process. Differences between processes are shown through shapes and connections between shapes. There are two aspects of the ISD process that can be interpreted through shapes. One is the sub-processes used to reach the goal, such as operations (rectangles) or decision-making (diamonds). The other is the overall configuration of all the shapes together. What basic shape does the whole process take? If you can answer this question, you've learned something about the process from the model.

Figure 7.1 presents five shapes that are common to ISD models.

Figure 7.1   Different Configurations of Models

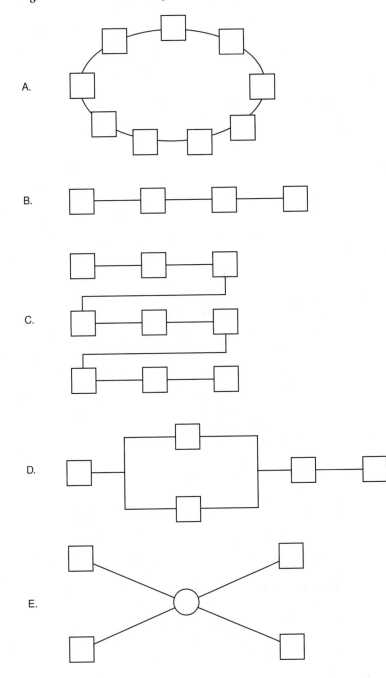

Shape A is an oval. It could also be drawn as a circle. This shape suggests no beginning and no end. The operations are connected so that wherever you start you complete all the steps. (This is not to be confused with the ovals used to begin and end a flowchart.)

Shape B is basically a short line of steps. It is a simple path to follow. Shape C is more complex. The basic shape is a large rectangle made from a path that allows for many steps in a line that starts at the top left corner and loops like a maze to the bottom right corner. More steps can be represented in a single path using this shape.

Shape D is a variation on B. You follow one path, but at points along that path you deal with two steps alternately or simultaneously. This path can be long or short and the number of concurrent steps can vary.

Shape E is a cross. The circle in the center is an intersection through which information passes. In this model, the steps are done in a specified order, but a step can be returned to at any point. The crucial element is the cross point, where information from each step is checked against information from another step and a decision is made to return to a step or proceed.

The basic shapes—oval or round, line, rectangle, cross, and line with squares projecting above and below—are some of the configurations ISD models can take. The oval indicates a flexible starting point; the line, a predetermined path; the rectangle, a long series of steps in a predetermined path; and the cross, steps that are returned to as information from other steps is checked. There are other configurations, but these examples show how the configuration of a model can reveal differences among ISD processes.

COMMON ERRORS

A designer should be aware of errors that occur commonly in the use of models. Boutwell (1979) lists several:

◆ Social variables are not taken into account.

◆ Training is generalized when it is situational.

◆ Other solution strategies are often ignored.

◆ Courses and materials are evaluated as single entities, rather than as interacting components of a larger whole.

◆ Models are often blindly adopted, rather than creatively adapted.

One common problem with the use of an ISD model is the use of an essentially structural model as if it were the complete procedure or paradigm. Because models are static and simplified, they lack the detail and dynamic interaction that must be provided in the ISD process. Designers should be aware of this and adjust accordingly. For example, some models lack a problem analysis phase and start with the assumption that an instructional problem exists. Yet for non-academic settings, the problem analysis phase is often necessary and important.

Therefore, when you adapt a model for the process you'll use to design instruction, don't do it blindly. Understand the assumptions of the model such as fixed path or starting point and why you chose it. Be aware, also, of the limitations of a model such as too few steps. In addition to the problems already mentioned, there can be errors in implementation such as not faithfully executing the steps, implementing the steps superficially, and rushing to completion due to unrealistic timelines (Hannum, 1983). In each of these cases, if you report that the model was used for your problem-solving process, you are not being accurate, because the process was not followed completely. In addition to applying a model completely, remember to question the appropriateness of the model. Remember also that the model does not represent the process exactly as it occurs in reality.

SELECTED ISD MODELS

The following is just a sampling of the models that have been published over the last 40 years.

The IDI Model (1973)

In 1965 a consortium was formed by instructional technology departments at the University of Southern California, Syracuse University, Michigan State University, and the U.S. International University in Corvallis, Oregon. In 1973–74 the consortium changed its name to the University Consortium for Instructional Development & Technology (UCIDT), and Indiana University became a member (Wittich & Schuller, 1973).

The U.S. Office of Education gave the consortium a grant to create IDIs for public school personnel. In the early 1970s the IDIs were used to train teams of administrators, teachers, and curriculum and media specialists in principles of instructional systems design. After a thorough review of the literature on systems approaches and design, the institute materials were developed by institutional members of the consortium (UCIDT, 1968). About 400 Instructional Development Institutes were conducted in 20 states. The subsequent evaluation was not thorough enough to determine impact. However, since then the components of the IDI workshops have been modified and used nationally and internationally with much success (Schuller, 1986).

The IDI model is noteworthy for its "organize management" step, which is missing from other models. This model also has the strength of being very detailed. The IDI project has nine steps in three stages called decision points in instructional development. Explanatory detail accompanies each step. Figure 7.2 shows the IDI model.

Figure 7.2   The IDI Model

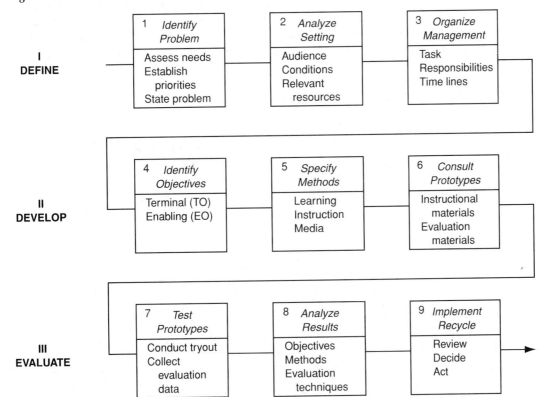

From *Instructional Technology: Its Nature and Use,* 5th ed. (p. 633), by W. Wittich and C. F. Schuller (Eds.), 1973, New York: Harper & Row Publishers, Inc. Copyright 1973 by W. A. Wittich and C. F. Schuller. Reprinted with permission.

The Air Force Model (1975)

The U.S. Air Force has been a pioneer in the application of instructional systems design concepts. It was the military that emphasized a systematic procedure for assuring application of instructional technology to course planning and development. The Air Force was among the first organizations to use a systematic approach to ISD. Today, the Air Force annually trains thousands from its ranks as instructional designers. Manuals for training instructors in ISD concepts were published from 1975.

Because training using the ISD approach is so important, Air Force policy states that ISD should be used to produce all training materials. The process requires the following:

1. determining job performance requirements;
2. determining training requirements (what is necessary to bring them to a skill level);
3. writing behavioral objectives and test items;
4. designing instructional procedures and materials; and
5. conducting and evaluating the instruction.

There is interaction between steps of the model, so sometimes portions of several steps can be revised simultaneously. The output of one step is intended to provide the information needed to accomplish a later step.

The Air Force Model is accompanied by adequate detail. Generally it is used by a team, although sometimes one person uses the model to perform the ISD process. This model emphasizes a thorough systems analysis before moving to the design phase. A lengthy process of collecting information about the learners, instructors, environment, subsystems, purposes, and policies is conducted, and task analysis is done thoroughly. The problem is examined until it is proved to be an instructional problem. After the first phase, decisions in other phases are based on the conclusions reached during the analysis stage. Classroom management techniques and individual differences are stressed at the "plan instruction" stage. The "conduct and evaluate" instruction stage includes support functions such as instructor training and facilities maintenance. Evaluation is conducted in both the field and the learning environment. This military model emphasizes analysis of content requirements and stresses instructional and systems management. The five-step model used by the Air Force is shown in Figure 7.3.

Figure 7.3   Air Force Model

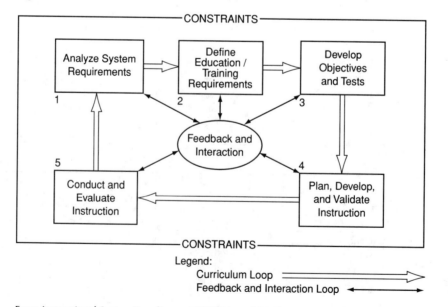

From *Instructional System Development* (UAF Manual 50-2) (pp. 50–52), by U.S. Air Force, 1975, Washington, DC: Author.

Figure 7.4   Stages in Designing Instructional Systems

System Level	1. Analysis of needs, goals, and priorities. 2. Analysis of resources, constraints, and alternate delivery systems. 3. Determination of scope and sequence of curriculum and courses; delivery system design.
Course Level	4. Determining course structure and sequence. 5. Analysis of course objectives.
Lesson Level	6. Definition of performance objectives. 7. Preparing lesson plans (or modules). 8. Developing, selecting materials, media. 9. Assessing student performance (performance measures).
System Level	10. Teacher preparation. 11. Formative evaluation. 12. Field testing, revision. 13. Summative evaluation. 14. Installation and diffusion.

From *Principles of Instructional Design* (p. 31), by R. M. Gagné, L. J. Briggs, and W. W. Wager, 1992, New York: Harcourt Brace Jovanovich College Publishers. Copyright 1992 by Harcourt Brace. Reprinted with permission.

The Gagné, Briggs, and Wager Model (1992)

In 1992 Gagné, Briggs, and Wager published a revision of the Gagné and Briggs text, *Principles of Instructional Design* (1974, 1979, 1988). Their model incorporates Briggs's theory on the use of levels of objectives to organize a course. Levels of objectives mean developing objectives from goals to specific objectives for each component of a course. In its procedural explanations this model combines Briggs's ideas on educational system design with Gagné's theories on types of learning and differing conditions for instruction. The educational system design part of their model is summarized in Figure 7. 4.

The Smith and Ragan Model (1993)

According to Smith and Ragan, the designer goes through a three-stage process: analysis, strategy development, and evaluation. They believe these three stages are common to most instructional design models. They qualify their model by cautioning that although designers usually follow the stages in the order listed, circumstances can cause the designer to modify the sequence or to do steps concurrently. Their model differs in that test items are written within the analysis stage right after tasks are analyzed. They also stress the iterative nature of design, which results in constant revision. Their model is shown in Figure 7.5.

The Kemp, Morrison, and Ross Model (1994)

This model differs the most from the other models. As it has evolved over the years, it has moved further from linearity. The model was introduced in a text in 1971. Figure 7.6 shows the 1994 model.

The 1994 model presents nine design elements that can be approached by different paths. In addition, two outer ovals indicate that revisions occur throughout the process. The first outer oval provides for formative evaluation and revision, the second for project management, summative evaluation, planning, and support services. A problem with the model is inadequate detail on doing instructional analysis. A strength of the model is its step of identifying delivery strategies (large group, small group, independent study).

Figure 7.5   The Smith and Ragan Model

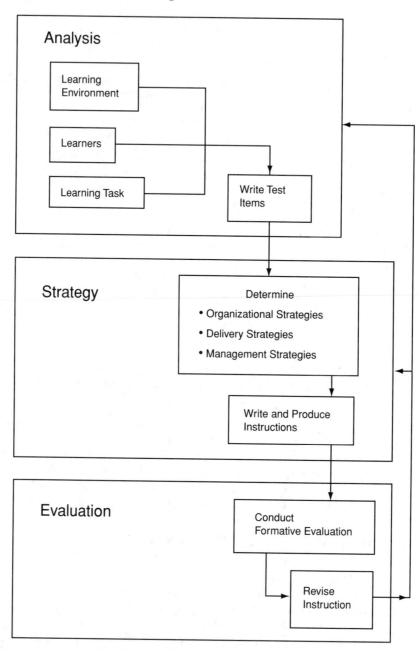

From *Instructional Design* (p. 8), by P. L. Smith and T. J. Ragan, 1993, New York: Macmillan. Copyright 1993 by Macmillan Publishing Co. Reprinted with permission.

The R2D2 Model (1995)

Willis (1995) describes a model that emerged from work at NASA's Johnson Space Center and the Center for Information Technology in Education at the University of Houston known as the R2D2 Model. He contrasts this model, which evolves from constructivist thought, with traditional models, which he believes come from the behaviorist tradition. He presents this model as more appropriate when designing for newer technologies because it allows for merging the steps of design and development as happens

Figure 7.6   The Kemp, Morrison, and Ross Model

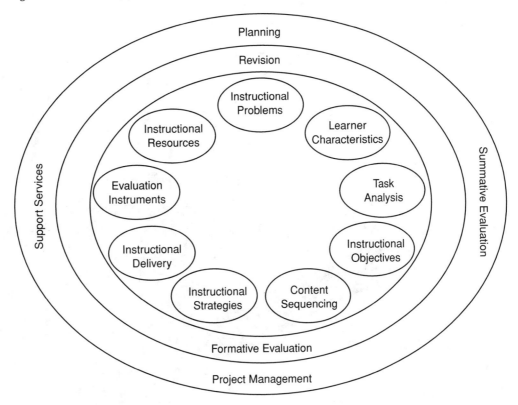

Elements of the Instructional Design Plan

From *Designing Effective Instruction* (p. 9), by J. E. Kemp, G. R. Morrison, and S. M. Ross, 1994, New York: Merrill/Macmillan College Publishing. Copyright 1994 by Merrill/Macmillan College Publishing. Reprinted with permission.

in rapid prototyping where parts of the project are conceived, produced, and evaluated quickly during the ISD process.

The name of the model stands for "recursive" and "reflective" and "design" and "development." "Recursive" in this context means "iterative" in that the same decisions may be addressed many times during the process. Final decisions emerge gradually over the course of the project. This characteristic is not unique to this model; although there is less emphasis in this model on front-end analysis, which includes needs analysis and determining objectives. "Reflective" means that the designer must give attention to the influence of context throughout the project. The stage of design and development also includes formative evaluation, which is emphasized because it occurs early enough in the process to allow for changes based on both objective and subjective data. This model will be discussed in more detail later in the chapter when the constructivist paradigm is considered. The R2D2 model is shown in Figure 7.7.

The Reiser and Dick Model (1996)

This linear model is intended for teachers. Unlike the Kemp, Morrison, and Ross Model, it does not allow you to choose the step you start with. It also presents a shorter process with fewer steps. Through the use of scenarios, the book that supports the model involves the teacher in a real life problem that instructional design can solve if this model is used. The Reiser and Dick Model is presented in Figure 7.8.

Figure 7.7   The R2D2 Model

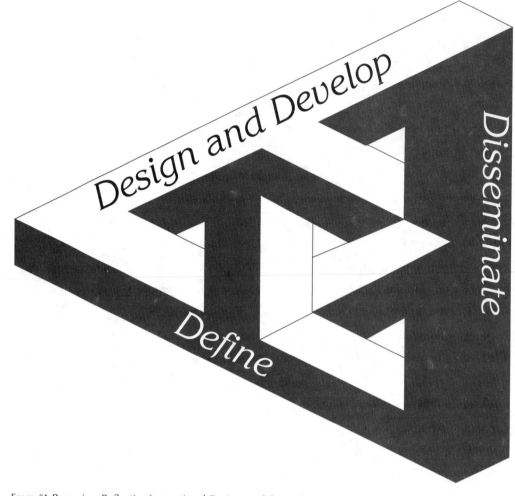

From "A Recursive, Reflective Instructional Design Model Based on Constructivist-Interpretivist Theory," by J. Willis, 1995, *Educational Technology, 35*(6), p. 15. Copyright 1995 by Educational Technology Publications. Reprinted with permission.

The Dick and Carey Model (1996)

This model was presented in a text for instructional designers published in 1978 and was revised in 1985, and 1990 (Dick, 1996). The text is used extensively in colleges to train instructional designers. Dick and Carey expanded the task analysis step to encompass instructional analysis. In the newest edition, they add the step of analyzing learners and contexts. The model describes the instructional design process from assessing needs to identifying goals through writing objectives to developing materials and evaluating instruction. Figure 7.9 presents the 1996 version of the Dick and Carey model.

The Seels & Glasgow ISD Model II: For Practitioners (1997)

As you have probably surmised by now, these models are variations on the generic ISD model and on each other. They are adaptations or redefinitions of previous models. This text introduces a new adaptation or variation intended for beginning students in instructional design. This is the Seels & Glasgow ISD Model II: For Practitioners presented in Figure 7.10.

Figure 7.8   The Reiser and Dick Model

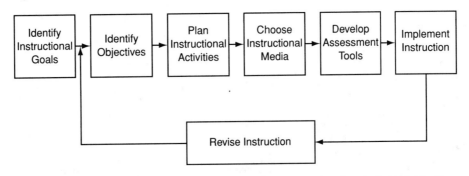

From *Instructional Planning: A Guide for Teachers* (p. 5), by R. A. Reiser and W. Dick, 1996, Needham Heights, Massachusetts: Allyn and Bacon. Copyright 1996 by Allyn and Bacon. Reprinted with permission.

The ISD process presented in the Seels & Glasgow ISD Model II: For Practitioners is based on the assumption that design happens in a context of project management. A project management plan is formulated and revised as necessary. This plan establishes roles, tasks, timelines, budget, checkpoints, and supervisory procedures. The steps are undertaken within the parameters of a project management plan divided into three phases:

1. needs analysis management;
2. instructional design management; and
3. implementation and evaluation management.

Diffusion, or promoting the adoption and maintenance of the project, is an ongoing process. Members of the design team may change depending on the phase in process. Each of the components of this model will be discussed separately.

The first phase of project management is to find the solution using needs analysis. This phase encompasses all of the decisions prompted by the questions associated with conducting needs analysis and formulating a management plan. This means questions related to needs assessment (goals), performance analysis (instructional requirements), and context analysis (constraints, resources, and learner characteristics) are addressed during this phase.

Figure 7.9   The Dick and Carey Model

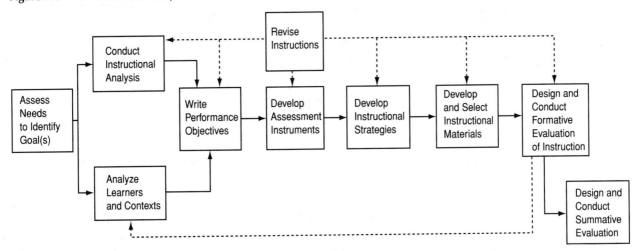

From *The Systematic Design of Instruction* (pp. 2–3), by W. Dick and L. Carey, 1985, New York: Harper/Collins College Publishers. Copyright 1996 by Harper/Collins College Publishers. Reprinted with permission.

Figure 7.10   The Seels and Glasgow ISD Model 2: For Practitioners

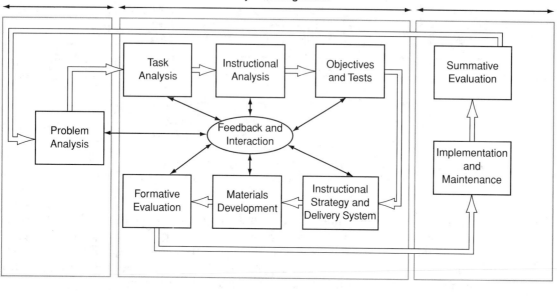

The second phase of project management includes all the steps related to design, development, and formative evaluation. These steps are done in order or, in some cases, concurrently, but the process is iterative. The steps can be returned to again and again, and decisions changed or adjusted as current data warrants. The designer can proceed to the next step before a step is finished and then return when ready. Each decision is followed by data collection and interaction with other members of the team. Consequently, changes are made as problems are revealed. There is flexibility to do task analysis at the same time instructional strategy decisions are considered and to do task analysis, instructional analysis, and writing objectives and tests concurrently. Similarly, objectives and assessment strategies can be evaluated formatively as they are developed.

The third phase of project management, implementation and evaluation management, involves transferring the program or product to a real life setting for continued use. For this to occur, several areas have to be attended to:

◆ Training materials and programs must be prepared.

◆ Training must be conducted and evaluated.

◆ Support systems and materials must be provided.

◆ Instruction must be evaluated summatively.

◆ The project must be disseminated.

◆ The ideas must be diffused.

◆ Instructors and learners must be trained to use new technology.

Even at this stage, revisions may be necessitated. Summative evaluation may yield data, impelling revision in the needs analysis and, consequently, in the design.

Diffusion, which means persuading others to adopt and maintain the innovation, is an ongoing process. The strategies that lead to diffusion are most effective if used during all the phases of a project. For example, designing an innovation that is user-friendly and has obvious benefits is a diffusion strategy. These characteristics can evolve from the first and second phases of project management. Another strategy is to involve potential participants, especially those likely to be early adopters. This can be done during all three phases. In the same vein, potential adopters can be moved through stages of awareness, interest, and trial during all three phases by targeted communication efforts. In the third phase, implementation management, opinion leaders and gatekeepers can be identified and targeted. Diffusion and dissemination of a project will be discussed in chapter 12, "Implementing Instruction."

In the Seels & Glasgow ISD Model II: For Practitioners, generally the steps are done in this order, at least for the initial attempt at outputs from a step. However, it is not necessary to complete a step before proceeding, and the order can be changed so that steps can be performed concurrently. For example, task analysis and instructional strategy decisions are sometimes considered concurrently. However, even in this case to some extent information about what is to be learned is gathered first. The order of steps can be modified to allow decisions about tasks and sequencing to be made in conjunction with each other. Similarly, it might be important to do the steps of objectives and tests and formative evaluation together in order to gather input on direction and approach early in the process. The rapid prototyping part of formative evaluation can necessitate doing several steps together or in brief. However, if the steps of the Seels & Glasgow ISD Model II: For Practitioners are assumed to be linear, then the flow would be as follows:

1. Find the problem through needs analysis. Determine whether there is an instructional problem: Collect information through needs assessment and context analysis techniques, and write a problem statement.
2. Plan for diffusion and project management.
3. Through task analysis collect more information on performance standards and skills and on attitudinal requirements. Then do an instructional analysis to determine the prerequisites.
4. Write behavioral objectives and criterion-referenced tests to match those objectives.
5. Determine the instructional strategy or components of instruction, such as presentation or practice conditions. Select delivery systems that will allow you to meet these conditions.
6. Help plan for production. Monitor materials development to assure project integrity.
7. Plan a formative evaluation strategy. Prepare to collect data. Revise as feasible and re-evaluate.
8. Plan for implementation and maintenance of the instruction.
9. Conduct summative evaluation. Revise goals if necessary. Adjust design accordingly.
10. Disseminate the innovation.

Table 7.2 compares the Seels & Glasgow ISD Model II: For Practitioners with the ISD model presented in Part I of this text as the ADDIE approach.

Exercises A, B, and C at the end of this chapter provide for practice on identifying ISD models.

THEORIES OF LEARNING

Instructional designers look to learning psychology for the answer to the question "What conditions lead to what outcome?" Out of theory about how learning occurs and associated research has come considerable knowledge regarding how to establish conditions to increase the likelihood that learning will occur. "Theory" is a global term used to specify particular ways of looking at things, explaining observations, and solving problems. Three major theories of learning are behaviorism, cognitive science, and constructivism. These theories can be described as philosophical paradigms or patterns that affect design decisions. The question of whether traditional ISD models are appropriate for all three paradigms is one being debated currently.

Table 7.2   A Comparison with the ADDIE Model

Steps in ADDIE Model	Steps in S & G Model	Questions Answered
1. Analysis	1. Needs Analysis	What is the problem?
		What are the parameters of the problem?
	2. Task and Instructional Analysis	What should the content be?
		What are the prerequisites?
2. Design	3. Objectives and Assessment	What should be assessed and how?
	4. Instructional Strategy	How should instruction be organized?
	5. Delivery System Selection and Prototyping	What will the instruction look and sound like?
3. Development	6. Materials Development	What should be produced?
	7. Formative Evaluation	What revisions are needed?
4. Implementation	8. Implementation and Maintenance	What preparation is needed?
5. Evaluation	9. Summative Evaluation	Are the objectives achieved?
	10. Diffusion and Dissemination	Has the innovation been disseminated and adopted?

The issue is whether existing models can be adapted to differing viewpoints or whether it is necessary to start with new assumptions and models. In other words, can the ISD paradigm encompass design based on cognitive science as well as constructivist paradigms, or is the ISD paradigm tied to behavioristic principles? If the latter is true, then processes developed for constructivist projects should be described as instructional design, but not ISD. Before we elaborate on this controversy, which is largely a definitional debate, we need to explain theories of learning and paradigm differences.

Behaviorism

Behaviorism is an orientation in psychology that emphasizes the study of observable behavior. It grew out of an attempt by early psychologists to make the study of behavior more objective. The premise of the behaviorist schools is that, instead of trying to understand vague internal processes, psychologists should concentrate on actions that are plainly visible, thereby making the study of behavior more scientific. Stimuli (conditions that lead to behavior) and responses (actual behavior) are the observable aspects of behavior. Behaviorists are concerned with discovering the relationship between stimuli and responses in order to predict and control behavior. That does not mean they are not concerned with thinking. Rather, they are interested in discovering the external controls which affect internal processes. They are less concerned with mental processes, since they can only be inferred.

The first application of behaviorism to instructional design came with the programmed learning movement. B. F. Skinner, one of the more prominent American behaviorists of the past half century, was chiefly interested in the learning process. He applied laboratory findings to complex forms of human learning by a technique called "programmed learning." In this technique the information to be learned is broken down into very small steps. At each step a single new term or idea is introduced and material previously covered is reviewed. Students respond to each step in a manner appropriate to the instruction, for example by answering a question or filling in a blank. The student is immediately told whether the answer is right or wrong. As the student progresses through the programmed materials, his or her behavior is gradually shaped until the learning objective is achieved. Textbooks, audiovisual devices, and computers have been used to present programmed materials.

Behaviorism influenced the course of instructional design for many years and continues to do so. It has provided precise prescriptions about what conditions lead to what outcomes. Its basic approach has been controversial, however, because it eschews references to mental events and does not adequately explain some complex human performance. For example, it cannot adequately explain how children learn grammar (Chomsky, 1969).

Cognitive Psychology

Psychologists have always been interested in mental processes. The first psychologists were chiefly interested in studying human consciousness and used a form of self-analysis called "introspection" to analyze the processes of their minds. This approach was rightly criticized as unscientific. In fact, behaviorism was a reaction against these methods, and for many years it was the major force in psychology.

There was a shift from behaviorism to an interest in the organization of memory and thinking. Among the factors that have shaped the cognitive science movement are computer programming and the work on artificial intelligence. For cognitive scientists, the basic model of the mind is an information processing system. Their orientation is a relative lack of concern with stimuli and responses and an interest in more holistic, internal processes (e.g., problem solving, comprehension, etc.).

Information processing and computer simulation are techniques used for theorizing about cognitive processes. Information-processing analysis is a technique for describing the presumed flow of information during cognitive processes. The flow diagrams show decision points and the sequences of the cognitive processes under study. In computer simulation a theory of cognitive operations is translated into a computer language and run as a program. If the performance of the computer matches human performance on the same task, then the theory that underlies the computer program is presumed a plausible one for human performance.

While the emphasis on cognition has focused attention on areas previously neglected, research on cognitive processes is based on a number of assumptions that are not easily verified, for example, that human thinking is analogous to computer programming. Likewise, the diagrams used to hypothesize about cognitive structures cannot be verified by direct means. In fact, it is generally true in cognitive psychology that the same performance can be accounted for by different theories about mental processes (Gagné, 1985). Nevertheless, the cognitive science movement has added many principles of design to our knowledge base (West, Farmer, & Wolff, 1991; Tennyson, 1995). Cognitive scientists are interested in how learners acquire knowledge and skills, rather than how behavioral responses are conditioned.

Instructional systems design has adopted many of the strategies developed by the cognitive science movement. The most important of these strategies is making a distinction between novices and experts especially when analyzing tasks and designing and evaluating instruction. Other important contributions are the comparison of mathemagenic and generative learning strategies, the role of schemata and imagery in knowledge acquisition, and the use of assessment for diagnosis. A brief explanation of each of these will help you understand this paradigm.

Mathemagenic approaches prescribe strategies by externally mediating instruction (Jonassen, 1988). For example, students may be given a cognitive map or asked to construct one given concept relationships. Generative strategies, on the other hand, require that students mentally construct the maps. Thus, instruction is internally mediated by the student. A schema is an organized knowledge structure. This means that frameworks for remembering are constructed and maintained. Schemas change as knowledge is acquired and stored. Some researchers believe that schemas incorporate both visual and verbal knowledge. Imagery refers to mental representations of knowledge that incorporate physical attributes. These "pictures in the mind" can serve as cues for memory. Because cognitive science emphasizes adjusting to a learner's thinking patterns, assessment data can be used to determine what content is delivered in what order or what remedial paths that are required.

Constructivism

Supporters of this paradigm claim that learning is more than conditioning or acquired knowledge, rather it is constructed knowledge. By constructed they mean that learners can only interpret information in the context of their own experiences. Learning must be personalized, set in authentic contexts, and oriented to problem solving. Constructivists are very interested in learning environments (spaces, places, settings) where learners can use tools and devices while interacting with others (Wilson, 1995, 1996).

Many constructivists believe that traditional ISD models are incompatible with the basic tenets of this paradigm. Among the reasons for this are beliefs that learning cannot be predetermined and that quantitative assessment is inadequate as a measure of personalized learning. Instead, constructivism, which has many roots in social psychology and other social learning paradigms, proposes that learning (a) allow students to assume roles and interact with others; (b) present problems, puzzles or challenges that must be solved; (c) emphasize intrinsic awards; (d) be personalized in meaning and assessment; (e) occur in realistic settings; (f) involve the learner in goal setting; and (g) encourage multiple perspectives. This paradigm has benefited from the development of interactive multimedia technology which makes realistic simulated environments practical.

On the other hand, some constructivists have developed ways to apply the paradigm within the basic ISD model (Willis, 1995; Wilson, Teslow, & Osman-Jouchoux, 1995; Bednar, Cunningham, Duffy, & Perry, 1995). To do this, they follow the essential steps but do this in ways consistent with the paradigm. They believe that ISD requires a systematic approach and the steps of design and evaluation but not behavioral objectives. Those who believe the ISD paradigm requires the use of behavioral objectives do not accept this constructivist adaptation. The issue thus becomes one of definition of ISD, not a debate about whether systematic constructivist design is possible. Therefore, constructivist design can be called instructional design or ISD depending on your definitional position (Seels & Richey, 1994). A more important issue is how learning is to be evaluated with constructivist design. For example, when can group activities provide acceptable criteria for assessment of individuals?

IMPLICATIONS FOR INSTRUCTIONAL DESIGN

Richey (1986) discusses the implications of behavioral and cognitive theory for instructional design. She notes that instructional design has been affected by both theories of learning, with the cognitive school having prominence at this time. As a result of the cognitive theorists' interest in mental processes, there is now interest in building instruction to facilitate thinking processes. However, Richey points out that instruction is still focused on behavioral outcomes. Her discussion of behavioral theories concludes with the following:

> Ultimately, the most fundamental application of behaviorist thought in instructional design is the reliance on observable behaviors as the basis for instruction. Performance, or behavioral, objectives describe goals using action verbs. All knowledge is cast in terms of the observable evidence of such knowledge. Test

items relate to such statements, and the entire delivery process is directed toward facilitating new learner behaviors. This orientation can also be extended to instruction related to values or attitudes. This is an almost universal approach among designers, and it stems directly from the behaviorist learning theories. (p. 65)

Since this was written the number of instructional design projects based on cognitive science and constructivist principles has greatly increased. Today, all three paradigms play a significant role in the generation of instructional design applications.

A Comparison of Design Dimensions

To understand the role that these paradigms play, we can compare the theoretical positions taken in relation to different aspects of instructional design. It is important to realize that those concerned with theory often have more interest in the purity of paradigm applications than those concerned with practice. Practice by its nature is more practical, which often translates into a more flexible and pragmatic application. Thus, when these paradigms are applied, it is not unusual to find some eclectic integration of principles from more than one paradigm. Examples and issues related to application of paradigms and implications for use of models will be discussed after the paradigms are compared.

Paradigms can be compared on several dimensions, including (a) definition of learnings, (b) the types of learning emphasized, (c) the instructional strategies employed, (d) the media preferred, and (e) the key concepts embodied. Table 7.3 compares the three paradigms on these dimensions.

Table 7.3 is based on publications in the instructional technology field that explain the viewpoints of the different paradigms. You can research a paradigm that interests you by using these sources:

Behaviorism: Gropper, G. L., 1983; *Behaviorism Today,* 1993; Seels, 1995; Ely & Plomp, 1996.

Cognitive Science: Brezin, 1980; Bonner, 1988; West, Farmer, Wolff, 1991; Seels, 1995.

Constructivism: Fosnot, 1984; Jonassen, 1991; Duffy & Jonassen, 1992; Seels, 1995; Wilson, 1995, 1996.

Issues Around Paradigms and ISD Models

Concerns about the use of traditional ISD models come mainly from constructivists, because the principles of cognitive science have been integrated in ISD models. The Dick and Carey Model (1996), for example, emphasizes information processing through the step of instructional analysis. The Smith and Ragan Model (1993) incorporates differences between novices and experts and instructional strategies appropriate to learning outcomes and domains.

Therefore, this review of the issues around paradigms and models addresses constructivist approaches to adapting models. Those who argue that it is impossible to adapt ISD models for this paradigm often are prompted by problems that arise when lock-step models are used for interactive multimedia development. One answer may be to adapt an ISD model based on a more flexible, cognitive or constructivist approach. One of the reasons traditional ISD models worked was that the teacher could adapt training as needed. This is not possible with interactive multimedia instruction ("To ISD or Not to ISD," 1996).

Bednar, Cunningham, Duffy, and Perry (1995) suggest aspects of ISD that must become more flexible when a constructivist paradigm is adopted. Content analysis is not important because content cannot be prespecified. Domains can be defined, but specific objectives must come from a student's perception of relevancy. Students should be encouraged to develop multiple perspectives on a task. Analysis of representative learners is not appropriate, because it is the individual learner that is important. The focus is on the learner's level of reflectivity. Here is their position on specification of objectives:

From a constructivist perspective, every field has its unique ways of knowing, and the function of analysis is to try to characterize this. If the field is history, for example, we are trying to discover ways that historians think about their world

Table 7.3   Instructional Design Paradigms

	Behaviorist	*Cognitivist*	*Constructivist*
Learning is	Change in overt behavior due to conditioning	Programming of a new rule for information processing	Personal discovery based on insight
Types of Learning	Discrimination, Generalization, Association, Chaining	Short-term sensory storage, short-term memory, long-term memory	Problem solving
Instructional Strategies	Present and provide for practice and feedback	Plan for cognitive learning strategies	Provide for active, self-regulating, reflective learner
Media Strategies	Variety of traditional media and CAI	Computer Based Instruction	Responsive environment
Key Concept	Reinforcement	Elaboration	Autotelic principle (intrinsic motivation)

From "The Instructional Design Movement in Educational Technology," by B. Seels, in *Educational Technology, 44*(3), p. 13. Copyright 1995 by Educational Technology Publications. Reprinted with permission.

and provide means to promote such thinking in the learner. Our goal is to teach how to think like a historian, not to teach any particular version of history. Thus constructivists do not have learning and performance objectives that are internal to the content domain (e.g., apply the principle), but rather we search for authentic tasks and let the more specific objectives emerge and be realized as they are appropriate to the individual learner in solving the real world task. (p. 106)

This is similar to the rationale made by Bruner (1966) for curriculum based on the "structure of the discipline" (Seels, 1995). However, the emphasis here is also on objectives evolving as tasks are tackled.

It is particularly difficult to reconcile positions on evaluation. Traditionally, ISD sets standards for success through predetermined objectives. This is impossible to do with the constructivist paradigm. Many employers want training to be done in groups with predetermined objectives and evidence of outcomes. While the constructivist paradigm does allow for evidence of outcomes, it is often primarily subjective evidence. Coupled with increased resource needs, the difficulty of determining outcomes and organizational outputs can create problems.

One approach that has been suggested is the use of different kinds of objectives. There are formats for writing objectives that are not behavioral. Formats appropriate for the constructivist approach are the problem solving or expressive objectives proposed by Eisner (1969, 1979). In a problem-solving objective a specific problem is presented to the learner, but there are many means by which the problem can be solved. The ends are closed and definite, but the means are an open system. With expressive objectives both the means and the ends are open-ended. The learner is provided with a rich experience. There are no preformulated behavioral objectives. For example, an expressive objective for early readers may be that given a mentor they will develop and publish a newspaper. Through this newspaper project they will develop new skills by being engaged with relevant material of intrinsic concern. Expressive objectives usually require a tutor or mentor to provide feedback and advice for the student.

The problems with using this approach for instructional design are evident. How do you determine to what extent you have achieved the goal? Will you be satisfied no matter what kind of newspaper the student produces? If this is a group project, what is expected of the individual student? Remember that according to constructivist theory, there must be allowances for individual differences in achievement. The expressive objectives format needs more theoretical and practical development. For example, innovative ways to measure achievement need to be identified. The Arts Propel Project ("Team Develops Exercises," 1987) has had some success with a portfolio used in conjunction with a tutorial as a way of measuring growth in aesthetic ability and following Eisner's (1969, 1979) recommendation to measure process instead of product.

Another issue is whether simply having no predetermined objectives and self-assessment means the design is constructive. It is not if the strategies used are traditional lecture/demonstration with no provision for constructing knowledge or solving challenging problems in the lesson.

> Rather, *authentic tasks* should be provided, within complex, real-world learning environments, allowing specific objectives to emerge that are relevant to the individual learner. Learning sequence should not be controlled, and multiple perspectives should be provided. Experts and teachers should model and coach, but not in a scripted or predetermined way. Evaluation should be goal-free and should examine the learner's process of constructing knowledge as well as the outcome or product. Constructivist perspectives are popular with some developers of hypermedia or multimedia instructional systems, in which it is possible to simulate reality and allow learners to select their own learning goals and sequence by navigating through various databases and media resources. (Gagné and Medsker, 1996, p. 12, authors' emphasis)

Other issues that relate to paradigms have to do with values. Rowland (1995) takes the position that the traditional criteria for ISD can interfere with creativity in design. Dick (1995) responds that that we can't have the same criteria for everything we design.

Current literature presents two positions: (a) ISD models must expand and become more open, or ISD will not survive; and (b) the basics of traditional ISD must be retained (Seels, 1995). It will be interesting to see how these positions are reconciled.

Characteristics of Design Based on Paradigms

So far, this discussion has been rather abstract. Let's turn now to more specific examples of the implications of these paradigms for design. We will do this in four ways:

1. a comparison of goals, assessment, and strategies as interpreted by the paradigms;
2. Dick's (1996) comparison of applications of the Dick and Carey model and the R2D2 Model;
3. an examination of problem based learning as a constructivist approach; and
4. RSVP TECH: Restructuring Social Science Via Progressive Technology.

Goals, Assessment, Strategies.   In Table 7.4 the goal, assessment, and strategy differences among the paradigms are compared. Some designers take a cognitive science viewpoint that includes aspects of behaviorism, and others take a constructivist viewpoint that includes aspects of cognitive science. The former are sometimes referred to as "neo-behaviorists" and the latter as "cognitive constructivists."

Each paradigm seems to have an affinity for different types of learning and delivery systems. For example, constructivism seems to be particularly appropriate for developing problem-solving skills; while cognitive science provides powerful tools for concept development. Research has shown that terminology is often learned best through behavioristic reinforcement of verbal association. Nevertheless, facts can be learned through cognitive science approaches, and problem-solving procedures can be learned through behaviorism. Each paradigm can be used for many types of learning. Still, it is possible that the theoretical basis for use of paradigms will eventually be clarified through affinity for types of

Table 7.4   Goals, Assessment, and Instructional Strategies Compared

	Goals	*Assessment*	*Strategies*
Behaviorism	Predetermined, behavioral	Of products and process	Cued practice reinforced through immediate feedback
Cognitive Science	Predetermined, goal-driven, statements of purpose	Diagnostic, of mental representation and processing	Chunking Concept mapping Advance organizer Rehearsal Imagery Mnemonics Analogy Visual frames
Constructivism	Not predetermined, negotiated, both goal-driven and personal goals	Of process and product, personalized	Argument Discussion Debate Collaboration Reflection Exploration Interpretation Construction

learning in a manner similar to the way delivery systems are distinguished to some extent by their relationship to paradigms (Seels & Richey, 1994).

It is equally possible that philosophical arguments will be reconciled, and there will be a merging of the paradigms within an ISD paradigm. This is in fact the trend today (Wilson, Teslow, & Osman-Jouchoux, 1995). It is important to realize that practicing instructional designers may not worry about whether an approach represents a consistent application of a paradigm. Often they make decisions instead on the basis of what works and find ways to use aspects of more than one paradigm. This situation reflects the researcher and practitioner roles in the field that were discussed in chapter 1.

Applying the R2D2 Model.   Dick (1996) compared the application of the R2D2 Model reported by Willis (1995) with applications of the Dick and Carey Model. The R2D2 Model is shown in Figure 7.7, and the Dick and Carey Model is shown in Figure 7.9. In his constructivist approach Willis' model purposively has no beginning or ending and implies continuous interaction among Design and Develop, Define, and Disseminate. The focus is on design and development because extensive front-end analysis is not necessary. The R2D2 Model is applied to a CD-ROM project about a simulation to enhance literacy skills. Dick's summary of Willis' instructional design process is given in Table 7.5.

Although task analysis was used, the output differs in that it leads to selection of an authentic reading task, a simulation of a job-hunting process, rather than a breakdown of tasks and sub-tasks. Pre-determination of objectives was not deemed important as long as teachers, students, and designers were involved in the process from the beginning. Because learning goals can be set individually, and the assessment uses methods such as journals, portfolios, and anecdotal reports, Willis does not try to do summative evaluation. Willis argues that this process represents a purer constructivist approach than modifications to traditional ISD models. He believes that these models cannot be adapted without major assumptions being questioned.

Table 7.5   Willis's Instructional Design Process

Willis's Instructional Design Model **Focal Points and Tasks**	
Definition Focus	Front-End Analysis Learner Analysis Task and Concept Analysis (No statement of instructional objectives)
Design and Development Focus	Media and Format Selection Selection of a Development Environment Product Design and Development Rapid Prototyping and Formative Evaluation
Dissemination Focus	Final Packaging Diffusion Adoption (No summative evaluation)

From "The Dick and Carey Model: Will It Survive the Decade?" by W. Dick, 1996, *Educational Technology Research and Theory, 44* (3), p. 61.

Problem-Based Learning (PBL).   Savery and Duffy (1996) describe problem-based learning as a way to link the theoretical principles of constructivism, the practice of instructional design, and the practice of teaching. Alavi (1995) describes PBL as

> A problem-based learning course is not a course in general problem solving, but focuses specifically on content (or subject-matter) central to the area of study by requiring students to acquire important knowledge in the process of tackling problematic situations . . . A problem-based course does not begin with a series of lectures; it begins with a problem-situation which the students have to begin to deal with in a problem-based tutorial . . . Typically, then, having been presented with a problem-situation, students will work co-operatively in small groups in coming to grips with the problem, in formulating it adequately, in identifying what they need to learn in order to deal with it, and so on . . . . (pp. 2, 4)

Problem-based learning was first developed by Barrows (1985) for training medical students to be effective at using information to solve problems rather than to become walking encyclopedias. It is compatible with the constructivist paradigm in that it establishes a situation in which learners interact with an information environment while working collaboratively with others to define a problem, generate hypotheses, gather data, and solve the problem. The problem presented is authentic and complex. For example, medical students would have to construct or use a patient's medical history, or make a diagnosis and compare it with actual outcomes. Students can decide to pursue sub-problems or to stay with one problem during the course. A structure for problem-based learning is provided (Alavi, 1995). Sometimes the structure involves defining a situation in need of improvement (SINI).

Because students have ownership of the problem and develop their own goals within a structure that creates an environment, this approach can be considered a constructivist approach. It follows systematic design principles in that goal setting, assessment strategies, and instructional strategies are consistent with each other. Assessment strategies include self-evaluation and peer-evaluation through surveys about process and rubrics.

RSVP TECH: Restructuring Social Science Via Progressive Technology.   Constructivist design requires a rich information environment that students can use to explore, interpret, and debate positions. One example of such an environment is provided by a project funded by the Office of Educational Research and Improvement (OERI) in the U.S. Department of Education. The primary focus of this project is to enhance student achievement by restructuring the standard classroom learning environment and refocusing traditional teaching practices so that students become more active participants in their own learning and share responsibility for that learning. Textbook materials were replaced by primary source such as documents, supplementary readings, and encyclopedias on CD-ROM. The design was implemented at Fullerton Union High School in Fullerton, California.

Juniors participating in RSVP TECH did more than just read about the American Revolution. Student groups (Rebels, Loyalists, Indians, French, British, Blacks) debated the causes of the Revolutionary War. Student pairs played delegates at a convention and constructed their own constitution. Electronic mail enabled them to "send" their proposals to the teacher, who then merged, copied, and distributed them for use in debate. Role-playing, debate, and technology also enlivened study of the Jacksonian Era and the Civil War.

After only one semester, RSVP TECH achieved documented results. When compared with their control group peers, students in the program achieved higher objective test scores, higher essay test scores for historical content, and higher ratings in history interviews. ("Making History Come Alive," 1993, p. 3)

Exercises D and E provide practice related to learning theory paradigms as they relate to ISD.

◆ EXERCISES

A. An Exercise Designed as a Test of Your Knowledge of ISD Models

1. Match the schematic with the name of the model it represents.

   _____1. Air Force Model
   _____2. Kemp, Morrison, and Ross Model
   _____3. IDI Model
   _____4. Dick and Carey Model

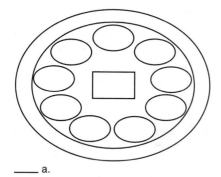

____ a.

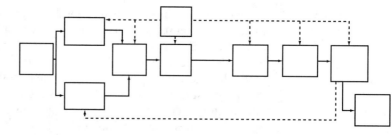

____ b.

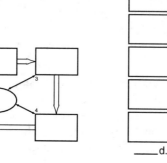

____ c.

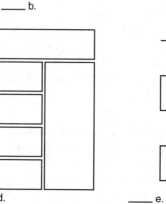

____ d.

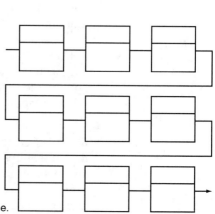

____ e.

Table 7.6

Model	Year	Configuration	Unique Characteristics
IDI			
Air Force			
Gagné, Briggs, & Wager			
Smith & Ragan			
Kemp, Morrison, & Ross			
R2D2			
Reiser & Dick			
Dick & Carey			
Seels & Glasgow			

2. Match the phrase with the model it describes.

_____1. There are three phases in instructional design: analysis, strategy, and evaluation.
_____2. Instructional design takes place in a context of project management.
_____3. The designer develops specifications for the system, course, and lesson level.
_____4. These two models emphasize the flexible nature of design because they have no beginning or ending.
_____5. There are few steps in this model for teachers.

a. Reiser and Dick Model
b. Gagné, Briggs, and Wager Model
c. Seels and Glasgow Model
d. Smith and Ragan Model
e. Kemp, Morrison, and Ross Model
f. R2D2 Model

B. An Exercise on Your Understanding of and Reaction to the Seels & Glasgow ISD Model II: For Practitioners

In an essay, explain and react to the nature and flow of the instructional design process presented in the Seels and Glasgow Model. Compare and contrast your reaction to this model with your reactions to some of the other models in this chapter.

C. An Exercise Designed to Help You Distinguish Among Models

Complete the chart in Table 7.6 for each of the models presented in the text.

How would you explain the variations among models? Speculate on reasons for these variations.

D. An Exercise to Check Your Knowledge About Theories of Learning

Answer true or false.

1. Programmed learning principles grew out of the behaviorist school of psychology.
2. Flowcharting is not a technique for describing mental processes.

Table 7.7

Instructional Problem			
	Behaviorism	**Cognitive Science**	**Constructivism**
Goals			
Assessment			
Strategies			
Delivery			
Systems			

3. Cognitive psychologists are interested in the organization of memory and thinking.
4. Constructivist psychologists are interested in learning environments.
5. Behaviorism adequately explains all types of learning.

E. A Group Exercise in Using Paradigms for Instructional Design

This is a dyad exercise in which one partner plays the role of a peer reviewer and the other the instructional designer. Then the roles are reversed.

Using the instructional design problem that you have been working on in previous group and application exercises, try to complete the chart in Table 7.7 for how the design would differ depending on the paradigm. You should be more specific to the topic than in Table 7.4 because you are applying the paradigms to a specific design problem.

◈ *REFERENCES*

Alavi, C. (Ed.). (1995). *Problem-based learning in a health sciences curriculum.* New York: Routledge.

Andrews, D. H., & Goodson, L. A. (1980). A comparative analysis of models for instructional design. *Journal of Instructional Development, 3*(4), 2–15.

Barrows, H. S. (1985). *How to design a problem based curriculum for the preclinical years.* New York: Springer Publishing Company.

Bednar, A. K., Cunningham, D., Duffy, T. M., & Perry, J. D. (1995). Theory into practice: How do we link. In G. J. Anglin (Ed.), *Instructional technology: Past, present and future* (pp. 100–112). Englewood, CO: Libraries Unlimited.

Behaviorism Today (1993). [Special Issue]. *Educational Technology, 33*(10).

Bonner, J. (1988). Implications of cognitive theory for instructional design: Revisited. *Educational Communication and Technology Journal, 36*(1), 3–14.

Boutwell, R. C. (1979). Instructional systems in the next decade. *Journal of Instructional Development, 2*(3), 31–55.

Brezin, M. J. (1980). Cognitive monitoring: From learning theory to instructional applications. *Educational Com-*

munication and Technology Journal, 28(4), 227–242.

Bruner, J. S. (1966). *Toward a theory of instruction.* New York: W. W. Norton Co.

Chomsky, N. (1969). *The acquisition of syntax in children 5 to 10.* Cambridge, MA: M.I.T. Press.

Dick, W. (1996). The Dick and Carey Model: Will it survive the decade? *Educational Technology Research and Development, 44*(3), 55–64.

Dick, W. (1995). Response to Gordon Rowland on "Instructional design and creativity." *Educational Technology, 35*(5), 23–24.

Dick, W., & Carey, L. (1996). *The systematic design of instruction* (4th ed.). New York: HarperCollins College Publishers.

Duffy, T. M., & Jonassen, D. H. (Eds.). (1992). *Constructivism and the technology of instruction: A conversation.* Hillsdale, NJ: Lawrence Erlbaum Associates.

Eisner, E. (1969). Instructional and expressive objectives: Their formulation and use in curriculum. In W. J. W. Popham (Ed.), *Instructional objectives: An analysis of emerging issues* (pp. 13–18). Chicago: Rand McNally.

Eisner, E. (1979). *The educational imagination: On the design and evaluation of school programs.* New York: MacMillan.

Ely, D. P., & Plomp, T. (Eds.). (1996). Classic writings on instructional technology. Englewood, CO: Libraries Unlimited.

Fosnot, C. T. (1984). Media and technology in education: A constructivist view. *Educational Communication and Technology Journal, 32*(4), 195–206.

Gagné, E. (1985). *The cognitive psychology of school learning.* New York: Little, Brown & Co.

Gagné, R. M., & Briggs, L. J. (1974). *Principles of instructional design* (1st ed.). New York: Holt, Rinehart, & Winston.

Gagné, R. M., & Briggs, L. J. (1979). *Principles of instructional design* (2nd ed.). New York: Holt, Rinehart, & Winston.

Gagné, R. M., Briggs, L. J., & Wager, W. (1988). *Principles of instructional design* (3rd ed.). New York: Holt, Rinehart, & Winston.

Gagné, R.M., Briggs, L.J., & Wager, W. W. (1992). *Principles of instructional design* (4th ed.). New York: Harcourt Brace Jovanovich College Publishers.

Gagné, R. M., & Medsker, K. L. (1996). *The conditions of learning: Training applications.* Orlando, FL: Harcourt, Brace & Company.

Gropper, G. L. (1983). A behavioral approach to instructional prescription. In C. M. Reigeluth, *Instructional-design theories and models: An overview of their current status,* (pp. 101–162). Hillsdale, NJ: Lawrence Erlbaum Associates.

Gustafson, K. L. (1991). *Survey of instructional development models* (2nd ed.). (ERIC Document Reproduction Service No. IR.-91.) Syracuse, NY: Clearinghouse on Information Resources.

Hannum, W. H. (1983). Implementing instructional development models: Discrepencies between models and their applications. *Performance and Instruction Journal, 22,* 16–19.

Jonassen, D. H. (1991). Objectivism versus Constructivism: Do we need a new philosophical paradigm? *Educational Technology Research and Development, 39*(3), 5–14.

Jonassen, D. H. (Ed.). (1988). *Instructional designs for microcomputer software.* Hillsdale, NJ: Lawrence Erlbaum Associates.

Kemp, J. E., Morrison, G. R., & Ross, S. M. (1994). *Designing effective instruction.* New York: Merrill/Macmillan College Publishing.

Making history come alive. (1993, Spring/Summer). *OERI Bulletin.* U.S. Office of Educational Research and Improvement, p. 3.

Reiser, R. A., & Dick, W. (1996). *Instructional planning: A guide for teachers* (2nd ed.). Boston: Allyn and Bacon.

Richey, R. C. (1986). *Theoretical and conceptual bases of instructional design.* New York: Nicols Publishing.

Rowland, G. (1995). Instructional design and creativity: A response to the criticized. *Educational Technology, 35*(5),17–22.

Savery, J. R., & Duffy, T. M. (1996). Problem based learning: An instructional model and its constructivist framework. In B. G. Wilson (Ed.), *Constructivist learning environments: Case studies in instructional design* (pp. 135–150). Englewood Cliffs, NJ: Educational Technology Publications.

Schuller, C. (1986). Some historical perspectives on the instructional technology field. *Journal of Instructional Development, 8*(3), 3–6.

Seels, B. (1989, May). The instructional design movement in educational technology. *Educational Technology, 29*(5), 11–15.

Seels, B. B. (Ed.). (1995). *Instructional design fundamentals: A reconsideration.* Englewood Cliffs, NJ: Educational Technology Publications.

Seels, B., & Richey, R. C. (1994). *Instructional technology: The definition and domains of the field.* Washington, DC: Association for Educational Communications and Technology.

Smith, P. L., & Ragan, T. J. (1993). *Instructional design.* New York: Merrill/Macmillan College Publishing.

Team develops exercises and portfolios to help teachers assess learning in the arts. (1987). *ETS Developments, 33*(1), 3–5.

Tennyson, R. D. (1995). The impact of the Cognitive Science movement on instructional design fundamentals. In B. B. Seels (Ed.), *Instructional design fundamentals: A reconsideration* (pp. 113–136). Englewood Cliffs, NJ: Educational Technology Publications.

To ISD or not to ISD? (1996, March). *Tech Trends,* 73–74.

U.S. Air Force. (1975). *Instructional system development* (UAF Manual 50-2). Washington, DC: Author.

University Consortium for Instructional Development and Technology (UCIDT). (1968). Syracuse, NY: Syracuse University, Instructional Design, Development and Evaluation.

West, C. K., Farmer, J. A., & Wolff, P. M. (1991). *Instructional design: Implications from Cognitive Science.* Englewood Cliffs, NJ: Prentice Hall.

Willis, J. (1995). A recursive, reflective instructional design model based on constructivist-interpretivist theory. *Educational Technology, 35*(6), 5–23.

Wilson, B. G. (Ed.). (1995). Constructivist learning environments [Special Issue]. *Educational Technology, 35*(5).

Wilson, B. G. (Ed.). (1996). *Constructivist learning environments: Case studies in instructional design.* Englewood Cliffs, NJ: Educational Technology Publications.

Wilson, B. G., Teslow, J., & Osman-Jouchoux, R. (1995). The impact of Constructivism (and Postmodernism) on ID fundamentals. In B. B. Seels (Ed.), *Instructional design fundamentals: A reconsideration* (pp. 137–158). Englewood Cliffs, NJ: Educational Technology Publications.

Wittich, W., & Schuller, C. (1973). *Audiovisual materials and their use.* New York: Harper and Row Publishers, Inc.

◆ ANSWERS

A. An Exercise Designed as a Test of Your Knowledge of ISD Models

1. 1. c
   2. a
   3. e
   4. b
2. 1. d
   2. c
   3. b
   4. e and f
   5. a

B. An Exercise on Your Understanding of and Reaction to the Seels and Glasgow ISD Model 2: For Practitioners
Your answer should address these points:

◆ ISD occurs in the context of project management.
◆ Although the process is generally linear, current theory and practice sometimes necessitate doing steps concurrently or incompletely.
◆ There are three stages of project management.
◆ ISD is an iterative, recursive, and reflective process with constant feedback, interaction, and revision.

◆ The first phase of project management is directed towards needs analysis.
◆ The second phase of project management includes all the steps necessary for design and formative evaluation.
◆ The third phase of project management involves tasks necessary for implementation.
◆ Diffusion activities should occur throughout the three phases.
◆ Sometimes data collected will necessitate a change in goals.

In addition to these points, the essay should describe your reactions to the models.

C. An Exercise Designed to Help You Distinguish Among Models
It is important that you complete the chart on your own first before checking with the answers given in Table 7.8. If you do not, you will remember less and be unclear on your reactions. This exercise is designed as a way to review models.

The models vary because they were developed or revised at different points in time and, therefore, reflect

Table 7.8

Model	Year	Configuration (shape)	Unique Characteristics
IDI	1973	box	step of project management, 3 stages
Air Force	1975	cross in rectangle	iterative nature
Gagne, Briggs, & Wager	1992	outline	levels of objectives
Smith & Ragan	1993	rectangle, ladder	assessment in analysis
Kemp, Morrison, & Ross	1994	circle	non-linearity
R2D2	1995	Escher waterfall	constructivist
Reiser & Dick	1996	simple line	few steps
Dick & Carey	1996	complex line	instructional & contextual analysis
Seels & Glasgow	1997	cross in center rectangle with piping across 3 rectangles	phases of project management, emphasis on decision making

earlier models. They were also developed for different audiences in some cases. For example, the Reiser and Dick and Kemp, Morrison, and Ross models are very popular with teachers. The IDI Model was used to disseminate the ISD approach to teachers and administrators. The Dick and Carey Model is intended for novices. There are also variations due to author preferences or experience.

D. An Exercise to Check Your Knowledge About Theories of Learning

1. True
2. False
3. True
4. True
5. False

E. A Group Exercise in Using Paradigms for Instructional Design

The answer to this exercise is shown in Table 7.9.

Table 7.10 is a contrasting example that shows that each paradigm can deal with other types of learning.

After performing this exercise, you should realize that in many cases delivery systems are interchangeable, depending on how they are used. In other words, the workbook could have been used within the constructivist paradigm and the videotape within the behaviorist as long as they were applied in a way consistent with the paradigm. While some technologies have an affinity for a particular paradigm, it is how the technology is used that determines its appropriateness.

Table 7.9

Instructional Problem: To learn about the human body's skeletal system			
	Behaviorism	**Cognitive Science**	**Constructivism**
Goals	Given a 30 item objective test on the body's skeletal system, you will answer 90% of the items correctly.	To learn about the parts of the body's skeletal system, how they relate, and health problems associated with this system.	Each learner develops a contract which specifies what their individual goal is in relation to the topic.
Assessment	Multiple-choice, completion, true/false, matching	generate visual representations of concepts and processes	peer and self evaluation through anecdotal reports
Strategies	questions providing practice, immediate feedback	cognitive mapping analogies flow-charts on diagnosing problems	collaboratively making decisions about authentic tasks
Delivery Systems	CBI with a computerized test.	a CBI tutorial with generative strategies	an environment providing information on the skeletal system including an interactive multimedia simulation of skeletal system problems

Table 7.10

Instructional Problem: To learn how to write a 500-word essay			
	Behaviorism	**Cognitive Science**	**Constructivism**
Goals	Given a topic, write a 500 word essay that scores 80 out of 100 points on a checklist.	Given criteria for a portfolio and 3 months, meet the criteria at a level of good or excellent.	The learner negotiates a personal goal related to this problem
Assessment	Writing product	Portfolio reflecting on drafts, process, and final products	Peer review and mentor comments
Strategies	Presentation, practice, and feedback	Imagery Brainstorming Cognitive Mapping	Discussion Debate Interpretation
Delivery Systems	A workbook on writing essays	A videotape on process writing and portfolios	A resource center on writing

8

Analyzing the Problem

OVERVIEW

The output of the problem analysis step is a description of all aspects of the problem. Problem analysis includes (a) needs assessment to determine performance discrepancies; (b) performance analysis to determine what part of the problem, if any, can be solved by instruction and through which format; and (c) contextual analysis to determine which learner and environmental factors should be considered in proposing a solution. These procedures are ways to identify different aspects of the problem. The step of needs assessment is used to identify discrepancies and goals. Performance analysis is used to determine which needs are instructional, and context analysis is used to identify learner and setting factors that constrain the solution. These phases are shown in Figure 8.1.

In ISD needs assessment procedures are used to identify discrepancies between what is and what ought to be. Needs, then, are gaps between the status quo and the ideal. These needs are prioritized and reformulated as goals or generalized statements of intent in regard to content. An instructional designer improves the instructional process in order to change learner outcomes, such as knowledge, skills, and attitudes.

Performance analysis procedures are used to determine whether the problem is one that can be solved by instruction. The instructional design process is appropriate only when performance analysis determines that a problem is an instructional problem. For a problem to be instructional it has to involve deficiencies in knowledge, skills, or attitudes. Performance analysis can also be used to determine the format for instruction that will be most cost effective, such as formal course or on-the-job training.

A problem statement is a summary of the results of needs assessment and performance analysis. The statement should clarify whether the problem is an instructional one and the nature of the performance discrepancy and the goals for improvement and priorities among goals.

The purpose of the contextual analysis process is to describe factors related to the learner and environment that should be taken into account, and to recommend strategies for doing so. Context analysis can be summarized in design notes about the learner, the environment, and the organization.

Figure 8.2 elaborates on the problem analysis step in the Seels & Glasgow ISD Model II: For Practitioners.

Figure 8.1   Phases of Problem Analysis

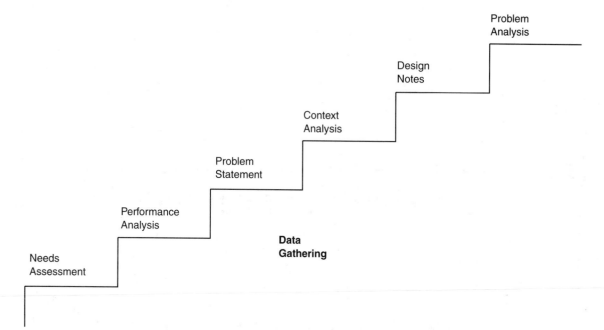

Figure 8.2   The Step of Problem Analysis in the Practitioner Model

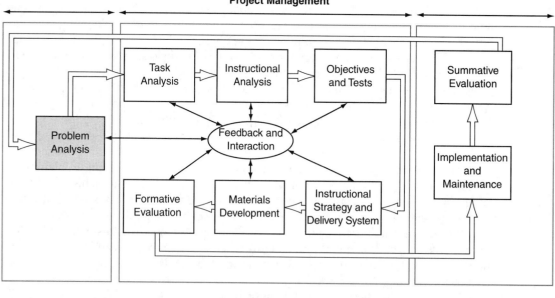

Problem Analysis
What are the discrepancies or gaps between what is and what ought to be?
What should be the goals and priorities for improvement?
What part of the problem, if any, is instructional?
What are the minimum requirements for instruction?
What characteristics of the learner, setting, and organization must be taken into account?

ORIENTING QUESTIONS

What are the components and outcomes of needs analysis?
How do you develop a plan for needs assessment?
How do you distinguish between instructional and non-instructional problems?
How do you do a contextual analysis?
How do you write a problem statement?

OBJECTIVES

1. Given a matching item, you will be able to identify the outcomes of each phase of problem analysis.
2. Given problem areas and a checklist, you will be able to develop a plan for gathering information.
3. Given problems, you will be able to classify them as instructional, non-instructional, or a combination of both.
4. Given a completion question, you will be able to identify appropriate instructional formats.
5. Given true/false questions, you will be able to identify statements about performance analysis as correct or not.
6. Given an outline for a needs assessment instrument, you will be able to complete the outline with questions that could be asked.
7. Given a table, you will be able to identify and classify related needs according to the Organizational Elements Model.
8. Given goals, you will be able to apply the card sort method for determining priorities.
9. Given the RUPS method, you will be able to write a problem statement.
10. Given the IDI method, you will be able to write a problem statement.
11. Given an information need and sources of data, you will be able to list contextual data that could be gathered.
12. Given an instructional situation, you will be able to apply the Seels and Glasgow Procedure for Contextual Analysis.

PHASES OF PROBLEM ANALYSIS

Although information may be gathered concurrently for each phase of problem analysis, this information must serve different purposes and lead to more than one outcome. For each of the phases you must gather information.

You may be given the results of a needs assessment, or you may need to do one. "Needs assessment" means developing a plan for gathering information about performance discrepancies and for using that information to make decisions about priorities. The priorities that must be determined are the goals for the problem solving effort. The data collected should provide a basis for stating goals. The problem is thus converted from needs statements to what should be achieved by the solution.

Thus, it is not enough to identify the needs as gaps or discrepancies. The designer must determine which of these needs should have priority. Methods for determining priorities, such as panels, card sorts, and storyboarding, are useful. Panels of experts can react to goal statements and be questioned about their reactions. Storyboarding requires putting goal statements on cards, displaying the cards, having participants change the groupings on the display, eliminating cards and consolidating them, and then reorganizing cards into priority categories. This process involves a lot of group movement and discussion and is especially suitable for prioritizing in a large group.

Performance analysis requires asking these questions: (a) Is this an instructional problem, one that can be solved by instruction?, and (b) What is causing the problem? The performance analysis step results in identifying the nature of the problem and its causes.

Table 8.1   Outputs of Problem Analysis

Input	Action	Output
Performance problem	Do needs assessment	Information on discrepancies, goals & priorities
Information on discrepencies and goals, data gathering	Do performance analysis	Whether it is an instructional problem, format requirements
Needs assessment, performance analysis	Write problem statement	Problem statement
Situation	Do context analysis	Context analysis
Context analysis	Write context notes	Context notes
Context notes	Select design factors, write design notes	Design notes

After analyzing performance you should be able to decide whether an instructional design solution is feasible and sufficient. In many cases instruction may be part of but not the whole solution, so it is important to justify any commitment of resources to instruction. During problem identification you ask what caused the problem and whether it can be eliminated by instruction. You may even find that solutions other than instructional design are warranted. Similarly, on-the-job training may be more justifiable than classroom instruction, and incentives may be more essential than instruction.

After data from needs assessment and performance analysis is analyzed, a problem statement can be formulated. A problem statement serves many purposes. It communicates the agreed-upon goals. If the team approach is used, the writing of the statement can become a process that facilitates the development of a common conceptual framework. If you are working independently, a problem statement is a way to clarify your thinking and facilitate communication with those you approach for assistance.

Information about the context of the problem helps the designer make decisions about feasible directions. To do context analysis, information about learner characteristics, the instructional environment, and the organizational situation is collected.

Table 8.1 gives the inputs, actions, and outputs of the problem analysis process.

Exercise A provides practice in learning the components of problem analysis.

DATA COLLECTION METHODS

You can use data collection methods for each phase of problem analysis: needs assessment, performance analysis, or contextual analysis. Sometimes, in order to collect information efficiently and thus not impose on busy people, the information needed for each of these components is collected simultaneously using a method appropriate to all the components. For example, you may use the same interviews to determine which part of the problem is instructional and which type of instruction is warranted, to determine content or skill goals and to determine which contextual factors need to be taken into account.

Each of these methods has advantages and disadvantages. Questionnaires reach a large number of people in a short time, but they take time to develop and may produce only superficial information. Records are a ready source, but require skilled review and often reflect the past rather than the current situation. Although interviews can be very revealing, the data collected may be biased. Observation provides useful in situ data but

Table 8.2   Data Collection Methods for Problem Analysis

Data Collection Techniques	Primary Strength	Primary Weakness
Business data review	Provides objective data	May take a long time
Interviews	Obtain in-depth information	Usually labor intensive
Focus groups	Provides qualitative focus	Direction of discussion may be swayed by informal leader
Questionnaires	Narrows direction of further investigation	Doesn't give in-depth information
Critical incident	Gathers observable investigation	Usually labor intensive
Observation	Provides a reality check	Usually labor intensive
Performance data reviews (e.g., performance appraisals)	Establishes criteria	May be confounded by other variables
Informal discussions	Provides input for other techniques	May be biased due to unsystematic approach
Job requirements review (e.g., job descriptions)	Provides objective data (if accurate)	Usually takes a long time

From "Maximize the Return on Your Training Investment Through Needs Assessment," by D. Georgenson and E. Del Gaizo, August 1984, *Training and Development Journal,* p. 46. Copyright 1984 by *Training and Development Journal,* American Society for Training and Development. Reprinted with permission. All rights reserved.

requires highly skilled observers. Tests can determine if deficiencies are causes but do not measure on-the-job use. Group discussion permits immediate synthesis, but the data is difficult to quantify (Newstrom & Lilyquist, 1979). The commonly used methods for problem analysis are compared in Table 8.2.

Some methods are better suited for one phase of problem analysis than another. When you want to gather just enough preliminary information to enable you to decide whether to pursue the problem, a review of records or a phone interview is quick and adequate. At the next phase or level where you need to collect information, tests and questionnaires are useful. If you want to be sure the information gathered from other methods is reliable, in-field observation is a good method. Forums, interviews, nominal groups, storyboarding, and card sort are useful for ranking priorities. Forums and group discussions are also effective ways to begin collecting information.

There are other less commonly used techniques, such as content analysis, which involves examining tests, articles, reports, or other print or non-print material in order to determine themes.

Exercise B provides practice in developing a plan for gathering information.

NEEDS ASSESSMENT

The phrase "needs assessment" can be confusing because it is sometimes used to refer to the whole process of needs analysis. It is also used to refer to the part of the process where content goals are determined by identifying discrepancies in learning and establishing priorities for instruction in the form of goals or statements of intent.

Making Decisions

In order to develop a plan for needs assessment, a series of decisions must be made. While there is no one model or conceptual framework for needs assessment, a model developed by Witkin for a project funded by the National Institute of Education is widely used in educational settings (Witkin, 1978a; 1978b). Witkin (1984) defines needs assessment as using information to make decisions, set priorities, and allocate resources. Her model includes nine questions:

1. Who wants a needs assessment?
2. Why is a needs assessment wanted?
3. What should be the scope of the needs assessment?
4. On whose needs will you focus and at what level?
5. What kinds and amounts of data should be collected for your purposes?
6. What sources and methods might you use for data collection?
7. What are your constraints on data collection?
8. What can you invest in people, money, and time?
9. What needs assessment products meet your purposes, constraints, and resources? (pp. 33–36)

It may be easier for you to remember that to devise any data collection plan you must answer at least three questions:

1. What do I need to know?
2. How will I collect information?
3. Whom or what will I use as a source of information?

You can make a table to summarize your plan by completing columns for the questions you'll ask, the information you'll need, and the sources or methods you'll use. You can also build a matrix to show your plans for data collection (Stufflebeam, McCormick, Brinkeroff, & Nelson, 1985). Across the top, list the questions you have developed. Down the side, list the data collection procedures you will use. Wherever a collection procedure will answer a question, put an "x."

Another approach to planning data collection is to use the checklist given in Figure 8.3. This checklist requires answering four questions.

Developing Instruments

In order to gather information, you have to prepare for writing questions and developing instruments. What kinds of questions do you want to ask? How do you want to phrase them? How will you analyze the answers? Before you develop an instrument, such as a survey questionnaire or interview protocol, you need to think about these questions.

Rossett's (1982, p. 30) typology for generating needs assessment questions is helpful. Her typology includes five areas of questioning: nature of the problem, priorities within the problem, subject matter/skills, attitude toward the problem, and cause of problem. You don't have to use all the questions and categories at once; you may omit some questions or categories completely.

Type 1 includes questions on problem finding. These questions deal with the discrepancy and the nature of the discrepancy. Rossett gives these examples:

◆ "Compared to other job seekers, I think that I . . . ."
◆ "What experiences have you had that have led you to enroll in this engine safety class?"

Type 2 questions cover problem selecting. It is important to give clear directions in this section. The respondents need to know on what basis you want them to rank items and whether you want them to describe their needs or a group's needs. Questions are longer in this section because you want them to select from several items or assign priority. For example:

Figure 8.3   Checklist for Decisions in Data Collection

1. What will be the scope of the needs assessment?
   ____ A. Phases
   ____ B. Resources
   ____ C. Schedule

2. What categories of information are needed?
   ____ A. Facts/Knowledge
   ____ B. Skills/Competencies
   ____ C. Feelings/Opinions
   ____ D. Causes/Relationships

3. What data collection methods will be used?

   A. Interviews
   ____ 1. Consultations
   ____ 2. Group debriefing
   ____ 3. Individual
   ____ 4. Forum/Panel
   ____ 5. Questionnaire
   B. Documents
   ____ 1. Records
   ____ 2. Literature
   ____ 3. Newspapers
   ____ 4. Test
   C. Observation
   ____ 1. Product
   ____ 2. Samples
   ____ 3. Settings
   ____ 4. Sociodata, e.g., sociogram
   D. Priority
   ____ 1. Card sort
   ____ 2. Delphi technique
   ____ 3. Storyboarding
   ____ 4. Nominal groups
   ____ 5. Other

4. What sources will be used?
   ____ A. People? Specify. _____
   ____ B. Services? Specify. _____
   ____ C. Reporting techniques? Specify. _____
   ____ D. Other? Specify. _____

◆ "Mark the skills below with the number that reflects how important it is to you to know how to do it."

Type 3 questions are on knowledge/skill proving. These items are like sample pre-test items. They will tell you what the learners know, if anything, about the skills. For example:

◆ "Please examine this resume. Render a judgment on its strengths and weaknesses."

Type 4 items deal with finding feelings. How does the learner feel about the problem? What are his or her emotions and attitudes? For example:

◆ "Which best describes your feelings about taking a class on alcohol abuse and automobile safety? Check one."

Type 5 questions center on cause finding. What do the learners think is causing the problem? For example:

◆ "Which of the following are contributing to your problem selling frangarams this year? Check all that apply to you."

Poorly designed questionnaires yield little information. When you prepare your instruments follow these basic rules (Spitzer, 1979; Maher & Kur, 1983).

1. Avoid ambiguous and technical language, negatively worded questions, hints at responses, and unnecessary or obvious questions.
2. Don't put the important items at the end.
3. Begin with easy items and personal data.
4. Emphasize crucial words, leave adequate space for comments, group and vary items, and include clear instructions and incentives.
5. Print your questions neatly and try them out first.
6. Plan how you'll analyze the data.

Classifying Needs

According to Burton and Merrill (1991), "a need is present when there is a discrepancy or gap between the way things 'ought to be' and the way they 'are' " (p. 21). They identify several types of needs all of which can be described as discrepancies:

◆ normative needs, when there is less than the established standard;

◆ felt needs, when people say they want something;

◆ expressed needs, when people create a demand through action;

◆ comparative needs, when similar services are not received;

◆ anticipated or future needs, when demands are projected; and

◆ critical-incident needs, when failures in training have serious consequences.

A discrepancy is a gap between desired behavior and actual or predicted behavior. An instructional design problem analysis is always done from the point of view that needs are gaps or discrepancies in instructional outcomes.

Kaufman and English (1979) classify needs differently. Their Organizational Elements Model (OEM) is shown in Figure 8.4.

Figure 8.4   Categories of Needs in the OEM Model

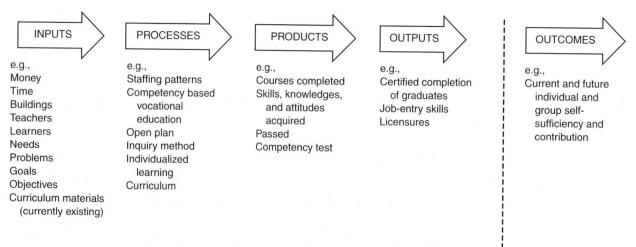

The OEM has five elements that relate means to ends and the individual to organizations and society. Two of the elements (inputs and processes) are means, or what organizations use and do. Three of the elements (products, outputs, and outcomes) are ends. Of the five, one element (outcomes) is external to the organization because it represents impact on society; the other four are internal to the organization. Thus, in their model, needs fall into three categories and five subcategories:

◆ quasi-needs: inputs and processes

◆ internal needs: products and outputs

◆ external needs: outcomes

The importance of this typology is that it helps us distinguish between needs that can become goals of instruction, needs that are long term goals based on society's intent, and quasi-needs, which are not needs in themselves but rather processes and resources that support instruction. A product can be an instructional goal for an individual. An output can be an instructional goal for an organization. Inputs, processes, and outcomes are not appropriate as goals for instruction although instructional goals should be related to them (Gentry, 1994).

Each of the elements in the model is defined. Inputs (things we use) and processes (things we do) are supportive of effects on individuals, organizations, and society, not effects in themselves. Examples of inputs are instructor or learner characteristics, and examples of processes are testing or managing.

Products and outputs are difficult to distinguish. They are results produced by an intervention through inputs or processes. Needs for products or outputs are internal to any organization. The difference between products and outputs is that outputs have more scope. Output refers to an aggregate of products and thus is a product of the organization as a whole rather than of an individual. A completed physics course is a product, whereas graduation is an output. A product must be combined with other products to create a useful output.

Outcomes are individual or organizational changes that contribute to society's survival. There should be logical consistency among all the elements. Each element should lead to the next element. By determining the status quo for each element and comparing it with the desired results, it is possible to identify gaps or discrepancies.

An example of the OEM model applied is given in Table 8.3.

Kaufman is describing a global societal level when he defines outcomes as the end result of the combined effects of inputs, processes, products, and outputs. Most instructional designers are concerned with less global needs. Designers often find it difficult to deal at the level of long-term benefits to individuals or society because time constraints confine them to short-term goals. This does not mean that the designer ignores long-term outcomes. Each need interacts with the other categories of needs (Kaufman, 1983; Kaufman & English, 1979). Typically, the instructional designer writes a problem statement that

Table 8.3   Example of OEM Model Applied to Computer Literacy Curriculum

Inputs	*Processes*	*Products*	*Outputs*	*Outcomes*
Grant money	Grant writing	Completed courses in computer skills	Certificates awarded	Trainees are employed and are off welfare; begin to display work habits to children, thus affecting future
Administrative support	Market research	Job-related skills	Trainees hired	
Curriculum objectives	Design of instruction	Competency test passed	College articulation	
Lab facilities			Agreement fulfilled	

includes the input (resources, such as development team), the action (processes to be used, such as systems models), and the product (results, such as competencies and attitudes), but this is done with awareness of long term goals.

Identifying Goals

Because the intent of needs assessment is to determine goals, a needs assessment is not complete until priorities have been identified. The purpose of a needs assessment is to clarify the scope of problem-solving efforts. The process should lead to a statement of priorities. The product of needs assessment should be goals, descriptions of intent stated in broad, not measurable, terms. Kaufman (1983) defines needs assessment as "the process for identifying, documenting and justifying the gaps between what is and what should be for results—products, outputs, and/or outcomes—and placing the gaps (needs) in priority order for closure" (p. 14).

Needs assessment is the process of defining the results (end) of the curriculum sequence (means). In instructional design the needs to be identified are the effects on individuals and organizations. The processes used to achieve the ends are needs of the designer, not of the learner.

There are several techniques for determining priorities from the data collected. Priority-ranking techniques include the Delphi Technique, expert panel, focus group, card sort, Q-sort, nominal group, and storyboarding. These methods are described in many sources (Kaufman & English, 1979; Murray-Hicks, 1981; Scott & Deadrick, 1982; Witkin, 1984; Stufflebeam et al., 1985). Three of these methods for ranking priorities will be discussed briefly: nominal group, storyboarding, and card sort.

A nominal group is a group constituted or named for a one-time task. It is used to prioritize items. Six to 12 people are seated around three sides of a rectangular table with a facilitator at the head of the U shape. During the first 10 minutes participants respond independently to an initial question about goals. Then, there is a round-robin listing of the items generated during the "no talking" period. Next, participants rank the most important items from the whole list. The accumulated ranks are determined along with the items on which there is the widest disagreement. During the discussion the participants can speak only to the facilitator. After discussion, the items are reassessed and assigned points. The resulting items are ranked and weighed, and a newly prioritized list of items is presented to the group. The group then discusses whether they agree with this list (Gentry, 1994).

Storyboarding as a technique for creative thinking was developed by the Disney Corporation. As used in needs assessment to establish priorities, it starts with many colors of index cards, soft display areas for tacking, tacks, and a group of people given a topic, theme, or question. Like the Delphi Technique, storyboarding requires a series of rounds. Participants are asked to write down as many ideas as they can in response to a question. Using different-colored cards, participants can generate categories, combine ideas, move, delete, or add ideas. Discussion is interspersed with the use of cards to visualize and manipulate ideas until categories and priorities in each category are generated and agreed on.

In card sort declarative sentences or themes are written on cards; then the cards are sorted and ranked. This is a forced choice method that usually requires sorting into five or fewer piles that represent degrees of importance. This technique is often used when large numbers of goals must be put in priority.

Exercises G, H, and I provide practice in needs assessment procedures.

PERFORMANCE ANALYSIS

The designer must identify which discrepancies require an instructional plan and which require other types of solutions, such as new management policy, better organizational structure, or improved equipment, tools, or materials. To do this you need to determine causes. Why are there deficiencies? Are the deficiencies due to instruction? Information on causes can be gathered during needs assessment. At this point problems are stated as goals to be accomplished, and causes have yet to be clarified. You may find that in order to reach a goal, it is necessary to attend to both instruction and management policy. The instructional designer may opt to deal only with the instructional aspect.

The other part of performance analysis is to identify minimal required instructional formats. By formats we mean formal courses, refresher courses, or on-the-job training. You can also use this information to decide whether this course should be required or elective and whether it should be for novices or practitioners.

Instructional or Non-Instructional?

As an instructional designer you effect changes in people. You must learn to distinguish among problems that call for effecting changes in knowledge, skills, and attitudes, and problems that call for alternative solutions, such as management or communication problems. For example, students forget to register by a certain date. This problem might be solved by posting a sign or by advertising the date. It could be a communication problem, not an instructional problem.

Your first task as a consultant may be to advise your client on whether the problem can be solved by instruction. The approach taken in this field is that instructional problems can be differentiated from non-instructional problems by whether the problem is due to a deficiency in knowledge/skills/attitudes or to poor organizational conditions. Both conditions can influence attitudes towards performance of tasks. The instructional design field deals only with deficiencies in knowledge, skills, or attitudes that can be remedied by formal training or practice (Kaufman, 1986).

Nadler (1982) distinguishes between problems stated in terms of obtaining or organizing resources and problems stated in terms of instruction. The distinction is useful because it reminds us that there are solutions other than training and that not all human resource problems are instructional problems. Instead of training, you may need to change the person in the job, the work team, the workplace, or the contingencies and rewards. Similarly, not all instructional problems require complex instructional design solutions. A job aid or on-the-job training may be sufficient.

The PROBE Approach.   Thomas Gilbert (1982), a psychologist/performance engineer, uses another approach, PROBE. PROBE, shown in Figure 8.5, uses a list of questions designed to elicit more than yes/no answers. Gilbert recommends PROBE when you are doing needs assessment on training for jobs. The more difficult the job, the more useful PROBE questions are. Gilbert has designed PROBE so that there are questions about two areas that affect behavior: environment and repertoire. Gilbert's PROBE approach yields information needed to determine whether a problem can be solved by instruction. If the answers indicate the problem lies in the behavioral repertoire, the solution is likely to be instruction; if the answers indicate the problem is the environment, instruction is not likely to be the solution. Figure 8.5 summarizes the PROBE Approach.

The Mager and Pipe Approach.   There are several flowcharts available for the designer to use for performance analysis. Kaufman (1986) offers an algorithm for identifying human performance problems. His flowchart requires identifying whether it is possible to solve the problems by changing the environment, people, or people's performance. Mager and Pipe's flowchart (1970) for determining performance problems is probably the most popular guide to performance analysis.

Mager and Pipe separate performance discrepancies into those due to skill deficiencies and those due to obstacles to and rewards for performance. Their method for analyzing whether performance problems are due to lack of instruction or lack of rewards is shown in Figure 8.6. At the skill deficiency decision box you choose one of two paths. One path takes you to instructional solutions and the other to non-instructional solutions. In some cases, you

Figure 8.5   Gilbert's PROBE Approach

E—QUESTIONS ABOUT THE BEHAVIORAL ENVIRONMENT

A. DIRECTIONAL DATA

1. Are there sufficient, readily accessible data (or signals) to direct an experienced person to perform well?

2. Are they accurate?

3. Are they free of confusion—"stimulus competition"—that slows performance and invites errors?

4. Are they free of "data glut"—stripped down to simple forms and not buried in a lot of extraneous data?

5. Are they up-to-date and timely?

6. Are good models of behavior available?

7. Are clear and measurable performance standards communicated so that people know how well they are supposed to perform?

8. Do they accept the standards as reasonable?

B. CONFIRMATION

1. Is feedback provided that is "work-related"—describing results consistent with the standards and not just behavior?

2. Is it immediate and frequent enough to help people remember what they did?

3. Is it selective and specific—limited to few matters of importance and free of "data glut" and vague generalities?

4. Is it educational—positive and constructive so that people learn something from it?

C. TOOLS AND EQUIPMENT

1. Are the necessary implements usually on hand for doing the job?

2. Are they reliable and efficient?

3. Are they safe?

D. PROCEDURES

1. Are the procedures efficient and designed to avoid unnecessary steps and wasted emotion?

2. Are they based on sound methods rather than historical happenstance?

3. Are they appropriate to the job and the skill level?

4. Are they free of boring and tiresome repetition?

E. RESOURCES

1. Are adequate materials, supplies, assistance, etc. usually available to do the job well?

2. Are they efficiently tailored to the job?

3. Do ambient conditions provide comfort and prevent unnecessary interference?

F. INCENTIVES

1. Is pay for the job competitive?

2. Are there significant bonuses or raises based on good performance?

3. Does good performance have any relationship to career advancement?

4. Are there meaningful non-pay incentives (recognition, and so on—for good performance (based on results and not behavior)?

5. Are they scheduled well, or so frequently as to lose meaning and so infrequently as to be useless?

6. Is there an absence of punishment for performing well?

7. Is there an absence of hidden incentives to perform poorly?

8. Is the balance of positive and negative incentives in favor of good performance?

---

may wish to use both paths because often performance discrepancies have both causes. The flowchart summarizes these steps:

1. Evaluate whether the discrepancy is important enough to warrant consideration.
2. Determine whether there is a lack of critical knowledge or skills. If so, look for an instructional solution; if not, look for a problem with motivation or obstacles.
3. Determine whether the workers ever had the required skills or knowledge.

Figure 8.5 *Continued*

P—QUESTIONS ABOUT BEHAVIORAL REPERTOIRES

G. KNOWLEDGE AND TRAINING

1. Do people understand the consequences of both good and poor performance?

2. Do they grasp the essentials of performance—do they get the "big picture"?

3. Do they have the technical concepts to perform well?

4. Do they have sufficient basic skills—reading and so on?

5. Do they have sufficient specialized skills?

6. Do they always have the skills after initial training?

7. Are good job aids available?

H. CAPACITY

1. Do the incumbents have the basic capacity to learn the necessary perceptual discriminations with accuracy and speed?

2. Are they free of emotional limitations that would interfere with performance?

3. Do they have sufficient strength and dexterity to learn to do the job?

I. MOTIVES

1. Do incumbents seem to have the desire to perform when they enter the job?

2. Do their motives endure—e.g., is the turnover high?

From "A Question of Performance—Part II Applying the PROBE Model," by Thomas Gilbert, 1982, *Training and Development Journal,* p. 87. Copyright 1982 by Thomas Gilbert. Reprinted with permission.

4. If they had the skills and knowledge, determine whether there has been opportunity for practice.
5. If the skill is used frequently, determine whether the feedback on performance is adequate.
6. If training, practice, and feedback are found adequate, consider simpler ways of solving problems, such as job aids (charts, diagrams, etc.), job redesign, or on-the-job training.
7. Determine whether workers are able to change. If not, transfer or terminate them.
8. Look at the reward structure. What kinds of behaviors are rewarded or punished?
9. Determine whether performance matters. Are the tasks worth accomplishing? How can you make the tasks worth accomplishing?
10. Determine whether there are obstacles to performance, such as policies, environment, expectations, demands on time.

Mager and Pipe (1970) distinguish between competence ("can do") and performance ("does do"). If workers can't do a task, then formal training is advised. If they can't do it but used to do it, practice and feedback are advised. If they can do it but don't do it, management of rewards and consequences (behavior management) is recommended. Mager and Pipe discuss performance problems that fall into the skill deficiency category. By skill deficiency they mean psychomotor or cognitive behaviors. They do not provide for instruction to develop attitudes. To determine whether a problem is instructional, an important question is whether workers could perform the task if their lives depended on it.

Instructional problems can be identified using the Mager and Pipe approach if knowledge and skills are considered competencies. Mager and Pipe do not deal with the distinction between attitudes affected by instruction and attitudes affected by organizational conditions. If you plan to use this approach to performance analysis, you need to obtain their book which includes a checklist and flowchart of the procedure. A poster is also available.

Figure 8.6   The Mager and Pipe Flowchart

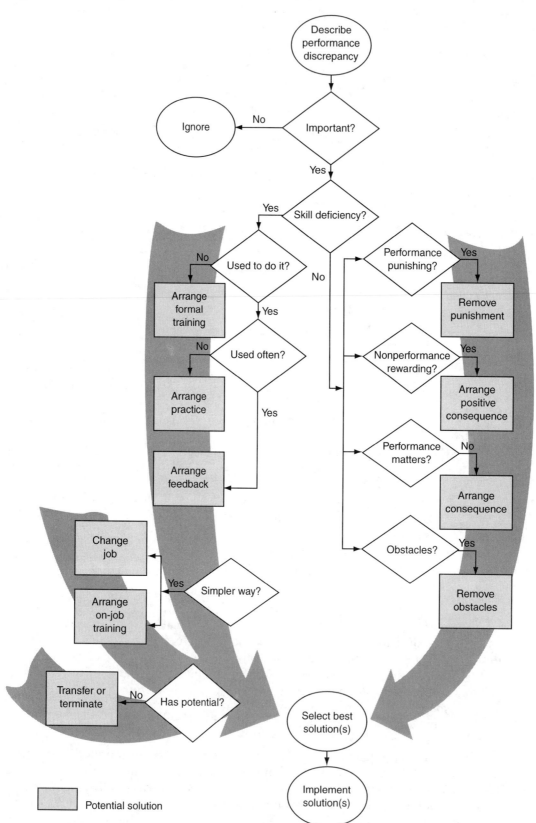

From *Analyzing Performance Problems* (p. 3), by R. F Mager and P. Pipe, 1970, New York: Globe/Fearon Publishers. Copyright 1970 by Fearon Publishers. Reprinted with permission.

Making Decisions About Instructional Formats

In addition to providing a basis for making decisions about which parts of the problem can be solved by instruction, the Mager and Pipe procedure provides a way to determine minimal instructional format requirements. Another approach to determining instructional formats is explained next.

The amount of instruction required to achieve proficiency varies depending on how critical, complex, and in demand the competencies are deemed. Students may already have some competencies, while others will be so easy to attain that merely telling a person what to do or providing a flowchart is all that is needed for successful performance. Some competencies are seldom required and incorrect performance has little serious consequence. On the other hand, other competencies are critical to successful performance, or level of the proficiency required with complex learning makes instruction essential.

Consider the job of an instructional designer whose responsibilities include performing task analysis. The job entails observing videotaped procedures and recording behavioral observations. Obviously, observing and recording accurate and complete task data are the most critical requirements of the job, and these tasks will be the focus of formal classroom instruction. In contrast, knowing how to operate the video playback equipment is necessary to perform the job, but clearly easier to perform and learn. In fact, if time for instruction is limited and someone on the job can demonstrate how to operate the equipment, instruction on this task can be delayed until the person is on the job.

In large-scale educational organizations where curricula are planned with career paths in mind, decisions must be made about when instruction will be most beneficial (When first entering a career field? After some experience in the job? In an advanced course? At the post-graduate level? In a refresher course?). Economic and time constraints, which are a part of virtually all design efforts, will also influence decisions about the format for instruction. When resources are limited, the objective is to emphasize instruction about the competencies that are most essential to successful performance and to present instruction in the most cost-effective format likely to be successful.

The U.S. Army developed a procedure to help instructional designers set instructional formats. This procedure involves asking questions that provide information on which to base decisions about which is the most desirable format for instruction: formal instruction, on-the-job training, refresher instruction, or no instruction. These questions cover seven dimensions: learning difficulty, consequences of incorrect performance, frequency of performance, immediacy of performance, availability of assistance, decay rate of skills, and performance difficulty. These questions, which are shown in Figure 8.7, are called "criticality dimensions."

Based on answers to these questions, one can recommend the minimal format required for instruction. Formats are related to their instructional requirements as this list shows:

◆ **Formal instruction.**   High levels of proficiency are required. The amount and scope of instruction should depend on what is required to achieve a high standard for performance. Extensive assessment is required.

◆ **Refresher instruction.**   Tasks are performed infrequently and forgotten quickly unless they are practiced often. If practice opportunities are not available on the job, refresher instruction can be used from time to time to maintain standards.

◆ **On-the-job Training (OJT).**   This instruction can be provided in the workplace rather than under formal conditions. This is appropriate for tasks that are easier to learn, and for situations where assistance is available.

◆ **Eliminate from Instruction.**   Tasks can be self-taught and a high degree of assistance is available on the job.

The shorter the instructional time, the more cost-effective. Therefore, it is desirable to provide alternates for formal instruction when appropriate. The less critical or difficult the task, the more likely one of these alternatives is appropriate. As part of performance analysis, the designer can analyze desirable formats for instructional requirements and make recommendations.

Figure 8.7   Seven Dimensions for Determining Instructional Formats

1. Learning Difficulty: the time, effort, and assistance required to achieve proficiency in a competency. Some *tasks* are so simple or familiar that they can be readily "picked up." Others are complicated that they are adequately performed only after extensive instruction.

```
1 . . . . . . . . . . . . . 2 . . . . . . . . . . . . . 3 . . . . . . . . . . . . . 4 . . . . . . . . . . . . . 5
```

Easy	Moderately	Hard
to learn	hard	to learn

2. Consequences of incorrect performance: whether failure to correctly perform the competency will result in overall failure of the job or function.

```
1 . . . . . . . . . . . . . 2 . . . . . . . . . . . . . 3 . . . . . . . . . . . . . 4 . . . . . . . . . . . . . 5
```

No	Will degrade	Failure
effect	or delay	

3. Frequency: how often a competency is performed in a field or job.

```
1 . . . . . . . . . . . . . 2 . . . . . . . . . . . . . 3 . . . . . . . . . . . . . 4 . . . . . . . . . . . . . 5
```

Quarterly	Monthly	Daily

4. Immediacy of performance: the time gap between completion of instruction and actual competency performance. Is the performer expected to be proficient at this task immediately after arrival on the job or start of the function? Or will there be a delay between initial learning and actual performance?

```
1 . . . . . . . . . . . . . 2 . . . . . . . . . . . . . 3 . . . . . . . . . . . . . 4 . . . . . . . . . . . . . 5
```

Three	One	One
months	month	week

5. Availability of assistance: any help the novice may have during actual performance of the competency after instruction. This includes supervisors, peers, and/or references.

```
1 . . . . . . . . . . . . . 2 . . . . . . . . . . . . . 3 . . . . . . . . . . . . . 4 . . . . . . . . . . . . . 5
```

None	Several	Many
	sources	

6. Decay rate: how quickly the skills associated with a competency are forgotten or lost if not performed regularly. How much practice is needed to retain the competency?

```
1 . . . . . . . . . . . . . 2 . . . . . . . . . . . . . 3 . . . . . . . . . . . . . 4 . . . . . . . . . . . . . 5
```

None	Every 3 months	Monthly

7. Performance difficulty: the time and/or effort required actually to carry out the competency once it has been learned. Performance difficulty should not be confused with learning difficulty. A psychomotor task may be very difficult to learn, but once learned, very easy to perform.

```
1 . . . . . . . . . . . . . 2 . . . . . . . . . . . . . 3 . . . . . . . . . . . . . 4 . . . . . . . . . . . . . 5
```

Easy	Moderately	Very hard
to do	hard to do	to do

Adapted from *Evaluation of a Training Developer's Decision Aid (TDDA) for Optimizing Performance Based Training in Marching Ascendant MOS* (p. 11), by E. W. Frederickson, J. Hawley, P. Whitemore, and M. M. Wood, 1980, El Paso, TX. Applied Science Associates. Copyright 1980 by Applied Science Associates. Adapted with permission.

Figure 8.8   Questions to Help Identify Instructional Formats

Are you presently involved in ___(give general competency)___ ?
        ____ Yes   ____ No
If you answered yes to this question, please complete items a through d.
    a. Rate the difficulty of performing this competency.
        ____ Easy to do
        ____ Moderately difficult to do
        ____ Difficult to do
    b. Were you expected to perform this competency immediately upon starting
       your present position?
        ____ Yes   ____ No
    c. Are there people in your organization to whom you can go for help with this
       competency?
        ____ Yes   ____ No
    d. What happens if you perform this competency improperly?
        ____ has no effect
        ____ has minimal effect
        ____ has moderate effect
        ____ has serious effect.

One way to collect the information you need about formats for instruction is to use a questionnaire or interview protocol. To collect this information you will need to have a very general list of competencies that you are interested in. You do not have to have completed a detailed analysis of content. A sample of questions appropriate for such instruments is given in Figure 8. 8.

Exercises C, D, E, and F provide practice in performance analysis.

PROBLEM STATEMENTS

Near the end of the needs analysis process, you should write a problem statement to guide you through the instructional design process. The problem statement will summarize the needs and the solution you are proposing. Problem statements should not be long. Usually one to three pages of discussion will suffice, but fewer or more can be acceptable. The problem statement itself is usually no more than a sentence to a paragraph or two. The rest of the information is background material on the problem.

RUPS Problem Statement

One easy format to use is RUPS, or Research Utilizing Problem Solving (Jung, Pino, & Emory, 1970). The purpose of the RUPS problem statement is to establish the background and context for the problem, state what type of problem it is, and give a general goal for improvement. The problem is stated as a goal. Figure 8.9 contains the guidelines for writing a RUPS problem statement. Use these guidelines to complete the exercise on writing a RUPS problem statement. The RUPS technique works best when you answer the questions in complete sentences.

You can use a RUPS problem statement to establish that your other team members or a client agree on the problem. Thus the process of writing a RUPS problem statement becomes a way to develop a common conceptual framework. That is, you can use the statement to communicate with others about your goals, or you can use the statement to gather input on the importance of the problem. The RUPS statement becomes a summary of the needs assessment and the nature of the problem. Figure 8.10 gives an illustration of a RUPS problem statement.

Figure 8.9   Guidelines for Writing a RUPS Problem Statement

1. Who is affected?

   You? Another person? A teaching team? Another group? An entire organization? The community or society?

2. Who or what is the cause?

   Is it a person or group? An entire organization or community? Is it lack of attention to details? Poor organization? Poor materials?

3. What kind of problem is it?

   Disagreement or confusion about goals? Lack of skills? Lack of resources? Lack of accurate communication? Lack of adequate means? Lack of support? Conflict about decision-making? (Obviously, not all these problems are instructional problems. In fact, only lack of skills should be solved by instruction. Perhaps instruction is related to accurate communication or adequate means, but why it is related has to be made clear.)

4. What is the goal for improvement?

   What will be different when the goal has been achieved? Who will be doing what to achieve what? What is the target? (Be as specific as possible. The goal is not just improved skills, but specific skills at a specific level.)

Figure 8.10   Example of a RUPS Problem Statement

Students and graduates in instructional design practica and positions sometimes prepare flowcharts and hierarchies incorrectly. Although they can pass tests on flowcharting symbols and prepare simple hierarchies and flowcharts, they make mistakes when they try to represent more complicated content. The instructor is causing this problem by not giving sufficient attention to the use of visual conventions in instructional design. A contributing cause is the frequency with which authors of articles and books in the field incorrectly label or draw hierarchies and flowcharts.

Thus there is a gap between what students know about hierarchies and flowcharts, such as recognition of symbols, and their ability to distinguish between correct and incorrect use of visual symbols and to develop flowcharts and hierarchies for complex content. This is an instructional problem because a deficiency in knowledge, skills, or attitudes must be eliminated. The goal will affect students' use of flowcharts and hierarchies on the job by ensuring their competency in using visual conventions correctly when they produce flowcharts and hierarchies. Students will be taught to differentiate between correct and incorrect use of flowchart and hierarchy conventions and to use symbols and conventions correctly when representing complex content. They will be taught to value correct use of visual conventions as a communication tool and as a way to establish professional credibility.

Figure 8.11   The IDI Problem Definition Stage

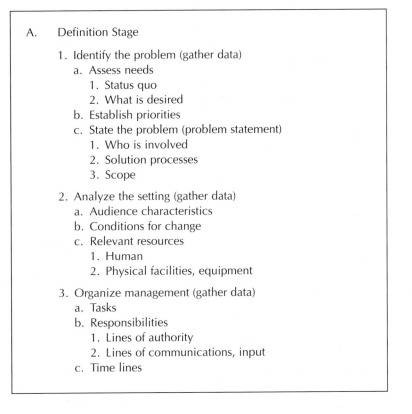

A.   Definition Stage

1. Identify the problem (gather data)
    a. Assess needs
        1. Status quo
        2. What is desired
    b. Establish priorities
    c. State the problem (problem statement)
        1. Who is involved
        2. Solution processes
        3. Scope

2. Analyze the setting (gather data)
    a. Audience characteristics
    b. Conditions for change
    c. Relevant resources
        1. Human
        2. Physical facilities, equipment

3. Organize management (gather data)
    a. Tasks
    b. Responsibilities
        1. Lines of authority
        2. Lines of communications, input
    c. Time lines

IDI Problem Statement

The Instructional Development Institute method of problem identification leads to a problem statement that proposes solution processes (University Consortium on Instructional Development and Technology, 1968). The results of your needs analysis can be summarized in an expanded problem statement by following the IDI format shown in Figure 8.11.

The IDI problem statement narrows the goal stated in the RUPS problem statement and forces the designer to be clear about the solution process. The IDI problem statement includes information on needs, priorities, scope, and solution. It draws this information from the needs assessment.

List the discrepancies identified from the needs assessment. Then explain which discrepancies are to be given priority and why. Finally, state the problem as how to achieve a goal. Tell who will accomplish the solution and how. Tell whether he or she will work on one phase of the problem (proposed solution) or on the whole problem.

Figure 8.12 is an example of an IDI problem statement that addresses the same problem presented in the RUPS problem statement in Figure 8.10.

Exercises J and K provide practice in writing problem statements.

CONTEXTUAL ANALYSIS

Through performance and needs analysis, the designer can determine the discrepancies and what part of the problem can be solved through instruction. The designer also needs to analyze the environment. The environment is created by the characteristics of the learners and instructors, the physical setting, and the support that management provides especially for transfer of training. The environment is systemic in that it has many parts that

Figure 8.12   Example of an IDI Statement

Instructional design students know visual conventions for flowcharting and hierarchies. However, when presented with examples from books or articles, they cannot distinguish between correct or incorrect use of visual conventions.

They can draw flowcharts and hierarchies for simple content, but make mistakes when asked to represent more complex content. When they accept practica assignments or positions in the field, they need to know visual symbols and conventions more thoroughly. They need to be able to distinguish between correct and incorrect use of visual/conventions and to construct flowcharts and hierarchies for complex content. It is also important that the students value using visual symbols and conventions correctly.

The most frequently used technique is flowcharting. This is also the most confusing technique because the conventions vary from field to field. The first priority will be to develop competencies related to flowcharting conventions. The instructor for the instructional design courses will develop improved instructional strategies for teaching and testing flowcharting competencies from the knowledge to the evaluation levels and from the responding to the valuing levels. An instructional design process will be used to improve the lecture and exercises on flowcharting.

combine to create a whole that is unique. By environment we mean the context in which learning and performance will take place. An analysis of this environment will reveal learner characteristics, constraints and resources that should be taken into account in formulating a solution to the instructional problem.

Richey and Tessmer's Theory of Contextual Analysis

There are many aspects to context analysis. Richey and Tessmer (1995) propose a comprehensive model that encompasses temporal stages and system factors. This model is shown in Figure 8.13.

According to Tessmer and Richey (1996), one must analyze the orienting (pre-instructional) context, the instructional (immediate) context, and the transfer (post-instructional) context. For each of these stages in instruction, factors that describe the learner, environment, and organization are analyzed. An example of an application of Tessmer and Richey's contextual analysis procedure is given in Table 8.4. Note that some factors such as attitudes or motivation need to be considered at all levels.

The concept of contextual analysis is a relatively new form of the old concepts of analyzing learner characteristics and constraints and resources. The authors who have published most extensively in this area are Tessmer and Richey (in press), Dick and Carey (1996), Tessmer and Richey (1996), Richey and Tessmer (1995), Tessmer and Harris (1993), and Richey (1992).

Dick and Carey's Procedure for Context Analysis

The Dick and Carey (1996) approach to contextual analysis is consistent but different. They propose gathering information on variables related to learners, learning, and performance in order to determine "the characteristics of the learner, the contexts in which the instruction will be delivered, and the context in which the skills will eventually be used" (p. 89). They believe that this information can affect content, strategy, and delivery decisions.

Their procedure is to have the designer complete three tables that call for identifying data sources and characteristics related to each variable. There is a table for learner characteristics which includes these variables:

Figure 8.13   Learning System Environments: Temporal Levels and System Factors

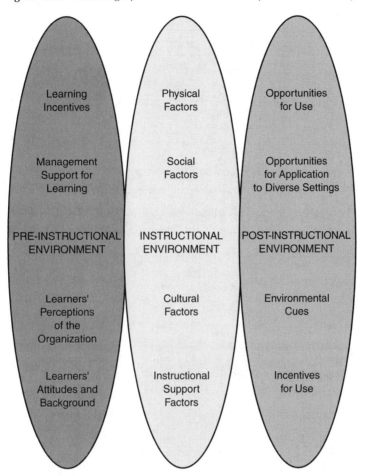

From "Enhancing Instructional Systems Design Through Contextual Analysis" (p. 198), by R. C. Richey and M. Tessmer, 1995, in Barbara Seels (Ed.), *Instructional Design Fundamentals: A Reconsideration*, Englewood Cliffs, NJ: Educational Technology Publications. Copyright 1995 by Educational Technology Publications, Inc. Reprinted with permission.

> (1) entry behaviors, (2) prior knowledge of the topic area, (3) attitudes toward content and potential delivery systems, (4) academic motivation, (5) educational and ability levels, (6) general learning preferences, (7) attitudes toward the organization giving the instruction, and (8) group characteristics. (p. 91)

The table for performance setting includes these variables: (a) managerial or supervisor support, (b) physical aspects of the performance site, (c) social aspects of the site, and (d) relevance of skills to the workplace. The table for the learning environment includes these variables:

> (1) the compatibility of the site with mandates associated with instruction, (2) the adaptability of the site for simulating aspects of the workplace or performance site, (3) the adapability of the site for using a variety of instructional strategies and training delivery approaches, and (4) the constraints present that may affect the design and delivery of instruction. (p.94)

Both the Richey and Tessmer and Dick and Carey approaches to contextual analysis are oriented towards training in the workplace; Dick and Carey, however, address the relationship of context analysis to public schools. They urge designers to see context analysis in school settings as equally important but to adjust the performance context to the curriculum context. In other words, where in the curriculum will these skills be used next?

Table 8.4 Levels and Factors of Contextual Analysis

Factors	Orienting Level	Instructional Level	Transfer Level
Learner	Demographics	Role perception	Experiential background
	Educational experience	Task perception	Attitudes towards training
	Work experience	Task motivation	
	Attitudes towards education and training		
	Attitudes towards work		
	Attitudes towards delivery systems		
	Attitudes towards content		
Immediate Environment	Peer and superordinate support	Seating	Environmental cues
	Perceived opportunity to perform	Sensory conditions	Peer and superordinate support
	Resources available	Teacher role perception	Incentives for use
		Learning schedules	Opportunities for use
		Perceptual quality	
Organizational Environment	Organizational culture	Learning schedules	Opportunities for application in diverse settings
	Incentives	School climate	Organizational culture
	Empowerment levels	Perceived administrative roles	
	Physical working conditions		

Adapted from "The Role of Context in Learning and Instructional Design" by M. Tessmer and R. C. Richey, 1996. Paper presented at the Annual Meeting of the American Educational Research Association in New York, NY.

They also suggest that the designer question the "real world" application of skills and how they can be built into instruction and performance settings.

The Dick and Carey approach recommends analyzing learners and contexts after goals are analyzed and while content is being considered during task and instructional analysis. The Seels and Glasgow approach, which is described next, suggests that contextual analysis be done before task and instructional analysis.

The Seels and Glasgow Procedure for Contextual Analysis

Just as with a needs assessment, to do a contextual analysis the designer needs to gather data. In this case, however, the data gathered has to do with variables which affect the learning environment and experience. The outcome of a contextual analysis should be a plan for considering contextual factors so constraints are taken into account and environmental resources utilized in order to maximize the effects of learning.

The Seels and Glasgow procedure is based on the theories of Richey and Tessmer, and Dick and Carey. It requires three steps:

1. Gather data to answer the questions on the Contextual Analysis Matrix.
2. Use that information to write context notes.
3. Use the context notes to write design notes.

The purpose of this process is to offer a structured way to (a) collect information about the situational context, and (b) winnow this information down until we can make inferences about design. It offers a way to sift extraneous from relevant information through structured deliberation and discussion. This approach can be used individually, in consultation, or in a group. This approach makes assumptions that simplify the information collected so that it is manageable.

Use the Matrix to Gather Information.   The first step is based on the matrix shown in Table 8.5.

Table 8.5   Contextual Analysis Matrix

Environment for:	Learner Characteristics	Instructional Setting	Organizational Support
Planning	What behaviors, prior knowledge, ability, and attitudes (e.g., towards content, delivery, and the organization) will the learner bring to the situation?	What constraints and resources will affect the selection and preparation of the social (e.g.,instructors, dynamics) and physical setting for instruction?	What resources will be availale for planning and development? What purpose will the instruction serve for the organization?
Learning	What are the characteristics of the group and how do they affect individual learners? Are individual learning preferences being met?	What characteristics of the social and physical setting affect learning? How credible is the instructor?	How will instruction be monitored? How will its relevance be established?
Performance	What support for transfer of training is needed? What other support is needed?	What social and physical constraints can hamper use of the new learning or skills? How can they be eliminated?	How will diffusion (adoption and maintenance) of the learning be encouraged (e.g., through rewards, norms)?

Write Context Notes.   Use these factors as a basis for context notes on the learners, setting, and organization. A context note is simply a description of what we know about the learners or setting or organization. Write separate context notes for each category. Figure 8.14 is an example of context notes made for a design project on training estimators for a moving company on a dedicated computer system.

Write Design Notes.   Review your context notes or share them with the design team. Consider which information has the most implication for content, delivery, or organizational support. Write design notes which summarize the conclusions you or your team members reach about important contextual considerations. Figure 8.15 presents the design notes derived from the context notes.

Other Suggestions.   The data you gather will reflect biases. Try to minimize biases by checking with several sources. Talk to the client, the potential students, the supervisors,

Figure 8.14   An Example of Context Notes

Learner Characteristics: The learners are all employees of a moving company. Their job is to go into the home and estimate moving costs and requirements for home owners. Most of the employees are men who started with the company as movers. Their average educational level is eleventh grade. Few have more than a high school education. Very few have ever worked with a computer before although most have at least three years' experience as estimators using a paper checklist format the company provides. The computer replaces a process that is already working for them. Although it may eventually save them some time, it is not necessary for them to complete their task. However, the company has decided they need to facilitate record keeping and that within a certain number of years all estimators will have to use the dedicated computer system. The employees do not know this now. Some are motivated to learn something new, and others are resistant. Most are anxious about their ability to learn the new system.

Instructional Setting: Most of the social climate in the company exists at the field office level. Employees will be given released time and travel funds to attend a two day training session at the home office. They will be trained in groups of 10 to 15 representing many offices so that no one office is without all its staff at the same time. The training will be done in the company classroom which is well furnished with tables and comfortable chairs, a white board, and audiovisual equipment. There is an adequate budget for refreshments during breaks and printed materials. The instructional team will be two people, a company employee from human resources and an employee of the design consulting company hired to develop the instruction. Employees will be told they will be provided with a computer system if they will use it.

Organizational Support: The company has invested significant resources in the development of the system and is commited to its implementation and increased use over the next five years until it is adopted by all estimators. It has not planned any diffusion activities other than formal instruction. Supervisors are going to be trained in the same groups as the estimators. The manager in charge of the training is the supervisor of human resources. He has had experience with training, but his expertise is in compensation. He wants to be kept informed, but does not feel the need to be involved other than overseeing progress. The plan is to do a follow-up telephone survey with supervisors to evaluate usage six months after the training. Records of requests for computers will also be kept. The company is very traditional, and the rate of change is not high.

Figure 8.15   An Example of Design Notes

Learner Characteristics: The employees are experienced in their job and are very comfortable estimating. Many have high anxiety about their ability to learn to use the computer system and their ability to be successful in the training sessions. They are somewhat uncomfortable with attending training classes where they will know no one else. While some are motivated to attend, many do not see the need for the system.

Instructional Setting: No social climate exists among the trainees. The instructors may have a credibility problem because they are not people who have actually moved or estimated in the home. If supervisors are part of the same training group, they may be defensive, and the employees may be intimidated. the facilities, equipment, and budget are adequate.

Organizational Setting: Anxiety about change may occur as the diffusion (adoption and maintenance of the innovation) process progresses. Little attention has been paid to preparing for acceptance of the innovation. Administrative support is strong but at a level that is formal and removed.

the instructors, the janitor and secretaries, the technical support people. Do not gather all data from your office. Get out and see the setting and the sites where training will be applied. Try to determine the organizational climate.

When you write your context notes, you are telling a story about an endeavor in process. Your context notes should capture the drama of the undertaking. Think of your learners and administrators as characters in a play and the facilities and organizational climate as a setting. Events and sources of conflict can be described as a plot in a play. Your context notes should bring the situation alive for your design team and client. Thus, you prepare those involved in the project for participation in decision making.

Exercises L and M provide practice in contextual analysis.

EXERCISES

A. An Exercise to Identify Phases in Problem Analysis

Match two outcomes given in column two with each phase of problem analysis given in column one.

    _____1. Needs Assessment   a. What will be the systemic influences on instruction?

    _____2. Performance Analysis   b. What are the prerequisites for learning?

    _____3. Contextual Analysis   c. Is instruction the solution?

                                   d. What are the goals of instruction?

                                   e. What tasks are to be taught?

                                   f. What factors will affect pre- and post-instructional phases?

                                   g. What priorities should be established?

                                   h. What format for instruction is indicated by instructional requirements?

B. An Exercise to Practice Developing Plans for Gathering Information

Use the checklist in Figure 8.3 to develop a plan for gathering information in one of the problem areas listed below. Report your plan in essay form, using graphics if you wish. Then repeat the exercise with another problem area.

1. There is a need to serve more nursing students with a limited professional faculty. One place to start is to develop a center for independent learning on certain aspects of the beginning nursing curriculum. There is first a need to identify what aspects should be programmed and to develop a procedure for producing software based on these aspects. The new learning resources center's director has experience in both nursing and media. The budget and clerical staff are limited, and the faculty is resisting involvement. It is felt that the best way to start is with a plan of attack in a specific area.

2. The social studies department wants to change to a more relevant curriculum. It plans to have units on economics throughout the world instead of organizing the curriculum by regional areas. The fear is that the content will be too diffuse to be retained. Teachers have been asked to submit proposals for this new curriculum, relating to activities, sequencing, content themes, and materials. The school is a suburban middle school.

3. A traditional elementary school reading program for grades K-6 has been re-evaluated. The results show that a majority of students are not reading at their grade levels. Library-use records document students' lack of interest in reading, which is probably due to poor reading skills. The reading supervisor has been charged with coordinating efforts to remedy the situation. After many group brainstorming sessions, the feeling is that too many unrelated ideas are being presented. It is suggested that some systematic goals be developed before further major policy changes are considered.

4. Students in high school biology fail to work on their own to discover concepts and facts about the subject. The school is located in a suburban area where the community income is above the national average. The school board and administration wish to try some innovative programs in the area of higher level thinking skills for biology. The BSCS series is being considered, but teachers are not enthusiastic.

5. The health educators for the county health department have recently been charged with upgrading the in-service training program for patrolman recruits in casualty care. The recruits represent the police for a city of 100,000. The previous program for recruits in casualty care consisted of lecture, textbooks, and films. It is important that the course be successful because patrolmen are usually the first on the scene of accidents, and their immediate first aid procedures may result in saving or losing a life. The department has considered determining the effectiveness of different learning situations (cognitive vs. predominantly psychomotor) in improving the retention and application of casualty care skills.

6. A large corporation is considering having all its management employees improve communication skills through training in areas such as transactional analysis, communication style, and listening skills. No determination has been made concerning the extent of the problem, or whether the problem exists at all.

C. An Exercise to Give Practice in Developing Questions in Topical Categories for Needs Assessment

Complete this outline for a needs assessment instrument by formulating three questions in each category. Choose a problem area, such as one of those listed in the previous exercise, and relate all questions to that area.

Part I. Nature of the Problem

1.
2.
3.

Part II. Priorities within the Problem

1.
2.
3.

Part III. Skills/Knowledge

1.
2.
3.

Part IV. Attitudes

1.
2.
3.

Part V. Causes

1.
2.
3.

D. An Exercise in Applying the Organizational Elements Model

In Table 8.6, fill in each of the categories in the Kaufman and English model as they relate to an instructional design need. Place a label under each column to indicate whether it contains one of the following:

    internal need (organizational)
    external need (societal)
    quasi-need (supportive)
    internal need (individual)

Star any need that can describe an instructional design product—in other words, a solution to an instructional design problem that can be realistically evaluated within the time frame usually allowed.

Table 8.6

Inputs	*Processes*	*Products*	*Outputs*	*Outcomes*

E. A Group Exercise in Applying a Method for Determining Priorities

This is a team exercise in using a card sort technique for establishing priorities. You are part of a team charged with developing a Master of Arts in Teaching (MAT) program for a university. In order to create a curriculum, the team has decided to begin by establishing goals for the program.

Each team member has been asked to imagine what successful graduates of the program will do, think, or feel. The next step is for each team member to write statements (one to a card) that describe how MAT graduates will be expected to perform. The statements should be complete sentences in active voice. Some of the other team members have written statements such as these:

> MAT graduates will accurately perceive their strengths and weaknesses.
> A MAT graduate will want to help others.
> Each MAT graduate will understand the role nonverbal communication plays in successful teaching.
> MAT graduates will understand how to identify and use learner characteristics.

Your first task, then, is to spend five to 10 minutes writing goal statements for a MAT program on separate cards. After each team member has finished writing goals, the cards are sorted. Each team member sorts his or her cards into groups that indicate priorities. In this case, sort your cards into the categories of (a) essential and critical, (b) very useful, and (c) slightly useful. After you have sorted your cards, rank order them within each group with no ties. If a statement seems vague, rewrite it.

Once statements have been written, sorted, and ranked individually, lay all the cards out on a table or display them on a board. The team members can inspect all the cards and ask questions beginning with the lowest category, slightly useful. The discussion continues until the cards in each category can be merged into a team rather than individual list. The decision-making process should be one of compromise, consensus, and creativity. Cards can be moved as decisions are made.

When the goal statements in each category are agreed on, the team must decide whether to include all the categories or all the cards in a category in the final goals. The team could decide that the program must focus on achieving essential goals only. Or the team could say that all "essential" goals and the first three "very useful" goals will become priorities.

As a team, use index cards and the card sorting technique to generate priority goals for a Master of Arts in Teaching program.[1]

F. An Exercise Designed to Help You Distinguish between Instructional and Non-instructional Problems

A problem could be described by more than one category. Which categories describe each of the problems below? Explain your classification of each problem.

Categories:

I. Non-instructional
   A. Contingencies and rewards
   B. Work conditions
   C. Work procedures
   D. Other

---

[1]Adapted from "The Card-Sort: A Tool for Determining Clients' Goals," by D. F. Leitzman and G.-R. Sisakhti, 1981, *National Society for Performance and Instruction Journal*, pp. 13–15. Copyright 1981 by *National Society for Performance and Instruction Journal*.

II. Instructional
   A. Skills
   B. Knowledge
   C. Attitudes
   D. Other

Problems:

1. An instructional designer is asked to develop additional training in telephone skills for volunteers at a United Fund Agency. The volunteers have already had two hours of training in how to represent the organization on the phone and in person. But they continue to give their opinions about controversial matters rather than merely stating the organization's position.

2. A training consultant is asked to develop training to make maintenance workers more productive. She analyzes the knowledge and skills needed and finds the workers already possess these competencies. She also finds that except for the end-of-the-year evaluation, there is no feedback on performance after the first three months.

3. An instructional designer is asked to improve the remedial reading curriculum for ninth-grade students. He finds that students are continually tested and evaluated on reading, that the current objectives are appropriate and clear, and that the materials for teaching are excellent. But the teacher is not using the materials as designed, nor is she reporting results correctly because she has minimal competencies in design and evaluation.

4. A government agency asks an instructional design consultant to develop instruction for repair technicians. When the designer does the needs assessment he finds the existing training program is excellent, but repair technicians are not performing well in the field. The technicians report that they are hampered by unavailability of parts, an impossible work load, and incompetent colleagues.

5. A school district has decided to offer enrichment social studies because many of the students already have the current curriculum competencies and are bored in class. The district will purchase materials and design a program to use these materials so that additional teacher time requirements will be minimal.

6. An educational specialist in a hospital setting is asked to improve the required certification course for radiation safety. He finds the current course teaches concepts well but gives no practice in safety skills. Consequently, workers return to their labs and continue to perform manual tasks carelessly. The course teaches concepts only, not attitudes or skills.

G. An Exercise Designed to Give Further Practice in Distinguishing Types of Instructional and Non-instructional Problems

For each problem, decide whether an instructional or non-instructional solution, or both, would be required.

1. Three graduates of a technical school motorcycle repair program are employed by Honda Corporation to be field representatives for sales and service. They stay in these roles for two years. During this time they do no maintenance; they consult on parts and procedures. Their duties are unrelated to their study in technical school. When they are reassigned to the main service center as repair personnel, they find they have forgotten how to execute motorcycle maintenance procedures. Is this an instructional problem? If yes, what kind of instructional solution would you suggest (Chenzoff, 1983)?

2. An oxygen bottle in a college chemical laboratory blows up when lab maintenance personnel try to fill it to 1850 psi, using an adapter without a blowout plug. The oxygen system has no relief valve. Maximum pressure is 450 psi. The directions placard had been painted over. The maintenance person had not been checked out on that piece of apparatus.

The lab supervisor recommends all lab maintenance personnel receive a course on servicing the oxygen equipment. Discuss the wisdom of this recommendation. What would you recommend (Chenzoff, 1983)?

3. Students in music are anxious to improve their skills in choral singing. The 90-member chorus meets twice a week for 40 minutes. Most of the time is spent on furious preparation for frequent musical events. The more talented members are frustrated and complain about the lack of opportunity to try innovative numbers or improve skills. Is this an instructional problem? What would you recommend?

4. You are operating the swimming program in a community center similar to a YWCA. The center is supported by county tax funds, and anyone can attend for a nominal fee. There are four age groups for which instruction is available: adults (over 18), teens (13–18), juniors (6–13), and beginners (6 and under). Average attendance at each instruction section is 100 per swim period. The swim periods are a half-hour long. There are one or two instructors, two lifeguards, and three in-the-water aides present at each period. The center would like to do a better job of teaching rules of water safety. They are planning to illustrate through media as well as class instruction. A lecture room is available nearby. Should they proceed as planned?

5. The student council at a junior high school is responsible for all after-school functions. The council has not been able to control the students or groups performing at council functions. As faculty advisor you would like to assure proper functioning of the council's activities. You would like to avoid problems which seem to be created as a result of student council action. For example, recently some students at a dance provoked the band members into a fight. Council members couldn't cope effectively with the disturbance; either the students involved in the fight didn't respect them, or the members themselves were reluctant to exert their authority. The council has discussed the problem many times. What is the nature of the problem? Is instruction recommended?

6. A private training school in an urban setting offers a 30 to 36-week secretarial training program for high school graduates. About 60% of the students are middle-class; 40% come from lower socioeconomic groups. Although graduates have quite a bit of manual and office practice skill, they are not careful about details. Therefore, graduates tend not to advance in their jobs. What, if any, instruction is recommended?

7. Several average classes of fifth-graders from a school district in a high socioeconomic area are found to be inadequately prepared for fifth-grade work. It is important that their problem-solving motivation and skills improve in order to meet the pre-entry criteria for a new middle school. Most of the students are unable to comprehend almost any fifth-grade textual material. They seem to lack enthusiasm for projects and problems. Many of the students have been frightened by their relatively sudden academic failure and are withdrawing in confusion. Is instruction the solution? What do you recommend?

H. An Exercise in Making Decisions About Instructional Formats

1. One example of an expensive format for instruction is _____.
2. One example of a less expensive format for instruction is _____.
3. One example of a format for instruction which is time consuming is _____.
4. A high level of difficulty combined with serious consequences if the task is not performed correctly indicates a need for _____ instruction.
5. When simple tasks are performed infrequently, _____ instruction may be warranted.
6. When a great deal of assistance is available, _____ may be warranted for instruction.

I. An Exercise Designed to Check Your Knowledge of Performance Analysis[2]

Label each item true or false.

1. Analyzing performance problems is necessary because a manager may fail to realize how best to solve performance problems.
2. A performance problem is a discrepancy between existing and expected performance.
3. An analysis of performance problems is not appropriate for every ISD effort.
4. An analysis of performance problems is especially necessary when nuclear plant operators are being trained on a new maintenance system.
5. Formal training is indicated when those who were once able to do a job are now unable to do it well.
6. Practice and feedback are useful for preventing the formation of bad work habits.
7. When workers or students receive punishment for performing well, poor performance often results.
8. Inadequate tools are obstacles to good performance.
9. Performance analysis can be done solely on the basis of available documents.
10. Formal training is usually the best solution when the proper sequence of steps in a procedure is not being followed.
11. If the learner is able to do what is required but still won't do it, a non-instructional solution could be warranted.
12. Formal instruction tends to be one of the more expensive ways to solve an instructional problem.
13. If a worker lacks the physical or mental capabilities to handle the job, either change the job to match the worker's capabilities or change the worker to match the job's requirements.
14. Obstacles obstruct performance.

J. An Individual or Group Exercise to Give Practice in Writing A RUPS Problem Statement

Choose a problem that meets the criteria for an instructional problem. Answer these questions about the problem. Then summarize your answers in a problem statement that includes the problem stated as a proposed solution.

RUPS Analysis:

1. Who is affected?
2. Who or what is causing it?
3. What kind of a problem is it?
4. What is the goal for improvement?

K. An Individual or Group Exercise to Give Practice in Writing an IDI Problem Statement

Choose a problem that meets criteria for an instructional problem. Answer these questions about the problem. Then summarize your answers in a problem statement that proposes a solution.

Problem Identification: IDI Method

1. Needs (status quo, what is desired, discrepancies)
2. Priorities
3. Problem Statement (who is involved, solution processes, scope)

---

[2] Adapted from *Module 9. Problem Analysis* (Contract No. F41689-83-C0048), by A. Chenzoff, 1983, Randolph AFB, TX: USAF Occupational Measurement Center (ATC).

L. An Individual or Group Exercise in Gathering Information Relevant to Contextual Analysis

Describe a situation in which you have identified the problem as instructional. You can use one of the problems you worked on in Exercises F and G, as long as the problem has been identified as instructional.

You are now gathering information that will be a basis for contextual analysis. In a team or individually, make a list of the kinds of information you could gather (e.g., topic, budget, personnel) and the sources of information you could use. Do this in response to each of these items (UCIDT, 1968). Be more specific than the descriptions given. In other words, what kind of statistics would you gather? Statistics about what? How would you present them? For example, in response to "Kinds of information about the community or society," try to give names to statistical graphs and to events. This exercise can also be done in a group through brainstorming or discussion. Be sure to choose an appropriate source for each kind of information.

Situation:

1. Kinds of information about the community or society. Sources of such information include interviews with VIPs, reports, statistics, projections, and media events. Give examples of types of information (e.g., perceptions) one can gather about a community, and suggest appropriate sources of information.

2. Kinds of information about the corporation or district. Sources of information include annual reports, proposals, statistics, and policy statements. Give examples of types of information (e.g., products) one can gather about a district or corporation, and suggest appropriate sources of such information.

3. Kinds of information about the division or department. Sources of such information include reports, charts, statistics, and interviews. Give an example of types of information (e.g., budget) one can gather about the organizational unit and suggest appropriate sources of such information.

4. Kinds of information about personnel. Sources of such information include employee records, questionnaires, evaluation reports, and statistics. Give an example of type of information (e.g., educational level) one can gather about personnel and suggest appropriate sources of information.

5. Kinds of information about the learners or audience. Sources of such information include peers, employers, parents, teachers, tests, sociograms, interviews, and observations. Give examples of types of information (e.g., attitude) one can gather about an audience, and suggest appropriate sources of such information.

6. Kinds of information about time. Sources of such information include schedules, calendars, deadlines, and opinions. Give examples of types of information (e.g., flexibility) one can gather, and suggest appropriate sources of such information.

7. Kinds of information about facilities. Sources of such information include inventories, floor plans, room schedules, and supervisors. Give an example of types of information (e.g., availability) one can gather about resources, and suggest appropriate sources of information.

M. An Exercise in Doing a Contextual Analysis

Hypothesize an instructional situation. You can use one of the situations presented in Exercises F and G as long as they are instructional, or you can use a situation familiar to you. Another option is to use the situation given here. Do an analysis of the situation using the Seels and Glasgow Procedure for Contextual Analysis.

Situation: You are an instructional designer assigned to a team to develop training for museum tour guides at a new regional history center devoted to social history. One of your responsibilities is to do a contextual analysis. The museum employs graduates in history to give tours to over 3,000 school children a month. The second and third floors of the museum take students through 300 years of local history. The fourth floor contains traveling exhibits and the library and archives. There is a discovery room for younger children. At least two costumed actors are present each day. What would be in your context notes and design notes?

REFERENCES

Burton, J. K., & Merrill, P. F. (1991). Needs assessment: Goals, needs and priorities. In L. J. Briggs, K. L. Gustafson, & M. H. Tillman, *Instructional design principles and applications* (pp. 17–44). Englewood Cliffs, NJ: Educational Technology Publications.

Chenzoff, A. (1983). *Module 9. Problem analysis* (Contract No. F41689-83-C0048). Randolph AFB, TX: USAF Occupational Measurement Center (ATC).

Dick, W. & Carey, L. (1996). *The systematic design of instruction* (4th ed.). New York: HarperCollins Publishers.

Frederickson, E. W., Hawley, J., Whitemore, P., and Wood, M. M. (1980). *Air defense training development decision aid (TDDA): Model extension and research requirement, final report* (Contract No. MDA 903-80-C-0160, Army Research Institute, Defense Supply Institute). Butler, PA: Applied Science Associates.

Gentry, C. G. (1994). *Introduction to instructional development.* Belmont, CA: Wadsworth Publishing.

Georgenson, D., & Del Gazio, E. (1984, August). Maximize the return on your training investment through needs assessment. *Training and Development Journal,* 42–47.

Gilbert, T. (1982, October). A question of performance—Part II: Applying the PROBE model. *Training and Development Journal, 17,* 85–89.

Jung, C., Pino, R., & Emory, R. (1970). Research utilizing problem solving (RUPS) (Leaders manual). Portland, OR: Northwest Regional Educational Laboratory.

Kaufman, R. (1983). A holistic planning model. *Performance and Instruction Journal, 22,* 3–12.

Kaufman, R. (1986). An algorithm for identifying and allocating performance problems. *Performance and Instruction Journal, 25*(1), 21–29.

Kaufman, R., & English, F. W. (1979). *Needs assessment: Concepts and application.* Englewood Cliffs, NJ: Educational Technology Publications.

Leitzman, D. F., & Sisakhti, G.-R. (1981). The card-sort: A tool for determining clients' goals. *National Society for Performance and Instruction Journal, 20,* 13–15.

Mager, R., & Pipe, P. (1970). *Analyzing performance problems.* Belmont, CA: Fearson.

Maher, J. H., Jr., & Kur, E. (1983, June). Constructing questionnaires. *Training and Development Journal, 37,* 17–19.

Murray-Hicks, M. (1981). Analysis techniques for management skills. *National Society for Performance and Instruction Journal, 20,* 15–20.

Nadler, L. (1982). *Designing training programs: The critical events model.* Reading, MA: Addison-Wesley.

Newstrom, J. W., & Lilyquist, J. M. (1979, October). Selecting needs analysis methods. *Training and Development Journal,* 52–56.

Richey, R. C. (1992). *Designing instruction for the adult learner.* London: Kogan Page.

Richey, R. C., & Tessmer, M. (1995). Enhancing instructional systems design through contextual analysis. In B. Seels (Ed.), *Instructional Design Fundamentals: A Reconsideration* (pp. 189–199). Englewood Cliffs, NJ: Educational Technology Publications.

Rossett, A. (1982). A typology for generating needs assessment. *Journal of Instructional Development, 6* (1), 29–33.

Scott, D., & Deadrick, D. (1982, June). The nominal group technique: Applications for training needs assessment. *Training and Development Journal,* 26–33.

Spitzer, D. (1979, May). Remember these do's and don't's of questionnaire design. *Training HRD,* 34–37.

Stufflebeam, D. L., McCormick, C. H., Brinkeroff, R. O., & Nelson, C. O. (1985). *Conducting educational needs assessment.* Boston: Kluvner-Nijhoff.

Tessmer, M., & Harris, D. (1993). *Analyzing the instructional setting.* London: Kogan Page.

Tessmer, M., & Richey, R. C. (1997). The role of context in learning and instructional design. *Educational Research and Theory, 45*(2), 85–116.

Tessmer, M., & Richey, R. C. (1996). *The role of context in learning and instructional design.* Paper presented at the Annual Meeting of the American Educational Research Association in New York, NY.

University Consortium on Instructional Development and Technology (UCIDT). (1968). Syracuse, NY: Syracuse University, Instructional Design, Development & Evaluation (IDDE).

Witkin, B. R. (1984). *Assessing needs in educational and social programs.* San Francisco: Jossey Bass.

Witkin, B. R. (Ed.). (1978a). *Before you do a needs assessment: Important first questions.* Hayward, CA: Office of Alameda County Superintendent of Schools.

Witkin, B. R. (Ed.). (1978b). *Needs assessment product locator: Available needs assessment products and how to select them for local use.* Hayward, CA: Office of the Alameda County Superintendent of Schools.

◆ ANSWERS

A. An Exercise to Identify Phases in Problem Analysis

1. d and g
2. c and h
3. a and f

B. An Exercise to Practice Developing Plans for Gathering Information

Choose two problems, and write a separate essay on collecting data for each problem. Each essay should address the major items 1, 2, 3, 4 in Figure 8.3. In addition, for terms 1, 2, and 4 all the sub-points need to be discussed. For item three in Figure 8.3 some sub-points under the option chosen should be considered. For example, What records? What newspapers? The plan should be logical and practical given the situation chosen and any other assumptions the student has explicitly stated.

C. An Exercise to Give Practice in Developing Questions in Topical Categories for Needs Assessment.

The questions formulated are correct if they meet the following criteria.

Part I: Questions should deal with the discrepancy and the nature of the discrepancy or discrepancies.

Part II: Questions should focus on having respondents rank priorities.

Part III: Questions should aim at finding out what the learners know.

Part IV: Questions should be aimed at ascertaining interest in and feeling about the content.

Part V: Questions should be aimed at determining why students need instruction in this area.

D. An Exercise in Applying the Organizational Elements Model

The purpose of this exercise is to help you achieve a deeper understanding of the Organizational Elements Model. To do this you need to elaborate by formulating an example. Your answer should be consistent with the theory presented in the text preceding the exercise.

Here is an example of an appropriate answer:

Description of Instructional Need: There is a need for high school students to be certified in CPR so that society eventually has many people skilled in this procedure.

Inputs:	Quasi-need
American Red Cross Course and manikin	(supportive)
Physical Education instructors qualified in CPR	
Goal to have 15% of every senior class competent	

Processes:	Quasi-need
Integrated in several physical education electives	(supportive)
Instructors give examinations regularly	

Products:*	Internal need
Certificate of competency in CPR skills	(individual)
Individual valuing of CPR skills	
Knowledge of guidelines for use of procedure	

Outputs:*	Internal need
15% of student body competent in CPR	(organizational)
Many students gain a job-related skill	
Many gain a skill valuable in recreational situations	

Outcomes:	External
Many in society competent in CPR	(societal)
Most in society value and support CPR training	
Increased awareness of prevention of illness	

The purpose of the OEM model is to check that you have related needs that contribute to a societal outcome and support an individual instructional need (product).

E. A Group Exercise in Applying a Method for Determining Priorities

At the conclusion of this exercise each group should select a spokesperson to report the goals selected and why. The goals should be limited as much as practical to the essentials. For examples, groups that report 20 goals all equally important should narrow their list of goals. A good range for the number of goals is 5 to 10.

F. An Exercise Designed to Help You Distinguish between Instructional and Non-instructional Problems

1. II c
2. I a, c
3. II a, b
4. I b
5. II a, b, c, d
6. II a, c

G. An Exercise Designed to Give Further Practice in Distinguishing Types of Instructional and Non-instructional Problems

1. This is an instructional problem. It could be solved by providing practice in a refresher course.
2. This is not an instructional problem. It could be solved through better supervision or a job aid (poster).
3. This is an instructional problem that requires formal instruction.
4. This is an instructional problem that could be solved through formal training, On-the-Job Training, or provision of other ways to practice.
5. This is a non-instructional problem. One way to solve the problem would be a system of incentives.
6. This is an instructional problem. In this case contingencies and rewards can become part of the classroom instruction.
7. This problem has both instructional and non-instructional components. It could be solved through a formal course combined with incentives.

H. An Exercise in Making Decisions About Instructional Formats

1. classroom instruction or formal instruction
2. on-the-job training
3. formal classroom course
4. formal instruction
5. refresher instruction
6. on-the-job training

I. An Exercise Designed to Check Your Knowledge of Performance Analysis

1. True
2. True
3. False
4 True
5. False
6. True
7. True
8. True
9 False
10. False
11. True
12. True
13. True
14. True

J. An Individual or Group Exercise to Give Practice in Writing a RUPS Problem Statement

—and—

K. An Individual or Group Exercise to Give Practice in Writing an IDI Problem Statement

Check to see that your statement covers each of the items in the outline. In addition, check to see that the statement ends by describing the solution in terms of immediate learner outcomes. Remember needs are the basis for finding a solution, but by the problem statement stage, needs should be translated into proposed solution. Students are never the problem, although learner characteristics influence determination of the problem.

L. An Individual or Group Exercise in Gathering Information Relevant to Contextual Analysis

Here is an example of a response that could be made in each category if the situation were to design a course in sex education for the middle school level.

1. A bar graph showing the number represented in each religion in the township with a summary statement of each religion's official position on sex education or instruction which addresses attitudes and values, as well as knowledge.
2. A district report on number of students in school who were known to be pregnant over the past seven years. The district policy statement on review of instructional materials and programs.
3. A report summarizing a review of state syllabi for areas of the curriculum relevant to sex education including health, social studies, and science.
4. A report on the number of teachers in the district who have had training in sex education, the number who are certified to teach in areas where it could be incorporated in the curriculum, and the number who have interest in teaching topics relevant to sex education. These teachers should be identified by subject area and level.
5. Interviews with representative students and parents about the possibility of adding sex education to the curriculum. These interviews should follow a protocol so that they can be summarized.
6. A timeline showing the proposed plan for consideration, development, implementation, and review of a pilot curriculum in this area.
7. An inventory of current library/media resources and a list of additional purchases that would be needed for support materials.

M. An Exercise in Doing a Contextual Analysis

If you applied the Seels and Glasgow Procedure for Contextual Analysis to the situation that required training museum educators, your context notes and design notes might look like this.

Context Notes:

Learner Characteristics: The new employees have been chosen competitively from many applicants. These novice museum educators initially have a strong background in history, although it is not as extensive in regional and ethnic history as they need to give tours. On the other hand, they may have no background in education or experience in teaching or working with children. For many of them this is their first professional job, which means that they are very motivated and anxious to be successful. They find the new museum is an exciting place to work; although it is suffering the pains of growing and being overextended. There are typically one or two educators in training at the same time. Therefore, group characteristics may not be important. When asked the trainees say they like on-the-job training but find it is often rushed and inadequate. As historians they are confident they can find information when they discover gaps in their knowledge of history. They are more worried about their ability to discipline and interest groups of varied ages. Disciplining excited groups ranging from third-graders to eleventh-graders is difficult. They are not sure who they would go to for help on discipline and management of groups. Another problem is the backing up of groups in exhibits especially when they arrive. Although these museum educators often have ideas for how to improve exhibits and tours, there is no formal method for recording these ideas or considering them for action. For example, they would like to see more actors dressed as sports heroes than as artists, because they can generate more interest in sports characters. They are frustrated because such observations aren't solicited or discussed.

Instructional Setting: A teaching area and the exhibit areas are available for the training sessions. In fact, any area of the center is available. The center contains a discovery area for children, several floors of exhibits, an entry area for large groups, a gift shop, snack shop, an area for changing exhibits, a teaching area with windows and a projection wall, and a library and archives. The exhibits are interactive. The instruction is typically done by professional staff from the Department of Education. Two half days are currently devoted to instruction with the instructor varying. Currently, instruction consists of giving information to the trainees as they walk through the exhibit. Existing brochures are used as handouts. Trainees have no experience with taking children through before they start giving tours. They usually find out which grades and schools are coming just before they give the scheduled tour. They receive no pre-information about the students from the teachers or schools.

Organizational Support: The Department of Education is the most successful area of the museum this year. There is a waiting list for school tours. Nevertheless, because of rapid expansion all areas of the museum are short of resources, especially personnel. Volunteers help in many areas as needed; however, professional personnel are used for the tours. The success of the tours is important for the museum's fundraising as it demonstrates meeting a regional need. When major contributors and special groups request tours, usually in the weekend, either senior staff or volunteer museum educators give the tours. The major constraint for training is time including preparation time, paid trainee time, and release time for instruction. There are resources for preparing printed materials and expertise in many areas, although few of the professional staff are historians or school educators. No evaluation of the tours or museum educators' performance is planned. Museum educators are paid an hourly fee. Currently, the educators do not assist with each other's training or record their experiences. Consequently, when one leaves an opportunity for diffusion of experience is lost.

Design Notes:

Learner Characteristics: The trainees would benefit from more extensive and formal instruction, especially in the areas of regional and ethnic history and education. They need help with the age, ability, and socio-economic differences especially as they relate to group behavior and discipline. The tour guides would probably be more confident if they knew more about regional education, such as about different school districts. Any negativity in attitude is minimal and comes from frustration from lack of discussion about improving the tours. They would like clearer direction about use of resources, what they need to read, and what they should recommend to students and teachers.

Instructional Setting: There is a need for more discussion with each other and with experts around critical incidents and maintaining interest.

Organizational Support: The organization could clearly express its increased commitment to training and ongoing evaluation of programs and performance. More competent museum educators can free up senior staff time.

Chapter

9

Managing a Project Team

OVERVIEW

Instructional design projects are almost always team efforts. Even when the designer has sole responsibility for instructional design, his work will have to be approved and accepted by others. Most likely, however, he will work as a member of a design or production team. In either situation, the designer's understanding of his role and his skill in relating to others can facilitate or hinder the design process.

The nature of the team will depend on a number of factors.

Size. Instructional design projects are often driven by deadlines. When a project is too big for one person to complete within schedule, the practical solution is to divide the work among two or more people.

Competencies. Some projects require more competencies than one person possesses. Then the designer must rely on someone else for subject matter expertise, or look "outside" the design department for special media production skills.

Acceptance. Eventually, the instruction will be used by others. It is important to gain acceptance of the course by those who will use it. Users may be within the organization where the designer works or in a client's organization. In any case, acceptance of the product requires participation by others.

Team membership changes as a function of where you are in the ISD process. As questions are answered and new questions surface, the competencies needed on the project change. In response to these new needs, some members leave or reduce their participation in the team while new members join the team. At the beginning, the team may include people from the client organization including managers responsible for overseeing development, current job-holders, subject matter experts, the end-users (including the instructors and administrators responsible for implementing the new course), and representatives of the target audience.

As the direction of the course is set and development begins, the emphasis will shift to a need for people with production skills—such as writers, directors, graphic artists, and computer programmers. To conduct the tryouts, the designer works with instructors, administrators, and representatives of the target audience. Throughout the design and development phases, SMEs and the client review products for accuracy and acceptance.

During implementation, the designer again works closely with the end-users, preparing to hand off the course to them.

The team approach is successful when three conditions necessary for effective teamwork are present: There is a plan in place for managing the work, team members have effective interpersonal communication skills, and team members have a team orientation and a shared vision that facilitates the team's collective effectiveness (Naval Air Warfare Center Training Systems Division, 1995).

Planning deals with clarifying tasks, procedures, and schedules. The team approach to instructional design requires clear specification of roles, tasks, objectives, and deadlines. There must be provision for someone to fulfill the leadership role of directing and coordinating communication. The leader is responsible for a plan that lets each group member know what is expected and when, but each group member needs to be familiar with the total plan as well.

The planning process answers the question, "How will we work together?" Basic to the use of the team approach are a set of knowledge requirements, skill dimensions, and attitudinal factors. Any team will function better if members have complementary expertise, good interpersonal communication skills, and shared values.

ORIENTING QUESTIONS

What are the criteria for an ISD project plan?
How can an ISD project plan be documented?
How do I plan projects in unfamiliar areas?
What competencies are needed to perform effectively on an ISD team?
In what settings are ISD jobs found? What are the trends in those settings?
How well am I prepared for ISD jobs in the setting where I choose to work?

OBJECTIVES

1. Given questions to assess your understanding of the planning process, identify and sequence the activities essential for effective planning.
2. Given the need to design instruction in an unfamiliar area, name the actions to take in order to get sufficient information to plan the work.
3. Given the need to conceptualize an output for a design and development activity, work with a design team to specify the outcome.
4. Given a plan for an ISD project, evaluate the adequacy of the plan.
5. Given an ISD plan of your own choosing, document the plan so that it satisfies all the criteria presented in this chapter.
6. Given the experience of working on an ISD team, evaluate whether the team engaged in behaviors that facilitated effective teamwork.
7. Given the environment where you expect to work, rate yourself on how well you are prepared to work in that area. Specify actions you will take to improve skills in which you are inadequate.

LEVELS OF PLANNING

Planning can be defined as laying out a course of action for yourself and others in order to accomplish a specific end. In an organization, planning takes place on several levels: strategic, operations, project, and activity. Let's take a look at some of these levels of planning.

Strategic Planning

Strategic planning takes place at the highest level of the organization. In strategic planning, the top people look at trends in social, economic, and political spheres and assess their probable impact on the organization. They try to envision the direction the organization should take in the immediate future.

As a hypothetical example, suppose the decision-makers in a corporation, as part of the strategy to stay competitive, decide they need to retrain their employees to use the new technologies that will increase productivity.

Operations Planning

Senior management has the responsibility for putting strategic plans into operations. This involves translating issues, needs, problems, and opportunities into specific goals and objectives, and establishing the time frames for achieving these goals and objectives. In our corporate example, operations planners might set two goals:

◆ Identify the new technologies and associated skills needed to increase productivity. The goal is to be achieved in six months.

◆ Conduct a needs analysis to determine how to prepare the work force to use the new technologies, and set priorities for the development of courses to prepare the work force for new ways of doing things. The prioritized list of courses will be identified within one year.

Project Planning

At the project level, middle managers and first-line supervisors outline the major efforts (projects) needed to achieve the goals. They specify who will carry out projects and resources which will be required.

For the second goal in our corporate example, the major tasks needed to achieve this goal might include the following:

1. Identify current performance levels of the work force.
2. Identify discrepancies between current performance levels and skills needed for new technologies.
3. Specify the solutions (e.g., instruction, job aids, incentive systems, work redesign, etc.) for bridging discrepancies.
4. Prepare statements that specify the requirements for each of the instructional solutions.
5. Identify constraints and resources needed to achieve the instructional solutions, and alternative methods for achieving the same goals.
6. Set priorities for development given the results of the previous task.

The project plan should specify the responsibility for each task, the time period within which it is to be accomplished, and budgetary or other constraints. For example, the manager in charge of the needs analysis would be responsible for:

◆ Establishing a schedule for completion of the analysis.

◆ Specifying the data collection methods and formats to be followed for recording the information.

◆ Assigning responsibility for collecting information about the problem.

◆ Coordinating with plant supervisors to allow designers access to workers and time to collect data.

◆ Arranging for support staff to enter the information into a database.

◆ Reviewing reports as they are generated.

In summary, ISD planning takes place at the project level, although it is generally true that the need for ISD planning stems primarily from planning decisions at higher levels. As the Seels and Glasgow Model indicates, project planning typically takes place at three points in the ISD process (see Figure 9.1).

1. A plan must be developed to carry out activities associated with needs analysis when the problem is defined and general goals and priorities are set.

Figure 9.1   Project Planning in the ISD Process

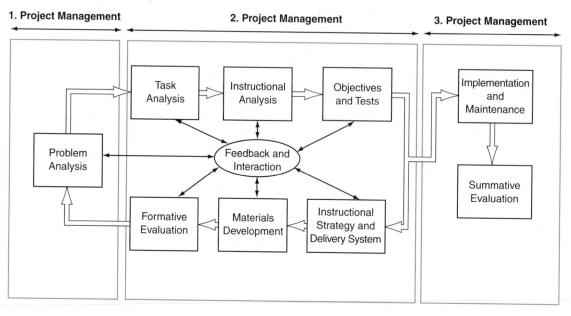

How do we work together?
What are the project objectives?
What steps must be taken to achieve the objectives?
How much time will the project take?
What competencies are needed to carry out each step?
What resources are needed to carry out each step?
How is the plan communicated to others?

2. If the problem has an instructional solution, a plan must be developed for carrying out ISD processes associated with developing the proposed instruction. The plan begins with task analysis and concludes with formative evaluation when the final instructional product is developed into its final form.

3. Once the instruction has been developed, the product must be installed in the real world and evaluated to determine if it has solved the problem. A plan must be developed for carrying out these phases of the ISD process.

Each planning point has a clear beginning and ends with an output that feeds into the next stage. The same people may or may not be responsible for carrying out all three projects.

BENEFITS OF PLANNING

The ability to control events is planning's greatest benefit. By carefully evaluating all aspects of the situation, problems are anticipated and dealt with effectively. Planning also enables you to make the best possible use of available resources.

A project may turn out well without adequate planning. However, it's much more likely that inadequate planning will result in one or more of the following events:

◆ A deadline is not met.

◆ A product does not meet quality standards.

◆ Clients are dissatisfied.

- Subordinates are confused and possibly resentful.
- Time and energy are wasted in handling problems that could have been foreseen and planned for.
- Resources are not available when needed.
- The budget is exceeded because of having to redo work that wasn't right the first time, because of downtime waiting for resources that weren't available when needed, or because planning was based on faulty assumptions.

Consider this example of ineffective planning: Two self-instructional manuals were to be written and printed by a certain date. Each manual was assigned to a different designer and a deadline set for completion. No schedule was established for each task. Standards for format and layout were not specified. As a result, the manuals had to go through several drafts, because each designer used a different format and each had a different idea of how the work should be done. The final drafts were sent to the printer only a few days before the deadline. The print shop had a number of other "rush jobs," and wasn't able to complete the job until after the deadline passed.

These problems could have been avoided by:

- setting standards for the work to be produced;
- establishing a schedule with checkpoints to monitor progress; and
- coordinating with the print shop, so that they could reserve a specific time period for the work.

ESSENTIAL STEPS IN THE PLANNING PROCESS

While management textbooks contain many variations of the planning process, there are certain basic steps common to every version. Figure 9.2 illustrates a version of the planning process that fits in an ISD environment. Some steps are always performed, while others are performed only when specific conditions exist. Only the steps that need further clarification are explained next. The step number corresponds to the one for that box on the flowchart.

Step 3: Collect and Examine Information about the Project

If you have actually developed similar instruction, you may be familiar enough with the task content to move on to the next step. However, if you are unfamiliar with the task content, you must collect and analyze information about the work procedures, and so forth, before you proceed with planning.

As an instructional designer, you may be given work in a new area. The less you know about an area, the greater the possibilities for error. Without a thorough understanding of the problem, you may proceed down blind alleys and dead ends. The wrong people may be assigned to the job, and you may have no good basis for measuring progress, allocating resources, and evaluating the output. Many mistakes could be made, and perhaps team members will learn from these mistakes. Eventually, they may get it right, but the trial and error approach to instructional design is expensive, time consuming, and frustrating. Table 9.1 shows two types of previous experience you may have and the implications of each for planning.

When effective designers take on an unfamiliar job, they assess their previous experience with the same or similar work; define the nature of their deficiency; collect information needed to remove the deficiency or accommodate it; and formulate a plan accordingly. They realize that if they do not take the time to define the problem, it will only have to be redefined later after resources have been expended. Effective planning means systematically defining the problem by assessing your experience on the factors shown in Table 9.2.

Figure 9.2   Steps in the Planning Process

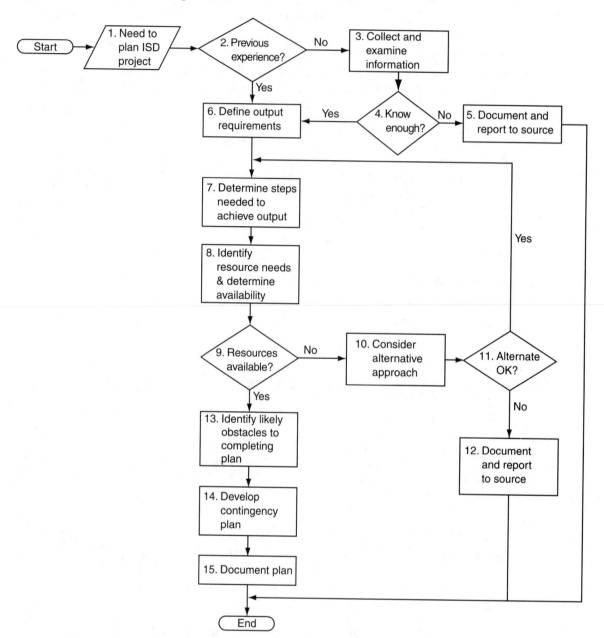

Table 9.1   Two Types of Experience and Implications for Planning

Direct Experience	*Vicarious Experience*
Actually working on all or part of the same or similar work	Taking a course Reading about the work Seeing others do the work
Results in SPECIFIC knowledge, and thus MORE LIKELY to be able to formulate an effective plan.	Results in GENERAL understanding, and LESS LIKELY to formulate an effective plan.

Table 9.2   Assessing Your Experience

Factors to Consider	Questions to Ask	Responses Indicating a Deficiency
Type of work	Have I done work requiring the same or similar duties, tasks, skills, knowledge, and abilities?	NO
Scope of work	Is the scope of work larger than any I've previously done in terms of size of staff, number of items processed or produced, or amount of coordination?	YES
Deadlines	Is the deadline shorter than any I've ever had with the same team and resources?	YES
History with Client	Do I know the client's preferences, work style, mind-set, and standards?	NO
Equipment and Supplies	Am I familiar with the hardware or software capabilities, maintenance requirements, or reliability?	NO

Once you've identified areas where your knowledge and experience is deficient, you should identify sources of information for acquiring the knowledge. Experts who understand the work can provide details, or information may be available in written form. Completing this task will require skill in extracting information from documents, persistence in working with people who may not give you the highest priority, the ability to resolve discrepancies from different sources, and the ability to synthesize the information into a coherent whole. In other words, you will need the same skills you needed to be an effective instructional designer. Table 9.3 lists potential sources of information and questions to ask for each unfamiliar area.

Step 6: Defining the Output Requirements

The next essential step in the planning process is to identify and specify exactly those outcomes that are expected from the project. Desired outcomes must be stated in qualitative and quantitative terms so that you know whether the objectives have been achieved. It is important to define the final results expected from the work for several reasons:

◆ Team members who will be doing the work need to know exactly what is expected of them.

◆ The outputs must meet the needs of the end-user and client. They need to know what will be delivered to them.

◆ Output requirements provide a basis for evaluating the final product.

Output requirements are specified by identifying the product to be produced. In an ISD project there are likely to be several products.

There will be several outputs from the analysis phase. The needs analysis output will be a goal statement describing the general requirements for the instruction. The outputs from the task analysis will be a task inventory and a document describing the task components.

Table 9.3 Potential Sources of Information When Planning a Project in an Unfamiliar Area

Non-Human Resources	*Human Resources*
Organization's rules, regulations, and policy	Managers within your organization
Documentation (user's manuals, reports, briefings, files on similar work, etc.)	Experienced staff at your organization
Books, journals, and magazines	Other organizations who have done similar work
	The client
	Outside specialists

Questions to ask experts who understand the work for an unfamiliar area

1. How long did the job take?

2. What resources were used?

3. What technical competencies were needed?

4. What training was needed for designers and support staff?

5. What steps were taken to achieve the objectives?

6. Were there any unusual obstacles?

7. What contingencies were taken?

8. What were the output standards?

9. What would you do differently?

The instructional analysis outputs will include hierarchies and prerequisites. All of these elements may be contained in a report prepared for the client, or it may be an internal document to be used by the project team during the design phase.

The output of the design phase is a document containing the objectives, test specifications, and instructional strategies. If a prototype was developed, the design document will contain the lessons learned from prototyping. The outputs of the development phase are the assessment instruments, the instructional materials, and records of the tryouts. The outputs of the implementation phase will include a number of documents on how to administer and maintain the course.

In order to adequately define the output, you may have to talk to a number of users to determine their exact needs. After reconciling differences, you must document the output requirements so that they will be useful to you as you continue with the planning process and so that you will provide others with a clear picture of what the outcome of the project should be. An adequate set of output requirements will specify:

◆ time frames within which the work is to be accomplished;

◆ a prescribed form or format for the output;

◆ quantitative standards (i.e., how many); and

◆ qualitative standards (i.e., performance standards for students, reading levels, etc.).

When the product is something tangible, it isn't difficult to specify objective, qualitative standards. Some products may be judged on a more subjective basis. For example, the standards for a presentation might include: effective use of audiovisuals, logical sequencing, smoothness of delivery, and conciseness. In documenting standards such as these, the criteria can be made more specific by including indicators that help define what you consider acceptable. For "smoothness of delivery," for example, you might include questions such as:

◆ Did the speaker frequently seem to be groping for words?

◆ Did the speaker use vocalizations such as "uh" excessively?

◆ Did the speaker use effective transitions from one point to another?

Even in these examples, there is room for disagreement (How often is "frequently"? What constitutes "excessive"?), but at least presenters have a better idea of what is needed.

In a seminar, for example, criteria might include the number of questions asked of speakers, the length of the discussions, ratings on evaluations forms, or voluntary comments during breaks.

Step 7: Determine Steps to Achieve the Output

It is important to break the work down into steps and substeps in order to determine the sequence in which each of the steps is to be performed. This helps reveal the most efficient path for achieving the desired outcomes. As with other aspects of the planning process, there are several reasons for making a list of the activities needed to achieve the output.

◆ The list will help make sure that no essential step is omitted.

◆ Breaking the work into steps and substeps will provide a basis for assigning tasks.

◆ The list will help when setting up a schedule. By identifying tasks that are independent of each other or dependent on the completion of other tasks, you will be able to select the best possible path to achieve the output.

◆ The schedule will help you monitor the work as it progresses.

Listing the steps involves the same processes you used when performing a task analysis, and the criteria for acceptability are similar. First, the list must be complete. No essential step should be omitted. Second, the steps should be at the appropriate level of detail. There should be from four to nine major steps, and two to five sub-steps for each step. Third, each step and sub-step should be written in behavioral terms. It should include an action verb (e.g., write, select, or develop) and the object of the verb (e.g., objectives, media, or prototype). The output of the activities should be stated explicitly. For example, the output for a project to motivate faculty and students to learn about a country could be an interactive CD-ROM disc which contains a tutorial, and functions for interactivity with the World Wide Web (WWW). It could also include databases that the tutorial could draw upon.

Team members must understand exactly what is expected of them when they perform each step. Finally, your notes should indicate:

◆ steps whose output must be reviewed;

◆ frequency of progress checks;

◆ steps that can be performed independently; and

◆ steps that must be performed sequentially.

Step 8: Identify Resource Needs and Determine Availability

This is one of the most important steps in the planning process. Resources (people, facilities, equipment, etc.) are identified for each of the major steps based on availability. If adequate resources are not available, alternatives to getting the job done are considered (e.g., requesting additional resources, reducing project scope, extending the deadline, or redefining the project).

Table 9.4   Time Estimates for One Hour of Instruction

Delivery System	Development Time
Conventional instructor led	40 to 100 hours
Self-paced (Programmed Instruction)	80 to 120 hours
Video	200 hours
Computer Based Training	200 to 400 hours

Adapted from "How Long Does It Take?" by C. Lee & R. Zemke, June 1987, in *Training*, pp. 75–80.

Planning requires the ability to schedule resources and staff to achieve objectives on time and within budget. Every project or activity requires resource support. The major resource categories are personnel, time, equipment, and supplies. Personnel assignments will depend on the number of individuals available, the match of capabilities needed with the planned activities, and the availability of individuals with the requisite skills. Every project or activity must be carried out within some time frame. Deadlines may be actual, such as a predetermined date set by regulation, or imposed by the seriousness of the problem that the effort is expected to solve.

Lee and Zemke (1987) asked experienced training managers what rules of thumb they used for estimating time lines. Managers in large corporations, the U.S. military, the U.S. Office of Personnel Management, and instructional development consultants were interviewed. The findings show that generally, time estimates were based on one hour of completed instruction for a given media delivery system. The more complex the delivery system, the more time was needed. Table 9.4 shows the range of estimated time for selected delivery systems reported to Lee and Zemke. In addition to the complexity of the delivery system, time allocations depended on the following factors:

◆ **Team members' experience with the same or similar work.** The less experienced a person is the longer it will take to do the job. It will take time to coach the individual, and then time to recover from mistakes that will inevitably be made. The CEO of a company specializing in computer-based training interviewed by Lee and Zemke warned that even the most experienced people will need time to adapt when working in a new setting. He said, "When starting a new venture, like a CBT group, it takes people a little time to get on board. Consultants have to learn to think like the company. If you hire a specialist, the same thing applies—the new person will have to get used to the organization and the organization used to him."

◆ **The stability of the content.** Course development will take less time if content is relatively stable. If subject matter is still in a fluid state (e.g., designing instruction on how to use a data management system while the system is still under development), then count on extensive time during the analysis phase, plus revision time later. As the system evolves the instructional content will have to be revised to reflect that evolution.

Equipment and Supplies.   Equipment includes computers, VCRs, CD players, etc. needed to perform the work. Supplies include items such as disks, paper, software programs, etc. needed to support the work.

In summary, when estimating resources use past experience to predict future requirements to the maximum extent possible. Keep good records of the actual time it takes for various activities and the resources needed so you can do a better job next time.

Exercises A and B at the end of this chapter provide practice in measuring your understanding of the planning process.

Step 15: Document the Plan

The last step in the planning process involves developing timeline charts, staging events to meet objectives, establishing checkpoints for reviewing and monitoring the work, and allocating personnel and other resources for each event. The plan becomes a blueprint for monitoring the project as it progresses.

Earlier in the chapter, four levels of planning were discussed: strategic, operations, project, and activity. Planning documents at the strategic and operations level have different requirements than the project or activity plans that are the instructional designer's responsibility. An acceptable project or activity plan should meet the following seven criteria:

◆ Areas of responsibility are designated.

◆ Plans for developing subordinates are indicated, if appropriate.

◆ Resources and work are aligned so objectives are met.

◆ Steps to accomplish objectives are spelled out.

◆ Vacations and other work requirements are considered.

◆ Due dates are specified.

◆ Check points are specified.

A well documented plan acts as a stimulus for exploring options and considering issues that might otherwise be ignored. It makes objectives visible by showing the planned checkpoints, due dates, timeframes, assignments, contingencies, equipment, and material requirements. It provides everyone with an understanding of how their work fits into a larger scheme—how what they do affects others, and vice versa. Usually when people have a "big picture" of the work, they can make more informed decisions about what to do and where to obtain information when they must act independently. For the team leader, it provides a tool for checking the status of the work. Finally, the plan creates a perception of being in control of the work, in control of yourself, and in control of the situation despite the problems and adversities that inevitably arise.

Format for Documenting a Plan.   The plan may be displayed using a number of formats. It may be constructed as a matrix or a list of tasks and associated responsibilities, milestones, and due dates. Any format is appropriate as long as it meets the criteria listed above. Most planning documents consist of a *Gantt chart* (see Glossary), like the one in the following example.

Perhaps an example from everyday life will give you a better idea of how a plan may be documented. Figure 9.3 shows the plan for a house tour in the form of a Gantt chart.

Situation: A house tour is the major fund raising event for an all-volunteer community group. The group raises approximately 75% of its revenue from this one-day event. The tour is held every year on the first Sunday in October, but planning the tour begins in late May. The group's President oversees the entire project. Task Leaders are responsible for the elements of the tour. All have worked on previous tours and are used to functioning autonomously. Each Task Leader recruits other members of the organization to work with them to accomplish the specific objectives. A budget is set for producing the brochure that describes the houses to the attendees, printing and mailing costs associated with promoting the tour and ticket sales, and the party for the more than 100 volunteers who work on the tour. A discussion of how the plan document meets the criteria is presented in Table 9.5.

Exercises C and D at the end of this chapter provide practice on documenting ISD plans.

Figure 9.3   Sample Project Plan

HOUSE TOUR ACTIVITIES	TASK LEADERS
Select homes	Jimmy
Identify candidate homes	
Obtain commitment from owners	
Send letters to home owners to verify commitment	
Notify brochure chair and artist as homes are identified	
Prepare Brochure	Vickie
Visit homes and write descriptions	
Verify write ups with owners	
Rewrite and Proof	
Prepare map...	
Authorize graphics/printer to start work on cover design	
Assemble copy, graphics, map & drawings for graphics/printer	
Proof galleys, arrange delivery of brochures	
Prepare Drawings	Kitty
Draw houses	
Deliver copies for brochure	
Frame original for home owners	
Sale Ads	Lew
Identify potential buyers	
Assign ads sellers	
Make sales	
Assemble copy & graphics for brochure	
Deliver for brochure	
Sell Advance Tickets	Mary
Assemble mailing lists	
Mail notices	
Print tickets	
Fill orders from mailed purchases	
Distribute tickets to advance ticket seller locations	
Distribute flyers and posters	
Publicize Tour	Wendy
Prepare and send press releases to newspapers	
Place television ads	
Design/print flyers & posters	
Put up banner	
Recruit & Train Tour Guides	David
Recruit/Assign Tour Guides	
Train Guides	
Plan Party for Home Owners & Workers	Bonnie
Obtain organization to host party	
Invite guests	
Assist host coordinate party	
Help set up on day of party	
Manage Day of Tour Activities	Mike
Obtain site for ticket booth	
Recruit ticket sellers	
Coordinate distribution of supplies	
Conduct day of tour sales	
Review Progress	Zita
Call Team Leaders	
Conduct monthly meetings	

Schedule columns: MAY (21, 28), JUNE (4, 11, 18, 25), JULY (2, 9, 16, 23, 30), AUGUST (6, 13, 20, 27), SEPTEMBER (3, 10, 17, 24), 1

Table 9.5 Criteria for Sample Project Plan in Figure 9.3

Criteria	*Corresponding Elements of Plan*
1. Areas of responsibility are designated.	Responsibility indicated by task leader column
2. Plans for developing subordinates are indicated, if appropriate.	Training for tour guides is specified under the task recruit & train guides
3. Resources and work are aligned so that objectives are met.	Timelines and diamonds show sequences for performing tasks and subtasks
4. Steps to accomplish objectives are spelled out.	Tasks and subtasks are spelled out to the level appropriate for these highly experienced individuals. More detail would be needed for less experienced people.
5. Vacations and other work requirements are considered.	Not applicable. Task leaders are responsible for fitting the work to their personal schedules.
6. Due dates are specified.	Time lines and diamonds show when steps are carried out. A diamond indicates a task with no subtasks. Ends of lines show completion dates for tasks involving substeps.
7. Check points are specified.	Weekly check points are shown. The President telephones the task leaders weekly to check on progress and to provide assistance as needed. Progress is also discussed at monthly meetings.

COMPETENCIES FOR TEAMS

Most experts on group theory and skills stress the knowledge requirements, skill dimensions, and attitudinal factors that are needed for effective teamwork. Research psychologists from the Naval Air Warfare Center (NAWC) Training Systems Division (1995) studied what makes effective teams. The knowledge, skills, and attitudes listed in Table 9.6 are those necessary for team members to work effectively together.

Knowledge that relates to how the specific tasks are performed on the project usually derives from your past experience working on similar projects. General knowledge about task performance evolves from your education and training. Knowledge about when specific duties and responsibilities are carried out and lines of communication within the team and with the client will vary from project to project. A well documented plan for accomplishing the work informs people about what is expected of them. Team members work better together if they know what to do and when to do it.

In a society that values individual initiative over group cohesion, the skills and attitudes necessary for effective team work are less well developed in our population than the knowledge base. Johnson and Johnson (1987) studied the skills and attitudes necessary for effective teamwork and developed behavioral descriptions of them. They classify effective team behavior as task and maintenance functions. Task functions are the skills necessary for a group to achieve its goals. Maintenance functions are not directly related to achieving

Table 9.6   Knowledge, Skills, and Attitudes for Effective Teamwork

Knowledge	Skills	Attitudes
Prescribe how the work gets done	*Help the group do the work*	*Promote group stability*
Possesses knowledge of the team's mission, objectives, norms, and resources	Assess and monitor the performance of the team and its members	Possess a team orientation, where thinking of teams is a natural way to approach issues
Understand the logical order to perform tasks	Be flexible and adapt rapidly to events	Possess a shared vision where there is agreement on what is the ideal state
Understand how to perform specific tasks	Resolve conflicts with mutual satisfaction	Team cohesion, with a strong sense of the collective "we"
Agree on a logical way to divide up tasks	Step in to correct and/or strengthen the actions of others	Mutual trust and confidence in each other's integrity, loyalty, and character
Know your role in exchanging information, handing off tasks, and other interaction patterns	Exchange complete, timely, and accurate information	Trust in the team's collective effectiveness
	Encourage and build the morale of other team members	A belief that the skills of dealing with others have value
	Communicate clearly and appropriately to others	
	Plan, cooperate, and share in approaches to solving problems	
	See problems or issues in their context and be sensitive to the environment of the situation	

Adapted from *Knowledge, Skills, and Attitudes for Effective Teams,* by Naval Air Warfare Center (NAWC) in Training Systems Division, 1995, Paper presented at the National Performance Management Conference, Washington, D.C.: U.S. Office of Personnel Management.

the group's goals; rather, they are the attitudes directed toward group stability and making sure that individual members are satisfied.

Task and maintenance functions require the ability to ask questions, perhaps for amplification or clarification, and to paraphrase or summarize. When you ask questions you force yourself to pay attention, to think, to be an active listener. Here is an example of each technique.

◆ Summarize—repeat using speaker's words (e.g., "You said that the X-Ray Department was understaffed and poorly managed.").

◆ Paraphrase—restate in own words (e.g., "I think you are implying that the department is inefficient.").

◆ Clarification—ask for confirmation or information (e.g., "Are you saying that the X-Ray Department is unlikely to meet the demand?").

◆ Amplification—request elaboration (e.g., "Have you a plan to suggest?").

Table 9.7 Task and Maintenance Functions

Task Functions *Skills that help the group do the work*	*Maintenance Functions* *Attitudes that foster group stability* *and satisfaction*
Information and Opinion Giver: Offers facts, opinions, ideas, feelings, and information.	*Encourager of Participation:* Lets members know their contributions are valued.
Information and Opinion Seeker: Asks for facts, opinions, ideas, feelings, and information.	*Communication Facilitator:* Makes sure all group members understand what others say.
Direction and Role Definer: Calls attention to tasks that need to be done and assigns responsibilities.	*Tension Reliever:* Tells jokes and increases group fun. *Process Observer:* Uses observations of how the group is working to help discuss how the group can improve.
Summarizer: Pulls together related ideas or suggestions and restates them.	*Interpersonal Problem Solver:* Helps resolve and mediate conflicts.
Energizer: Encourages group members to work hard to achieve goals.	*Supporter and Praiser:* Expresses acceptance and liking for group members.
Comprehension Checker: Asks others to summarize discussion to make sure they understand.	

Adapted from *Joining together: Group theory and group skills,* by D. W. Johnson & F. P. Johnson, 1987, Englewood Cliffs, NJ: Prentice-Hall.

Task and maintenance functions and the types of activities team members must engage in to be effective are shown in Table 9.7. There is a great deal of similarity between Johnson and Johnson's task and maintenance function and the NAWC's skills and knowledge requirements for effective teamwork.

NAWC stresses that good teams don't just happen. Team members must learn to work together, and this implies some type of training. According to NAWC, training individuals separately in the knowledge, skills, and attitudes listed in Table 9.6 is not as effective as training the team as a group using simulation, role playing, and guided task practice.

The kind of training recommended by NAWC is seldom conducted for ISD teams. However, the skills and attitudes that help the team do the work and contribute to group stability can and do develop over time. Initially the effectiveness of a group will depend on the guidance provided by the group leader. The less experienced a group, the more necessary it is that task and maintenance functions are provided by the leadership. As the team members gain experience, they learn to work together more effectively and require less and less supervisory guidance. When a team is working effectively, task and maintenance functions are performed by every member of the group.

Team Behaviors and ISD Activities

The four ISD activities where team behaviors are especially important include the following:

Planning the tasks to be performed when you are a member of a design team.   Working cooperatively and constructively with other team members will advance the work toward the agreed-upon goals. There are certain steps that facilitate teamwork. At the start of each new project, a meeting should be held with all personnel who will have any involvement in the project. The purpose of the meeting is to gain the team's inputs regarding schedules and levels of effort for each activity. Clients' expectations for delivery schedules and output requirements should be clearly established before the meeting. If feasible, the client should participate in the meeting. Leaving clients out of the loop until time to review the plans can result in unexpected delays and changes in the plans for the overall development effort. Once a plan is formulated, it should be distributed to all team members including the client. Team members and the client must have a shared vision, shared standards, and shared understanding of roles and responsibilities.

Gathering information from content specialists to determine learning requirements.   A designer often works with specialists who are experts in their field. The designer elicits information, clarifies ambiguity, and directs the discussion toward gathering precise information from people who are adept at performing their jobs but who may not be adept at describing what they do. Under these circumstances, the designer will need persistence, tact, and diplomacy to extract information in sufficient detail.

Access to SMEs for the amount of time needed for analysis and review will require the cooperation of the SME's direct supervisor. Acting as an SME for the project may conflict with the performance of a worker's usual activities on the job. If the organization values the instruction and understands the level of effort required of the SME, it will make him available to support the development effort. If not, there will be a conflict between the SME's commitment to his job and his commitment to training development, which he may not perceive as being a part of his job. To avoid such problems, it is important to meet with upper management, who authorized the ISD project but may not have fully understood its implications, to clarify and explain why the SME's input is important to the project and the benefits for the organization in the long run. A project that does not have support from the top will almost invariably run into trouble. If the management is not perceived as being committed to the effort, there is no reason to expect a different attitude from the workers who are expected to provide subject matter expertise.

Working with the media production team during the development phase.   The more complicated the delivery system, the more competencies are needed on the team and the more costly the production process will be. It is the instructional designer's responsibility to ensure that the presentation's look and sound support rather than interferes with the achievement of the instructional objectives. Media production teams used to working on projects intended to entertain or to sell a product may not understand when these approaches conflict with sound instruction. Production will run more smoothly and will cost less if team members all understand the goals and objectives of the project, and the production process is carefully planned to achieve these goals.

Gaining the client's commitment to the approach.   Ultimately, the instruction will be used by others. The user organization, whether an internal or external group, must be committed to the product if it is to be useful over the long run. Commitment will be easier to gain if during every step in the project, the client is kept informed about the what, how, when, and why of ISD activities.

Just because an organization has funded a project does not mean that everyone in the organization supports the project. If there is not widespread support for the effort, it will be necessary that every member of the ISD team who interacts with client staff be a goodwill ambassador. It will be easier to overcome resistance to a project if instructional designers are flexible, can rapidly adapt to change, can resolve differences, can gain the respect of skeptics and otherwise perform the team skills set out by the NAWC.

Ways to Reach an Agreement

In any group work there must be ways to reach agreement. Johnson and Johnson (1987) suggest seven ways to reach agreement during group work. They are decision by the following parties:

◆ authority without discussion

◆ expert member

◆ average of members' opinions

◆ authority after discussion

◆ majority control [vote]

◆ minority control [committee]

◆ consensus (pp. 104–105)

Although each method has its advantages and disadvantages, one generally effective method is to reach consensus by discussion until all ideas are accepted, rejected, or revised by the group as a whole. According to Johnson and Johnson, even though the consensus method takes the most time, it often reduces implementation time. When implementation is considered, consensus turns out to be the least time-consuming method.

Consensus is the way the League of Women Voters reaches its positions on national issues. The League holds study meetings in preparation for a meeting where consensus or agreement on a position must be reached and stated. Agreement cannot be reached by majority vote or minority committee, or expert opinion or authority; it must be achieved by action of the group as a whole. It is important that you experience consensus and understand how it works before undertaking the team approach. Although many decisions are of necessity resolved by authority or expert opinion, other decisions need the efforts of all to generate the best solution.

Exercises E and F at the end of this chapter provide practice on using and assessing the skills for being an effective member of a team.

ISD JOBS AND SETTINGS

An instructional design practitioner's job may vary in the expertise required, the product produced, and the job setting. The ISD practitioner may do a task analysis under a project manager's supervision in a research and development organization, or he or she may lead a team that develops a three-day workshop for industry. Design is not always a team effort. In a smaller organization, a single person may do the instructional design tasks and more. You must prepare yourself to adjust to different situations by understanding how jobs, products, and settings vary in the field of ISD.

There are a range of jobs available across settings and at different levels of expertise. Sometimes the instructional designer acts as a specialist in one of the steps in the process. Other jobs call for the designer to be a generalist competent to carry through a project from start to finish. This range of jobs is due not only to the variety of specialized functions, but also to the different levels of expertise required by certain jobs. Figure 9.4 illustrates three levels of expertise in ISD jobs.

Jobs in public schools usually incorporate instructional design functions as part of other positions such as curriculum supervisor, media specialist, instructional technologist, and director of instruction. Compared to other settings the impact of instructional design in schools has been low. Some of the reasons for this low impact are the teacher-intensive nature of traditional schooling, the rigidity of the daily schedule, and the low amount of discretionary funding available to schools.

Figure 9.4   Levels of Expertise in ISD Practitioner Jobs

Basic: The instructional designer works on parts of a project under the direction of another designer. She works with others to improve existing instruction. She works on small projects or parts of projects.

Intermediate: The instructional designer takes responsibility for developing an entire course or for major redesigning projects. He can be a team leader on small or medium-sized projects.

Advanced: The instructional designer is heavily involved in project management and proposal writing. She may direct needs assessment or evaluation studies which determine project directions. She supervises team leaders. She can oversee large projects.

Differences among these settings can lead to differences in ISD processes and products. Designers moving from the academic world to the consulting world should remember the following: (a) your proposal may have to include much of the front-end problem solving and analysis in order to win the contract; and (b) you may have to propose a less costly project, even if it is a less desirable one, in order to be competitive.

Similarly, those moving from the academic world of higher education to the K–12 school system need to be aware that differing norms mean differing constraints. Higher education routinely constrains through admissions standards. Public schools routinely constrain through budget and community values.

The options in instructional design vary with settings, jobs, and products. These options are shown in Figure 9.5. In the figure each cell stands for an ISD position and the limitations on that position.

Figure 9.5   Products, Settings, and Jobs

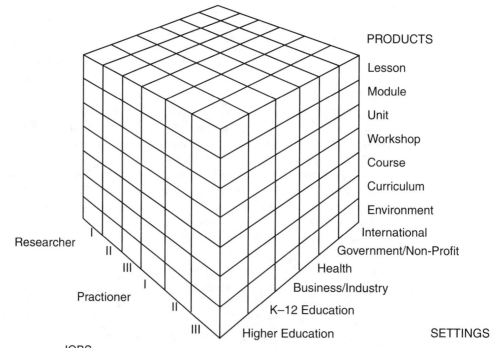

Any milieu that has an instructional function can become a setting for instructional design. This includes ISD efforts in international settings, business and industry, health and nonprofit associations, and schools and informal education. All of these need systematic development of instruction that utilizes instructional media and technology.

The prospects for instructional design positions in industry and government are excellent. The impact of deregulation, decentralization, downsizing, and the increasing level of sophistication required for jobs have led to a need for retraining. Just as technology is changing the way people work, it is also changing the way people learn.

The *New York Times* reports that more and more businesses are embracing new technologies to deliver training because the economic arguments are persuasive (Murphy, 1996). Although the up-front capital investments are high for training programs using high-tech multimedia, the operating costs are low because the ongoing expenses of instructors and materials are eliminated. The *Times* article cites GE Capital, a unit of General Electric, as a company who has moved in this direction. GE Capital's program manager for training and development projects that a training program using CD-ROM pays for itself within 15 months in savings on the costs of student travel to receive training and instructors.

Due to the reduction in the size of the federal government, the U.S. Office of Personnel Management (OPM) is looking to high tech media as a way to produce high quality training for less. In a request for proposals, OPM described its training requirements for the next five years as follows:

> A substantial portion of the work . . . will be accomplished using Instructional Systems Design (ISD) principles. . . These projects will typically result in the production of materials ranging from traditional classroom training to a wide variety of alternative training methods and distance learning technologies. However, a majority of the work will result in non-classroom products and methodologies. Projects will require significant research and front-end analysis because of the substantial investment required in the production of distance learning technologies. (U.S. Office of Personnel Management, 1996, p. 28)

Exercise G at the end of this chapter provides practice on evaluating your readiness to work as an instructional designer in your area of interest.

EXERCISES

A. An Exercise to Assess Your Understanding of the Planning Process

1. From the list below, what are the five essential activities to plan work successfully?

    ____ a. reach consensus with other ISD team members
    ____ b. document the plan
    ____ c. consult with subject matter experts
    ____ d. determine alternative media delivery systems
    ____ e. determine resource availability
    ____ f. specify the output requirements
    ____ g. determine resources needed
    ____ h. determine the steps to achieve the output

2. Sequence your five choices from question 1 in the order in which they should be performed to plan work successfully.

3. What is the best way to ensure that a job is completed efficiently?

    ____ a. weigh the alternatives
    ____ b. discuss all approaches with ISD team members

_____ c. prepare a detailed budget
_____ d. perform the job as in the past
_____ e. predetermine a course of action

4. Assume you must plan interviews to determine the job performance requirements of mental health practitioners who counsel troubled teens. You have no direct experience doing this type of interview. What should you do?

_____ a. document the reasons for stopping
_____ b. go ahead as best you can
_____ c. consult with someone who has interview experience with this population
_____ d. read a text on mental health practices

5. You have no information about a particular job. What are five sources from which you can obtain relevant information about the job so that you can devise a plan to collect job/task data?

6. You have been given the task of developing materials for a medium unfamiliar to you. What kinds of information are needed to plan the task? List the nine questions below.

B. A Group Exercise in Conceptualizing the Output for a Design Project

You are in the furniture design business and a customer wants you to design a chair. Your task is to determine the requirements for the chair. That is, you must conceptualize the output by specifying the following:

◆ time frame in which the design is to be completed;

◆ features that the chair must have;

◆ qualitative standards for the materials and construction of the chair; and

◆ quantitative standards for any dimensions that the chair must have.

This is a group exercise. To determine the output requirements, you may ask the customer 10 questions. No follow-up questions are allowed. Each person should individually write 10 questions to ask the customer. Then, with the other members of the group, arrive at a list of the final 10 questions to ask the customer in order to specify the requirements for the design of the chair.

C. An Exercise in Evaluating ISD Plans

The following case study contains two parts: a situation, and a plan in the form of a Gantt chart. Determine if the Gantt chart meets the criteria for a project plan given in the situation.

Situation:
A Blue-Ribbon Panel reviewed the Air Force's process for forecasting budget requirements. It concluded that the Air Force failed to receive full funding for a number of major projects because individuals who generate the basic data have no standardized training.

Since the job is not the responsibility of an established career field, there is no Air Force school for developing such training. For this reason, and because of personnel shortages in the training community, the Air Staff decided that the training would be the responsibility of the Air Force Accounting and Finance Center.

The section supervisor, Master Sergeant (MSgt.) Wilmer worked in training development during his last assignment so he was familiar with ISD principles. He developed the following plan (see Table 9.8) for identifying tasks performed by unit resource advisers. MSgt. Wilmer reports to Korea in 60 days. (MSgt. Wilmer uses Air Force jargon in his plan. OJT means on the job training; TDY means travel duty.)

Table 9.8 MSgt. Wilmer's plan

PLAN FOR DEVELOPING THE RESOURCE ADVISOR TRAINING SYSTEM

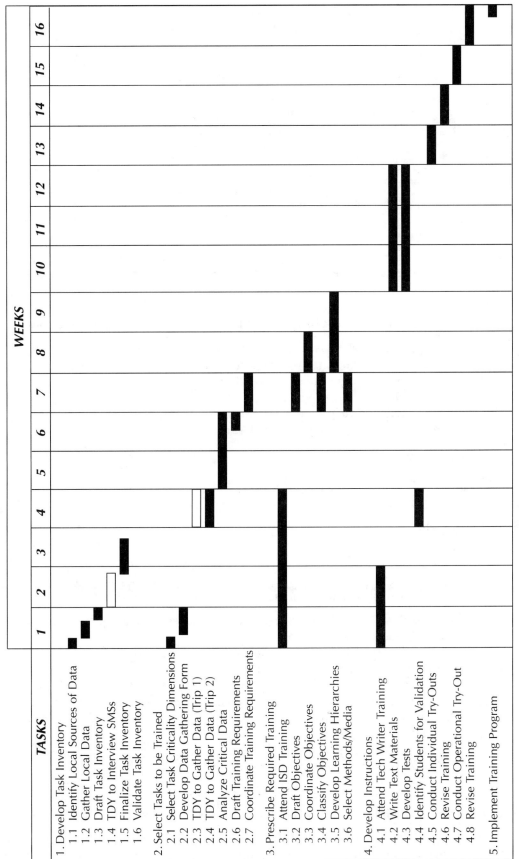

Note: ▢ MSgt. Wilmer will conduct OJT in data gathering. Also, MSgt. Wilmer will direct all non-TDY tasks through Week 7.

Source: Glasgow and Bulmer (1985), p. 21.

251

Table 9.9   Evaluating MSgt. Wilmer's plan

Criteria	Yes	No
1. Areas of responsibility are designated.		
2. Plans for developing subordinates are indicated, if appropriate.		
3. Resources and work are aligned so that objectives are met.		
4 Steps to accomplish objectives are spelled out.		
5. Vacations and other work requirements are considered.		
6. Due dates are specified.		
7. Check points are specified.		

Evaluate MSgt. Wilmer's plan and determine if it is adequate. In Table 9.9 place an X in the Yes column if the plan fulfills the criterion. Place an X in the No column if it does not.

D. An Exercise in Documenting of Plan for a Project of Your Own Choosing

This exercise is designed to let you apply what you have learned about planning to a situation of your own choosing. Working with your assigned partner or team members, analyze a project that you expect to undertake during the term.

Briefly describe the project.

Now, define the output requirements so that the instructor will have a clear idea of what you intend to develop as your class project.

Time Frames:

Forms or formats to be used:

Qualitative standards:

Quantitative standards:

Develop a plan to accomplish the project.

1. Make a list of all the steps and sub-steps to achieve the output.
    a. Include all essential steps.
    b. Use the appropriate level of detail.
    c. Write steps in behavioral terms.
2. Estimate the time, personnel, equipment, and supplies you will need to do the project. Write overall estimates for each resource. Then allocate the resources to each step.
3. Plan for any special skill or knowledge that team members will have to acquire to carry out the steps.
4. Accommodate schedules and other work requirements of the team members
5. Document the plan to meet the requirements in Table 9.10.

E. An Exercise in Using Encouraging Phrases as a Member of a Team

Brainstorm lead-in phrases that could be used as listening skill techniques during a team meeting. For example, "Are you saying _____ ?" or "Is it your contention that _____ ?" Following are phrases to encourage:

Table 9.10

Criteria	Yes	No
1. Areas of responsibility are designated.		
2. Plans for developing subordinates are indicated, if appropriate.		
3. Resources and work are aligned so that objectives are met.		
4 Steps to accomplish objectives are spelled out.		
5. Vacations and other work requirements are considered.		
6. Due dates are specified.		
7. Check points are specified.		

◆ Paraphrasing (e.g., "Is that what you said _____ ?")

◆ Summarizing (e.g., "How would you describe that idea?")

◆ Clarification (e.g., "Would you explain your point about _____ ?")

◆ Amplification (e.g., "Please elaborate on what you mean by _____ ?")

F. A Group Exercise Performing Teamwork Skills and Evaluating the Team's Performance of Task and Maintenance Functions

This group exercise consists of three parts. In part 1 you will work as a member of a team to perform a task. In part 2, the group will assess the team's performance of task and maintenance functions. In part 3, you will individually indicate your satisfaction with the ratings.

1. In item 7 of Exercise A you worked with a group to develop ten questions that you would ask a customer to determine the specifications for a chair. Now, working with the same group, prepare a set of answers to the questions in order to develop the specifications for a chair. The chair specifications must be acceptable to all members of the group. That is, the group's decision must be made by consensus.

2. Reflect on the experience of working as a group to arrive at specifications that were mutually acceptable to all members. Using the scale shown in Table 9.11, the team should rate itself on each of the task and maintenance functions defined by Johnson and Johnson (1987). The ratings may be determined by consensus, by majority vote, or by one person taking the responsibility for determining the ratings for everyone. Enter the team's ratings in the table shown in Figure 9.12.

3. What method did the group use to arrive at its ratings?

_____ a. Consensus
_____ b. Majority rule
_____ c. Authority of one person without discussion
_____ d. Other (please specify)

Were you satisfied with the ratings? _____ Explain why you felt as you did.

Table 9.11   Team rating scale

1	2	3	4	5
Poor		Average		Outstanding

Based on this experience, what method of group decision making do you think is most effective? Explain your answer.

G. An Individual and Group Exercise in Evaluating Your Readiness to Work as an Instructional Designer in Your Area of Interest

The first part of this exercise is for your use only. It is not designed as a test. First check the type of environment where you expect to work.

_____ 1. Business and industry
_____ 2. Government services
_____ 3. School system
_____ 4. Higher education
_____ 5. Health

If you do not have a good understanding of the job requirements in the field you have checked, review position descriptions, job advertisements, and literature describing the direction the field is headed to get an idea of the requisite competencies. This can be done individually or in a group.

For each of the competencies listed in Table 9.13, check the column that reflects how you view your ability to perform the competency. For each competency where you rated yourself as having no skill or some skill, indicate an action you can take to develop that competency in the "To improve" column (e.g., take a course, do an internship, complete an independent study project). Be specific about courses, books, and sites.

Finally, identify your three top priorities to improve your competencies given the trends and directions in your chosen field. In a group discussion with others wishing to work in the same field, share your priorities to get feedback on your perceptions about trends in instructional design and about the practicality and usefulness of what you intend to do.

Table 9.12

Task Functions _Skills that help the group do the work_	Maintenance Functions _Attitudes that foster group stability and satisfaction_
_____ 1. **Information and Opinion Giver:** Offers facts, opinions, ideas, feelings, and information.	_____ 7. **Encourager of Participation:** Lets members know their contributions are valued.
_____ 2. **Information and Opinion Seeker:** Asks for facts, opinions, ideas, feelings, and information.	_____ 8. **Communication Facilitator:** Makes sure all group members understand what others say.
_____ 3. **Direction and Role Definer:** Calls attention to tasks that need to be done and assigns responsibilities.	_____ 9. **Tension Reliever:** Tells jokes and increases group fun.
_____ 4. **Summarizer:** Pulls together related ideas or suggestions and restates them.	_____ 10. **Process Observer:** Uses observations of how the group is working to help discuss how the group can improve.
_____ 5. **Energizer:** Encourages group members to work hard to achieve goals.	_____ 11. **Interpersonal Problem Solver:** Helps resolve and mediate conflicts.
_____ 6. **Comprehension Checker:** Asks others to summarize discussion to make sure they understand.	_____ 12. **Supporter and Praiser:** Expresses acceptance and liking for group members.

Table 9.13

Competencies	No Skill	Some Skill	Strong Skill	Action to Improve
ISD Competencies				
a. Conduct needs analysis				
b. Assess learner characteristics				
c. Analyze jobs and content				
d. Write behavioral objectives				
e. Develop criterion tests				
f. Specify instructional strategies				
g. Select delivery systems appropriate for instructional events				
h. Conduct formative evaluation				
Media production competencies				
Design and develop instruction for: (Rate each technology)				
a. Print technologies				
b. Audiovisual technologies				
c. Teleconferencing technologies				
d. Computer technologies				
e. Integrated technologies				
Teamwork competencies				
a. Skills that help the group to do the work				
b. Attitudes that foster group stability and satisfaction				

Background:

ISD competencies are those skills needed to apply a systems approach to instructional design. Media production competencies are abilities to design instruction using the presentation and response requirements of the specific technologies and work with media production specialists to develop the material. (Consult chapter 5 and the glossary for definitions of each technology.) Teamwork competencies refer to the skills and attitudes identified in Tables 9.6 and 9.7.

My three top priorities for a plan of action are as follows:

a.

b.

c.

◆ REFERENCES

Glasgow, Z., & Bulmer, S. (1985). *Managing the ISD process; A course for first line supervisors: Student guide* (Contract No. F41689-83-C-0048). Randolph AFB, TX: USAF Occupational Measurement Center (ATC).

Johnson, D. W., & Johnson, F. P. (1987). *Joining together: Group theory and group skills.* Englewood Cliffs, NJ: Prentice-Hall.

Lee, C., & Zemke, R. (1987, June) How long does it take? *Training,* pp. 75–80.

Murphy, K. (1996, May 6). Pitfalls vs. promise in training by CD-ROM. *The New York Times,* p. C3.

Naval Air Warfare Center (NAWC) Training Systems Division. (1995). *Knowledge, skills, and attitudes for effective teams.* Paper presented at the National Performance Management Conference, U.S. Office of Personnel Management, Washington, D.C.

U.S. Office of Personnel Management. (1996). *Research and development in instructional systems, development performance, management, workforce productivity, compensation, and employee relations* (Solicitation OPM-RFP-96-01595VHB). Washington, DC: Author.

◆ ANSWERS

A. An Exercise to Assess Your Understanding of the Planning Process

1. b. Document the plan
   e. Determine resource availability
   f. Specify the output requirements
   g. Determine resource needs
   h. Determine the steps to achieve the output
2. f. Specify the output requirements
   h. Determine the steps to achieve the output
   g. Determine resource needs
   e. Determine resource availability
   b. Document the plan
3. e. Determine a course of action
4. c. Consult with someone who has interview experience with this population
5. Any five of the following are correct:
   ◆ Organization's rules, regulations, and policy
   ◆ Documentation (user's manuals, reports, briefings, files on similar work, etc.)
   ◆ Books, journals, and magazines
   ◆ Managers within your organization
   ◆ Experienced staff at your organization
   ◆ Other organizations who have done similar work
   ◆ The client
   ◆ Outside specialists
6. a. How long did the job take?
   b. What resources were used?
   c. What technical competencies were needed?
   d. What training was needed for designers and support staff?
   e. What steps were taken to achieve the objectives?
   f. Were there any unusual obstacles?
   g. What contingencies were taken?
   h. What were the output standards?
   i. What would you do differently?

B. A Group Exercise in Conceptualizing the Output for a Design Project

There is no one correct answer. The output should meet the requirements in the exercise.

C. An Exercise in Evaluating ISD Plans

The answer to this exercise is shown in Table 9.14.

1. This plan does not specify areas of responsibility with the exception of MSgt. Wilmer providing OJT. This could result in missed tasks.
2. Although OJT and formal training are specified for tasks 1, 2, and 3, there are none for task 4. This is a default "no."
5. MSgt. Wilmer's assignment to Korea is not considered.
7. Checkpoints are not specified.

Overall, despite its many problems, this plan could succeed while MSgt. Wilmer is around because people are being developed and the ISD process is being followed. However, events between weeks 8 and 16 are not controlled.

D. An Exercise in Documenting of Plan for a Project of Your Own Choosing

There is no one correct answer to this exercise. Your plan should satisfy the criteria in the exercise.

E. An Exercise in Using Encouraging Phrases as a Member of a Team

There is no one correct answer to this exercise. The phrases you used should be designed to encourage team participation.

F. A Group Exercise Performing Teamwork Skills and Evaluating the Team's Performance of Task and Maintenance Functions

There is no one correct answer to this exercise. The more task and maintenance functions that were performed, the better the team's performance. Decisions made by consensus are more satisfactory, however, there will be times when the team does not have the knowledge to make a correct decision, or there is not time for consensus building.

Table 9.14

Criteria	Yes	No
1. Areas of responsibility are designated.		X
2. Plans for developing subordinates are indicated, if appropriate.		X
3. Resources and work are aligned so that objectives are met.	X	
4 Steps to accomplish objectives are spelled out.	X	
5. Vacations and other work requirements are considered.		X
6. Due dates are specified.	X	
7. Check points are specified.		X

G. An Individual and Group Exercise in Evaluating Your Readiness to Work as an Instructional Designer in Your Area of Interest

There is no one correct answer to this exercise. You must make the decisions for your own professional development.

Chapter

10 Determining Prerequisites

OVERVIEW

The behavior to be attained at the end of instruction is defined by the task analysis. When the task analysis is completed, a database exists to answer the question "What is the job or content?" Then the tasks defined by this process are subjected to another type of analysis, called instructional analysis. Instructional analysis is intended to answer the question "What must be learned?" The distinctions between task and instructional analysis were covered in chapter 2 and are summarized in Table 2.1. Instructional analysis consists of three functions: analyzing task and content levels to determine the type of learning required, sequencing tasks or content in the order in which they should be learned to determine prerequisite relationships, and setting the entry requirements for the course. Figure 10.1 shows where instructional analysis is conducted in Seels & Glasgow's ISD Model II: For Practitioner.

ANALYZING TASKS AND CONTENT TO IDENTIFY THE TYPES OF LEARNING

Instructional analysis is the process by which tasks are classified according to the types of learning required to acquire the task or knowledge. This usually takes the form of using some sort of learning classification system. In this text, we use the taxonomy developed by Robert M. Gagné and Leslie J. Briggs (Gagné, Briggs, and Wager, 1992). The Gagné taxonomy is probably one of the best known and most frequently used taxonomies in the field. Its acceptance is most likely based on the fact that it alone, of the many taxonomies, helps the designer make the transition from the abstract definitions of learning to the concrete action that will bring learning about. The instructional strategies prescribed by Gagné and Briggs for their categories of learning are covered in chapter 11. In this chapter, you will learn to distinguish among them.

SEQUENCING INSTRUCTION

Instructional analysis also makes explicit the prerequisites that lead to the learning outcomes and have implications for sequencing instruction. Prerequisites are subordinate competencies that "enable" the learning of another task. To identify prerequisites, the

Figure 10.1   Instructional Analysis in the Practitioner's Model

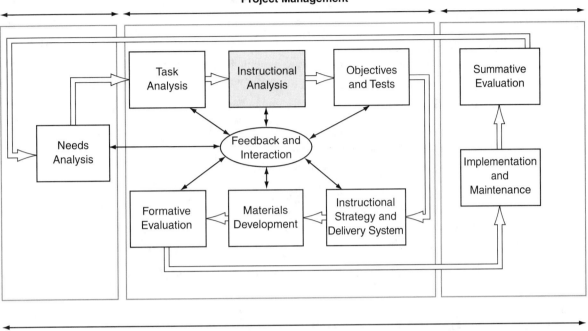

What types of learning are required by the objectives?
In what order must learning occur?
What skills or knowledge must students have
at the onset of instruction?

instructional designer asks, "What must the learner know in order to perform this task?" The answer to this question will be one or more subordinate competencies to be acquired before learning the final task. The designer continues to ask the same question with regard to the subordinate competencies, thereby identifying lower and lower levels of subordinates.

SETTING THE ENTRY REQUIREMENTS

Not all tasks and content are included in instruction. As discussed in chapter 8, the needs analysis process may have uncovered noninstructional solutions for some tasks. Also, limits on time, money, or staff may mean setting priorities for tasks that warrant subsequent development. Such limitations may mean that instructional development for some tasks may have to be put off until another time. During instructional analysis, the designer finalizes the decisions about which tasks will be included in instruction and which will not.

The intent is to avoid designing instruction on content students already know. To this end, the instructional designers assesses the capabilities of the "target audience"—the students expected to take the instruction—to determine which subordinate competencies were learned previously and which have yet to be learned. The result of this activity establishes the entry requirements for the course and has implications for how much instruction is needed to achieve the learning outcomes.

ORIENTING QUESTIONS

What implications do types of learning have for instructional design?
What are the outcomes of an instructional analysis?
How does an instructional analysis differ from a task analysis?
How are hierarchies constructed?
How do you determine the entry requirements for a course?

OBJECTIVES

1. Given learning outcomes, classify them as examples of verbal information, motor skills, attitudes, or intellectual skills.
2. Given a hierarchy, answer questions about relationships among the tasks.
3. Given an incomplete hierarchy and a list of tasks, complete the hierarchy.
4. Given a list of tasks, use the list to construct a hierarchy.
5. Given learning outcomes, identify the information needed to define the entry-level behaviors.
6. Given a list of tasks and associated test results, select the tasks that can be considered entry-level behaviors.
7. Given a hierarchy, describe the target audience and identify the entry-level behaviors.

TYPES OF LEARNING

The taxonomies discussed in chapter 3 are distinguished by their content. Bloom, Englehart, Furst, and Krathwohl (1956) distinguish between subcategories such as "knowledge of terminology" and "knowledge of classification categories," although the requirements for acquiring such knowledge are not distinguishable. That is, there is no difference between the instructional strategies for learning each subcategory. Likewise, "acceptance of a value," "preference for a value," and "commitment" in the affective domain (Krathwohl, Bloom, & Masia, 1964) are difficult to distinguish on the basis of their requirements for learning. The lower categories in the psychomotor domain (Harrow, 1972) are acquired through maturation, although some can be facilitated by instruction. Only the two highest categories, "skilled movements" and "non-discursive communication" are learned, and the strategies for acquiring them are the same.

Robert M. Gagné and Leslie J. Briggs (1974) have approached the classification of learning from a different angle. Their scheme includes five kinds of learned capabilities: intellectual skills, cognitive strategies, verbal information, attitudes, and motor skills. It can be characterized by its comprehensiveness and by its prescriptive nature. Learning outcomes are organized into categories that can be taught by similar instructional strategies. Each outcome represents a type of learning. Intellectual skills is an outcome that encompasses several forms of learning. For each category the internal and external conditions for learning are prescribed. Internal conditions are those that must be present within the learner in order for the type of learning to occur. These are usually prerequisite competencies that were previously developed or remembered. External conditions must be established by the instructional designer. The intellectual skills and external events components of the taxonomy are based on work done by Gagné over many years (Gagné, 1989; Ragan & Smith, 1996). The categories of Gagné and Briggs's taxonomy and associated conditions for learning are defined in Table 10.1.

Gagné's (1985) contribution to the taxonomy concentrates largely on the intellectual skills central to school learning. Four levels of hierarchically-ordered intellectual skills are defined, with each requiring different instructional conditions. Martin and Briggs (1986) note several studies that validate the hierarchical order of the intellectual skills. In contrast, levels of learning outcomes not differentiated are motor skills, attitudes, and cognitive strategies. To promote learning of skills in the psychomotor domain, similar internal

Table 10.1   Definitions of Gagné and Briggs' Five Learned Capabilities

Intellectual Skills

Problem solving

↑

Combining lower-level rules to solve problems in a situation never encountered by the person solving the problem. May involve generating new rules that receive trial-and-error use until the one that solves the problem is found.

Examples: **Generates** a strategy which incorporates rules and concepts previously learned, tries it out, modifies it, tries it out again, and continues until the problem is solved, e.g. develops a strategy for analyzing and synthesizing ideas in order to write an essay about an issue.

Rule using

↑

Demonstrates the application of a rule to a given situation or condition by responding to a class of inputs with a class of actions. Relating two or more simpler concepts in the particular manner of rule. A rule states the relationship among concepts.

Examples: **Demonstrates** procedure for solving a mathematical problem. It is helpful to think of rules or principles as "if then" statements. "If a task is a procedure, then use flowcharting to analyze the task." If you can convert a statement into an "if-then" statement, then it is a rule or principle.

Defined concept

↑

Classifying a particular class of objects, events, or relations by classifying in accordance with a definition and explaining component concepts included in the definition.

Example: **Classifying** aliens as citizens of foreign countries or identifying boundary lines by relating the concepts of area, line, and endpoints to show limits.

Concrete concepts

↑

Responding in a single way to all members of a particular class of observable events. Identifying the essential similarity among a class of objects, people, or events, which calls for a single response.

Example: **Identifying** music as jazz, country western, rock, etc.; saying "round" upon seeing a manhole cover, a penny, and the moon.

Discrimination

Making different responses to the different members of a particular class. Seeing the essential differences between inputs and responding differently to each.

Example: **Discriminates** yellow finches from house finches on the basis of markings; distinguishes the differences on an instrument panel.

Cognitive Strategy

An internal process by which the learner adopts a strategy to control his or her own way of thinking and learning.

Example: **Adopts** self-testing as a way to decide how much study is needed; knowing what sorts of questions to ask to best define a domain of knowledge; is able to form a mental model of the problem.

Verbal Information

Labels and facts

Making a verbal response to a specific input. The response may be naming or citing a fact or set of facts. The response may be vocal or written.

Example: **States** objects, people, or events. Stating a person's birthday or hobbies. Stating the capitals of the United States.

Bodies of knowledge

Recalling a large body of interconnected facts.

Example: **States** in his own words the meaning of textual materials. States rules or regulations.

Attitude

An internal state that affects an individual's choice of action toward some object, person, or event.

Example: **Chooses** to visit an art museum; writing letters in the pursuit of a cause. (See Krathwohl's Affective Taxonomy)

Motor Skills

Bodily movements involving muscular activity.

Example: **Executes** starting a car; shooting a target; swinging a golf club. (See Harrow's Psychomotor Taxonomy)

Adapted from *Principles of Instructional Design* (4th ed.), by R. M. Gagné, L. J. Briggs, & W. W. Wager, 1992, New York: Harcourt Brace Jovanovich College Publishers. Copyright 1974, 1979, 1988, 1992 by Harcourt Brace Jovanovich College Publishers.

conditions (the acquisition of lower level prerequisite motor skills) and identical external conditions apply whether the motor skill to be learned is simple or complex. In the next chapter, you will learn more about the internal and external conditions for acquiring the different types of learning.

Gagné, Briggs, and Wager (1992, p. 128) associate a verb with each learning outcome. If these verbs are used consistently, it is easier to tell the type of learning represented by a task or objective statement. As you describe a task, construct a hierarchy, or write an objective, use the verb Gagné, Briggs, and Wager suggest and others will find it easier to react to your ideas. You will find that following this procedure also helps you analyze and critique your own work. The verbs are as follows:

Intellectual Skill
    Discrimination   *discriminates*
    Concrete Concept   *identifies*
    Defined Concept   *classifies*
    Rule Using   *demonstrates*
    Higher-Order Rule (Problem-Solving)   *generates*
Cognitive Strategy   *adopts*
Verbal Information   *states*
Motor Skill   *executes*
Attitude   *chooses*

Motor Skills

Motor skills involve muscles, the senses, and the brain. They are nonverbal capabilities that usually require some degree of hand-eye coordination and manipulative abilities. Examples are starting a car, unlocking a door, shooting at a target, swinging a golf club, writing with a pencil, and calibrating an instrument.

Usually, motor skills can be broken down into part skills that when chained together constitute the total performance. For example, the actions for unlocking a door include

1. positioning the key with the serrated edge properly oriented;
2. putting the key into the lock as far as it will go;
3. turning the key in the proper direction; and
4. opening the door.

In the example, steps 2 through 4 are stimulated by the specific input of completing the last action of the previous step. Most motor skills can be divided into part skills that are performed in a specific sequence and no other sequence, and can be diagrammed as input, action, output sequences as shown in Figure 10.2.

As the learner becomes more proficient at performing the part steps, the actions flow seamlessly together until performance is so internalized that the person seems to do it "without thinking."

Attitude

R. M. Gagné (1985) defines *attitudes* as complex internal states that affect an individual's choice of personal action toward people, things, and events. Thus, you can infer something about a person's attitudes based on the things he chooses to do or avoids doing. For example, a person's concerns about crime can be inferred from the security measures he takes. The number and types of locks he puts on his doors, whether he installs anti-theft devices in his car, whether he participates in a neighborhood block watch, etc., are all actions that reflect his level of concern about crime. A number of instances of the person's behavior in a number of different situations suggests that person's attitude about people, objects, places, or events.

Attitudes are very important but very difficult to define and to measure. If attitudes can be inferred by the personal actions chosen by the individual, then it follows that the

Figure 10.2   Diagram for a Motor Skill

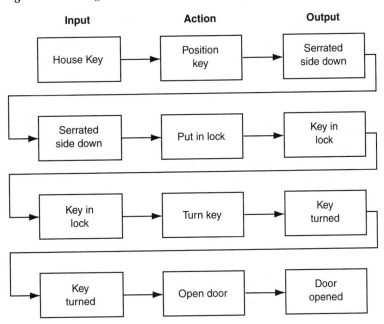

best way to assess attitudes is by recording observations of the person's behavior over a period of time. A teacher wanting to instill the attitude of "working cooperatively" may record observations of students' behavior over several weeks to ascertain the effect of instruction on this objective. However, observational measures are difficult to obtain; therefore, attitude measures are frequently based on self-reports. Simply asking someone to put a check mark on a rating scale does not necessarily result in anything being measured. For this reason, attitude scales should be developed with the assistance of an expert in this type of assessment.

Finally, although we as a society often speak of the need for schools to instill certain "values" in students, attitude change is seldom achieved by a specific lesson or course of instruction. Attitude learning is usually a long-term goal that often cannot be achieved within the time frame of a course offering.

Verbal Information

Learning Labels.   Learning labels means associating names with objects, events, or things. Such an association is a simple input, action, output chain. An example is connecting a name with a face. The input is a person's face; the action is a vocal, subvocal, or written response; the output is the person identified by name, as shown in Figure 10.3.

Learning Facts.   Facts are verbal chains expressed as a relationship between two or more named objects or events. An example is, "Pittsburgh is in Pennsylvania." The statement refers to the relationship between the city called "Pittsburgh" and the state called "Pennsylvania." The relation is shown by the words "is in."

Figure 10.3   Diagram for Learning Labels

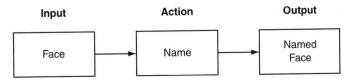

Learning Organized Knowledge.   This type of verbal information refers to larger bodies of interconnected facts. The key word is "organized" as a network of propositions that are linked to larger propositional networks already existing in memory. For example, a student may learn a number of new facts about Pittsburgh that are related to each other, such as those pertaining to the city's economy, geography, and history. One way of organizing the facts in memory is to relate them to facts already known about the city or to facts already known about similar cities, such as Cleveland.

Intellectual Skills

Intellectual skills are the mental processes that are central to school learning. They make it possible for an individual to respond to his environment through symbols (Gagné et al., 1992). There are four types of intellectual skills: discriminations, concepts, rules, and problem solving.

Discriminations.   Discriminations require the student to make different responses to inputs that differ from each other along one or more physical dimensions. Examples that children learn in school include distinguishing between simple shapes such as a circle and a square. Finer discriminations are required to distinguish a square from a rectangle or a parallelogram—all are four-sided figures, but they differ in other ways. The student must be able to see the essential differences among many inputs and connect the appropriate response to individual inputs.

Figure 10.4 shows four different triangles. All triangles are similar in that they are bound by three lines and three angles, but the four triangles can be distinguished along two physical conditions: namely, the length of the lines relative to each other and the type of angles formed by the lines. Triangle 1 is an equilateral triangle because all lines are of equal length; triangle 2 is a right angle triangle because the lower left angle is a 90° angle; triangle 3 is an isosceles triangle because only two lines (the legs) are equal; and triangle 4 is a scalene triangle because none of the lines are equal. To evaluate a student's ability to discriminate among the various types of triangles, you would show him the four types of triangles without the labels, and ask him to point to each as you named them.

Here's an example of a discrimination from everyday life. Suppose you have several different keys on a single key ring. The keys may all be the same general size, shape, and color, but you can still learn to distinguish among them. You distinguish the keys by the number of notches, the general pattern of the notches, and the depth of the notches. You would be distinguishing among several inputs (which are similar in some ways) and responding differently to each. Once you were able to discriminate the office key, you would not attempt to use the house key to open your office door. Discriminations can be diagrammed as input-action-output chains, as shown in Figure 10.5.

Concrete Concepts.   *Concrete concepts* require the student to make the same response to many different inputs that may or may not resemble each other. Concept learning is different from discrimination learning. In concept learning, students must learn to see the similarities among inputs. In discrimination learning, the student must learn to see the differences among inputs. A concrete concept identifies the attribute such as color, shape, textures, etc., that a group of objects have in common. Such concepts are called concrete because the performance they require is recognition of a *concrete object*.

Figure 10.4   Discriminating among Four Types of Triangles

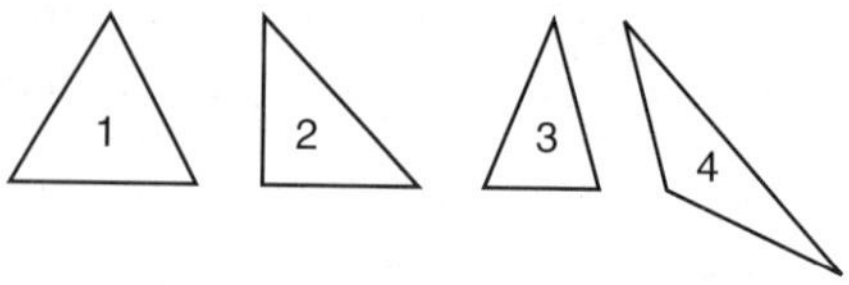

Figure 10.5 Diagram for a Discrimination Task

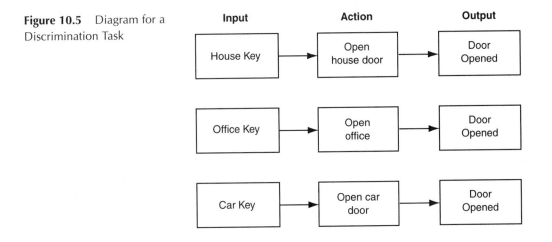

Take the concept "chair." The attributes of a chair are that it is a seat for a single person and has a back. It may or may not have arms. We say a person has learned the concept "chair" when she can identify several examples of a chair. Stating the definition of a chair is evidence of learning a verbal chain; it is not an indication that the person has acquired the concept. One can tell whether a concrete concept has been acquired by asking the student to point to or label two or more members of the object class. In the case of the concept "chair," we could be confident that a person has acquired the concept if she identified pictures of a rocker, a high chair, a folding chair, a throne, and wheel chair as members of the same class of objects known as "chair" because they share certain attributes, although they are quite different in other respects. She would also recognize that a love seat, a bench, a stool, and a couch are not chairs because they lack the attributes of a chair.

Figure 10.6 shows how concrete concepts can be diagrammed.

As we can see, concrete concepts are so named because they refer to actual objects. They may also refer to an object's position in space. The position of an object is in relation to that of another object. So an object's position may be over, under, beside, right, left, middle, etc. Since one can point to an object's position, position qualifies as a concrete concept (Gagné et al., 1992).

Defined Concepts. An individual is said to have acquired a *defined concept* when she can classify some particular class of objects, events, or relations on the basis of its definition.

Concrete concepts differ from defined concepts in that they refer to the actual object. Suppose you have some keys to doors, several keys for padlocks, and a couple of keys for trunks. Each type of key has similarities that make it a member of a particular class of objects called "key." In this instance "key" is an actual object; therefore, it is a concrete concept.

In addition, "key" can be a defined concept when its meaning refers to something that, like a key, opens or closes a way, or reveals or conceals a place. The statement "Vicksburg was the key to the lower Mississippi" means that the location of the city gave access to the region. A key might also be a code that explains or reveals something, such as a key to a map, or an answer key to a test. We also speak of a person as being key in the sense that he dominates or controls an organization.

Defined concepts are acquired when we can classify the meaning of some particular class of objects, events, or relations by reference. Defined concepts often cannot be identified by pointing to them, as can concrete concepts. Many are more or less abstract notions such as "community," "justice," "liberty," "equality," etc., that must be demonstrated to show that they have been learned. In the case of the defined concept "key," a student may point to a test key or a key to a map, but in reference to key people or places, the student will have to demonstrate understanding of the concept by citing examples of key locations and individuals and telling why they are key. Simply stating the definition would be indication of having learned verbal information, not of having acquired the defined concept.

Figure 10.6   Diagram of a Concrete Concept

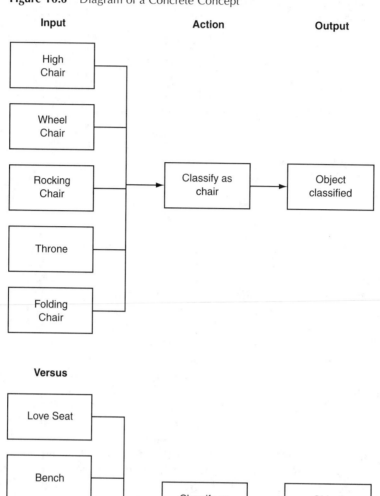

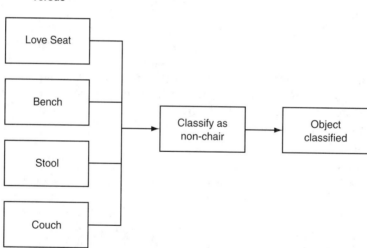

Rule Using. In *rule using*, the student relates two or more simpler classifications according to a rule or principle. A rule or principle states the relationship among classifications. It is helpful to think of rules as "if-then" statements. Consider the rule, "Round objects roll." The student must know the class of objects that can be classified as "round." He must also know the defined concept of "rolling." In defining rolling, he must discriminate rolling from other types of movement, such as sliding, bouncing, etc. Combining the concepts of rolling and roundness, he may chain them into the principle: "Round objects roll."

There are many examples of rule-governed behavior. Language is governed by the rules of grammar; the principles of science are rules, and troubleshooting the cause of defective equipment involves the use of rules. Obviously, knowledge of rules is not demonstrated by stating the definition of a rule, but rather by applying the rule to some task.

Problem Solving.   *Problem solving*, the most complex form of learning, incorporates all the lower level skills. Here the student must recall and select rules, and formulate new rules that may apply to the problem at hand. The new rule must be tested to see if it works in the situation. If it works, it is retained. If it doesn't, it is rejected and a new rule is devised. So, problem solving involves trial and error learning to some degree. Troubleshooting malfunctioning equipment is a good example of problem solving.

Problem solving can be shown by this simple example: "John is taller than Harry, shorter than Bill, and the same height as Jim. Who is the tallest?" To solve this problem, the student must understand the concepts of "taller than" and "shorter than," generate "if-then" rules, and combine these rules to solve the problem. So, to arrive at the solution, the student must go through these problem solving steps:

1. If John is taller than Harry, and shorter than Bill, then Bill is taller than both John and Harry.
2. If John is the same height as Jim, then Bill (who is taller than John) is also taller than Jim.
3. Therefore, Bill is the tallest man in the group.

Cognitive Strategies

A *cognitive strategy* is a special kind of intellectual skill whereby learners modify their ways of attending, learning, remembering, and thinking. (R. M. Gagné, 1985). Cognitive strategies include highlighting or underlining text the learner considers important, outlining materials, mental rehearsal of information, organizing information in some meaningful way, using mnemonics or visual imagery, and engaging in other activities to facilitate learning and remembering. Unlike intellectual skills, cognitive strategies have as their object the learner's own internal cognitive process. Discriminations, concepts, and rules are oriented toward external objects and events (Gagné et al., 1992).

Cognitive strategies may be used as instructional techniques in designing instruction, but employing them in this way supplements learning. For example, you may help a learner remember a name through the use of a visual image. Using the visual image is a technique for recalling a name; it is not the object of instruction. There is evidence that instruction on the use of cognitive strategies is beneficial, but "teaching students how to think" is an enormously complex undertaking and the likelihood of success is dependent on a great many variables that are beyond the instructional designer's control.

Another Approach to Classification

Ellen Gagné (1985) discusses another approach to classification of types of learning, based on cognitive theories of learning and information processing (Ragan & Smith, 1996). She describes two forms of knowledge that represent types of learning. These are declarative and procedural learning. Declarative and procedural knowledge are similar to verbal information and intellectual skills learning as classified by R. M. Gagné and L. J. Briggs.

Exercise A at the end of this chapter provides practice in identifying learning outcomes.

SEQUENCING INSTRUCTION

When children enter first grade, instruction is directed at teaching them to read, write, and do simple arithmetic. Mastery of these skills is important; they are the basis of all future school learning and they are necessary for effective day-to-day living. Because they are prerequisites for virtually all future learning, they are called basic skills.

A prerequisite is a task that enables or aids the learning of another task. Reading, writing, and arithmetic are basic prerequisites for everyday living. Gagné et al. (1992, pp. 150–151) define two types of prerequisites: essential and supportive. An essential

Figure 10.7 Simple Hierarchy of Learning Relationships

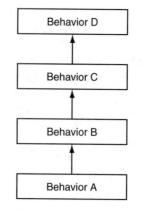

prerequisite is a subordinate task essential to the learning of a higher order task. For example, before a child can learn division, he or she must first learn to add and subtract. Addition and subtraction are essential to learning division because they are actually part of the total skill of dividing.

Supportive prerequisites, as the name implies, support learning by making it easier. A child who enjoys math is likely to learn math skills, but the child's attitude is not essential for learning. That is, a positive attitude is supportive of learning math skills, but not essential.

In order to determine the prerequisite skills and knowledge for a task, the designer asks, "What must the learner know in order to perform this task?" Usually the designer arrives at the answer by constructing hierarchies. As each set level of prerequisites is identified, the designer asks the same question again until enough levels are specified for the task and target audience.

A hierarchy is an organization of elements that describes the path of experiences a learner must take to achieve any single behavior that appears higher in the hierarchy. Figure 10.7 illustrates a simple hierarchy. The order of learning proceeds upward. The sequential nature of the prerequisites is represented by the vertical axis of the hierarchy. A must be learned before B, which must be learned before C, and so on. The hierarchy does not preclude the possibility that a student may skip a particular learning step. In this figure, a student may begin the learning sequence at behavior B if he or she has already acquired behavior A. The top of the hierarchy represents the terminal behavior.

The term "hierarchy" is used rather freely. For our purposes, a hierarchical relationship means you cannot do task B unless you know how to do task A. The question you will ask again and again in preparing hierarchies is this: What must the student already know in order to learn how to do this task or subtask? Figure 10.8 shows a visual display that looks like a hierarchy, but is not. It shows the temporal relationship of what is done. Although it has the vertical construction of a hierarchy, the display is in fact a flowchart.

Do not confuse a procedural relationship with a hierarchical relationship. Hierarchies do not show procedural relationships. In analyzing procedural relationships you ask "What does the experienced person performing this task do first? What is the next step? What step comes after that?" and so on. When analyzing procedural relationships you focus on the expert performer, but when analyzing hierarchical relationships you focus on the learner. As the hierarchy in Figure 10.9 illustrates, the concepts associated with an education problem must be learned before students can perform the more complex behaviors associated with that problem.

Exercise B at the end of this chapter provides practice in determining prerequisite competencies.

Figure 10.8   Procedural Diagram for the Task "Remove Main Drive Shaft from OH058 Helicopter"

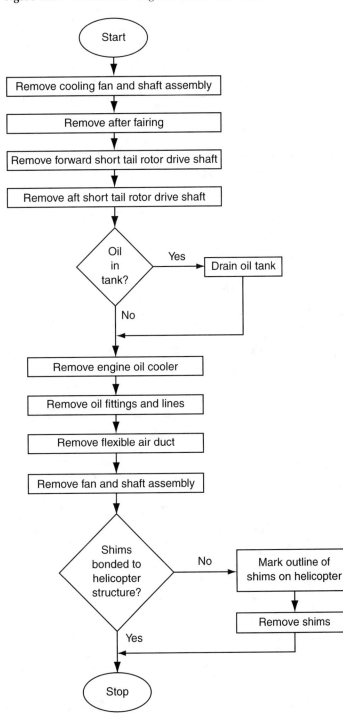

From *Module 9: Preparing Task/Content Hierarchies: Student Resource Book*, by D. Frezza, 1985, Butler, PA: Applied Science Associates.

CONSTRUCTING HIERARCHIES

Just as you must follow conventions for constructing flowcharts, you also must follow conventions for constructing hierarchies that can be understood.

Figure 10.9   Hierarchy for an
Educational Problem

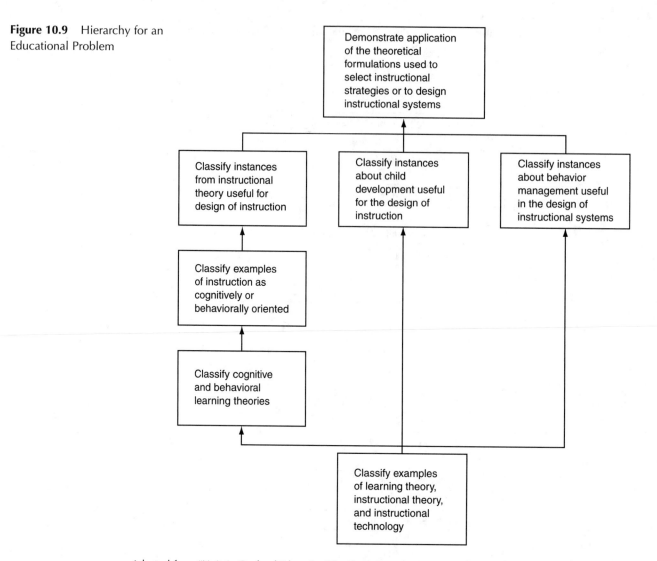

Adapted from "Unit 1. Goals of Education" by D. T. Gow, in *Design and Development of Curriculum Materials: Vol 1* (pp. 1–22), by D. T. Gow (Ed.), 1976, Pittsburgh, PA: University Center for International Studies, University of Pittsburgh.

Reading Hierarchies

Hierarchies are read from the bottom up. The block at the top is the end point. It contains the most comprehensive, complex action in the diagram. The blocks at the bottom—the starting points—contain the simplest, most basic actions.

Levels.   Subtasks of roughly equal complexity and without an essential prerequisite relationship are placed side by side. Blocks at the same level of the diagram are of equal rank and have no prerequisite relationship.

Annotations.   The boxes in a hierarchy may contain annotations. When they are too long, annotations are listed separately and referenced by numbers in the boxes.

Symbols.   Learning outcomes that are related to the main part of the hierarchy are shown by symbols indicating associated types of learning. These symbols will be explained under "Procedures for Creating Hierarchies."

Procedure for Creating Hierarchies

The starting point for constructing a hierarchy is a comprehensive list of the tasks that make up a job or function. There are four major steps to constructing a hierarchy:

1. **Cluster or group the tasks.**   For inclusion in a group, select tasks that bear a close relationship to each other. Each task must be included in at least one of the groups, but a task may also be common to several groups. Label the groups with terms that emerge from the job or function being analyzed. Initial clustering or grouping of tasks may be tentative. The composition of the groups may change as a result of decisions you make later on. Do not hesitate to regroup tasks when it seems appropriate.

2. **Organize tasks within each group to show the hierarchical relationships for learning.** Ask yourself "What would the learner have to learn in order to do this task?" Once the essential prerequisite relationships are shown, reevaluate the relationship between each pair of tasks with the question "Can this superordinate task be performed if the learner cannot perform this subordinate task?" The lower-level skill must be integrally related to the higher-level skill.

3. **Confer with a subject matter expert to determine the hierarchy's accuracy.**   This step occurs concurrently with steps 1 and 2.

4. **Analyze associated types of learning and add them to the hierarchy using symbols to indicate the relationship.**

> Each of these steps will be illustrated next.

Hierarchical Relationships of Outcomes

Gagné's taxonomy of intellectual skills provides the basic structure for constructing hierarchies that show the relationships among learning outcomes. These hierarchies are sometimes called types of learning hierarchies. Whatever they are called, they are a way to represent visually a continuum of lower to higher level intellectual skills and other associated learning outcomes. Figure 10.10 illustrates the application of Gagné's taxonomy for constructing a hierarchy for a problem-solving procedure. The hierarchy dictates the order for learning.

Figure 10.10   Hypothetical Analysis of Steps in a Problem Solving Procedure

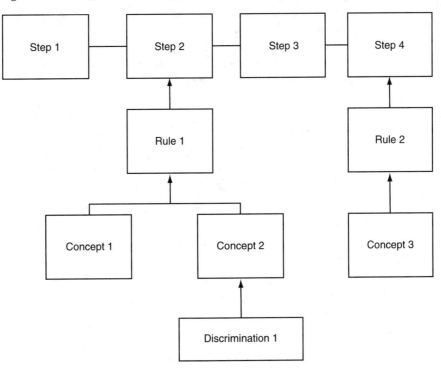

Figure 10.11 Verbal Information Diagramed as a Prerequisite

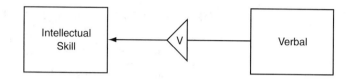

When more than one type of learning outcome must be shown in an instructional analysis, a line is drawn to the related outcome in a different domain and a symbol is inserted in the middle of the line to show that associated learning must occur. There are at least two approaches to the symbols used to show associated learning. One approach is used by Gagné, Briggs, and Wager (1992, p. 24) and consists of using triangle shapes with the letters describing the outcome in them. For example, a hierarchy can include triangles with the letters for type of learning in them. Dick and Carey (1996) and this book use a slightly different approach in that different shapes are used for each learning outcome. Thus, the symbol for motor skill is an "M" in a square, for attitudes is an "A" in a circle, for verbal information is a "V" in a triangle, and for intellectual skills is a dotted line. The "V" points towards the intellectual skill with which it is associated (Briggs & Wager, 1981).

For example, simple verbal information tasks, such as learning labels or lists, usually do not lend themselves to hierarchical analysis. In such cases the most meaningful analysis is to identify major categories of information implied by the task. Dick and Carey (1996) refer to the creation of information categories as "cluster analysis." The clusters are lists of related information organized into categories that have no dependency relationships for learning. Thus, learning can proceed in any order.

Verbal information, however, may be a prerequisite for certain complex communication tasks, and in these cases, hierarchies do apply. For example, knowledge of facts about an era in history may be partly the foundation for performing certain intellectual skills such as writing an essay to compare and contrast the impact of historical events. To represent verbal information as a prerequisite to an intellectual skill, simply connect the verbal information as shown in Figure 10.11.

Whether procedural tasks are intellectual or motor skills, they will be in flowchart form. The type of analysis will depend on the type of learning involved in the subtask. Hierarchical analysis should be done for intellectual and motor subtasks; the analysis may reveal that certain subtasks performed later in the procedure are in fact prerequisites for subtasks performed earlier.

Several studies demonstrate the relationship between the cognitive taxonomy and the affective taxonomy (Martin & Briggs, 1986, p. 92). The following relationships between the two domains have been supported:

1. Receiving/awareness is directly prerequisite to knowledge and responding. One must be aware of information and ready to receive it in order to learn it and to respond to it.
2. Knowledge and responding are directly prerequisite to valuing. Attitude tasks are often defined in terms of choosing to engage in some observable and measurable behavior. The implication is that behaviors have been previously learned. If not, they must be acquired before the attitude can be learned.

To represent an attitude that is essential for learning a motor skill or an intellectual skill, simply connect the two types of learning with a line as shown in Figure 10.12.

Dick and Carey (1996) suggest that attitudes also be subjected to a second level of analysis to find out why the learner makes a particular choice. The answer to this

Figure 10.12 Attitude Diagramed as a Prerequisite

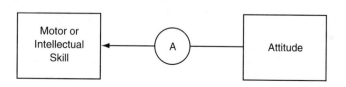

Figure 10.13   Diagraming an Attitudinal Task

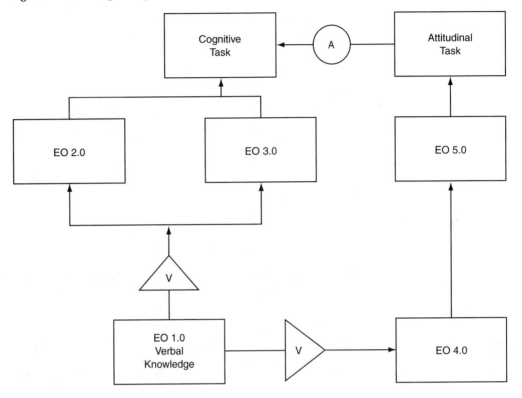

question is the verbal information that constitutes the persuasive part of attitude shaping. See Figure 10.13 as an example of the interrelationship between cognitive and affective behavior.

At this point, it may be helpful to review when you use hierarchies and when you don't. As the discussion in chapter 2 on analyzing tasks explained, the form for visual representation of the instructional analysis depends on the learning outcome given in the TPO. If the major learning outcome is intellectual skills, a hierarchy is appropriate. Associated types of learning can be shown separately using other forms of representation such as learning clusters or flowcharts. If a hierarchy has a TPO at the rule using level, an annotated flowchart is usually included. If, however, the primary learning outcome is verbal information, a cluster diagram will be used instead. If the primary outcome is a motor skill, a flowchart may be sufficient. Regardless, it is important to remember that the product of an instructional analysis is a visual representation usually in the form of a hierarchy, flowchart, or cluster diagram or some combination of these.

EXAMPLE OF AN INSTRUCTIONAL ANALYSIS

When children learn French, they are often immersed in French conversation. After many dialogues to help them learn French words and sentences and their English equivalents, students are led to discover rules for French pronunciation and to use the vocabulary they have learned to create their own dialogues.

To analyze the tasks involved in this learning problem, let us assume that we have interviewed some French teachers and reviewed several French textbooks. As a result, the two major components of this learning problem are identified. The first component is memorizing English/French equivalents and their meanings. The second component is applying rules for pronunciation. A separate task and instructional analysis is needed for each component. Then there must be an analysis of how the two major components relate.

Figure 10.14   Association Analysis for French Words for Food

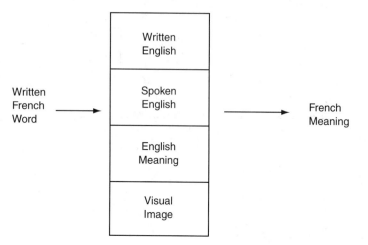

Let's start with the verbal information component. The task analysis reveals associations that must occur during information processing. These tasks can be shown in a diagram of the association process, as shown in Figure 10.14.

Next, the types of verbal information that must be learned are translated into a more specific goal: "Be able to state the English equivalent of a French word for a food and the meaning of the word (verbal information—names, labels, and organized knowledge)." The instructional analysis for this verbal information goal takes the form of a cluster analysis as shown in Table 10.2.

Now let's turn to the task analysis for the demonstrated pronunciation component. The tasks identified are visualized in a hierarchy in Figure 10.15.

Table 10.2   French Words for Food

Entrées	*Principal*	*Desserts*	*Boissons*
Avocat	Quiche	Dessert	Thé
Vinaigrette	Carotte	Fruit	Café
Concombre	Boeuf	Abricot	Chocolat
Crème	Lentilles	Banane	Limonade
Radis	Porc	Figues	Perrier
Salade	Mayonnaise	Poire	Jus D'Orange
Tomate	Saumon	Orange	Vin
Pâté	Crabe	Pêche	Bière
Escargot	Soufflé	Raisin	Champagne
Oignon	Mouton	Chocolat	
Céleri	Sauce	Crêpes	
Soupe	Olives	Pruneau	
	Moutarde		

Figure 10.15 Learning Hierarchy for Pronouncing French Words

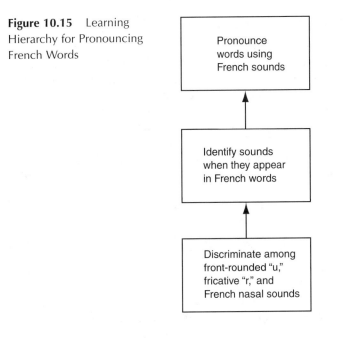

- ◆ Be able to distinguish among sounds for (French front-rounded "u," a French fricative "r," and French nasal vowels (a, e, i, o) followed by "n" or "m". Be able to distinguish among either printed or spoken sounds. (Discrimination)
- ◆ Be able to identify instances of French sounds for front-rounded "u," fricative "r," or nasal vowels when they appear in spoken or written French words. (Concrete Concept)
- ◆ Be able to pronounce in French new or familiar words for foods. (Rule Using)

The visual form of the completed instructional analysis would be a hierarchy showing the intellectual skills and associated verbal information learning. The instructional analysis for the intellectual skills component can be combined with the verbal information tasks. This is one way to do an instructional analysis on learning French restaurant words.

Exercises C, D, and E at the end of this chapter provide practice in constructing hierarchies.

DETERMINING THE ENTRY LEVEL FOR INSTRUCTION

Most people have experienced reading a text or being in a class that is "over their heads." And most people have also had the opposite experience—dealing with subject matter that is too simple. These all too common experiences demonstrate mismatches of instructional material and student abilities. The instructional designer can avoid mismatches by identifying competencies in the target audience—students who will take the course—and then designing the instruction to build on those competencies. What the target audience knows or can do are the entry level behaviors.

Entry level is a key concept in instructional design. If entry level is incorrectly set, initial instruction will be either too hard or too easy for the target audience and therefore will be ineffective. Entry levels are often hard to set because the type of data needed for accuracy are often difficult to come by.

Information is collected about what students know and can do with respect to the tasks to be taught. Once this information is known, the instructional designer determines which skills the target audience has already mastered and which must be taught.

Type of Data Needed

It is important to distinguish between two types of information about the target audience: general characteristics and entry level behaviors. General characteristics describe the educational level, achievement level, socioeconomic background, motivation, interests, and other information about the target audience. Categories such as high school biology majors, eighth-graders, undergraduate psychology majors, and persons with two years' experience on the job give a general idea of the target audience for the instructional materials. Information about the target audience's interests and preferences and about their expectations regarding instruction is helpful when planning a strategy for engaging students in learning tasks. However, such information is too general and inclusive for setting entry levels.

When assumptions about what students should be taught are based on general characteristics, the result can be the mismatch previously described. Assume that the target audience for an automotive repair course scores in the upper 25th percentile on a norm-referenced mechanical ability test. What can you conclude about this group's ability to set the timing on a carburetor? Exactly where should the entry level be set? Entry-level behaviors define the specific prerequisites for the tasks to be learned. Without knowledge of exactly what the test measures, it is impossible to determine with any precision the entry behaviors for the carburetor task. Assumptions can be based only on the instructional designer's preconceived notions about what students with these characteristics should know rather than what they do know.

Here is the recommended procedure to determine entry-level behaviors using test results:

1. Examine test items to determine whether any correspond to prerequisite skills.
2. For items that correspond, examine the test results to identify those that were and were not successfully performed by the target audience. Those that nearly everyone performed correctly need not be taught.
3. Where no correspondence is found, obtain other information to define the entry level. If time is available, entry-level behaviors should be determined empirically. Construct and administer tests for a representative sample of the target audience to determine the entry-level behaviors, or interview members of the target audience to ascertain what they can and cannot do.

What can the designer do if there is no opportunity to collect the task-specific data necessary for accurate determinations of entry-level behaviors? If time does not permit verification of assumptions before materials are developed, then verification is delayed until materials are developed and tried out. The dangers of such an approach are obvious, but the instructional designer is often faced with this dilemma.

To reduce the margin of error, assumptions should be based on the best information available. In lieu of test data, you should consult several other sources. Materials and tests from courses the target audience has taken can be examined to find whether prerequisites were covered. Dick and Carey (1996) recommend determining whether it would be worthwhile to test for a particular skill before permitting a student to begin instruction. If the answer is yes, you probably have defined an entry-level behavior. This question can be asked of instructors or supervisors with first-hand knowledge of the target audience. They can examine the instructional analysis and answer this question for each of the entry levels. SMEs and/or job incumbents can be asked to respond to the same question based on their own experience.

Setting the Entry Level

The procedure to identify entry-level behaviors is fairly straightforward if prerequisite requirements have been fully identified. Evidence about what students know and can do is

Figure 10.16   Identifying Entry-Level Behaviors in a Hierarchy

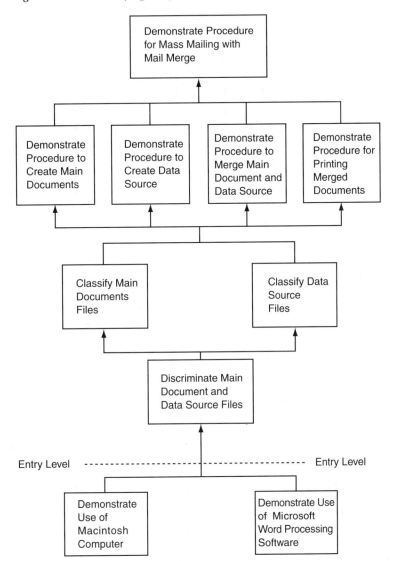

compared to the prerequisites for performing the tasks to be taught. Most likely, the comparison will show that a majority of the target audience already has some of these skills; therefore, it is not necessary to teach them.

When prerequisites are in hierarchical form, identify the skills that a majority already can do, and draw a line above these skills in the hierarchy. The skills above the line are those you must teach; those below the line are the entry-level behaviors necessary to begin instruction. An example of how entry-level behaviors can be identified for a hierarchy is shown in Figure 10.16.

The same approach can be taken with cluster analysis and procedural flowcharts where prerequisites are clear-cut. Figures 10.17 and 10.18 show how entry-level behaviors are identified for a verbal information task when students need no previous knowledge of the competency to be learned, and for a motor skill when students can perform some of the basic procedures. Information items in a cluster analysis are reviewed, and those already known by a majority of the target audience are checked and noted as entry-level behaviors.

Exercises F, G, and H at the end of this chapter provide practice in setting entry levels.

Figure 10.17   Identifying Entry-Level Behaviors for a Verbal Information Task

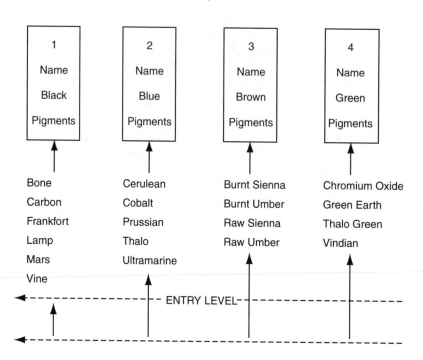

Figure 10.18   Identifying Entry-Level Behaviors for a Motor Skill

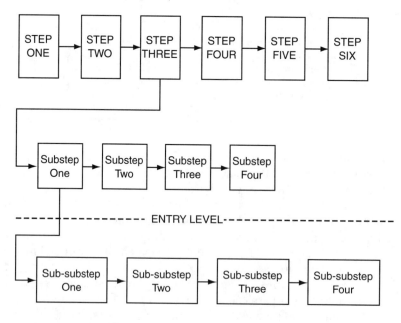

◇   ***EXERCISES***

A. An Exercise to Classify Learning Outcomes According to Gagné's Learned Capabilities
Classify each of the learning outcomes according to Robert Gagné's learned capabilities. Identify the type or level of learning required as shown in Table 10.3.

Table 10.3

Learning Outcome	Type of Learning
1. Wraps an ankle, given an elastic bandage and a plastic model of an adult's foot.	
2. Lists the U.S. Air Force enlisted and officer ranks from memory.	
3. Lists five causes of the Civil War as cited in *The Civil War and Reconstruction* by D.S. Randall.	
4. Given a list of chemical elements, recalls and writes the valences of at least 30.	
5. Analyzes electrical circuits, using Ohm's Law.	
6. Interprets written instructions to determine sequence of two or more actions.	
7. Encodes data for radio and teletype transmission.	
8. Using a year's data from atmospheric data-gathering systems, computes the annual mean wind velocity.	
9. Finds West 33rd Street on a map of Manhattan.	
10. Labels the components of a carburetor.	
11. Participates in a public discussion on the transportation of hazardous materials.	
12. Changes an automobile tire in 10 minutes.	
13. Attends the theater regularly.	
14. Volunteers to answer a crisis hotline telephone.	
15. Contributes to a political party.	
16. Types 60 words a minute.	
17. Visually tracks a moving object.	
18. Uses visual imagery to remember names.	
19. Troubleshoots defective equipment to detect cause of breakdown.	
20. Follows investment guidelines to obtain highest possible income.	
21. Diagnoses disease from clinical symptoms.	

B. A Group Exercise in Defining Prerequisites

This is a group exercise for three or four students. Doing the exercise in a group empha-sizes the fact that in practice instructional design is carried out by several people. The group should do an analysis of the following goals or two similar goals approved by your instructor.

Your analysis will be judged by the following criteria:

◆ The analysis answers the question: "What must the learner know in order to perform this task?" and the answer is clear to a person unfamiliar with the content area.

◆ The analysis is carried to the level appropriate for the target audience.

1. For 12th-grade students of U.S. history: The students should be able to select and list appropriate historical examples of four common sources of conflict (economic, social, political, and religious) during the 1930s (Gow, 1976, p. 74).

2. For elementary school students: The students should be able to write a complete simple sentence and identify the subject, verb, and object (Gow, 1976, p. 74).

C. An Exercise in Applying Knowledge of Hierarchy Conventions

Refer to the hierarchy diagram shown in Figure 10.20 in answering the following questions.

1. Which of the following subtasks is at the highest level?
   a. Identify graduation marks.
   b. Read values with interpolation.
   c. Align points with scale.
2. Which of these statements is correct?

Figure 10.20

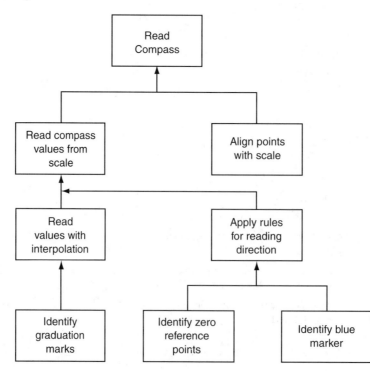

Adapted from *Module 9: Preparing Task/Content Hierarchies: Student Response Book* (p. 72), by D. Frezza, 1985, Buler, PA: Applied Science Associates.

a. "Read compass values from scale" is essential for performance of "Read values with interpolation."
b. "Read values with interpolation" is essential for performance of "Read compass values from scale."
3. How does the subtask "Apply rules for reading direction" relate to (contribute to the performance of) subtask "Align points with scale"?
4. How does the subtask "Read compass values from scale" contribute to the performance of the subtask "Apply rules for reading direction"?

D. An Exercise in Constructing a Hierarchy

Figure 10.21 is a blank hierarchy diagram and a list of tasks. Fill in the diagram by writing the appropriate task in each block.

Figure 10.21

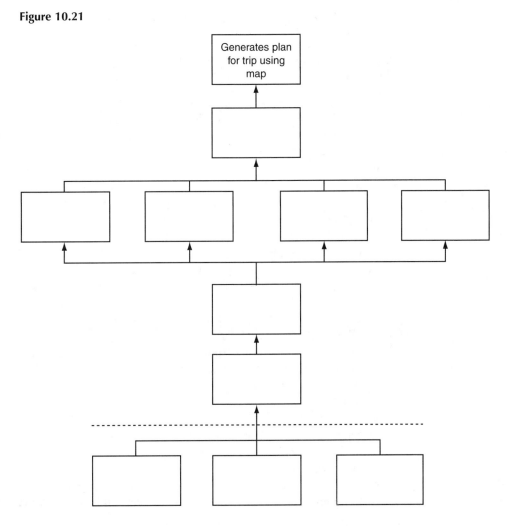

List of Subtasks

Discriminate and identify shapes   Classify symbols re: routes, highways
Demonstrate using legend to read map   Discriminate and identify size
Identify symbols used on map   Discriminate legend from rest of map
Discriminate and identify colors   Classify symbols re: distance
Classify symbols re: recreation   Classify symbols re: transportation

E. A Group Exercise in Constructing a Hierarchy

Divide into groups of three or four. Each group will prepare a task hierarchy using the conventions described in this chapter. Examine the sets of randomly listed tasks below for the job of troubleshooting FM radios. Your assignment is to use the tasks to construct a hierarchy. All tasks must be included in the hierarchy.

1. Recognize symptoms
2. Use Form XYZ to record results of troubleshooting
3. Identify component parts
4. Classify test results as normal or abnormal
5. Troubleshoot FM radios
6. Use test equipment
7. Obtain knowledge of normal test results[1]

F. An Exercise in Identifying Information Relevant for Determining Entry-Level Behaviors

Select the information most likely to provide the specific information needed for defining the entry-level behaviors for each learning outcome.

1. Learning outcome: Locate positive and negative numbers on a number line.
   a. Results from a test of scientific concepts and skills.
   b. Test results on the same task from students with similar backgrounds.
   c. Outline of most recent math course.
   d. None of the above.
2. Learning outcome: Read for comprehension of paragraphs.
   a. Percentile ranking of the target audience on a standardized reading test.
   b. Survey of the target audience's reading preferences.
   c. Judgments of the target audience's previous reading teachers.
   d. None of the above.
3. Learning outcome: Troubleshoot radio repeater sets.
   a. Previous instructor's assessment of target audience.
   b. Objectives of courses previously taken by the target audience.
   c. Personnel files giving previous experience with radios.
   d. All of the above.
4. Learning outcome: Name a microcomputer and state the function of each component.
   a. Mechanical aptitude scores.
   b. Interviews with people in the target audience.
   c. Interviews with supervisors.
   d. All of the above.
5. Learning outcome: Name and define the purpose of each type of test used in an individualized, structured curriculum.
   a. Transcripts showing courses in test construction.
   b. Descriptions of work history in training development.
   c. Judgments by test developers who have no first-hand knowledge of the target audience.
   d. None of the above.

---

[1] From *Module 9: Preparing Task/Content Hierarchies: Student Response Book* (p. 56), by D. Frezza, 1985, Butler, PA: Applied Science Associates.

G. An Exercise in Determining Entry-Level Behaviors from Test Results

Below are six learning outcomes for a lesson on toxoplasmosis. The intended audience is third-year medical students. The percentage of the target audience who successfully answered pre-test items associated with each objective appears after each learning outcome. Check which, if any, are entry-level behaviors.

_____ 1. State the factors contributing to toxoplasmosis. (81%)

_____ 2. Recognize the characteristics of congenital toxoplasmosis. (40%)

_____ 3. Recognize the signs of acquired toxoplasmosis. (43%)

_____ 4. Describe the potential for differential diagnosis. (45%)

_____ 5. Identify the lab findings associated with toxoplasmosis. (25%)

_____ 6. State the recommended treatments for toxoplasmosis. (46%)

H. A Group Exercise in Defining the Prerequisites and Entry-Level Behaviors for a Procedural Task

Review the task analysis you developed for Exercise F in chapter 2. Expand upon that analysis to define the prerequisite requirements, write a description of the target audience, and identify the entry-level behaviors for students. Your product must meet the following criteria:

◆ Entry levels are based on behaviors, not general characteristics.

◆ Entry-level behaviors must be essential prerequisites, not supportive prerequisites.

◆ REFERENCES

Bloom, B. S. (Ed.), Englehart, M. D., Furst, E. J., & Krathwohl, D. R. (1956). *Taxonomy of educational objectives: Handbook I: Cognitive domain.* New York: David McKay Co.

Briggs, L. J., & Wager, W. (1981). *Handbook of procedures for the design of instruction* (2nd ed.). Englewood Cliffs, NJ: Educational Technology Publications.

Dick, W., & Carey, L. (1996). *The systematic design of instruction* (4th ed.). New York: Harper/Collins College Publishers.

Frezza, D. (1985). *Module 9: Preparing task/content hierarchies: Student resource book* (Randolph AFB TX: Contract No. F41689-83-C-0048, USAF Occupational Measurement Center [ATC]). Butler, PA: Applied Science Associates.

Gagné, E. (1985). *The cognitive psychology of school learning.* New York: Little, Brown, & Co.

Gagné, R. M. (1985). *The conditions of learning* (4th ed.). New York: Holt, Rinehart and Winston, Inc.

Gagné, R. M. (1989). *Studies of learning.* Tallahassee, FL: Learning Systems Institute.

Gagné, R. M., & Briggs, L. J. (1974). *Principles of instructional design.* New York: Holt, Rinehart and Winston, Inc.

Gagné, R. M., Briggs, L. J. , & Wager, W. W. (1988; 1992). *Principles of instructional design.* New York: Holt, Rinehart and Winston, Inc.

Gow, D. T. (1976). *Design and development of curricular materials: Self-instructional text* (Vol. 1). Pittsburgh, PA: University Center for International Studies, University of Pittsburgh.

Harrow, A. J. (1972). *A taxonomy of the psychomotor domain.* New York: David McKay Co.

Krathwohl, D. R., Bloom, B. S., & Masia, B. B. (1964). *Taxonomy of educational objectives: Handbook II: Affective domain.* New York: David McKay Co.

Martin, B. L., & Briggs, L. J. (1986). *The affective and cognitive domains: Integration for instruction and research.* Englewood Cliffs, NJ: Educational Technology Publications.

Ragan, T. J., & Smith, P. L. (1996). Conditions-based models for designing instruction. In D. H. Jonassen (Ed.), *Handbook of research for educational Communications and technology* (pp. 541–569). New York: Simon and Schuster MacMillan.

◆ ANSWERS

A. An Exercise to Classify Learning Outcomes According to Gagné's Learned Capabilities

1. Motor Skills
2. Verbal Information
3. Verbal Information
4. Verbal Information
5. Rule Using
6. Rule Using
7. Verbal Information
8. Rule Using
9. Rule Using
10. Verbal Information
11. Attitudes
12. Motor Skills
13. Attitudes
14. Attitudes
15. Attitudes
16. Motor Skills
17. Motor Skills
18. Cognitive Strategy
19. Problem Solving
20. Rule Using
21. Problem Solving

B. A Group Exercise in Defining Prerequisites
This group exercise should be evaluated using the criteria given in the exercise. Each group can critique another group's work.

C. An Exercise in Applying Knowledge of Hierarchy Conventions
1. c
2. b
3. It doesn't. These two subtasks are discrete.
4. It is essential for performance.

D. An Exercise in Constructing a Hierarchy
The answer to this exercise is shown in Figure 10.22.

Figure 10.22

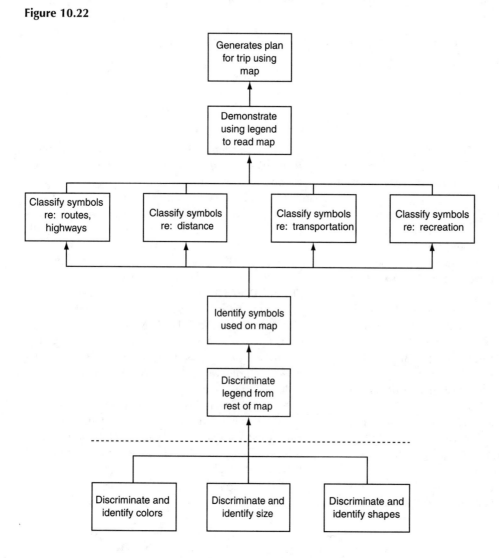

E. A Group Exercise in Constructing a Hierarchy
The answer to this exercise is shown in Figure 10.23.

F. An Exercise in Identifying Information Relevant for Determining Entry-Level Behaviors
1. b
2. c
3. d
4. b
5. d

G. An Exercise in Determining Entry-Level Behaviors from Test Results
1. State the factors contributing to toxoplasmosis. (81%)

H. A Group Exercise in Defining the Prerequisites and Entry-Level Behaviors for a Procedural Task
The exercise should be evaluated using the criteria given in the exercise. One strategy is to have students critique each other's work.

Figure 10.23   Hierarchy for troubleshooting FM radio

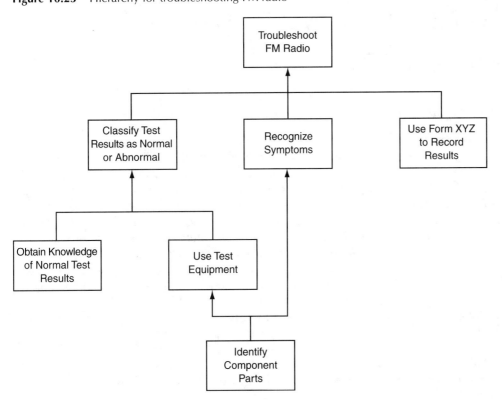

11

Planning Instructional Strategies

OVERVIEW

Once you have written and sequenced the objectives and constructed tests, you are ready to develop your strategy for designing the learning events that will accomplish the objectives. Figure 11.1 shows the point in the ISD process at which this occurs.

Generally, there is a set of events prescribed for all learning situations. The diagram by Virginia Johnson in Figure 11.2 shows the basic instructional events of a simple instructional segment. The same events should be included in most types of instruction, whether it is self-paced or group-paced, and no matter what medium or methods of instruction are employed (e.g., computer-assisted instruction, films, simulations, etc.).

The introduction directs students' attention to the learning task, motivates them by explaining the benefits of achieving the objectives, and relates the new learning to previous learning. The presentation is the stage during which the information, facts, concepts, principles, or procedures are introduced to the student. Presentation requirements will vary depending on the type of learning to be accomplished and the students' entry-level behavior. The criterion test measures the students' accomplishment of the terminal objective(s). Criterion practice occurs under the same conditions as the final test. The purpose is to determine whether a student is ready to take the final test, or whether remediation is necessary.

Transitional practice is designed to help the students bridge the gap between entry-level behavior and behavior required by the terminal objective(s). Less difficult situations are presented at the beginning of instruction, and gradually practice becomes more difficult. The important thing to remember about transitional practice is that it prepares students to perform the criterion practice.

Guidance is the coaching and prompting that helps students perform correctly. The shape of the figure representing guidance shows that more assistance is present at the beginning of practice, and that it is gradually reduced until the students can perform unassisted. As the diagram shows, assistance is provided only during transition practice, not during criterion practice.

Feedback, an integral part of practice, tells students whether they are right or wrong, and how they can improve performance. Feedback is provided during transitional and criterion practice. Practice alone is not sufficient for effective learning.

Figure 11.1   Instructional Strategy in the ISD Process

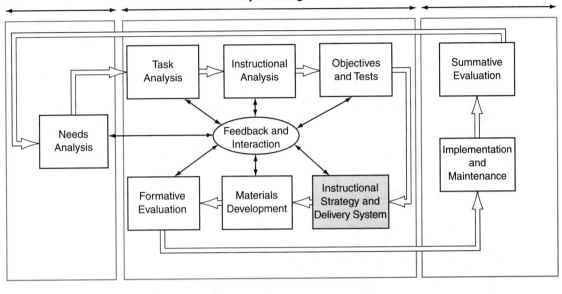

Project Management

Task Analysis → Instructional Analysis → Objectives and Tests

Needs Analysis

Feedback and Interaction

Formative Evaluation ← Materials Development ← Instructional Strategy and Delivery System

Summative Evaluation

Implementation and Maintenance

Diffusion

What must happen for learning to occur?
How will the content be presented?
What instructional strategies are preferred for the types of learning involved?

How much practice is needed? What form of feedback is best? How should new information be presented? Research on instructional design variables that facilitate learning provides many of the answers. The body of research on instructional design variables is quite large, however, and beyond the scope of a single text. Therefore, this chapter will concentrate on some of the basic events of instruction—introduction, presentation, practice, and feedback—that apply in most circumstances. While the events of instruction are generally the same irrespective of the learning objectives, the specific applications of

Figure 11.2   Instructional Events

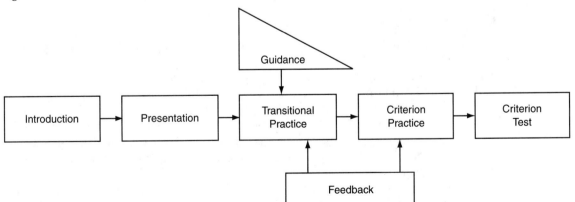

Guidance

Introduction → Presentation → Transitional Practice → Criterion Practice → Criterion Test

Feedback

From *Module 13: Principles of Learning: Student Resource Book* by V. Johnson (p. 17), 1985, Randolph AFB, TX: USAF Occupational Measurement Center.

some of these events are different in part for learning intellectual skills, verbal information, attitudes, and motor skills. For each type of learning, Gagné specifies the internal conditions that must be present in the learner in order to acquire a new competency, and the external conditions that can be manipulated by the instructional designer in order to influence the internal events of learning.

Internal conditions refer to the student's state of readiness to learn, his motivation level, his existing mental structures, and the previously acquired information in his working memory. External conditions refer to the actions that the instructional designer prescribes to gain and maintain the student's attention, to present new information so that it builds on existing cognitive structures, and to provide the opportunities for practice and feedback that aid retention. This chapter elaborates on how the external events that are controlled by instruction apply to each type of learning.

ORIENTING QUESTIONS

What forms can practice take?
What forms can feedback take?
What are the ingredients of an effective introduction?
What variables affect how information will be presented to the learner?
What instructional strategies apply to the different types of learning?

OBJECTIVES

1. Given learning situations, identify effective introductions of what is to be learned.
2. Given ineffective introductions, revise them to make them more effective.
3. Given instructional objectives, develop introductions to the new material.
4. Given learning situations, identify effective presentations of what is to be learned.
5. Given ineffective presentations, revise them to make them more effective.
6. Given instructional objectives, develop presentations on the new material.
7. Given learning situations, identify practice schedules that will facilitate learning.
8. Given learning situations, identify transitional practice that will facilitate learning.
9. Given inadequate practice situations, revise them to make them more effective.
10. Given practice situations, identify effective feedback for the situation.
11. Given ineffective feedback, revise the feedback to make it more effective.
12. Given instructional objectives, produce transitional practice and feedback.

EVENTS OF INSTRUCTION

Introducing the Lesson

The first activity in the teaching/learning process is to direct the students' attention and prepare them to learn. As noted earlier, an introduction should explain the objectives of instruction, describe the benefits of achieving the objectives, and relate the new learning to previously learned material. Students accomplish objectives more effectively if they know exactly what is expected of them. Then, they can focus on those activities that lead to achievement of the objectives. For example, if nutrition is being studied, it may not be obvious to a student whether the objective is to identify foods in each food group or to plan a menu with foods in each food group—two quite different outcomes. Students should not have to guess what is expected of them.

It is important to communicate objectives in a language students understand. For older students, it may be sufficient simply to give them the actual objectives devised by the instructor. For younger students, the objectives must be restated at a level they comprehend.

This may entail providing an example or demonstration of the performance expected at the end of the lesson or samples of the types of questions asked on the final exam.

Gagné and Medsker (1996) suggest that a clearer picture of the designed performance may be created by providing an example of the desired outcome. For intellectual skills one may demonstrate the activity; for verbal information, state the information learned; for cognitive strategy, demonstrate the adoption of the strategy; and for motor skills, execute the actions learned.

Many teachers erroneously assume that students understand the value of what is being taught. In fact, students may not understand how what they are being asked to learn fits into a larger goal. Yet considerable evidence suggests that students who see a real purpose to the learning task will learn it better. The instructional designer should include a statement in each lesson about why the material or task is of value. Sometimes a straightforward statement about the benefits of instruction is enough, but other times it takes ingenuity to convey the long-term benefits to students. For the course on loan documentation discussed in chapter 1, the pre-test served to raise participants' awareness about what they needed to learn about loan documentation. If you cannot devise a good reason for learning the topic or task, perhaps you should reassess your task analysis and instructional analysis data to determine whether the instruction is really necessary.

Learning is more effective when it can be related to previously learned information—for instance, by a brief recall of a previous lesson to show how the current lesson relates to it. The idea is to provide a framework or schema familiar to the learner that helps him relate to the new learning.

In the case of rule learning, you may review the concepts that comprise the rule to be learned. Or, you can compare the concepts to be learned to concepts already known to the students. For example, electrical current is often explained by comparing the flow of electricity to the flow of water. Outlines or summaries of the prior knowledge may be used for relating previously learned verbal information to learning new bodies of information. In the case of motor skills, learners may be reminded of component skills already in their repertoire. For cognitive strategies, learners may be asked to recall strategies currently used by them so that new strategies may be related to them.

In summary, an effective introduction

◆ describes the objective of the lesson and how students will be evaluated;

◆ describes the benefits of learning; and

◆ relates the new learning to previous learning.

Exercises A, B, and C at the end of this chapter provide practice in developing effective introductions to lessons.

Presenting New Content

When new content is to be learned, the lesson should present the facts, concepts, and rules, and/or describe and demonstrate the skill. New material is easier to remember when it is presented in an orderly, highly structured form that is meaningful to the student, reduces extraneous information and confusing stimuli, and contains a great deal of redundancy.

When planning presentations, avoid information overload. Substantial research evidence suggests that information chunked into limited bits (seven bits plus or minus two is recommended) is more easily stored in memory. The appropriate number of chunks depends on the students' previous experience with similar material and the rate of delivery. Rapid delivery increases information load.

The presentation cues help the student to learn by doing the following:

◆ Calling attention to important characteristics of the material.

◆ Providing examples (and non-examples) of concepts.

◆ Providing verbal or pictorial cues to call attention to critical elements of the new material. Visual presentations are more effective for difficult or even meaningless concepts; while aural presentations facilitate reception of familiar, fairly simple, and very meaningful material.

◆ Using mnemonic devices to help students learn arbitrary associations.

In summary, an effective presentation has the following attributes.

◆ The structure is logical.

◆ Information is chunked to prevent memory overload.

◆ Cues direct attention to relevant aspects of the learning.

Presentation Requirements for Intellectual Skills

Discrimination Learning.   Discrimination learning enables the student to distinguish the distinctive features of objects, sound, tastes, smells, textures, and symbols. The most common method for teaching discriminations is contrast practice. The learner observes a series of stimuli and indicates which stimuli display key features (Gagné and Medsker, 1996). Preferably, instruction starts with asking the students to distinguish between two extreme cases where the differences are readily apparent. Feedback is given after each response. Progressively, the discriminations become finer and finer, until the student is able to make the distinctions called for in the objective.

In the early 1960s, David J. Klaus conducted an unpublished study at the American Institutes for Research that taught adolescents to distinguish good paintings from bad. Experts ranked the artistic quality of slides of the paintings. Paintings that experts did not agree on were eliminated from the study. Students viewed the slides in pairs starting with those with the most extreme rankings (worst painting vs. best painting). They were given immediate feedback about the correctness of their response. They were simply told that they were right or wrong. No explanation was given for why the answer was right or wrong. The difference between pairs of paintings became progressively smaller as students were able to make finer and finer discriminations. In time, through contrast practice, students were able to make distinctions like those of the experts.

No verbal information other than feedback was given in Klaus' study. Judging the artistic merit of paintings is not a verbal process. The basis for the distinctions is purely visual. In most cases, however, the efficiency of discrimination learning can be enhanced and the trial and error nature of this process reduced by providing verbal cues. For example, to distinguish visually between different breeds of cattle, one might point out the features that distinguish them. In the discriminating among cattle the student is learning to distinguish cattle based on physical features, not to simply state the distinguishing features verbally. The latter would be an example of verbal learning.

Concrete Concepts.   In concept learning, a person classifies objects or object qualities on the basis of certain attributes. Concrete concepts learning occurs when examples and nonexamples are encountered. For example, to learn the concept wrench, a workman could look at various types of wrenches (adjustable wrench, Allen wrench, pipe wrench, socket wrenches, etc.). He would also observe tools that might be confused with wrenches (channel-type pliers, slip joint pliers, etc.). In addition, the instructor would provide verbal guidance to point out the attributes of wrenches that distinguish them from other tools.

Gagné and Medsker (1996) point out that, because of the close dependent relationship between discriminations and concepts, it may be difficult to decide whether a particular learned capability is a discrimination or a concept. They use the example of a building superintendent learning to distinguish keys. Initially, the keys all look alike. Soon, the superintendent is able to tell them apart. She can sort the keys according to purpose: door keys, padlock keys, mailbox keys. She is also able to identify an entirely new key as belonging to one of these categories.

To teach a concrete concept, you would do the following:

◆ Ensure that the students have the prerequisite discriminations.

◆ Show specific examples and nonexamples exhibiting the range of relevant and irrelevant attributes. Nonexamples should include those that might be confused by the students as being a member of the class to be learned.

◆ Provide verbal cues calling attention to the relevant and irrelevant attributes. For example, in teaching the concept "chair" you would point out the relevant attribute (seat with a back, for one person) and the irrelevant attributes (i.e., arms, the type of legs or base).

◆ Provide classification practice and feedback about the correctness of responses.

Defined Concepts.   Defined concepts must be learned by the use of language because they are abstract rules for classifying objects and events that cannot be defined by physical attributes alone. A verbal definition is essential to act as cues to the learner. Otherwise, instruction is the same as for concrete concepts.

Consider the case of a mental health worker learning to assess the behavior of patients with a type of psychiatric disorder. The disorder would be defined first by identifying the behavioral attributes the worker might expect to observe in the patient. Then, the mental health worker might observe examples of the disorder and nonexamples of patient behavior in video simulations of patients with and without the disorder. He would be given classification practice and feedback. It is important to include in examples the full range of the disorder from mild to severe. It is also important to include nonexamples that share attributes with the disorder and, therefore, can be confused with the disorder.

Rules.   Rules are typically thought of as an if-then relationship, exemplified by the following example of how to read an electric meter: "IF the needle is between two numbers, THEN read the lower number."

Instruction on the rule for reading electric meters would include:

◆ A verbal statement of the rule and a demonstration of its application.

◆ Presentation of a variety of examples of rule applications.

◆ Practice in applying the rule. Reviews spaced over time have a marked effect in enhancing the learning of rules. (Gagné and Medsker, 1996)

Presentation Requirements for Learning Verbal Information

Labels.   Labels are the names associated with people, objects, and events. The learning of labels is called paired associate learning. The more labels to be learned, the more difficult the learning task. Interference is also a problem with paired association. This occurs when a previously learned association interferes with learning a new association, or a new association interferes with recalling a previously learned association. In other words, labels get misapplied or cannot be remembered.

Mediating links which cue the response facilitate the learning of labels, and may take the following forms:

◆ *Imagery* where the learned uses a pictorial image to aid learning and recalling a label. For the name "King," the learning may think of the image of a king in a deck of cards.

◆ *Clustering* labels into common categories also aids learning. Clustering is used in Exercise D at the end of this chapter.

- *Elaboration* places the word or phrase to be learned in a sentence. The sentence: "*Peter* picked a *pot* of peppers" may help you remember the name Peter Potts.
- *Mnemonics* (memory enhancing) devices such rhymes as pegwords aid recall of labels.
- *Superimposed meaningful structures* such as the sentence: "*All Good Boys Do Fine.*" helps to remember the names of the lines in a musical scale.

Sheer repetition is important to learning labels, as well as all verbal information. Continued practice after initial mastery has been reached has also been shown to aid recall of verbal information.

Facts.   Facts are not just strings of words, but meaningful propositions that a person can communicate in his own words. New facts can be more easily learned if they are assimilated into an existing cognitive structure. Ausubel (Ausubel, Novak, & Hanesian, 1978) found that students learned facts about Buddhism more readily when they first read a summary of the tenets of Christianity. The summary of Christianity, called an "advance organizer," provided a cognitive structure for assimilating the new information about Buddhism. In addition to advance organizers, the mediating devices used in learning labels apply to learning facts. Repetition is also critical.

Organized Verbal Knowledge.   Organized verbal knowledge requires the recall of main themes or generalizations, as well as recall of facts. According to current theory, the strangest influence on learning is previously acquired knowledge already organized into what is called a schema (Gagné and Medsker, 1996). In other words, the more a person knows about a topic, the more readily new information is learned. The critical events for verbal information learning are as follows:

- Providing a meaningful context to which students can relate the new information. An advance organizer is one technique.
- Using effective recall cues such as diagrams, figures, tables, etc. in print media, and sound or motion in film, video, and computerized media.
- Providing a logical structure for the presentation.
- Providing repeated practice and feedback.

Presentation Requirements for Learning Attitudes

Social learning theory (Bandura, 1986) postulates that people learn by imitating other people and by behavior being reinforced. Bandura distinguishes between learning and performing. In his studies, a highly credible model is observed acting out the behavior and receiving a reward for the behavior. The credibility of the actor and the observation of positive reinforcement predisposes the viewer to adopt the same behavior. The behavior is learned through observation, or what Bandura calls "vicarious learning." Later, if the opportunity presents itself, the learner will perform the behavior learned vicariously. The actor may be live or on any audiovisual medium.

The implications of these studies for attitude formation is that attitude change follows behavioral change. The instructional steps are as follows:

- Presentation of humans modeling the attitude (e.g., a professional demeanor with patients undergoing radiological exams).
- The actors are reinforced for exhibiting the appropriate behavior.
- Students practice the behavior in highly structured role plays.
- Detailed feedback on the role play performance is provided.

Presentation Requirements for Learning Motor Skills

In motor skill learning, the student passes through three overlapping phases:

Early Phase.   With the help of the instructor, the student comes to understand the task. The instructor may demonstrate and describe the task as she performs it and tells the students what to expect. She may provide detailed diagrams or flowcharts that students may study. When the student tries her hand at the task, the instructor may provide cues about what to do next and give feedback on how to correct the performance.

Middle Phase.   The correct behaviors are practiced until they become fixed and established. The student learns to link component parts of the chain into their proper sequence. This phase lasts until the student can smoothly perform the task with minimal error. For many skills, the proficiency reached at the end of this phase will satisfy the criterion objective of instruction.

Late Phase.   The skill becomes so efficient, effortless, and errorless, that the performer is sometimes said to perform the task "without thinking." The performance is involuntary and does not deteriorate under stressful and interfering conditions. Reaching this level of proficiency may span years and usually is achieved after instruction is completed.

Exercises D, E, and F at the end of this chapter provide practice in developing effective presentations.

Practice

Learning is an active process. It is more effective when students produce, practice, or try their hand at the task to be learned. Practice is the single most important ingredient of effective instruction; it speeds up learning, aids long-term retention, and facilitates recall. It is especially critical for learning verbal information and motor skills.

Instruction is less effective when there is no opportunity to perform the task or when practice is delayed until after the instruction has been completed. Unfortunately, much of the instruction in our classrooms provides little or no opportunity for practice. Too often, instruction is designed so that students passively receive information; they listen to lectures, read texts, or watch demonstrations.

Cognitive psychologists believe effective practice creates cognitive structures for efficient storage and retrieval of information from long-term memory. Behaviorists are less concerned with what goes on inside the student's head than with the conditions that make practice more effective. Regardless of their theoretical orientation, however, all scientists agree on three aspects of practice:

1. Practice opportunities must allow students to perform the task actively.
2. Practice is most effective when it occurs immediately after the presentation of new material, while information is still fresh in the students' minds.
3. There must be multiple opportunities for practice. Learning very seldom occurs after only one try at a task.

Overt vs. Covert Practice.   Practice may be either overt or covert. An overt response, such as writing an answer, performing a procedure, or repeating a word or phrase, is observable. A covert response, such as thinking of an answer, mentally practicing a verbal chain for later recital, or silently selecting the correct answer from a series of options, is not observable.

Experiments that address whether covert or overt responding facilitates learning have mainly dealt with verbal learning. Findings show that students who respond covertly learn and retain verbal material as well as students who respond overtly. Learning from films, lectures, or similar presentations can be increased by using techniques to elicit covert responses. For example, the lecturer can strategically pause to pose a direct question or to allow the students to complete a sentence.

During the past several years, an increasing number of studies have examined how learning from written materials takes place. A related issue is the use of questions embedded in textual material. Questions designed to evoke higher level cognitive processing (e.g., compare, synthesize, evaluate, problem solve, etc.) are preferable to questions that require lower level learning, such as recall of facts. Presumably, the higher level questions cause the student to study the written material more thoroughly to get the correct answer. When the questions require only simple recall, however, students study only those parts of the text specific to the questions.

Under certain circumstances overt responding is preferable because it allows the teacher to verify the accuracy of students' responses, especially with less able students who require more assistance. In addition, overt responding facilitates rote memorization. Overt responding is also preferred for psychomotor skills and for procedural tasks that have not been well established.

Schedule of Practice. In general, the more opportunities the student has to respond, the more learning occurs. Practice opportunities should not be massed into one session. Cramming for an exam is an example of massed practice. Cramming may result in high performance on the test, but it is subject to rapid forgetting. For long-term retention of material, practice should be distributed over a period of time with short rest periods between each practice opportunity. "Distributed" practice is preferable for all learning, but it is needed more for less able students. It is essential for learning long, difficult tasks.

Shortening the rest period is better than lengthening the work period. Rest periods should not be too long because after a certain point they fail to pay off. Intervals between practice should be shorter when error tendency is high than when it is low. There are no hard and fast rules. For example, if students forget between sessions much of what was learned, it may be because weekly practice sessions are spread too far apart. Daily sessions may be more effective for some learners, but two or more brief sessions per day may be necessary for others.

Transitional Practice. Transitional practice bridges the gap between entry-level behavior and criterion performance. It is intended to provide students early in learning with situations they can handle. Gradually, practice becomes more difficult until students can perform at the criterion level. In other words, practice starts easy and ends hard.

Transitional practice may take several forms. One way is to break down the task into its component parts and have students practice solving part of a problem before the whole problem, or practice the separate steps in a procedure before combining them in the proper sequence. (The component subtasks or sub-steps were identified earlier—during the task analysis phase of the instructional design process.)

Another common way of making practice less difficult is by starting with easier responses and building to harder ones. Gropper (1971) recommends providing recognition practice, then editing practice, and finally production practice. In recognition practice, students merely select a correct answer from two or more options. In editing practice, students are shown an incorrect performance and asked to correct it. Production practice is the closest to criterion performance (assuming the criterion performance requires students to produce rather than merely recognize a correct performance). Unlike criterion practice, during production practice students may receive guidance. Table 11.1 shows examples of recognition, editing, and production practice. Notice the guidance in both examples of production practice. The exercises at the end of this chapter are an example of Gropper's REP strategy.

Table 11.1 Examples of Transitional Practice

Recognition practice

- Which of these two carburetors is assembled correctly?

- Is this a nimbus or cumulus cloud?

Editing practice

- This carburetor has been assembled incorrectly. Assemble it correctly.

- This cloud was incorrectly labeled a nimbus cloud. What kind is it?

Production practice

- Assemble this carburetor. Don't forget that the choke must be completely assembled first.

- Look at the shape and color of this cloud. What kind of cloud is it?

From *Module 13: Principles of Learning: Student Resource Book* by V. Johnson (p. 17), Randolph AFB, TX: USAF Occupational Measurement Center.

Practice may be made easier by lowering the standards for performance (such as speed, accuracy, completeness, quality, etc.) during the early stages of learning. As learning proceeds, students are brought progressively closer to criterion standards. For example, a timed task may have no time limits at first. Gradually, time limits are applied and shortened to what the criterion performance will require.

Another important principle of learning is that practice should be as error-free as possible. Once made, a correct response is likely to recur. The same is true for an incorrect response. (Ask any skier or golfer who has tried to correct a bad technique.) Therefore, it is up to the designer to provide guidance and prompts during the early stages of practice in order to reduce guesswork and make sure the student's initial response is correct. Having to "discover" the correct response by trial and error wastes time; it confuses and frustrates the learner. There is a place for discovery learning in some educational settings, but the method is difficult to implement when instructional time is limited. Error-free learning is especially important in learning motor skills.

Since it is impossible to ensure that every student will always respond correctly the first time, the designer should plan cues. Cues help guide students to the correct response, but they should not be so obvious as to reveal the response. Cues may, for example, tell the form of the response (e.g., "your answer should be a fraction"), depend on meaningful associations or past knowledge, or draw attention to key properties (by means of arrows, charts, diagrams, etc.).

Exercises G, H, and I at the end of this chapter provide practice in developing effective practice.

Feedback

Another way to minimize errors is to let the student know immediately when a response is incorrect. Knowing when they are right or wrong helps students correct their actions during subsequent trials and focus on parts of the task that require refinement. Again, this is especially critical in learning motor skills.

Feedback may take two forms. It may arise naturally out of the task environment—during learning and later during the criterion performance on the job or on a test. Target practice is one example of a task where feedback is natural. But often feedback does not arise naturally from the task itself, and in these cases the instructional designer must devise methods for providing it. Such "artificial" feedback is present only during learning.

The requirements for feedback are the same for all types of learning. Feedback devised by the instructional designer should be as follows:

◆ **Complete.**   Provide the entire correct answer. Simply telling students they are wrong doesn't tell them how to be right.

◆ **Specific**.   Identify errors in the performance and provide information about the magnitude and direction of the error. This information allows students to make the appropriate correction.

◆ **Corrective.**   Explain the logic of the correct answer. Students who are told why their answers are right or wrong learn more effectively than students who receive no feedback until they get the right answer.

◆ **Immediate.**   Give the correct answers after each practice trial.

◆ **Reinforcing.**   Reward correct responses with praise, recognition, or something else you know to be reinforcing. A student who is reinforced for doing something is more likely to do the same thing again. Often, simply knowing that one has performed correctly is in itself rewarding.

Exercises J, K, and L at the end of this chapter provide practice in developing effective feedback and practice.

EXERCISES

A. An Exercise in Recognizing Effective Introductions

Below are examples of instructional objectives and an introduction for each. Evaluate each introduction by the following criteria.

◆ Describes the objective of the lesson and how students will be evaluated.

◆ Describes the benefits of learning.

◆ Relates the new learning to previous learning.

1. Objective for mail room clerk: Determine how much postage is required for different classes of mail.

   The amount of postage needed for a package will depend on its weight, content, destination, and the mailing class selected. Mailing classes include parcel post, first class, second class, and third class. Packages with too much postage waste money. Those with too little postage are returned to the sender and are late reaching their destination. In this lesson you will learn how to determine the right amount of postage to use.

   Check those that apply:

      ✓ a. Describes the objective of the lesson and how students will be evaluated.
      ✓ b. Describes the benefits of learning.
      ✗ c. Relates the new learning to previous learning.

2. Objective for coal miners: Follow procedures for putting out fire in underground coal mines.

   It is important that miners be trained in fire fighting—for their own safety and because they are the ones who can attack a fire while it is still small and while the chance of putting it out is greatest. In this lesson you will learn the procedures to follow in fighting small mine fires. At the end of the lesson, you will review written descriptions of miners' actions when fighting fires and determine whether they followed the correct procedures.

   Check those that apply:

      ✓ a. Describes the objective of the lesson and how students will be evaluated.
      ✓ b. Describes the benefits of learning.
      + c. Relates the new learning to previous learning.

3. Objective for first lesson of a fitness program for beginners: Take a 45-minute walk, do three to five modified pushups, abdominal curls, and leg raises.

This is a ten-week fitness program for people who have yet to incorporate exercise into their lives and want to start it. It is based on four workouts a week. At the end of the 10 weeks, you will be able to walk eight miles a week at three miles an hour, burning 650 calories a week. . . . From simple beginnings like this, totally sedentary people have permanently altered their lives, discovering new energy, losing weight, stopping smoking, and boring family and friends with incessant talk about their new obsession.[1]

Check those that apply:

  ✓ a. Describes the objective of the lesson and how students will be evaluated.
  ✓ b. Describes the benefits of learning.
  ✓ c. Relates the new learning to previous learning.

B. An Exercise in Editing Ineffective Introductions to Make Them More Effective

Select one of the deficient introductions from Exercise A and rewrite it to satisfy all of the criteria.

C. An Exercise in Producing Effective Introductions

Select three objectives from a course of study with which you are familiar. Prepare introductions for each objective. The introduction must meet all of the following criteria. When you have completed the exercise, write a brief statement describing how you met each criterion.

◆ Describes the objective of the lesson and how students will be evaluated.

◆ Describes the benefits of learning.

◆ Relates the new learning to previous learning.

D. An Exercise in Recognizing Effective Presentations

Below are examples of instructional objectives and presentations prepared for each. Evaluate each presentation against the following criteria:

◆ Structure is logical .

◆ Information is chunked to prevent memory overload.

◆ Cues direct attention to relevant aspects of the learning.

1. Objective: Recall a list of words.

Presentation: During the introduction, the instructor says: "Here is a list of words that you are expected to learn. On the test, you may recall the words in any order." Then the instructor writes the following list on the board and tells the class to copy them.

Summer	Noon
Blue	Red
Night	Winter
White	Spring
Fall	Night
Morning	

---

[1] From Stockton (1989), p. B-12, for a series of articles on fitness.

Check the criteria that apply:

_____a. Structure is logical.
_____b. Information is chunked to prevent memory overload.
_____c. Cues direct attention to relevant aspects of the learning.

2. Objective for infantry soldier: Ignite smoke pots using manual ignition, electric ignition, and manual chain firing.

Presentation: The instructor distributes a checklist of the steps for each procedure. There are four steps in the manual ignition procedures:

1. Strip off waterproof tape and the metal clamp.
2. Remove the outer cover to expose the match head.
3. Remove the scratched block from its envelope.
4. Draw the scratcher block rapidly across the match head.

The eleven steps in the electric ignition procedure and three steps in the chain firing procedure are similarly detailed on the checklists.

The instructor starts with the manual ignition because it is easy and most familiar to the students. As he demonstrates the procedure, he describes what he is doing and why.

He demonstrates the chain firing procedure next because it is also a manual procedure. During the demonstration, he describes what he is doing and why.

Finally, he demonstrates the electric ignition procedure using the same instructional strategy. The entire presentation takes 50 minutes.

Check the criteria that apply:

_____a. Structure is logical.
_____b. Information is chunked to prevent memory overload.
_____c. Cues direct attention to relevant aspects of the learning.

3. Objective for a salesperson: Identify a customer's style in risk taking, decision making, and communicating. The styles are Active Positive, Active Negative, Active Neutral, and Dominant Negative.

Presentation: The instructor presents a definition of the four styles and discusses how to negotiate with each. He then distributes scripts of how each type might respond to a salesperson's call. Key phrases that signal the prospect's type are underlined. The instructor reviews and elaborates on each underlined segment.

Check the criteria that apply:

_____a. Structure is logical.
_____b. Information is chunked to prevent memory overload.
_____c. Cues direct attention to relevant aspects of the learning.

E. An Exercise in Editing Ineffective Presentations to Make Them More Effective

Select one of the deficient presentations from Exercise D and revise it to satisfy all of the criteria.

F. An Exercise in Producing Effective Presentations

Prepare presentations that follow the introductions you prepared in Exercise E. The introduction must meet all of the following criteria. When you have completed the exercise, write a brief statement describing how you met each criterion.

_____a. Structure is logical.
_____b. Information is chunked to prevent memory overload.
_____c. Cues direct attention to relevant aspects of the learning.

G. An Exercise in Recognizing Effective Practice Schedules

Below are examples of instructional objectives and two practice schedules prepared for each. Indicate which is the better schedule and tell why.

1. Objective: Given a distribution curve, select the appropriate average (i.e., mean, median, or mode) and calculate it.

   _____ Practice Schedule A: A statistics teacher will lecture on the topics and conclude with a series of 30 exercises on all averages.

   _____ Practice Schedule B: A statistics teacher will lecture on the topics. After each topic is presented, it will be followed by 10 exercises.

   Explain your choice.

2. Objective: Classify food items into four food categories: milk, grain, meat, and vegetable.

   _____ Practice Schedule A: The instructor will assign reading as homework, directing students to think of two examples of each food group. The next day, students will be asked to write them on the board.

   _____ Practice Schedule B: The instructor will assign reading as homework assignment. The next morning, students will be asked to think of two examples of each food group and write them on the board.

   Explain your choice.

H. An Exercise in Recognizing Effective Transitional Practice

Below are examples of instructional objectives and two transitional practice strategies prepared for each objective. Indicate which is the better strategy and tell why.

1. Objective: Packs grocery bag so that fragile items are on top.

   _____ Practice A: Student is given a list of fragile items. He discusses the items on the list. He is directed to pack three orders.

   _____ Practice B: Student is given a list of fragile items. He critiques a videotape of a clerk packing fragile items. He is directed to pack three orders.

   Explain your choice.

2. Objective: Associate colors on resistors with resistance values.

   _____ Practice A: Column A shows the resistance values and associated colors. Write the correct value in Column B.

Column A	Column B
black-0	red _____
brown-1	green _____
(. . . and so on for 10 colors)	

   _____ Practice B: Write in the proper resistance values for the following colors.

   brown _____
   black _____
   red _____
   green _____
   (. . . and so on for 10 colors)

   Explain your choice.

3. Objective: Distinguish between examples of term and revolving loans.

_____ Practice A. (1) With the aid of a written definition and verbal cues, select examples of each type of loan. (2) With only the definition, select examples of each. (3) Select examples unassisted.

_____ Practice B. (1) With the aid of verbal cues, select examples of each type of loan. (2) With the aid of only a definition, select examples. (3) Select examples unassisted.

Explain your choice.

I. An Exercise in Editing Ineffective Practice to Make It More Effective

Below are examples of practice devised by instructional designers. Revise each to improve it.

1. Objective: Inspect tires for defects. No more than five percent of the defects are missed.
   Practice: Using a checklist of defects to look for, the student inspects four tires. Then practice is unassisted.
   Revision:

2. Objective: Produce a design by (a) drawing a design with water soluble paint on a water-color board, (b) covering the entire board with non-soluble ink, and (c) washing off the soluble paint to reveal the design delineated by the ink.
   Practice: After a demonstration of the process, students use the technique. The instructor circulates around the room offering help as needed.
   Revision:

3. Objective: Plan seating arrangement to facilitate discussion and consensus among participants.
   Practice: Distinguish among several proper and improper seating arrangements, then develop a seating plan for a room of own choosing.
   Revision:

J. An Exercise in Recognizing Effective Feedback

The following are examples of instructional events. Indicate which feedback option is better and tell why.

1. Instructional event: A man is learning to develop black and white film.
   Feedback A: Stop him after a mistake, and demonstrate what he should have done.
   Feedback B: After he completes the procedure, summarize what he did wrong.
   Explain your choice.

2. Instructional event: A woman is undergoing on-the-job training to be a supervisor.
   Feedback A: Comment about effective and ineffective performance at the end of each day.
   Feedback B: Comment about effective and ineffective performance at the end of each week.
   Explain your choice.

3. Instructional event: A man is learning to complete income tax forms. He is given several problems using the short form.
   Feedback A: A model of a correctly completed short form using another exercise.
   Feedback B: A model of a correctly completed short form using the same exercise.
   Explain your choice.

K. An Exercise in Editing Ineffective Feedback to Make It More Effective

Below are examples of feedback devised by instructional designers. Revise each to improve it.

1. Practice: A woman learning tennis is practicing her backhand.
   Feedback: After practice, she watches a video replay of herself.
   Revision:

2. Practice: A woman is learning to recognize clinical signs of depression. Using a checklist, she observes several dramatizations on videotape of interviews with clients and checks off the signs she observes.
   Feedback: After she completes the task, she verifies her answer against a completed checklist in the back of her workbook.
   Revision:

3. Practice: A trainer is learning how to use questions to draw students into discussion groups. In response to an exercise he prepares three questions.
   Feedback: The instructor reviewing his questions says, "Those will never do. Try again."
   Revision:

L. An Exercise in Producing Effective Practice and Feedback

Select three objectives from a course or field of study with which you are familiar. Devise practice and feedback opportunities for each. The practice must meet all of the following criteria. When you have completed the exercise, write a brief statement describing how you met each criterion.

◆ Scheduled immediately after presentation of the task to be learned.

◆ Multiple practice opportunities.

◆ Practice is distributed.

◆ Practice progresses from easy to hard.

◆ Practice opportunities are designed to be as error-free as possible.

The feedback must meet all of the following criteria:

◆ Complete

◆ Specific

◆ Corrective

◆ Immediate

◆ Reinforcing

◈ *REFERENCES*

Ausubel, D. P., Novak, J. D., & Hanesian, H. (1978). *Educational psychology: A cognitive view* (2nd ed.). New York: Holt, Rinehart and Winston.

Bandura, A. (1986). *Social foundations of thought and action: A social-cognitive theory.* Englewood Cliffs, NJ: Prentice-Hall.

Gagné, R., & Medsker, K. L. (1996). *The conditions of learning: Training applications.* Fort Worth, TX: Harcourt Brace College Publishers

Gropper, G. L. (1971). *A technology for developing instructional materials: Handbook.* Pittsburgh, PA: American Institutes for Research.

Johnson, V. (1985). *Module 13: Principles of learning: Student resource book* (Contract No. F41689-83-C-0048). Randolph AFB, TX: USAF Occupational Measurement Center (ATC).

Stockton, W. (1989, January 23). A slow but sure way to get in shape. *The New York Times,* p. 19.

◆ ANSWERS

A. An Exercise in Recognizing Effective Introductions

1. b.
2. a and b.
3. a, b, and c.

B. An Exercise in Editing Ineffective Introductions to Make Them More Effective

Item 1 from the previous exercise should be revised to include:

◆ A statement on how the students will be evaluated (e.g., "You will have to calculate the postage for five packages given the destination, content, and mailing class.").
◆ Relate the new learning to previous learning (e.g., "In the last lesson, you learned that there are different costs associated with different classes of mail. In this lesson, you will learn the right amount of postage to use.").

Item 2 should be revised to relate the lesson to previous learning. For example, "In the last lesson you learned the sources of fires in underground mines. In this lesson . . . ."

C. An Exercise in Producing Effective Introductions

The introduction should include statements that

◆ describe the objective of the lesson and how it will be evaluated;
◆ describe the benefits of learning; and
◆ relate the new learning to previous learning.

D. An Exercise in Recognizing Effective Presentations

1. None of the criteria apply.
2. a and c. The lesson starts easy, with the known, and ends with the unknown, which is more difficult. However, 50 minutes is too long for a lecture. The instructor's descriptions direct attention to relevant aspects of the learning. The checklist also cues performance.
3. c. Underlined scripts direct attention to key phrases to be learned.

E. An Exercise in Editing Ineffective Presentations to Make Them More Effective

Item 1 should be improved if the list were organized as follows, it would be structured logically and chunked to prevent memory overload:

Spring	Red	Morning
Summer	White	Noon
Fall	Blue	Night
Winter		

The instructor could cue the learning by saying something like: "Here are three lists of words. The first list contains the words for the four seasons; the second list, the colors of the American flag, and the third list the three periods in a day. You are expected to learn them. On a test you will be asked to recall them."

Item 2 should be revised to prevent information overload by presenting it in three parts: manual ignition, chair firing procedure, and electrical procedure. Each presentation would be followed by an opportunity for students to practice the procedure.

Item 3 would be structured better and information chunked better for recall if the presentation of each style was immediately followed by a discussion of the scripts associated with each. Instead, the instructor covered all four scripts. This organization is less likely to help the students differentiate among the types and communication strategies appropriate for each.

F. An Exercise in Producing Effective Presentations

Check that the presentations meet the criteria specified in the exercise.

G. An Exercise in Recognizing Effective Practice Schedules

1. Practice Schedule B. Practice is distributed.
2. Practice Schedule A. Practice is covert (i.e., thinking of examples) and immediate. In Schedule B, practice is delayed until the next day.

H. An Exercise in Recognizing Effective Transitional Practice

1. Practice B. The video presentation provides a demonstration that is close to the actual behavior on which practice can be modeled.
2. Practice A. The behavior is cued by Column A during the first practice opportunity.
3. Practice A. Initial practice is more heavily cued by both verbal and visual cues. Then, the cues are gradually reduced.

I. An Exercise in Editing Ineffective Practice to Make It More Effective

1. The student first practices identifying defects on a series of slides. A greater variety of defects can be shown on the slides than on four tires. Then the student can practice spotting defects unassisted using actual tires.
2. Practice should follow each step. Then the whole chain can be practiced.
3. Distinguish proper and improper seating arrangements shown in pictorial form. Then, critique a room arrangement. Finally, prepare a room of her own choosing.

J. An Exercise in Recognizing Effective Feedback

1. Feedback B. Feedback is more immediate and specific.
2. Feedback A. Feedback is more immediate.
3. Feedback B. Feedback is more specific.

K. An Exercise in Editing Ineffective Feedback to Make It More Effective

1. Feedback is too delayed and not corrective. The instructor should coach her while she plays.
2. Feedback is immediate. It could be made more specific if the feedback was presented by video instead of in the text. Then the clinical signs that led to the diagnosis would be shown explicitly.
3. The feedback is too vague. The instructor should point out how to improve each of the questions prepared by the student.

L. An Exercise in Producing Effective Practice and Feedback

Check that the feedback meets the criteria specified in the exercise.

Chapter

12

Implementing Instruction

OVERVIEW

Part One of this book presents a decision making procedure for novices (Figure 2.1) developing instruction using the ISD approach. In Part II this procedure is incorporated in a more elaborate model for experts (Figure 7.11). Both of these models, the Seels & Glasgow ISD Model I: For Novices and the Seels & Glasgow ISD Model II: For Practitioners, include a step called implementation. We present both models so that beginning designers and designers who prefer a linear approach can use one. Once novice designers know the essentials of ISD, they can progress to the more realistic and less linear model, the one for practitioners.

For the ISD project to be successful a course must be implemented as intended. This means that the proper support in terms of admissions, time, facilities, materials, equipment, and instructors must be provided. It is the job of the designer or the design team to specify the requirements for implementation. Because problems often arise during implementation, this phase must be monitored. The client must be ready to take responsibility for the course. It takes time for people to accept new materials and methods and to use them effectively.

Implementation, then, is the process of installing the project in the real world context. To do this, the environment and other variables must be managed. Implementation can involve training teachers and administrators, planning for resource allocation, and developing maintenance systems. Only after implementation is successful can the effectiveness of the project be determined. An expansion of the steps of implementation and summative evaluation are shown in Figure 12.1.

There are at least four major steps necessary to implementing instruction and determining its effectiveness: ensuring diffusion of the innovation, planning for implementation, evaluating summatively, and disseminating information about the project. Diffusion means others adopt your ISD project. Diffusion of the innovation requires that a climate for acceptance, trial, and maintenance of the project is created. This is done by using a variety of strategies to involve people with the project throughout the process. Diffusion requires attention to to characteristics of the innovation and to phases, personalities, and strategies from the earliest steps in the process through the last steps. If you are successful in diffusion, the project will be implemented and maintained. If you are not, there may be a trial period, but the project will be discontinued relatively quickly.

Figure 12.1   The Step of Implementation and Maintenance in the ISD Process

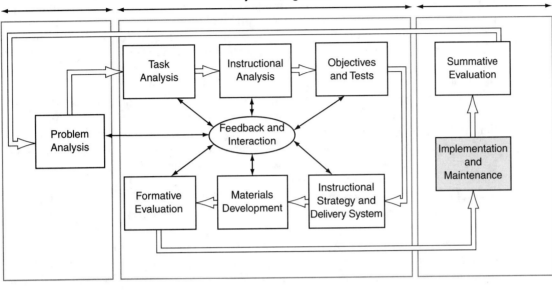

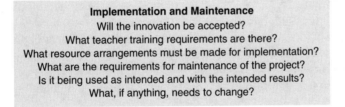

Implementation and Maintenance
Will the innovation be accepted?
What teacher training requirements are there?
What resource arrangements must be made for implementation?
What are the requirements for maintenance of the project?
Is it being used as intended and with the intended results?
What, if anything, needs to change?

When you develop a diffusion plan you have to be concerned primarily about what communication strategies to use. The choice of strategies, however, depends on the stage in adoption and the personalities of the people selected to diffuse the innovation. A diffusion plan should use communication channels and opinion leaders effectively. Begin diffusion planning by identifying whom you want to communicate with and why. The next step is to select communication strategies for each of the stages in diffusion: knowledge, persuasion, decision, implementation, and confirmation (Rogers, 1995). The phases or stages can also be described as awareness, interest, trial, and adoption. An adopter who goes through each stage will be more likely to maintain the adoption. At the initial stage, sending printed materials or using mass media can be effective, but such measures will be less effective at later stages. To move people further towards adoption, you need to offer a strategy, such as a pilot test, demonstration, or work session, that involves them. Consider who talks to whom, especially through informal channels, and who controls access to resources and users because you must have their support for some of the strategies. Informal channels, such as social groups, are often more powerful than formal channels, such as committees. Allow enough time for many communication strategies.

The step of implementation requires determining the budget needed for maintenance and training requirements. The implementation and maintenance requirements of a self-paced course differ from those of a group-paced course, although the categories of concern are similar. A course or program must have a plan for administration and staff development in order for implementation to proceed smoothly. Administration plans typically include registration, scheduling, record-keeping, personnel assignment, reporting, acquisition or allotment of equipment and facilities, and acquisition and distribution of materials. Staff development plans include instructor training and administrative staff training. At this point a realistic budget can be prepared for implementation and maintenance. Once implemented, a maintenance plan ensures quality through staff competencies, equipment, and materials. A plan for updating content as changes occur in the field will also maintain quality.

After the course has been implemented, summative evaluation can be conducted. Summative evaluation is for the consumer. Formative evaluation gathers information that the developer will use in revising the system, whereas summative evaluation gathers information that will help potential users of the system decide whether to adopt it. Summative evaluation yields descriptive reports and conclusions about effectiveness. One aspect of summative evaluation is comparing cost effectiveness. Traditional instruction and the instruction developed by the ISD project may be equally effective in terms of student achievement, but the new instruction may be more cost effective, especially over time.

After the project is adopted, implemented, and evaluated summatively, the results should be disseminated to the client. Dissemination means informing others of your research results. There are few federally funded ISD projects that do not have a dissemination component.

ORIENTING QUESTIONS

How does one assure diffusion of the ISD project?
What preparations are required to successfully implement instruction?
How does one do summative evaluation?
What are cost effectiveness measures?
What should a final report on an ISD project cover?

OBJECTIVES

1. Given a completion question, you will be able to list the characteristics an innovation should have in order to enhance its potential for diffusion and define each characteristic listed.
2. Given phases of the diffusion process, you will be able to match appropriate strategies for communication.
3. Given costs, you will be able to amortize development, startup, and ongoing costs.
4. Given a form for budgeting for implementation, you will be able to complete the form for at least five appropriate categories or subcategories.
5. Given a form for budgeting for maintenance, you will be able to complete the form for at least five appropriate categories or subcategories.
6. Given statements of different types of evaluations, you will be able to distinguish between formative or summative evaluation.
7. Given completion questions, you will be able to classify the approach to summative evaluation or the type of effectiveness described.
8. Given research abstracts, you will be able to identify those that are examples of comparative experiments.
9. Given objectives for a summative evaluation, you will be able to conceptualize the associated outcomes, indicators, and data sources.
10. Given an outline of sections in a final report, you will be able to identify some of the missing elements in the outline.

DIFFUSION OF THE ISD INNOVATION

Schiffman (1995) describes ISD as a synthesis of theory and research including that related to diffusion skills. Her list of diffusion skills includes: relationship building, diagnosis, acquiring resources, choosing the solution, gaining acceptance, and generating capability for self-renewal. Garland (1996) lists the barriers to diffusion usually encountered by instructional technologists: cultural traditions, risk aversion, lack of knowledge, lack of user acceptance, cost, and infrastructure issues.

Rogers (1995) describes diffusion as: "the process by which an innovation is communicated through certain channels over time among the members of a social system. It is a special type of communication, in that messages are concerned with new ideas" (p. 5). The main elements in diffusion appear in this definition: innovation, communication, channels, time, and a social system.

Characteristics of the Innovation

The designer works at diffusion throughout the ISD project. He tries to develop an innovation that has characteristics that promote diffusion. If the new instruction is perceived as better than the previous instruction, it is said to have a *relative advantage*. Relative advantage is a characteristic of innovations that diffuse well. Another such characteristic is *compatibility* with existing values and norms of the social system. If the instruction as designed is incompatible with the client's values, it will be less likely to be adopted. For example, if instruction is designed for an open classroom and the community does not accept open classroom education, the ISD innovation will be incompatible. *Complexity* is also important. A complex innovation that is hard to understand or use is less likely to be adopted. If instruction is perceived as difficult or hard to use, it may be rejected. One always tries to develop user friendly instruction. Similarly, if instruction has high *trialability*, it is more likely to be adopted. Trialability means that it is easy to experiment with the instruction on a limited basis. This process can lead to more confidence in the innovation. Finally, an innovation which has high *observability* will be more likely to diffuse because it will be easily visible to others. The design team, therefore, needs to develop instructional innovations that have these characteristics.

Communication Strategies.   There are many ways to communicate with others about the project including providing them with literature, talking to them, asking for their help, taking them on a site visit, providing a demonstration, presenting a workshop on the project, and having them develop products for the project. The strategies used have to be appropriate for the people you wish to involve. For example, it is not advisable to ask the president of a corporation to adopt the innovation before sufficient awareness of and interest in the project is developed.

Communication Channels.   In order for people to become aware of the innovation, messages must be sent through channels. Both mass media and interpersonal channels are available. Although mass media channels can be used to inform many people quickly, the designer mainly uses the interpersonal communication strategies just described. In addition, the design team can use both formal and informal communication channels to diffuse the innovation. It is important to remember that informal channels are often stronger than formal channels and that it is usually better to use the informal channels.

Over Time.   Individuals are more likely to maintain an innovation if they go through all the stages of diffusion: awareness, interest, and trial.[1] During the awareness stage the

---

[1] In addition to the research of Everett Rogers (1995), the principles of diffusion presented here are based on the work of Michael Molenda of Indiana University at Bloomington, IN.

Table 12.1   Strategies for Different Stages in Diffusion

Stage	Effective Strategies for Specific Stages	Effective Strategies for Most Stages
Awareness	Distributing printed material, local mass media	Talking to people, asking for help, site visits
Interest	Presentations, pilot tests	
Trial	Demonstrations, workshops	

designer should talk to as many people as possible. Printed information is also a way to create awareness. For example, a brochure on the project could be created. To move people to the interest stage, more powerful communication strategies are needed. You can ask for help or provide demonstrations. One way to generate interest is to have clients visit the project and review materials under development. If you want to encourage diffusion through the trial stage, you need to involve potential users in focus groups, formative evaluation and planning for implementation. Table 12.1 suggests some communication strategies that are very effective for a stage in diffusion. This does not mean that the strategy can only be used at that stage.

A Social System.   All the individuals engaged in meeting the instructional goal through ISD (i.e., the clients, designers, developers, users) form a social system. It is important to remember that communication occurs within the structure of this social system. This means that there are networks by which communication occurs. A design team can encourage diffusion of the instructional innovation by communicating with opinion leaders (those who have the power or credibility to persuade others to accept the innovation). As a change agent (someone who is trying to bring about change) you will need the support of these people.

Exercises A and B provide practice on diffusion of innovations.

IMPLEMENTATION

Much of what we know about implementation comes from case studies. This means generalization to other situations is difficult because the variables may be very different. According to Ely (1995), "Implementation not only means that educational technology ideas have been diffused and accepted, but that there has been actual use of new media or technology in an educational setting" (p. 43).

Burkman (1987) sums up many designers' feelings about implementation:

> Do you want to see an instructional designer wince? Just ask to be shown a situation in which one of his or her design products is working as planned within an organization. Such a request almost always results in a blank stare or an evasive response. Standard evasive responses include giving a list of the constraints that prevented superior efforts from being implemented, gnashing of teeth over the incompetence of the people on the firing line that sabotaged some really noble project, or passing along a dusty example of a 10-year-old product along with a tale about how well it worked before being abandoned. (p. 429)

Burkman continues by saying that implementation is a critical problem for designers, especially for those who develop products for public schools. There is more attention to implementation and maintenance today than when Burkman wrote this statement because as resources become more precious we cannot afford large investments in projects that are not continued. The capability for continuation is an important criteria for many contracts now. Furthermore, we are far more aware of the need for characteristics such as user friendliness which facilitate diffusion, implementation, and maintenance or utilization.

Gentry (1994) includes diffusion activities plus implementation activities such as training and budgeting in a step he calls "product installation." He defines this step as the "process of establishing the necessary conditions for effective operation of a new instructional product or process when initially placed in a targeted system" (p. 177). He states, however, that adoption or diffusion techniques are also used earlier. Gentry's tasks for carrying out product installation are as follows:

1. Get agreement to support a new product or process from organization decision makers and gatekeepers.
2. Identify others in the target system who will be affected by the product's installation.
3. Convince others affected by the product's installation of its value.
4. Make sure that supporting structures required by the product are in place (e.g., policies, procedures, evaluation, and maintenance).
5. Make sure that the resources required by the product or process have been formally allocated.
6. Identify system personnel who will be teaching or managing the ongoing operation of the instructional product.
7. Provide training for teachers and/or managers (build training into the product, where possible).
8. Establish access to the appropriate instructional facilities for operation of the product's first use.
9. Support the instructors and managers during the first uses of the product in the client system. (pp. 178–179)

Gentry separates the ongoing operation (i.e., maintenance) of the product or process from product installation (i.e., implementation).

In order to prepare for implementation, the design team has to address training and budgeting. These topics have probably already been discussed during the needs analysis and project planning stages. It is unlikely a commitment has been made for financial support of the project without a discussion of hypothetical costs and savings to result from the project and product. Similarly, discussion of training requirements would have occurred when the project plan was developed. Based on agreed-upon assumptions, the client will have considered whether they could afford the project or not. Although these discussions have occurred, so far decisions about implementation have been hypothetical. This is the point at which planning becomes more realistic. Throughout the project adjustments have been made in the budget and product. Now you need to adjust your planning for implementation to reflect these changes. Our discussion of implementation will be divided into decisions that must be made about training and decisions that must be made about budgeting and resource allocation.

Training

The U.S. Department of Education compiled a database of 100 distance education projects in 1990. Over half of the projects offered teacher training or staff development (Ely, 1995). Because technological applications often involve unfamiliar procedures or equipment, training becomes an important part of implementation. Often there is a need to train management and staff as well as instructors.

A project at the Western Pennsylvania School for the Deaf provides an example of planning for both diffusion and the training component of implementation. After receiving a Buhl Foundation grant, the school began a major infusion of technology into the curriculum in 1993. The grant was for integrating multimedia technology into the science, English, and social studies curricula over a three-year period (Bernauer, 1995; 1996). The overall goals were to (a) establish an Interactive Technology Lab, (b) develop and apply interactive technology materials in three major content areas over a three-year period, (c) to integrate this technology fully into the curriculum process, (d) to provide release

Table 12.2   Development Team for Integrating Technology into the Curriculum Project at the Western Pennsylvania School for the Deaf

Year 1 (Science and English)	Year 2 (English and Social Studies)	Year 3 (Social Studies)
1 Science Teacher (consulting teacher)	1 Science Teacher (consulting teacher)	1 Science Teacher (consulting teacher)
1 English Teacher	1 English Teacher (lead teacher)	1 Social Studies Teacher (lead teacher)
1 Project Coordinator	1 Social Studies Teacher	1 English Teacher
	1 Project Coordinator	1 Project Coordinator

time for training on the technology, (e) to evaluate teacher concerns regarding such technology, and (f) to evaluate the effects of technology on student achievement and attitudes. To encourage continuity and a growing base of expertise within the school, the implementation spiraled from one year to the next. Thus, the development team for each year changed as shown in Table 12.2. A teacher who had received previous grants in this area was appointed consulting teacher. This plan provides a structure for diffusion, implementation, and training.

This plan allows for on-the-job training of teachers in time for them to be prepared to assume development and implementation responsibilities in their subject matter when the year focusing on their area arrives. The plan works because the teams are small enough to work efficiently and effectively with each member supporting the others. This is just one approach to training for implementation. It is called the peer-training approach (Gentry, 1994). Another approach to training is to use workshops for groups. This is often used when large numbers of teachers need to be trained.

In order to plan for training to implement the product, the designer needs to ask "Who will be trained, for how long, in what, how and why?" Like instructional material training materials and processes need to be tried out through formative evaluation. To make decisions about training you can use the same ISD processes you used to make decisions about the instruction to be implemented. For example, you can do a performance analysis to determine whether training is the only solution needed and the type of instruction warranted. It may be sufficient for the team to train a few teachers or staff using on-the-job training such as peer-training or a formal workshop may be required. You need to have objectives for the peer-training or workshop. It is important to provide support materials for those being trained, such as lesson plans, workshop outlines, and coordinator's or independent study manuals. The intent of the training should be that the instructors deliver the instruction as planned. You do not want an instructor to spend 10 minutes on a portion of the instruction that you planned to devote 40 minutes to covering. One way to avoid this situation is to train thoroughly.

Resource Allocation

In order to implement instruction and training, management must make a commitment to resource allocation. Requests for facilities, equipment, release time, and personnel must be approved. Some of this may already have been done according to the project plan. If not, it is time to reserve space, schedule events, and arrange for instructors. You are now at Stage III of project management. If ISD projects haven't been specified completely yet for this stage, now is the time to make sure all these tasks are accounted for in your project plan. You are probably planning for ongoing operation as well as initial implementation; therefore, you need to provide a relatively permanent facility that is adequate. You may have to modify as well as maintain the space. This means giving attention to the learning environment, security, policies, and staff needs. You will also have to consider supervision of instruction and facilities. To do all this you will need to fine-tune your budgeting. We turn, therefore, to budgeting techniques.

Budgeting

There are principles of budgeting that will help you communicate with your client. Some of these principles, such as amortizing and cost analysis, were discussed in chapter 5, "Selecting and Developing Delivery Systems."

Amortizing.   Instructional technology often has high development or delivery costs that are offset by use over a long period of time by many students. One way of illustrating that, in the long run, costs are justifiable is to amortize development and operating costs. Let's say that your development costs are $10,000 and it will cost $2,000 a year to deliver and maintain the system for five years. Each year 100 students will use the instruction. If you amortize the costs in your budget, the cost of instruction will be $20,000 for five years which can be divided by 500 students to make a per student cost of $40 including development and maintenance. If you do not amortize, you would tell the client that the cost per student would be $20 plus $10,000 for development.

Contingency Budgeting.   When you originally budgeted, you worked with estimated costs. At this point you should be able to develop actual costs to compare with projected figures. When you contingency budget you provide estimated figures that can be compared with more realistic figures. You must then adjust the budget to cost overruns and over-estimates. When you contingency budget, you provide some extra funds in the overall budget or specific categories, to allow you to adjust to differences between actual and estimated costs. For example, you may have budgeted $15,000 for computer equipment. The actual cost may be $20,000. By building an extra 10% into a budget of $50,000 you have provided a contingency that will cover the difference. This advantage is often offset by the need to propose a budget low enough to be awarded the contract.

Cost Analysis.   The most important job of the instructional designer in budgeting is to identify the categories of expenses that must be estimated. This function is often assumed by the project manager. The categories will differ from project to project because the technology and content will differ as will the setting and development team. Nevertheless, categories of expenses are associated with each step in the ISD process. Therefore, the designer or project manager can start budgeting by hypothesizing the cost of completing each task associated with a step. By Stage III of project management, though, realistic costs should be available and taken into account. Estimated costs can be compared with actual costs and the budget adjusted accordingly. Because the list of costs for each task can become unwieldy, and there are costs that are not specific to each task such as personnel who work throughout the project, after a task-based analysis is done, the budget is summarized into general categories. For example, these categories are typical of a simple ISD project budget: salaries, professional and non-professional, benefits, travel, supplies, consultants, communication, equipment, production, training, operation, and overhead. As you can tell from this list, it is sometimes difficult to decide where to list costs. Will salaries for trainers and operators be placed under salaries or under training? Will communication costs such as telephone, fax, and mail that are related to the development of instruction be placed under administrative communications or under production? Where will computer time be provided for in the budget? The answers to such questions vary depending on the project. It is important that the budget communicate what is included in a category clearly and that the categories encompass the costs of a project in the areas of development, implementation, and maintenance.

A major part of cost analysis is determining cost per unit and quantity of units required. If three instructors are to be paid $20 per hour for two hours of training, the unit cost is $20 and the quantity is two; butj320 the sum of 2 × $20 ($40) must be multiplied by

Table 12.3   An Example of a Budget for Implementation

Category	Unit Cost	Quantity	Total Cost
Training:			
Release time for 3 instructors	$20/hr	2 hrs × 3 instructors	$ 120
Expendables—			
coordinator's manual	$10/manual	3 manuals	30
handouts	$5/set	3 sets	15
Refreshments—			
coffee	$10		10
Paperware	$2		2
Bagels & cream cheese	$10		10
Juice	$3		3
Start-Up:			
Computer stations	$1,000/station	5 stations	5,000
Expendables—			
disks	$5/disk	5 disks	25
handouts	$10/set	30 sets	300
3 instructors	$20/hr	8 hrs × 3 instructors	480
Lab assistant	$10/hr	10 hrs	100
TOTAL			$6,095

three ($120). This is still not the total cost for instructor training, however. To this must be added any costs not covered elsewhere in the project such as the cost of the expendables used for training or the cost of renting training facilities.

An example of a budget for implementation is given in Table 12.3.

A budget for maintenance of the project once it was implemented would require some of the same categories and some other categories. Table 12.4 is an example of a budget for maintenance.

Table 12.4   An Example of a Course Maintenance Budget for a Year

Category	Unit Cost	Quantity	Total Cost
3 instructors	$2,000/term	3 terms	$ 18,000
Lab assistant	$200/term	3 terms	600
Supplies	$100/term	3 terms	300
Equipment	$200/term	3 terms	600
Handouts	$10/set	100 students	1,000
Disks	$5/disk	100 students	500
Maintenance	$500/term	3 terms	1,500
Communications	$200/term	3 terms	600
Administration	$200/term	3 terms	600
Overhead	$975/term	3 terms	2,925
TOTAL			$26,625

Implementation can be planned to include maintenance costs, or these costs can be presented separately.

Exercises C, D, and E provide practice on budgeting for implementation.

SUMMATIVE EVALUATION

After the project is implemented, it is important to arrange for summative evaluation. The reason for this is that the client and others interested in using the project need information on which to base decisions about adoption. It is not necessary for the designer to do the summative evaluation. In fact, the results are more credible if the design team does not do the summative evaluation because they are so involved they are less likely to be objective.

The purpose of formative evaluation was to intervene in the development process so that changes could be made. Summative evaluation has a very different purpose—to make statements about effectiveness. Sometimes the summative evaluation of one course can provide formative evaluation data for the next course (Kifer, 1995).

Summative evaluation addresses the question, "Have we solved the problem?" The purpose of the evaluation is to collect, analyze, and report findings on the summed effect of instruction to decision makers in the client organization. Summative evaluation may be undertaken to assess instructional effectiveness, efficiency, costs, acceptance, and long term benefits. The exact evaluation questions asked will depend on what decision makers want to know. The answers to the evaluation questions usually lead to conclusions about whether to continue the instruction or to change it in some way.

Sometimes the question may be comparative: "Do students taking the instruction learn more than students taking another type of instruction on the same subject?" Comparative research can be used to answer many questions about other program outcomes: "Does the instruction take less time to complete? Does it consume fewer resources? Does it cost less? Do end-users prefer it more?"

Decision makers may be interested in other results. Evaluators can look at end results by asking questions such as: "What percentage of the students taking the course reach mastery?" "What is the instruction costing us?" and "What are the long term benefits?" They may also compare before and after effects, e.g., "Has worker productivity improved as a result of the training?"

Summative evaluation takes place after implementation because at that phase end-users are often working through the problems of conducting a new course for the first time. Data collected at this time is highly suspect since it is unlikely to represent the course as it will eventually be delivered. The purpose of summative evaluation is to gather information about permanent effects, not the transient effects that are likely to be in place during implementation.

Measures Used in Summative Evaluation

There are three aspects of projects that are measured during summative evaluation: effectiveness, efficiency, and benefits. Each of these elements is measured differently.

Instructional Effectiveness.   Summative evaluation is similar to formative evaluation when it asks about levels of achievement of students taking the course. To do this the evaluator determines (a) the research objectives, (b) the research design, (c) the measurement instruments, (d) the data to be collected, and (e) the results to be analyzed so conclusions can be drawn. There are at least four areas that can be measured: cognitive learning, attitudes, performance, and organizational impact of learning effectiveness. Summative evaluation differs from formative evaluation in the way that questions are asked and the level at which the data is analyzed.

Summative evaluators are more global in their outlooks. They are interested in overall scores and grades on tests presented as group means and standard deviations. The purpose of summative evaluators differs from those of the instructional designers during formative evaluation where the focus is on diagnosing specific learning failures in order to improve the instruction.

An area of great interest currently is how to summatively evaluate programs that measure through the use of performance assessment with portfolios, seminars, performances, and exhibits. According to Johnson (1996a, 1996b), to do this, school districts have to establish standards and develop criteria and rubrics. Documentation must also be collected through triangulation, that is from at least three sources. Johnson urges districts to involve both students and teachers in the development of these standards and criteria.

Instructional Efficiency.   Measures of instructional efficiency are the time to complete the instruction, the number of faculty and support staff needed to implement the instruction, and the facility and equipment needs. Time to complete the program is usually associated with some sort of self-instructional materials where there are individual differences in completion rates. Completion time is less applicable to traditional programs designed in terms of classroom periods or semesters where time in class is fixed. The less time taken to achieve the objectives, the more efficient the program is judged to be.

Efficiency is also measured by the level of effort required to implement the program. Level of effort translates into how many faculty members, administrators, and support staff are needed. Use of facilities is also a measure of efficiency. Evaluators may look at the number of hours the facility is available, as well as the number of students using the facility. Outcomes from evaluations of efficiency can lead to decisions to narrow or expand the use of the program.

Benefits of Instruction.   The benefits of instruction are often harder to evaluate than other aspects of a program. Evaluating benefits means having clear objectives about what the program is intended to achieve then collecting data from sources directly associated with the program (students, faculty, administrators, etc.) or indirectly associated with the program (the community, the family, the workplace) to ascertain whether the benefits were achieved.

You are probably already familiar with the indicator approach to determining benefits. Mass media reports on the best places to live, the best places to raise a family, the best graduate programs and undergraduate colleges or universities are all examples. In each of these examples, a series of indicators of best in a category was developed, and final determination was based on all of these indicators. In instructional systems design the indicators are used to determine success of instruction rather than the best in a category.

Another type of benefit analysis is a cost effectiveness study. One way to do such a study is to compare the costs of two treatments. The cost of instruction can also be compared with indicators, such as increase in productivity.

Approaches to Summative Evaluation

The literature suggests that there are at least four approaches to summative evaluation: expert judgement, operational tryout, comparative experiment, indicators, and cost benefit analysis. The next section will elaborate on each of these approaches.

Expert Judgment.   Dick and Carey propose expert judgment as one basis for deciding whether the instruction will meet an organization's defined needs (Dick & Carey, 1996;

Carey & Dick, 1991). Experts are advised to render judgments based on four strategies for evaluation:

1. evaluating the congruence between the organization's instructional needs and the candidate instruction;
2. evaluating the completeness and accuracy of the candidate instruction;
3. evaluating the instructional strategy contained in the candidate instruction;
4. evaluating the utility of the instruction; and
5. determining current users' satisfaction with the instruction. (Dick and Carey, 1996, p. 323)

They recommend that expert judgment be used in conjunction with other approaches to summative evaluation.

Operational Installation.   After formative evaluation and revisions are completed, the course can be implemented in a field setting under actual conditions. The purpose of this field implementation is to collect data that will establish the effectiveness of the instruction with a target group of learners—in other words, with the intended audience in the intended setting. Installation in the field can provide information about learner and instructor attitudes, learning and performance, and resource and time requirements. This information is then conveyed to clients to help them make adoption and audience decisions.

Comparative Experiment.   This is another form of field implementation. The same information is collected using experimental and control groups. It allows the client to make decisions about the best form for instruction under clearly identified conditions.

Experimentation on learning involves the introduction of some new or untried element and evaluating its effects. The experiment is designed to determine whether a direct relationship exists between the introduction of the new element and the learning outcome. This determination is accomplished by comparing groups that differ with respect to the element being evaluated but are similar in all other relevant dimensions.

Assume, for example, that a researcher wishes to evaluate a new method for teaching spelling to third-graders. If the method is effective, the curriculum committee will introduce it into the entire school system. To evaluate the new method, the researcher constructs two matched groups of third graders typical of the school system. At the beginning of instruction, the groups are equal in spelling ability, intelligence, background, and attitudes toward school. The researcher uses the new method with Group A, the experimental group. The method currently employed in the school system is used with Group B, the control group. The researcher strives to ensure that, in terms of all factors that affect performance, administration of both methods is the same. (Class schedule and teaching staff, for example, may affect performance.) After a period of time judged reasonable to evaluate the teaching methods, the researcher tests both groups on the same spelling test, or a battery of tests may be used. Results are compared to determine whether there is a difference in the groups' spelling competencies. Given the outcome, the curriculum committee has a sound basis for deciding whether the expenditure of time and resources required to make the change is warranted. If the research is published, other school systems will look to it and to findings from related research to guide them in making curricular decisions.

Because there are so many variables that can affect learning, controlled experimental designs are difficult to implement. Results frequently are not consistent from one study to the next, and often no significant differences appear. Part of the difficulty can be explained by problems in the research design. Wilkinson (1980) cites minimal acceptable standards for comparative studies. These are the acceptance criteria:

1. Experimental and control groups must have at least 25 subjects.
2. Experimental and control groups are equal on all relevant dimensions. This is accomplished best by randomly selecting and assigning subjects from the same population to the experimental and control groups.

3. Both groups are taught by the same instructor (or comparable instruction).
4. Performance is measured by a testing instrument that is valid and reliable.
5. Test results are evaluated by acceptable statistical procedures.

The requirement for the same instructor has been modified to take into account newer technologies which may use other approaches to instruction such as simulation. To be comparable instruction must call for similar amounts of practice and be equally interesting. Today it is common to define the characteristics of the learners the groups were selected from so that conclusions can be reached about the type of learner who found the instruction effective.

Indicators.   An example of a summative evaluation effort may help you to understand the process. The mission of the Star Schools Program funded by the U.S. Office of Education is to improve access to instruction and instructional effectiveness in a wide range of subjects through the use of distance learning technologies. A number of studies were conducted to evaluate the Star Schools. The Office of Education structured their evaluation into the following components:

◆ Five major objectives were specified.

◆ Two to three outcomes were specified for each objective.

◆ Indicators associated with each outcome were specified. There were a total of 46 indicators.

◆ Data sources were specified for each indicator. These included surveys, interviews, reviews of school records, focus groups, and case studies.

Table 12.5 shows the relationship of these components for one of the program's objectives and two of its outcomes. The objective counts participation only. It does not consider what happens as a result of that participation. Indicators and the likely sources for the outcomes are given in columns four and five.

Cost Benefit Analysis.   As discussed previously in chapter 5 on delivery systems and in the preceding implemenation section, there are three types of costs associated with an instructional program:

◆ *Development costs to design and produce the instruction.* These costs run from the Analysis Phase of ISD through the Development Phase of ISD. The more complex the media, the higher the costs are likely to be.

◆ *Start-up costs.* These are one-time costs associated with the implementation phase of ISD. They include capital improvement costs, acquisition costs for equipment such as computers or simulators, staffing costs, and any other expenses associated with installing the course.

◆ *Operating costs.* These are the costs associated with running the course on a day to day basis. They include the salaries for faculty and administrators responsible for delivering instruction; student costs (most applicable in a business or government environment) including travel and lodging; the employee's salary while at training, the downtime or the cost of a replacement while the employee is being trained, etc.; direct costs for replacement of consumable supplies; overhead; and maintenance and repair costs.

Cost effectiveness is often looked at in terms of cost per student. High-technology delivery systems often translate into high development costs and high startup costs, but because they are usually self-instructional, the operating costs are often lower. Low-technology delivery systems may cost less to produce and implement but usually cost more to operate because they are dependent on faculty to deliver the instruction. There are also higher overhead costs associated with the need for classrooms and office facilities for faculty and administrative personnel.

Summative evaluation of a course across several measures—effectiveness, efficiency, and benefits including cost benefits—may reveal differences in some areas and

Table 12.5   Example of Performance Indicators for the Star Schools Program

1. Objectives	2. Outcomes	3. Indicators	4. Data Sources
Reach underserved learners of all ages throughout the U.S. and its affiliated territories.	A. The scope of the program includes different types of learning communities.	1. Number & characteristic of K–12 schools (urban, rural, suburban). Characteristics = grade levels, rural, urban, suburban, state.	School records, district records, registration forms, school principal/building administrator.
		2. Number and characteristic of other settings where learners participate in the program.	Case studies, interviews.
		3. Number and percentage of districts classified as Title 1.	
	B. Learners of all ages participate in the program.	4a. Number and percentage of K–12 students (ethnicity, socio-economic, grade level, gender, special needs, status-Title 1), teachers (ethnicity, level of experience), and others participating in the program.	School records, district records.
		4b. Total learners' program hours.	

Adapted from *The Star Schools Program: 1996 Reflections,* by C. Lane and S. Cassidy, 1996, Office of Education Research and Improvement, U.S. Department of Education.

not in others. For example, when traditional recertification courses in cardiopulmonary resuscitation (CPR) for nurses were compared with independent study through interactive video and a manikin with sensors, there was no difference in learning effectiveness. However, the interactive video format proved more efficient and cost effective (Aukerman, 1986).

Exercises F, G, H, and I provide practice in summative evaluation.

DISSEMINATION

After the project is adopted, implemented, and evaluated summatively, the results are disseminated to the client and other interested parties. Dissemination means informing others of the results of your developmental research. Richey (1996) explains the nature of developmental research and its products. Sometimes a final report is not necessary because deliverables or interim reports have been provided throughout the project. At other times, the contract calls for a final report that summarizes the activities and outcomes. This final report is often used to disseminate information about the project.

Project activities should be documented through record-keeping systems, correspondence, minutes of meetings, drafts, interim reports, and evaluation data. This is important for several reasons. First, expert designers keep complete records to use as a basis for being reflective about the process and project including their actions. Second, these records are a source of detail for reports to the client and other consumers. Third, if major revisions are made after summative evaluation, these records may be useful. The moral of the story is to keep everything throughout the project and after it finishes or until you are sure the materials won't be needed for case studies or revisiting the project.

It is helpful to develop a database for the project. Gentry (1994) suggests using any of several excellent database software programs "to store and retrieve ISD project information and to generate reports" (p. 302). He lists these tasks as essential to creating an ID project database:

1. Select appropriate database software
2. Determine database objectives
3. Design the database
4. Develop the database
5. Enter and edit the database records
6. Retrieve the records for deletion or alteration
7. Prepare to generate reports from the database
    a. Determine the objectives of the specific report
    b. Design the report: determine the records to be used; the form of the report . . . and the order in which records should be placed
    c. Develop the report
8. Generate reports from the database
9. Evaluate/edit the report
10. Evaluate the database (p. 303)

Sometimes it is difficult to separate dissemination from diffusion. For example, if a brochure about the project is printed, it can be used to promote awareness of the project which leads to diffusion, or it can be used to disseminate information about the project. Sometimes these functions overlap.

For your purposes, the most important aspect of dissemination is the final report for a client. The final report should explain why the project was done, how it was done, the results of the tryouts, and the recommendations for revision. If summative evaluation was done that should be reported too. The outline for a final report can vary depending on the project, the writer, and the client. Figure 12.2 presents one outline for a final report on an ISD project.

In the instructional strategy section it is helpful to include a flowchart showing the order of events in instruction, including evaluation activities. If you include an appendix, refer to it in the text and label it. If there are many appendices, you can group several under one label by category. Be sensitive to protecting the privacy of some of the people involved, especially volunteers and clients.

Notice that this outline follows the Seels & Glasgow ISD Model II: For Practitioners in that it is divided to some extent by the stages of project management: (a) needs analysis; (b) design and development; and (c) implementation and summative evaluation.

An outline for a final report, then, can vary with the ISD model used. An outline based on the model for experienced designers is more extensive than an outline based on a model for novices. The outline can also be varied to suit the client. For example, a report to business or industry could emphasize cost effectiveness and use many relevant charts and graphs. A report to a health area such as nursing could use a research report approach since areas in the sciences are comfortable with experimental research. A report to schools could use a curriculum proposal approach. Regardless of the approach, you are required to incorporate the elements of developmental research, which include discussion of phases in a process, examples of evolution through revision, data on effectiveness, efficiency, and benefits. Of course, it is always important to be clear about goals, inputs, and outcomes.

Exercise J provides practice in dissemination.

Figure 12.2   An Example of an Outline for a Final Report

I. Statement of the problem

    A. What did the needs analysis indicate?

    B. What was proposed as a solution to the problem?

    C. How was task analysis done?

    D. What was the output of the instructional analysis?

    E. What diffusion strategies were used?

    F. How was this phase of the project managed?

II. Design

    A. Was a model or paradigm applied?

    B. What were the objectives?

    C. What assessment strategies were used?

    D. What instructional strategies were used?

    E. What delivery systems were selected?

    F. What diffusion strategies were used?

    G. How was this phase of the project managed?

III. Development

    A. How was the course developed?

    B. What strategies were used for formative evaluation?

    C. What revisions were made?

    D. What diffusion strategies were used?

    E. How was this phase of the project managed?

IV. Implementation and Maintenance

    A. What conditions are necessary for implementation?

    B. What conditions are necessary for maintenance?

    C. What teacher or instructor training is required?

    D. What are the results of summative evaluation?

    E. What plans are there for dissemination?

    F. What diffusion strategies were used?

    G. How was this phase of the project managed?

V. Appendices

    A. What instruments were used for data collection?

    B. What charts and graphs were generated and used?

    C. What sample materials illustrate the project?

◆ EXERCISES

A. An Exercise to Check Your Understanding of Characteristics of Innovations

List the characteristics an innovation should have in order to enhance its potential for diffusion. Then define each characteristic listed.

B. An Exercise in Matching Strategies for Communication with Stages in Diffusion

Although any of the communication strategies can be used at any of the stages of diffusion, a strategy is often more effective at one stage than another. Match the strategy most effective at that stage. Match one strategy with each stage.

Stages in Diffusion	Communication Strategies
_____ 1. Awareness	a. Offer a hands-on workshop
_____ 2. Interest	b. Circulate a memo
_____ 3. Trial	c. Talk to people
_____ 4. Most stages	d. Join a club
	e. Make a presentation

C. An Exercise to Provide Practice in Amortizing Costs

Development costs are $5,000 and per-year operating costs are $1000. The course will be used by 50 students a year for five years. What is the cost per student if development and operating costs are amortized? How much less is the figure if costs are not amortized?

D. An Exercise in Budgeting for Implementation

Complete the form shown in Table 12.6 for at least five appropriate categories or subcategories.

E. An Exercise in Budgeting for Maintenance

Complete the form shown in Table 12.7 for at least five appropriate categories or subcategories.

Table 12.6

Categories	Unit Cost	Quantity	Total Cost

Table 12.7

Categories	Unit Cost	Quantity	Total Cost

F. An Exercise to Help You Distinguish Summative Evaluation from Formative Evaluation

Read the following statements about evaluation practices. Put an "S" in front of the ones that refer to summative evaluation and an "F" in front of the ones that refer to formative evaluation.

_____ 1. The instructional designer observes individual students as they work through a computer based program.

_____ 2. The mean test scores of students taking a computer based program are compared with the mean test scores of students studying the same subject in a traditional classroom.

_____ 3. Based on feedback from the field regarding problems that airmen are having with certain maintenance tasks, the commander of an Air Force training wing tells the staff to revise a repair and maintenance course.

_____ 4. A three-day course designed for first-line supervisors is offered for the first time. Instructional designers monitor the course. They record performance data and debrief the participants at the end of each day. As a result, the designers decide that certain case study exercises need refinement before the course is fully implemented.

G. An Exercise in Classifying Approaches to Summative Evaluation and Types of Effectiveness

1. A field trial in which information is collected using experimental and control groups is called _____.
2. When the costs of instruction are weighed against the outcomes of instruction, the approach is called _____.
3. A final tryout conducted in a realistic setting with one large group is called _____.
4. Evaluating congruency, completeness, accuracy, instructional strategy, and user's satisfaction is using the _____ approach.
5. Evaluating learning achievement, learner attitudes and performance, and organizational impact is measuring instructional _____.
6. When indicators associated with outcomes and objectives are used it is likely evaluators are measuring the _____ of instruction.
7. Measures of time to complete instruction and resource needs are ways to determine instructional _____.

H. An Exercise in Distinguishing Comparative Experiments from Other Types of Research

Read the following research abstracts and check those that are examples of comparative experiments. For each item checked, name the variables being compared and the groups used in the experiment.

1. Three spatial tasks were created in two forms, as video and as computer graphics. Both forms of each task were presented to third graders, middle schoolers, and university students. Middle-schoolers and adults preferred working with the video, but were more accurate working with computer graphics. Third-graders preferred the computer, but were equally successful working with both displays. The study suggests that the expectations with which students approach an instructional technology may determine the effectiveness of that technology more than characteristics of the technology in question (Acker & Klein, 1986).

Variables compared:

Groups used:

2. College students wrote compositions that elicited their technical knowledge of three topics. Then they completed a questionnaire that assessed which of four informational sources had contributed to their knowledge of the topics—formal education, mass media, social interaction, and direct experience (Graesser, Hopkinson, Lewis & Bruflodt, 1984).

Variables compared:

Groups used:

3. Varying approaches to mathematics were explored in a philosophy of mathematics course. Students were asked which foundational schools they preferred and their preferences were compared with scores on hemispheric tests. The results indicate that preferences may be related to the brain's hemispheres (Fidelman, 1985).

Variables compared:

Groups used:

4. The purpose of this study was to determine the effects of various mastery criteria on student performance and attitude in a course in which mastery strategies were employed. Undergraduates in an introductory course in educational psychology were randomly assigned to one of three treatments—one in which mastery criteria were gradually increased from 70% to 90%, a second in which mastery criteria gradually decreased from 70% to 90%, or a third in which mastery criteria remained constant at 80%. Results indicated that although the high mastery criterion (90%) had a positive effect on some aspects of quiz performance, it had no effect on final examination performance. Results also indicated that students preferred mastery criteria to remain constant during a semester. When examined in light of previous research, these findings call into question some prior notions regarding the levels at which mastery criteria should be set (Reiser, Driscoll, Farland, Vengara, & Tessmer, 1986).

Variables compared:

Groups used:

5. Ideas on teaching-learning theory of ratio are presented. Views of children and of members of an international panel are presented, and five questions and their responses are compared with real classroom experience (Streefland, 1984).

Variables compared:

Groups used:

I. A Group Exercise to Help You Conceptualize Elements of a Summative Evaluation Plan

As Table 12.5 illustrated, one way to do summative evaluation is to identify indicators of success in achieving the objectives. Using the objectives from the Star Schools Program, the group should discuss the associated outcomes, indicators, and data sources that could be used for summative evaluation. Then, the group should complete Table 12.8 by listing these items opposite the appropriate objective.

Table 12.8

1. Objectives	2. Outcomes	3. Indicators	4. Data Sources
1. Expand instruction in core subject areas as well as literacy skills in vocational education.			
2. Provide professional development that is sustained over a period of time.			
3. Employ a variety of electronic technologies and tools for distance education.			
4. Foster partnerships.			
5. Demonstrate improved cost-benefit ratio.			

Adapted from *The Star Schools Program: 1996 Reflections,* by C. Lane and S. Cassidy, 1996, Washington, DC: Office of Education Research and Improvement, U.S. Department of Education.

J. An Exercise in Organizing a Final Report

Identify some of the missing topics and subtopics in this outline for a final report.

Design
>Model or paradigm
>Objectives
>Assessment
>Instructional Strategies
>Management Strategies

Implementation
>Conditions for Implementation
>Conditions for Maintenance
>Summative Evaluation
>Plans for Dissemination

Appendices

◆ REFERENCES

Acker, S. R., & Klein, E. L. (1986). Visualizing spatial tasks: A comparison of computer graphic and full-band video. *Educational Communications and Technology Journal, 34*(1), 21–30.

Aukerman, M. E. (1986). *Effectiveness of an interactive video for CPR recertification of registered nurses.* Unpublished doctoral dissertation, University of Pittsburgh, Pittsburgh, PA.

Bernauer, J. A. (1995, April). *Integrating technology into the curriculum: First year evaluation.* Paper presented at the Annual Meeting of the American Educational Research Association, San Francisco, CA.

Bernauer, J. A. (1996). The power of partnering. *T.H.E. Journal: Technological Horizons in Education, 24*(3), 71–73.

Burkman, E. (1987). Factors affecting utilization. In R. M. Gagné (Ed.), *Instructional technology: Foundations* (pp. 429–455). Hillsdale, NJ: Lawrence Erlbaum Associates.

Carey, L. M., & Dick, W. (1991). Summative evaluation. In L. J. Briggs, K. L. Gustafson, M. H. Tillman (Eds.), *Instructional design: Principles and applications* (2nd ed.), (pp. 269–314). Englewood Cliffs, NJ: Educational Technology Publications.

Dick, W., & Carey, L. (1996). *The systematic design of instruction* (4th ed). New York: HarperCollins College Publishers.

Ely, D. P. (1995). Trends in educational technology 1991. In G. J. Anglin (Ed.), *Instructional technology: Past, present, and future* (2nd ed.), (pp. 34–58). Englewood, CO: Libraries Unlimited.

Fidelman, U. (1985). Hemispheric basis for school in mathematics. *Educational Studies in Mathematics, 16,* 59–74.

Garland, K. P. (1996). Diffusion and adoption of instructional technology. In G. J. Anglin (Ed.), *Instructional technology: Past, present, and future* (2nd ed.), (pp. 282–287). Englewood, CO: Libraries Unlimited.

Gentry, C. G. (1994). *Introduction to instructional development: Process and technique.* Belmont, CA: Wadsworth Publishing.

Graesser, A. C., Hopkinson, P. L., Lewis, E. W., & Bruflodt, H. A. (1984). The impact of different information sources on idea generation: Writing off the top of our heads. *Written Communication, 1,* 341–364.

Johnson, B. (1996a). *The performance assessment handbook: Volume 1: Portfolios and seminars.* Princeton, NJ: Eye on Education.

Johnson, B. (1996b). *The performance assessment handbook: Volume 2: Performances and exhibitions.* Princeton, NJ: Eye on Education.

Kifer, E. (1995). Evaluation: A General View. In G. J. Anglin (Ed.), *Instructional technology: Past, present, and future* (2nd ed.), (pp. 384–391). Englewood, CO: Libraries Unlimited.

Lane, C. & Cassidy, S. (1996). *The Star Schools Program: 1996 reflections.* Washington, DC: Office of Educational Research and Improvement, U.S. Department of Education.

Reiser, R. A., Driscoll, M. P., Farland, D. S., Vergara, A., & Tessmer, M. C. (1986). The effects of mastery criteria on student performance and attitude in a mastery-oriented course. *Educational Communications and Technology Journal, 34,*(1), 31–38.

Richey, R. C. (1996). Developmental Research. In D. H. Jonassen (Ed.), *Handbook of research on educational communications and technology.* New York: MacMillan.

Rogers, E. M. (1995). *Diffusion of Innovations* (4th ed.). New York: The Free Press.

Schiffman, S. S. (1995). Instructional systems design: Five views of the field. In G. J. Anglin, *Instructional technology: Past, present, and future* (2nd ed.), (pp. 131–144). Englewood, CO: Libraries Unlimited.

Streefland, L. (1984). Search for the roots of ratio: Some thoughts on long term learning process (towards . . . a theory). Part I: Reflections on a teaching experiment. *Educational Studies in Mathematics, 15,* 327–348.

Wilkinson, G. L. (1980). *Media in instruction: 60 years of research.* Washington, DC: Association for Educational Communications & Technology.

◇ ANSWERS

A. An Exercise to Check Your Understanding of Characteristics of Innovations

Characteristic	Definition
Relative Advantage	when new instruction is perceived as better than previous instruction
Compatibility	when new instruction is compatible with existing values and norms of the social system
Complexity	when instruction is perceived as difficult, it is less likely to be adopted
Trialability	when it is easy to experiment with instruction on a limited basis
Observability	when instruction is easily visible to others

B. An Exercise in Matching Strategies for Communication with Stages in Diffusion

1. b
2. e
3. a
4. c

C. An Exercise to Provide Practice in Amortizing Costs

If costs are amortized, the per student cost is $40. If they are not, the cost per student is $20 less or $20 plus $5000 in development costs.

D. An Exercise in Budgeting for Implementation

Check your answer against Table 12.3.

E. An Exercise in Budgeting for Maintenance

Check your answer against Table 12.4.

F. An Exercise to Help You Distinguish Summative Evaluation from Formative Evaluation

1. F
2. S
3. S
4. F

G. An Exercise in Classifying Approaches to Summative Evaluation and Types of Effectiveness

1. comparative experimentation
2. cost benefit analysis
3. field implementation
4. expert judgment
5. effectiveness
6. benefits
7. efficiency

H. An Exercise in Distinguishing Comparative Experiments from Other Types of Research

1. Variables compared: Video vs. computer graphics
   Groups used: Third-graders, middle schoolers, and university students
2. Variables compared: Formal education vs. mass media vs. social interaction vs. direct experience
   Groups used: College students
3. Variables compared: Learner preferences and hemispheric dominance
   Groups used: Mathematics students
4. Variables compared: Mastery criteria that increased vs. mastery criteria that decreased vs. mastery criteria that remained constant
   Groups used: Undergraduates in an introductory course in educational psychology randomly assigned to each treatment
5. Variables compared: Informational presentation and classroom experience
   Groups used: Not clear

I. A Group Exercise to Help You Conceptualize the Elements of a Summative Evaluation Plan

A partial list of how the U.S. Office of Education conceived of some of the elements is shown in Table 12.9. Your group probably thought of many more.

J. An Exercise in Organizing a Final Report

The following sections are missing from the report:

Statement of the Problem
    Needs Analysis
    Proposed Solution to the Problem
    Task Analysis
    Instructional Analysis
    Diffusion Strategies
    Management Strategies

Design
    Diffusion Strategies
    Delivery Systems

Development
    How Developed?
    Formative Evaluation
    Revisions
    Diffusion Strategies
    Management Strategies

Implementation
    Instructor Training
    Diffusion Strategies
    Management Strategies

Appendices
    Instruments
    Charts and Graphs
    Sample Materials

Table 12.9

1. Objectives	2. Outcomes	3. Indicators	4. Data Sources
1. Expand instruction in core subject areas as well as literacy skills in vocational education.	A variety of sources are offered that had not been available.	Number and types of courses provided to participants (by educational institution) including K–12 students (by grade/group), adult learners, educators, parents, and community members.	School records, project director interviews.
2. Provide professional development that is sustained over a period of time.	Teachers and other educators participate in staffing development activities.	Number of people who completed a program (which may consist of several programs or modules) and number of people who enroll in future programs. Reasons for noncompletion.	Program providers, school records (difficult but maybe impossible to access during interviews).
3. Employ a variety of electronic technologies and tools for distance education.	a. Project uses a variety of electronic technologies and tools in providing distance education. b. Schools use a variety of electronic technologies and tools while participating in distance education.	a. Number and types of distance education technologies used by projects. b. Number of schools acquiring technology through Star Schools sources within the last 10 years.	a. Project records b. School and project records.
4. Foster partnerships.	Partnerships include a variety of entities.	Number, type, and role of entities in the telecommunication partnerships	Project records, interviews of project directors.
5. Demonstrate improved cost-benefit ratio.	Determination of project costs.	Determine fixed and variable costs.	Project records, district/school records.

Adapted from *The Star Schools Program: 1996 Reflections,* by C. Lane and S. Cassidy, 1996, Washington, DC: Office of Education Research and Improvement, U.S. Department of Education.

Glossary

The glossary that follows includes only the key terms used in this book. It is not intended to be an exhaustive list of the terms used by instructional designers or of multiple meanings of terms. This list can be used in conjunction with glossaries for specialized areas, such as *delivery systems*, which require more pages than are available for this text. Terms are defined as they are used in this book.

ABCD   Format for writing behavioral objectives. Objectives that describe the audience, behavior, condition, and degree. Mnemonic for remembering the components of a behavioral objective.

Acquisition   Knowledge or procedures are learned and stored in long-term memory.

Activity Planning   Detailed and specific project planning for parts of a larger effort. Includes assigning and scheduling tasks, arranging for information flow, specifying methods, and reviewing reports. See *Project Planning*.

ADDIE Model   A generic model extracted from common features of ISD models. Includes the steps of Analysis, Design, Development, Implementation, and Evaluation.

Affective Domain   A taxonomy for classifying objectives that deal with feelings, attitudes, and other indicators of emotionally-based behavior.

Amortizing   Basing cost analysis figures for ISD on total costs over years to obtain a per student cost.

Analysis   Collecting and analyzing data to determine needs, tasks and content, and instructional requirements. The process of defining what is to be learned. See *Needs Analysis, Task Analysis,* and *Instructional Analysis.*

Assessment   Estimating or judging the degree of learning. Can serve the functions of measuring, diagnosing or instructing. The information gained can be used for secondary functions such as formative evaluation or grading.

Attitudes   An acquired mental state that influences choices for personal action, such as preferences, avoidance, or commitment.

Audience Specialists   Instructors or teachers experienced with teaching the content.

Audiovisual Technologies   Ways to produce or deliver materials by using mechanical or electronic machines to present auditory or visual messages.

Authentic Assessment   Examining performance on "real" tasks rather than paper and pencil tasks. See *Performance Indicators*.

Behavioral Objective   Instructional objective which makes the expected behavior explicit by identifying the required behavior or performance conditions and criteria for acceptable performance.

Behavioral Statement   Describes learning outcomes in terms of observable student activity which indicates what was learned. Through this observable activity learning can be measured.

Behaviorism   A paradigm in instructional design that holds that learning occurs by reinforcement of stimulus-response bonds, also a school of psychology.

Channel   In media selection theory, the perceptual mode. In diffusion theory, the context, such as mass media or interpersonal communication. In either case, the means for delivering the message.

Channel Characteristics   Perceptual mode requirements (i.e., audio, visual, kinesthetic, tactile, olfactory) for presentation, practice, and feedback. In the Seels and Glasgow Model for Selection of Delivery Systems, these characteristics are used to determine task requirements.

Cluster Diagram   A drawing that graphically indicates the relationship among terms or facts.

Cognitive Domain   A taxonomy for classifying objectives that deal with verbal knowledge and intellectual skills such as concept learning and procedural skills.

Cognitive Science   A paradigm in instructional design which is devoted to the study of how individuals acquire, process, store, and use information. Also a school of psychology.

Cognitive Strategy   An internally organized cognitive skill that allows learners to control their learning and thinking.

Communication Channels   Messages are sent through channels. In the Diffusion of Innovation Theory, channels are mass media or interpersonal communication and formal or informal.

Communication Strategies   Ways to communicate with others such as providing literature, asking help, or demonstrating.

Comparative Experimentation   Information is collected during field implementation from both experimental (treatment) and control (nontreatment) group.

Computer-based Technologies   Ways to produce or deliver materials using microprocessor-based resources.

Concrete Concepts   Identifying instances of a class of objects having common physical features.

Consensus   A method for reaching agreement during group or teamwork. Discussion continues until all ideas are accepted, rejected, or revised by the group as a whole. Usually requires compromise as a conflict management strategy. Does not always lead to the best decisions.

Consistency   A requirement for reliability. Single items are insufficient to determine reliability. If a student answers several items that address the same competency correctly, the answers are said to be consistent.

Constraints   Limitations that must be taken into account.

Constructivism   A school of psychology which holds that learning occurs because personal knowledge is constructed by an active and self-regulated learner who solves problems by deriving meaning from experience.

Contextual Analysis   Information is gathered about learner characteristics, the instructional environment, and the organizational situation related to pre-instruction, instruction, and post-instruction.

Cost Analysis   Estimating costs for an instructional systems design project including development, startup, and ongoing costs.

Cost Benefit Analysis   Collecting data on the cost to achieve program objectives. A process designed to identify preferred options by weighting costs against benefits.

Covert Response   Mental practice or internal response. A covert response, such as thinking of an answer, mentally practicing a verbal chain, or silently selecting the correct answer from a series of options, is not observable; however, mental processing can be inferred from overt responses.

Criterion Item   An assessment item designed to determine the extent to which the learner meets standards for achieving the objective (criterion). These may be embedded throughout instruction or in post-tests. Response to items are compared with an objective standard.

Criterion Practice   When practice occurs under the same conditions as the final test. The purpose is to determine whether a student is ready to take the final test, or whether remediation is necessary.

Criterion-Referenced Text   Assessment instrument used to determine whether the learner has mastered prespecified content; measures performance against a predetermined standard.

Cues   Part of a stimulus that directs attention to key features. May consist of graphic devices such as arrows, underlining, highlighting, or auditory signals, such as vocal emphasis and sounds.

Declarative knowledge   Verbally stable knowledge represented in the form of propositions.

Defined Concepts   Type of learning outcome that is part of Gagné's intellectual skills hierarchy. Classifying instances in accordance with a definition.

Delivery Systems   Ways to carry information from a source to a receiver or vice versa for the purpose of instruction. Delivery system options include print, audiovisual, computer-based, and integrated technologies. Synonymous with media.

Design   The process of specifying how learning will occur.

Development   The process of authoring and producing the materials.

Diffusion of Innovations   The process of communicating through planned strategies for the purpose of gaining adoption of an innovation.

Discrimination   A type of learning outcome which is part of Gagné's hierarchy of intellectual skills. Distinguishing one object from another.

Dissemination   Systematically making others aware of an innovation by circulating information.

Distance Learning Technologies   Delivery systems which permit instruction at points physically distant from the point of origin.

Document Review   Collecting information by examining written material, e.g., using manuals, books, information sheets, policy manuals, or job aids to analyze problems or tasks.

Embedded Items   Items which appear throughout instruction in order to judge achievement of a criterion. See *Criterion Item.*

Enabling Objective   Subobjectives. Prerequisite learning requirements stated in behavioral format. Differs from an instructional activity in that it must be assessed.

Entry Behavior Behaviors that will be required prerequisites because they will not be addressed during instruction.

Entry Level A dotted line on a hierarchy indicates entry level. Behaviors below the line will be required prerequisites. Behaviors above the line will be addressed during instruction. See *Entry Behavior.*

Error Matrix Method for recording data from test assessments. One axis of a table indicates the numbers of items on a test and the other axis indicates student names or codes. Each cell shows whether the student responded to the item correctly or not. See *Item Matrix.*

Evaluation The process of determining the adequacy of instruction and learning.

Feedback Responses to student responses. Information about errors in responses.

Flowchart Visual representation of procedures for performing a task.

Formative Evaluation Gathering information on the adequacy of an instructional product or program, and then using this information as a basis for further development.

Gantt Chart A chart that shows part of a project plan. Tasks to be done are given on the vertical axis. Dates during the project are given on the horizontal axis. Cells show when each task will be done.

Gatekeeper A person who can control the dissemination and diffusion of an innovation by facilitating or blocking the flow of information or the success of communication.

Generic ISD Model An integrated set of steps that evolved from general systems theory into a basic ISD model known as the *ADDIE Model.* The steps are analysis, design, development, implementation, and evaluation.

Goal Analysis A procedure for deriving observable and measurable statements from general statements of intent (goals). Behavioral indicators of goals are listed. Each sub-behavior yields other sub-behaviors.

Goals General statements of intent.

Grouping The learning situation can be described as large group, small group, or independent study. One of several criteria for the selection of a delivery system.

Guidance The coaching and prompting that helps students perform correctly.

Hierarchy A graphic representation that organizes elements according to prerequisite relationships. It describes the path of experiences a learner must take to achieve any single behavior that appears in the hierarchy.

Implementation The process of installing the innovation in the real world.

Innovations Something new or altered. In the case of ISD: projects, programs, environments, materials, and delivery systems.

Input/Action/Output Chart A chart with three columns—one for input, one for action, and one for output. It can be used to show a chain of behavior by repeating the output as input or a non-chain series of behaviors, in which case the input and output are not repeated. Used to record data during task analysis.

Instructional Analysis An analysis of tasks to determine the types of learning involved and ascertain their prerequisite relationship in order to verify a sequence for learning. Presented graphically through flowcharts, hierarchies, or cluster diagrams.

Instructional Design An area of theory and practice that forms a knowledge base in the field of instructional technology. Processes for specifying conditions for learning.

Instructional Designer An instructional technologist who makes decisions about specifications for conditions for learning. A designer can assume the role of a researcher or a practitioner.

Instructional Effectiveness Levels of achievement of students that indicate cognitive learning, attitudes, performance, and organizational impact.

Instructional Efficiency   Measure of time to complete the instruction and resources needed, e.g., faculty, equipment, facilities, and staff. The level of effort required to implement the program.

Instructional Environment   The context in which instruction and learning will take place.

Instructional Events   Actions that an instructional designer prescribes to gain and maintain the students' attention, to present new information so that it builds on existing cognitive structures, and to provide opportunities for practice and feedback. Events such as introduction, presentation, practice, and feedback that are controlled by instruction.

Instructional Formats   Level of instruction required such as formal courses, refresher courses, and on-the-job training.

Instructional Paradigms   A model or pattern for the ideas of a school of psychology as they relate to instruction. See *Learning Paradigms.*

Instructional Problem   A problem involving deficiencies in knowledge, skills, or attitudes. Can be solved by instruction.

Instructional Setting   The physical, social, and cultural factors that characterize the environment in which instruction takes place.

Instructional Systems Design (ISD)   An organized procedure for developing instruction that includes the steps of analyzing (defining what is to be learned), designing (specifying how the learning should occur), developing (authoring or producing the materials), implementing (using materials or strategies in context), and evaluating (determining the adequacy of instruction).

Instruments   Assessment device such as a test, attitude inventory, or checklist, used to measure learning or opinions.

Integrated Technologies   Ways to produce and deliver materials that encompass several forms of media under the control of a computer.

Integrity of the Design   Specified objectives are met consistently in development. The designer can ensure this by monitoring steps, participating in decision making, and assuming roles that strengthen the likelihood that quality will be maintained.

Intellectual Skills   Symbolic knowledge, such as concepts, procedures, principles, and rules, that requires transfer of prerequisite learning before higher levels of learning can be achieved. Intellectual skills are a type of learning outcome that requires understanding relationships. Gagné's hierarchy of intellectual skills proceeds from discrimination to concrete concept to defined concept to rule using.

Interactive Instruction   Instruction that requires frequent responding from the student as in computer-assisted instruction where information is presented, a question or problem is posed for the student to answer, and feedback is given. Also, a system designed to permit learners to influence variables in instruction, such as sequence and content, because they become active participants.

Interactive Multimedia   An integrated technology consisting of a collection of media sources in digitized form that allows the user to interact with the media and determine the direction of the program or presentation.

Internal Review   A step in formative evaluation during which a variety of knowledgeable people review the instruction and provide comments and criticism.

ISD Models   Graphic representation of a systematic approach to the design and development of instruction.

ISD Practitioner   An instructional designer who is interested in applying research and theory in the development of methods and materials.

ISD Process   An orderly process for the development of instruction.

ISD Researcher   An instructional designer who is interested in studying variables and developing theories related to instruction.

ISD Steps   Stages in the ISD process that fulfill different functions. These stages vary depending on the ISD model.

ISD Teams   Group undertaking the task of design and development. The team usually includes a variety of expertise. Changes in team membership depend on where you are in the ISD process.

Item Matrix   Synonymous with *Error Matrix*.

Iterative   Repeating a step. Returning to steps throughout the ISD process or doing steps concurrently (i.e., going back and forth continually).

Job Performance Aids   A tool that assists workers in performing parts of their job by minimizing the need for recall. Also called "job aids." In print form, often presents procedures through graphical display.

Kinesthetic   The channel of motion or movement. Related to task requirements, one of the criteria for selection of delivery systems.

Learned Capabilities   Synonym for Gagné's learning outcomes. Each learned capability has an associated verb that is used in an instructional objective to signify the learning outcome. The capability verbs are discriminates, identifies, classifies, demonstrates, generates, adopts, states, executes, and chooses.

Learner Characteristics   Those facets of the learner's experimental background that impact the effectiveness of the learning process.

Learning   A relatively permanent change in a person's knowledge, behavior, or attitudes due to experience.

Learning Paradigms   Synonymous with instructional paradigms that describe principles of schools of psychology. See *Instructional Paradigms*.

Level of Objectives   Types of objectives which serve different functions. They are organized from general to specific, e.g., program objectives, course objectives, unit objectives, lesson objectives, or sub-objectives.

Levels of Planning   Planning is laying out a course of action in order to accomplish a specific end. Planning in an organization takes place on different levels: strategic, operations, project, and activity. Each level serves a different function.

Listening Skills   The ability to be an active learner because one asks questions for amplification or clarification and paraphrases or summarizes.

Mager and Pipe Performance Analysis   Procedure used to determine to what extent a problem can be solved by instruction and what instructional formats are required. Summarized in a flowchart used to determine instructional and non-instructional aspects of a problem.

Maintenance Functions   Attitudes that foster group stability and satisfaction. Teamwork competencies not directly related to achieving the group's goals; rather, they are the attitudes and behaviors directed toward group stability and making sure individual members are satisfied. Includes being an encourager of participation, a communication facilitator, a tension reliever, a process observer, an interpersonal problem solver, and a supporter and praiser.

Management Skills   The ability to plan for project management and to lead ISD project teams. Requires clarifying tasks, procedures, and schedules, and identifying and obtaining resources. Results in clear specification of roles, tasks, objectives, and deadlines.

Motor Skills   Consists of the execution of goal-directed muscular movements, characterized by smoothness and precise timing.

Needs Analysis   The process of problem analysis. Encompasses needs assessment, performance analysis, and contextual analysis.

Needs Assessment   A systematic process for determining goals, identifying discrepancies between goals and status quo, and establishing priorities for action.

Norm-referenced Test   Comparing test scores with those of other learners in order to determine achievement.

Observable Behaviors   Statements of behavior that can provide evidence of learning.

On-the-job Training   Instruction provided in a workplace setting by a supervisor or peer. Suitable for easy to learn content and where assistance is available.

Operational Tryout   Materials are tried out under conditions that simulate those of the actual instructional environment.

Operations Planning   Translating issues, needs, problems, and opportunities into specific goals and objectives and establishing the time frames for achieving these goals and objectives.

Organizational Elements Model   A model classifying needs using five elements that relate means to ends and the individual to organizations and society.

Organizational Support   A category that addresses resources available for developing, monitoring, and diffusing instruction, e.g., rewards for learning.

Overt Response   Response, (such as writing an answer, performing a procedure, or repeating a word or phrase) that is observable.

Performance   Applying learning in order to demonstrate a skill or procedure.

Performance Indicator   Way to assess performance, such as examination of products, observation of process, and review of portfolios and projects. Measure of a student's ability to do something.

Portfolio   A purposeful and integrated collection of a student's work showing progression. Includes self-reflection on extent to which performance standards are met.

Post-assessment   Assessment done after instruction such as post-tests used to add reliability to embedded items.

Post-instructional Environment   The stage in instruction when transfer to real life settings takes place. Context for learning at this stage includes environmental cues, incentives, and opportunities for use.

Practice   To perform an activity repeatedly for the purpose of acquiring skill or proficiency.

Pre-assessment   Assessments used prior to instruction, such as pre-tests.

Pre-instructional Environment   The context in which planning for instruction takes place. Affected by variables such as learner perceptions, attitudes, and background.

Presentation   A routine instructional event that provides stimuli for learning.

PROBE   Gilbert's approach to performance analysis. Consists of questions about two areas: behavioral repertoire and environment. Allows you to determine what part of the problem can be solved by instruction.

Problem Analysis   Step in the ISD process that includes needs assessment, performance analysis, and contextual analysis. The purpose of the step is to describe the problem, goals, priorities, learners, constraints, and resources. See *Needs Analysis.*

Problem Solving   A learning outcome that requires applying previous learning (i.e., of rules) to a novel situation.

Problem Statement   Summarizes the needs and solution you are proposing and the priorities you have identified.

Procedural Knowledge   Knowledge of how to do something. Such knowledge is dynamic and transforms information.

Process Objectives   Describe procedures for problem solving or other ways of doing things that students are to learn, such as a process for articulating issues.

Product   The outcome of a procedure is a product which is evaluated against a standard. Products can take many forms such as reports, charts, or dramatic performances.

Project Management   Involves planning, monitoring, and controlling instructional systems design projects.

Project Plan   Outlining the steps, staffing requirements, timelines, and resources required to achieve goals. Entails defining the project objectives and setting priorities.

Project Planning   Outlining the projects and resources required to achieve goals. Describing problems, proposed solutions, and priorities.

Prototype   An original exemplar of the design. Developed so that formative evaluation can occur. A version of a product in an unfinished form that can be used to test effectiveness and efficiency.

Psychomotor Domain   Area of learning associated with physical movement and skills.

Rapid Prototyping   Quick construction of a design approach in order to evaluate its effectiveness before full-scale development. Design and development of part of a product are often done concurrently.

Refresher Instruction   Providing formal practice opportunities from time to time in order to maintain standards, e.g., CPR recertification.

Reliability   Characteristic of a dependable measure. If the assessment is repeated the results will be the same. See *Consistency* and *Temporal Dependency*.

Resources   Sources of support for carrying out a design project or implementing instruction. Includes staffing, funding, physical facilities, equipment, and instructional materials needed to perform the work.

Retention   Remembering what was learned and maintaining learning in memory.

Rubric   Criteria presented in graphic form that enable an evaluator to give feedback that stimulates reflection.

Rule Using   Type of learning outcome. Appears at the highest levels of Gagné's intellectual skills hierarchy. Demonstrating the application of a regular relationship between classes of objects. Combining concepts to make principles and rules.

Script   For print technologies, written dialogue. For audiovisual technologies, a written version of the narration (audio) and shots (visual) in the order they will appear. For computer-based and integrated technologies, the screens with text and visuals in the order they will appear.

Seels & Glasgow ISD Model I: For Novices   A linear model that elaborates on the ADDIE model and presents a series of questions to cue the designer about decisions that must be made.

Seels & Glasgow ISD Model II: For Practitioners   A non-linear model that incorporates the Seels and Glasgow ISD Model I and adds to and elaborates on its steps. Provides for steps being done concurrently and continually. Presents a series of questions to cue the designer about decisions that must be made.

Small Group Tryouts   Groups of 2–10 students who experience the instruction during formative evaluation. Useful for estimating the duration of instruction because it is group-paced. This tryout does not have to occur in a real life setting.

Social System   Networks within which communication occurs. Individuals, informal groups, or organizations engaged in joint problem solving to accomplish a common goal.

Storyboard   A way to represent audio and visual components. Gives directions for angles and distances and for shots and special effects.

Strategic Planning   People at the highest level in an organization look at trends in social, economic, and political spheres and assess their probable impact on the organization. A vision of directions the organization should take in the immediate future.

Subject Matter Expert (SME)   Person knowledgeable about the content of instruction. Consulted extensively during task analysis, but also used to review products from each phase of the ISD process.

Summative Evaluation   Involves gathering information on adequacy and using this information to make decisions about utilization.

Table of Specification   A blueprint for a test or assessment plan. Specifies content and learning outcomes to be assessed.

Target Audience   Intended learners and the characteristics that describe them.

Task Analysis   Step in ISD process where tasks and content are identified, and relevant data is collected.

Task Characteristics   Criteria for selection of delivery systems and instructional strategies. Requirements for learning such as visuals (see *Channel Characteristics*). Requirements related to learning goals which include appropriateness to types of learning and channel requirements.

Task Functions   Skills that help the group do the work. Necessary for a group to achieve its goals.

Task Schedule   See *Gantt Chart* and *Project Plan*. List of tasks and deadlines for completion.

Technology Options   Delivery systems that can be selected for ISD project. Can be categorized as print, audiovisual, computer-based, or integrated technologies.

Teleconferencing   Two-way (audio or video) electronic communication between two or more groups or individuals in separate locations.

Temporal Dependency   A requirement for reliability. If a student achieves similar scores on a test and retest, or on two forms of the same test, results are said to be consistent.

Terminal Performance Objective   The objective learners are expected to accomplish after sub-objectives (enabling) have been achieved. The highest level of objectives in a system.

Time   A variable in diffusion of innovations. Encompasses the time individual requires to pass through stages of adoption and the rate of adoption of individuals and groups.

Transfer   Applying skills learned in one context to another context.

Transitional Practice   Practice that bridges the gap between entry-level behavior and criterion performance. Often proceeds from easy to difficult practice.

Treatment   A description of how the material will be organized, the approach to be taken, and the content.

Tutorial Tryouts   Students go through a prototype of the instruction individually as part of formative evaluation, in order to identify trouble spots that continue to occur.

Types of Learning   System of task classification by learning outcomes, such as Gagné's or the Domain of Educational Objectives.

Verbal Information   Learned knowledge indicated by stating names, facts, and passages.

Author Index

Page numbers in boldface indicate figures or tables.

Subject Index

Page numbers in boldface indicate tables or figures.